For the caring people
of Weston, Massachusetts

especially
John A. Fiske, Esquire,
who put the trust back in my soul.

In memory of my grandparents,
who brought me up
to have the courage of my convictions
no matter what.

And for my children –
we got off the train together.

Author's Note

This work is a nonfiction novel. The situations and characters described in this book are true-to-life. Pseudonyms have been used for individuals who are not in the public domain — out of respect for their privacy and in keeping with their wishes to remain anonymous.

In some instances, I have gone one step further, altering actual character descriptions. To move the narrative along, certain conversations have been condensed or merged (and a few created after consultation with those involved).

Despite these liberties, the narrative remains faithful to the spirit of what took place. Readers should understand that *Snow Job* is not an unusual story. Rather, scenarios much like those described herein play out daily in family and probate court systems across the United States of America.

Acknowledgments

I wish to acknowledge the help and support of the many people whose wisdom and insights shaped the final version of this work. First and foremost, I thank these three: my editor Lynne Raughley, for her painstaking care, willingness to educate, and ability to "duke it out" with me on matters large and small in the reshaping of this manuscript; my former boss, Charles T. Casale, for encouraging me to find a way to bring *Snow Job* to the reading public and for his guidance in the ways of business; and my dear friend/attorney Sharon L. Keller, for her steadfast support and legal expertise in the birthing of Hang On To Your Hat! Press.

Over the six years that *Snow Job* was in progress, more people than can be mentioned here talked or corresponded with me about aspects of the manuscript. In every instance, their input made a difference, and wherever possible, I tried to incorporate their suggestions and advice. Any shortcomings that remain are mine alone. To the following individuals I am particularly indebted . . .

For their literary insights: Bill Whitworth of *The Atlantic Monthly*, who convinced me that *Snow Job* should be produced as a work of nonfiction and Jayne Young of *The Atlantic Monthly*, who originally brought the manuscript to his attention.

For their spiritual insights: the Revs. Harry H. and Judith L. Hoehler; Dr. Arthur R. Kennedy, Jr.; attorney John A. Fiske; Dr. Michael P. Teter; Robert Nelson; Marina V. Baker; Julie and D. Joseph Gersuk; Lisa A. Breit; and one very special person who wishes to remain anonymous.

For their clinical insights and encouragement: Joseph A. Califano of Columbia University's Center on Substance Abuse and Addiction; Dr. Frank A. Momany of the Tulane University School of Medicine; Bevin Carmichael, former Substance Abuse Prevention Coordinator of Weston, Massachusetts; Dr. Charlotte Modahl of Boston City Hospital; Dr. Alan Barry of McLean Hospital; Dr. Paul Arkema of Westwood Lodge; Constance Bean; Cathleen Buchanan; Dr. Myron Fink; Dr. Robert Goodman; Dr. Ralph Lilly; Dr. Richard L. Pickett; and Dr. David Treadway.

For their insights on the banking and financial community: Robert E. McCarron, Jr., formerly of the Boston Safe Deposit and Trust Company and his colleagues there, Richard Reynolds, Karen King, and Steve Palombi; also Frank J. Sennott of KPMG Peat Marwick.

For their community perspectives: Weston Selectman Joseph W. Mullin and Madeleine W. Mullin; Deputy Chief Roland Anderson and Sergeant Robert Allenberg of the Weston Police Department; Dr. Christine Bishop; Holly Condit; Connie Davis; Marsha Gleason; Dr. Marcia K. Green; Martha B. Hahn; Lisa S. Horowitz; Linda May; Peggy O'Neill; Joan Vernon; Marsha Walker; and Liz Williams.

For taking the time to teach me about the business of making books, Massachusetts publishers: Ilene Horowitz and Sam Schlosberg, founders of Font & Center Press in Weston; Mary Ann Hales, founder of the Cottage Press in Lincoln; and Carol and Dave Hohle of the Christian Science Publishing Society in Boston. For providing the artistic skills which made this project a reality: cover designer Laura J. Anderson; portrait photographer Dianna J. Rust; and Hat Press logo designer Lee Ann Jacob.

To my special New York friends for their constancy and gracious hospitality when I often visited in "re-write mode": Dick and Marian Bott; George A. Ikeda; Linda Urben and Ron Peterson, I am forever grateful.

To many nurturers of children across this land – whether they've survived betrayal by our current legal system or remain embattled in the struggle to keep their homes and children intact – my thanks for sharing your most personal stories with me. Your suffering inspired me to begin *Snow Job* in 1989; but it was your countless examples of marathon courage that gave me the power to see it through.

Last but not least, I gratefully acknowledge the *many* lawyers from coast to coast who read or spoke with me about portions of this book. Those named here and above, in all their dealings with me, brought high standards of ethical conduct to their work – and are a credit to the legal profession. From west to east: Elizabeth F. Enayati of San Francisco; Gordon I. Fink, Deputy Attorney General of Nevada; Joyce Stamp Lilly of Houston, Texas; Jonathan A. White of Weston; and Kevin Curry, Tucker Drummond, Stephen N. Lander, Mark G. Lappin, and Jeremiah Lynch of Boston. The remainder, a far larger number, have requested anonymity and in keeping with their wishes will not be listed here. But they know who they are – and in ways beyond my telling they have profoundly shaped this work.

– Barbara F. Graham
Weston, Massachusetts
Summer, 1995

<u>RELEASE</u>

_____, 1991

In consideration of One Dollar and other good and valuable consideration and in consideration of the promise not to use the firms name or the name of its partners or any of its employees or any reasonably identified references thereto in any publication authored by the releasee or to which the releasee contributes or in the course of the releasee's appearance as a public speaker, such consideration and promise to the undersigned given by Barbara F. Graham (hereinafter "releasee"), the receipt whereof is hereby acknowledged,   , Esquire and the partners and employees of the law firm   hereby remise, release and forever discharge the said releasee from all debts, demands, actions, causes of action, suits, dues, sum and sums of money, accounts, reckonings, bonds, specialties, covenants, contracts, controversies, agreements, promises, doings, omissions, variances, damages, extents, executions, liabilities, and any and all other claims of every kind, nature, and description whatsoever, both in law and equity, which against the said releasee or the heirs, executors, administrators, successors, or assigns of the releasee the undersigned now has or ever had from the beginning of the world to this date and more especially on account of all those matters which were or could have been raised in the   Municipal Court Civil Action No.   captioned "   v. " or which were or could have been raised in the Bar Association Fee Dispute Committee Case No.   , and all matters related thereto.

Executed as a sealed instrument this day and year above written.

Signed in presence of

on his own behalf and on the behalf of the partners and employees of the law firm

25relatw

This is a copy of the Release Form drawn up by "Heyward Cutting" and signed by "Gabriel G. Reed" and an associate. In keeping with this agreement, portions have been expunged to protect the actual identities of the lawyers, their firm, the court jurisdiction, and the bar association named herein.

Dramatis Personae

The Charbonniers
Ursula Larkin Charbonnier — Writer/Editor, *Molecular Modelling News*
Duncan Charbonnier — Executive at Germane Engineering
Spencer and Amanda Charbonnier — Their Children
Jock and Darcy Charbonnier — Duncan's Father and Stepmother
Elsie Charbonnier — Duncan's Mother

The Hollidays
Julia Holliday — Conover Caterer and Ursula's Friend
Hobart Holliday — Founder of Westbury Ventures
Ethan, Enoch, Evan and Ezra — Their Sons

The Lawyers
Sue Sage, Esq. — Ursula's Divorce Attorney (#1)
Gabriel G. Reed, Esq. — Ursula's Divorce Attorney (#2)
Jillian Frost, Esq. — Ursula's Divorce Attorney (#2A)
Merrill Crosby Esq. — Ursula's Divorce Attorney (#2B)
Jonah McCoy, Esq. — Ursula's Divorce Attorney (#3)
Heyward Cutting, Esq. — Ursula's Bar-Appointed Attorney (#4)
Chubb MacIntyre, Esq. — Duncan's Divorce Attorney
Seth Wright, Esq. — Duncan's Divorce Attorney
Sandy Straps, Esq. — Julia's Divorce Attorney (#1)
Robert P. Rhana, Esq. — Julia's Divorce Attorney (#2)
Jeannie Curtin, Esq. — Julia's Divorce Attorney (#3)
Quentin Corey, Esq. — Julia's Divorce Attorney (#4)
Sherman Franklin, Esq. — Julia's Eviction Attorney (#5)
Burton Marshall, Esq. — Julia's Bankruptcy Attorney (#6)
Roger Cornwallis, Esq. — Hobart's Divorce Attorney
Frank Niccolini, Esq. — Hub Safe's Attorney, Charbonnier Case
Mortimer Hives, Esq. — Hub Safe's Attorney, Holliday Case
Lilly Lockhart, Esq. — Their Boss at Hub Safe
Ian Ruddway, Esq. — Ursula's Friend; a New York Attorney
Elspeth Antioche, Esq. — Law Editor, *Molecular Modelling News*
Denny Goferbucks, Esq. — Attorney for the Day Family
Max Canfield, Esq. — Ursula's Neighbor; a Boston Attorney

The Judges
Judge Joseph Tracy — Judge in The Charbonnier Matter
Judge Simon Rumborough — Judge in The Holliday Matter

The Doctors
Asa Larkin, M.D. — Ursula's Father; an Ainstree Cardiologist
John Arthur, M.D. — Charbonnier Family's Internist
Wally Post, D.M.D. — Ursula's and Duncan's Dentist
Wilson Garry Culp, M.D. — Duncan's Psychiatrist at Westbury General
Irena Cossell, Lic.S.W. — Social Worker Associated with Culp

Davis Dalton, Ph.D.	A Psychologist at Appleton Hall
Harry Ballard, M.D.	A Psychiatrist at Appleton Hall
Junius Moropoulos, M.D.	Ursula's Surgeon
R. W. Brixon, D.M.D.	Amanda's Orthodontist
Bruce Pfizer, M.D.	Duncan's Neurologist (#1)
Richard Thorensen, M.D.	Duncan's Neurologist (#2)
Bruce Landsberg, M.D.	Duncan's Neurologist (#3)
Hugo Schell, M.D.	Duncan's Neurologist (#4)
David Madden, M.D.	Charbonnier Family Friend; a Psychiatrist
Dahlia Sutherland, M.D.	Psychiatrist at Governor Chandler Clinic
Gavin Roberts, Ph.D.	Charbonnier Children's *g.a.l.*
Camden Crosby, M.D.	Husband of Merrill; a Neurologist
Davis Fenway, M.D.	A Family Therapist in Conover

The Bankers at Hub Safe Deposit & Trust

Kip Whitaker	President, the Hub Company
Richard Rapp and Rod McLaren	Officers in the Mortgage Department
Simon Semple	Director of Corporate Communications

Colleagues

Archie McGowan; Leslie Drew; and Frank Morrow, Ph.D.	The Three Founders of Genesis Labs Frank Morrow was also Chief Science Editor for *Molecular Modelling News*
Vladimir Siegfried	Chief Financial Officer at Genesis Labs
Shea Phillips	Business Manager for *MM News*
Ike Peters, PhD	Wheaton Glass Scientist and the Ceramics Technology Sector Advisor for *MM News*
Jeff Abbott	CEO, Genesis Labs; Successor to Leslie
Kevin Wilder	CEO, Molecular Innovations
Paul Sudo	A Vice President at Genesis Labs
Ivy Parrish	An Executive at Germane Engineering

Friends and Conoverians

Jackie Melrose	Ursula's Friend; Harvard Medical Librarian
Jeff Melrose	Jackie's Husband; a Conover Selectman
Elise Priest	David Madden's Wife; Ursula's Friend
Christa Walsingham	Caretaker of the Charbonnier Children
The Revs. Trudy and Matt Hale	Co-Ministers, First Parish Church, Conover
Rob and Frank Stoughton	Financial Advisors at Westbury Ventures
Ted Talbot	Ursula's Friend and Neighbor; a Publisher
Bud Alden	Ursula's Friend and Neighbor; an Architect
Ally Everett	Teacher in the Conover Schools
Mary Francis	Counselor in the Conover Schools
Devon Carmody	Substance Abuse Prevention Coordinator for the Town of Conover
Eliza Pickering	The Peripatetic Secretary
Chief Avery Boland	Deputy Chief of Police, Conover
Ginny Bartlett	Ursula's High School French Teacher

Table of Contents

Part III
A Canticle of Dawn

"Jimmie, do you know what a Snow Job is?"

"You mean, the kind of Snow Job that goes on around this place?"

"Yes, Jimmie."

"Yeah, I know what a Snow Job is!"

> — Ursula and Judge Tracy's Court Officer
> At Middlesex County Probate Court
> Cambridge, Massachusetts
> 29 October 1990

Part I

A Narrative of Deception

I

Security

And you all know security
Is mortals' chiefest enemy.

— William Shakespeare, *Macbeth*

Security is a very visible illusion. Striking in its clarity; comforting in its tangibility. You can find a lot of it in Conover, Massachusetts — if you don't look too deeply or too far back. Over the years, I have seen it shine from the cobalt skies that shelter our Memorial Day parades, and I have felt it in the warm crush of carolers on the Town Green at Christmas. Sometimes it's in the predictable creaking my boots make on the aging footbridge in the woods. But I find it most when the seasons change — in the V-formations of the Canada geese that sortie at dawn and in the whistle that blows when the B & M passes through Hastings Green. I don't remember now if the Canada geese arrived early or late that autumn, but I do remember how safe I felt, the way I'd always felt with Duncan.

Hastings Green is my station, the fourth stop in Conover on the train that spokes west from Boston. From there, it's just a short walk up the hill and around the corner to our stone cottage on Inverary Lane. The train makes three other stops in Conover: in front of Westbury General, the community hospital on the Westbury-Conover line; or across from the Police Station in Conover Center; or in front of the cemetery on the Post Road, next to First Parish Church, where the track snakes briefly into Beaumont, then crosses the line back into Conover.

In 1983 Duncan and I used to frequent a French-style bistro, not far from the stretch of track that runs west from the cemetery. It was called Conover Crossing. A superb chef in his own right who liked to cook as much as I, my husband seldom suggested going out for a meal. But Duncan was usually happy to dine at Conover Crossing. The food was reliably good and the atmosphere serene — when the trains weren't roaring by. We had only to remember to bring our own wine, for Conover has been "dry," you know, since the Puritans settled here in 1638.

In those rushed years of early parenthood and career-building, quiet dinners at Conover Crossing were our Friday night prelude to getting back on track. How often they'd helped Duncan put an intense week at Germane Engineering behind him! And both of us always liked to see Steve, the Crossing's artist-owner – and his changing mix of art displayed, for sale, on the walls above the banquettes.

Of all the evenings we dined there, only one stands out in memory now. It comes back to me in a soundless wind, slow-motion layers of confusion swirling through layers of apparent order, the way clouds pass over a moon. There and gone, gone and there – or were they? It depends on who looked, and when, doesn't it?

". . . The road conditions were good that night. There was no reason to have any trouble . . . The road conditions were good that night. There was no reason to have any trouble . . ."

That's how it always begins, those minutes witnessed by no one else, an event that can neither be confirmed nor denied. Except by me. What cannot be proved doesn't frighten me anymore; but it did in 1983. So I waited two years to confide in a doctor and chose to live in silent fear. Silent fear, holy fear, a confirmation and denial all in one. The fear that makes people treasure every "normal" day: drinks before dinner, and the laughter of children, and the key in the lock when the sun goes down. And a warm hand to hold when your fingers turn cold.

"Forget your gloves, Ursula?" said Duncan.

"I guess I left them on the table. You know how it is with last-minute instructions to a new sitter. Do you think she'll be all right with them?" Amanda was four then, and Spencer recently six.

"I'd say Mr. Spencer had things well in hand, wouldn't you? And give me yours, please, before it turns white!" he said, as he reached for more than my hand.

I was thirty-three that autumn – an age that had worried Mieko, my friend from Japan. She had taken me aside the previous New Year's, during a party in our home: "Ursula, thirty-three is most unlucky for a woman. Something bad will happen to you in this year. Please be careful," she implored. After Seiji and Mieko went home that night, Duncan and I had laughed about it in bed. What in the world could happen to me? I was safe in the arms of my darling Duncan, the miracle love of my life.

"What are you thinking about, Ursula? I see a furrowed brow."

"Oh, just my biggest problem in the world," I bantered.

"What's that?"

What to give you for Christmas, I didn't say. The only person on my list whose present wasn't selected and safely tucked away in the attic.

And then it happened. I looked up, and we were no longer on the road.

"Oh my God! Duncan! No!" I screamed. "We have to get off of these railroad tracks!" Oh God, I thought, please don't let there be a train!

We couldn't be off the road. But we were. NO. This wasn't really happening, but it was. I grabbed for the wheel, but Duncan was locked onto it, and I couldn't move him, a man close to twice my weight. His eyes were wide and unblinking, frozen on the strip of track before us, as we climbed and the road fell away from us. The car lurched and bumped over the railroad ties. Duncan's pale red hair was caught by the light and for an instant merged with the harvest moon. Please don't let there be a train! Don't let there be a train. And then just as abruptly as the horror began, the car came to a stop.

"Duncan, we have to get off of these railroad tracks," I repeated in the firmest, calmest tone I could muster.

He grinned at me impishly, as though nothing extraordinary had occurred. There were no scratches, no bruises, no evidence, no concern on Duncan's part. We had crashed into air, you see, an unreported and unreportable incident, whose full impact I would not feel for years. And what had happened to the moon?

Duncan said nothing and put the car into reverse. And we lurched and bumped along the railroad bed, in the exact way we had come. He beamed broadly at me. A long, mad, stupefying grin. Safely back on the road to Conover Crossing, I tried again. "What just happened?" I asked.

"What do you mean?" he replied blankly. "We're going to dinner at Conover Crossing."

I tried twice more during the meal, tempering my need to know what had happened with patience and space for him to explain. But he wouldn't discuss it, and instead launched into an enthusiastic monologue about the lithograph on the wall behind my head. It was a trumpet, garishly orange and grey, ultramodern, and in no way suitable for our home. His remarks bordered on euphoria, as though he had disappeared into the picture and somehow been sucked up into the trumpet. This was not my laid-back Duncan, who rarely ventured beyond verbal neutral. Not our resident master of diplomacy, who was mostly amused and seldom annoyed, at my habit of taking a position on everything.

I excused myself, to negotiate with Steve. Duncan's Christmas present this garish trumpet would be, whether I liked it or not. We could pick it up in a few days. Would that be all right? I returned to the table, and dinner was lovely. Duncan was back to his old sweet self, even though it was clear he wasn't going to discuss the railroad tracks with me. Maybe he was embarrassed, I reasoned. But I couldn't just forget something like that, unless I thought I was losing my mind, and I really didn't think I was.

The following month, when Duncan opened his Christmas present, the first thing he said was, "What's this? Why would you buy me anything like this?"

"But you said you loved it! Don't you remember last month at Conover Crossing, when you went on and on about it?"

He shrugged.

"Duncan, don't you remember!?"

"Ursula, it doesn't go with our house, and it wouldn't look good in my office. Why would you buy me such a thing?" He put it aside.

And it sat in a corner for the next two years, until Genesis Labs came into our lives, and then it hung in my office for another five years, before the light went on in my brain, so slow was I to see all that was happening.

In the winter that followed, I played back the railroad track incident in my mind and wondered about the trumpet lithograph, now in the corner on my dining room floor. And finding no sense in these thoughts, I would put them aside, mentioning the railroad tracks episode only to Duncan's long-time friend, Dick McCall, when he came to Boston in early 1984.

One afternoon, I started to tell him over a peaceful cup of tea in the sunroom, when we were interrupted by a phone call. I walked over to my desk to answer it. "Look, he's not here I tell you. You have the wrong number. You always have the wrong number! Stop calling us."

Then I returned to the cozy wraparound sofa, taking a moment to steady my thoughts. I focused on the calming mix of blue prints and paisleys, which I'd scattered about this small room where I wrote. Their interplay of pattern so often helped center me when I worked over new ideas or apparent inconsistencies. But today my mind would have no part of this tactic.

"What was that all about?" asked Dick.

"It was just that same wrong number. Look, I know this is going to sound a little strange, but for ten years we've been getting calls for 'Duncan Charbonnier, The Potter.' People keep wanting to buy stuff from him. Anyway, Duncan used to get calls for him in New York, even before we were married. And then we got them repeatedly during our Michigan years, and now we're getting them again in Massachusetts. Dick, sometimes the people are very persistent and nasty. They tell me I'm lying, and that I know where he really is. Once I asked a caller what The Potter looked like, and she said he had dark hair, so I know it isn't Duncan!

"Anyway, let me finish telling you about the railroad tracks." And when I got done, I said, "What do you make of it, Dick?"

"I don't know, Ursula," he replied evenly.

Then a child walked into the room, calling me back to the safe routine of a mom in Conover, a place as tidy as a family closet – until it is opened by someone else.

What is order to one can be chaos to another, and comfortable Conover had its share of both. Incorporated in 1713, Conover was already a well-established farm town when Paul Revere galloped through on his Midnight Ride, with a warning to folk "to be up and to arm." The church of First Parish had stood tall the next morn, an oasis of reason in battle, even then.

Years after the war, Paul Revere had occasion to return to Conover, arriving with his sons in 1801. They climbed the steps of an earlier tower at First Parish, where the bell he cast still chimes. Working together, they set the bell in place. And when they had finished hanging it in the belfry, Revere paused to survey the countryside below. His view to the west must have been much like ours, minus cars, power lines, and other illusions of twentieth-century advancement. From the tower, he saw rolling hills covered with green clouds of treetops, stone walls edging the farmers' fields, and a cluster of proprietorships on Center Street. Though we have fewer orchards today, and Westbury General and the B & M were still a century away from being built, the bell-maker imagined steady growth and prosperity. Then he took a moment to remember the War and bless the peace of this summer day: "May it extend to all people who will hear my bell."

What has Time brought? The flock that the Revs. Trudy and Matthew Hale now shepherd fight new and darker battles, in a world Paul Revere would not recognize. In this hidden, more cunning and baffling war, battles play out not on open meadows streaked with blood in the light of day — but behind closed doors, in suitably chill conference rooms, over proper luncheons at the Iroquois Club. And sometimes on the train — no, always on the train and at its stops along the way. I have come to know them all.

And it has taken a long time. In the beginning, in our early Conover years, I saw the stops only as they appeared. To a young mother, Westbury General was a convenient emergency room for moments, thankfully few, when Amanda or Spencer sprained a limb or needed to be stitched up. Not for years would I meet Dr. John Arthur and a parade of neurologists, followed by Wilson Garry Culp and a platoon of paid enablers.

The Police Station was simply a place to get a bike license. And Deputy Avery Boland was the jolly fellow who taught the children about safety, and fingerprinted them when it became the prudent thing to do after a child in nearby Wilmot was snatched from her yard. Vanilla, law-abiding person that I was, why would Ursula Charbonnier — wife, mother and editor — ever have serious dealings with the Conover Police? As for the cemetery and the grey stone church, they were simply picture postcards I sped by in the car. Or gazed at from the train.

Only in years to come, when I got off the train and ventured inside, would I see all these places for what they were: critical waystations on a turbulent journey; and for what they ultimately became: beacons in our storm.

War has changed a lot in Massachusetts, since that season the British marched into Boston. We don't brandish bayonets anymore. The enemies in this story are far too subtle and modern for that. But their uniforms you will recognize: three-piece suits, black robes, white coats. And their rules you will come to know: hands are to appear clean at all times; weapons are never displayed. That the casualties, in the end, learn exactly where the weapons are stored (in locked glove boxes, briefcases, file cabinets, and secret bank accounts) does them no good, for this knowledge almost always comes too late. Publicity is strictly forbidden. *The Boston Globe* does not cover our story.

For this war only thrives in silence, a silence that never forgets that "the road conditions were good that night. There was no reason to have any trouble . . ."

Six Years Later

II

Gabriel G. Reed

If you'll believe in me, I'll believe in you.
— Lewis Carroll, *Through the Looking-Glass*

In that first phone conversation, he had sounded like the futsy-dutsiest old man in the world, "Well I don't know if I'll even take your case, but if Angus MacKenzie recommended you, then why don't you come in one day next week?"

". . . believe my story and take my case . . . You will believe my story and take my case . . . believe my story and take my case, believe . . ." my mind turned with the tires of Shea Phillips's car as we exited the Mass Pike at Copley Place and skimmed along the rows of brick townhouses that line the Back Bay avenues. But I was too charged up to appreciate Boston at its shining best this mellow September day. As we headed down Newbury, I heard Shea say something about the scent of the late summer flowers, but their fragrance eluded me. My senses were wrapped in gauze that afternoon, so intent was I on only one thing. "He has to believe me Shea. How much longer can this go on? My God, someone has to believe me!"

"He will," she tried to reassure. "Remember what Angus said — Reed is the best in Boston. Just tell him the truth: the railroad tracks, the doctors, Appleton Hall, and what we found in Duncan's car at Armstrong Field this summer. He'll believe you, Ursula."

"Ringling & Haycroft didn't."

"Ringling & Haycroft weren't the best in Boston!" Shea replied, with a confidence in Reed I didn't necessarily share. It was based on her unbounded belief in Angus MacKenzie, our company's General Counsel, who over the past four years had extracted Genesis from one legal scrape after another.

Fortunately none of them had involved our part of the business: *Molecular Modelling News* — read in chemical and pharmaceutical houses worldwide. As its Business Manager, Shea had immediately taken ownership of all non-editorial aspects of running the publication. "You do the words, Ursula, and I'll do the music," she had said from day one. To Shea, "music" only began with the business and financial; it extended to *anything* that distracted me from editorial work — an editor's dream. And during this hardest summer of my life, "music" had come to encompass unstinting moral support, in any manner, way, shape, or form, including interviewing new attorneys.

We found a parking place around the corner on Exeter, and scanned the street for the Perry House, which turned out to be the only grey stone building in a row of elegant red-brick manses, a dilapidated gatehouse sort of affair, which had seen better days. A huge cracked pot of wilted impatiens sat on the top step. Reed seemed to have deliberately allowed the exterior to go. Flakes of black paint chipped off the massive wood door as I let fly a brass knocker that needed polishing, and I brushed them off my white linen suit as we waited for someone to answer. I could see that the foundation was in good condition, but the stone facade had started to crumble over the years. Was Gabriel G. Reed thumbing his nose at the neighbors, I wondered, or merely making a political statement? When I tried to peer in the dusty side window, my eye fell on a doorbell nearly hidden by ivy. Shea and I were buzzed in and told to wait in a small, dark alcove enlivened only by a cyan, floor-to-ceiling reproduction of the Statue of Liberty, swathed in an American flag. Her lit torch pointed to the landing of a double staircase, where two outsized Cigar Store Indians from the Old West flanked an Art Deco rendering of the Mona Lisa. I couldn't take my eyes off the resolute "trois of the ménage," as I immediately dubbed them.

"Which one of you is Ursula Charbonnier?" bellowed a voice that was half bark and half flirt, all in one. "[Bow-wow,] I am!" I repressed, as I stood up and shook his offered hand, a piece of New Hampshire granite with skin pulled over it. He motioned me into his office, a potentially grand room, decorated in what could only be described as Ralph Lauren Reject: Orientals loomed in North Carolina, plaid throws tossed over worn chintz sofas, piles of Brookstone catalogs and Farmers' Almanacs strewn on a second desk in the corner, and a glowering moosehead mounted above the mantle. "What's the old boy's name?" I asked gamely.

"Infidelity. Now what has brought you here today?" he beamed broadly, deliberately enjoying his juxtaposition, which was not as on target as he probably thought.

Over the next hour and a half, doors opened and closed many times, and people with notepads came and went at his direction. I lost count of them after the fourth one was introduced. When Gabriel is in a room, it's hard to pay attention to anyone else. I sat taut and still in the leather wing chair by the window, where from time to time, I could hear his voice, questioning and probing — then my voice, replying and elaborating, fully engaged in the difficult effort of telling all that had happened.

Never was he still. As he listened, he alternately leaned against walls and lumbered about the room, in just the way I always moved through the two years of back pain which followed a 1983 car accident. Tortoise-shell reading glasses went on as he reached for papers and books, and came off as he fielded phone interruptions and occasional questions from the note takers. About an hour into the meeting, I began to think about his age. The head of close-cropped sandy waves wasn't giving away any clues, nor were the hands that hadn't gotten calloused and firm from pushing Montblanc pens in a law office all day. Something about his body struck me as rough and tumble, almost spoiling for a fight. Should my imagination garb him in boxing gloves or farm overalls? I wondered. And what was it about him that made me think of hay?

Certainly he didn't look like a lawyer. Except for his brows. They were finely drawn and dramatic, twin bronze expressors of a finely honed legal mind. The brows presided over a ruddy, windswept face, and in it I thought I saw early pain.

"Who has been representing you?" he asked early on.

"Sue Sage, from Ringling & Haycroft."

"Does your husband have a lawyer?"

"Yes. Chubb MacIntyre at Candice & . . ."

"We used to be in practice together – years ago. Oh, don't look so worried! We are not drinking buddies. And if your husband's as cheap as you say he is, first we'll start out with Mr. MacIntyre, and then we'll move down to Mr. Wright, and after that we'll get down to Mr. Hammermann . . . and when we get down to Mr. Hammermann . . ." At this Reed rubbed his hands together in anticipation of God only knows what. He certainly seemed happy about Duncan's choice of counsel.

"And do you know that MacIntyre had the nerve to ask how much money I was going to inherit from my father!" I chimed in.

"Well, that's customary in these cases."

"Well, it's offensive!" I protested.

"It is offensive, and your father is going to live for a long time."

"That's right. His parents lived into their mid-nineties. Look, my father just wants me out of this."

"Now tell me when your problems began," he said, as he paused beneath Infidelity.

"I first knew for sure there was a problem, one night in 1983. The road conditions were good that night. There was no reason to have any . . ." And in the hour that followed I talked, and I talked, and he walked and I talked and the note takers wrote and I talked. I don't remember much more about it than that until he asked about the children's health.

"It's fine, and their mental health is fine too, and *it* is going to stay that way!" I rumbled at him, like a verbal locomotive crashing into what I wanted the future to be.

"Well that's what I meant," he said extra softly, as if to calm me down. "And . . . *that's* the way it's going to be!" he roared, for contrast, as he turned and jauntily stomped his foot on the Carolina Oriental.

"Yes, that's the way it's going to be!" I roared back. Reality was beginning anew. I could actually detect a little fight in my voice.

"Tell me about Ivy Parrish," he said.

"All right. In one sentence – she's been with the same man for seventeen years, had a kid with him nine years ago, built a house with him five years ago, and married him two years ago."

"Soooooo . . . she's living life backwards," he said, throwing his arms in the air. "Maybe next year she'll fall in love with him!" Then he turned serious. "Ursula, it doesn't matter if people are from Conover or Ashton, their problems are all the same."

"And most people don't know what real trouble is," I added.

"Most people don't know what real trouble is," he agreed. He saw me squinting in the low afternoon sun and moved to adjust the wooden shutters, the old-fashioned kind where you could control every panel. Like the ones Grandfather had in his office, when I was a little girl.

This made the room darker, and he walked over to his large desk to turn on a light and thumb through my Ringling & Haycroft file. I had brought copies of our wills, tax returns, financial statements, and the medical logs which so dryly delineated my rapidly splintering life.

"Sue Sage said . . ."

"I don't want to hear about anything Ms. Sausage said," he broke in sharply. "You are never going to mention her name again!"

This sounded promising. "Well, if you'll take this case . . ." I ventured.

"Yes, I'll take this case!" he boomed, pausing in front of the floor-to-ceiling bookcases which framed the window. "And may I call you Uh-sah-lah?"

"Yes," I said, since he had been all afternoon, anyhow.

"And you will call me Gabriel," he commanded grandly. (Where were the trumpets? I wondered.)

"Now *you* are going to be quiet! And *I* am going to talk for awhile." The gravel voice had gone into command mode. "You are going to come back here next Thursday, and before that, you are going to write a letter to Ms. Sausage. I'll dictate it, but you can change it if you want . . . 'Dear Ms. Sausage, As you may have perceived, I have grown increasingly . . .'" He fell silent, in search of the next word.

". . . uncomfortable?" I ventured.

". . . restless . . . with the legal services with which you have . . ."

"Restive!" I interrupted. When he went stone quiet, I realized the invitation to edit had not been intended to be taken seriously.

". . . restive," he continued after a still longer pause, the hard turquoise eyes boring in on me as I scribbled what followed.

But my pace was too slow. "Ursula, Uh-sah-lah! . . ." he interrupted impatiently. I continued to write with one hand and indicated that he wait for me to finish with the other. I don't think he was used to waiting, but I am not used to missing a word. "Oh, do you take shorthand too?" he jeered.

"No, I have my own system: Greek, Chinese, hieroglyphics . . ." I smiled.

"Now, you are going to go home and write two narratives," he continued briskly. "The first will be a Financial Narrative . . . by the way, does Duncan have any lines of credit?"

"Why yes, a $40,000 line with Hub Safe Deposit & Trust."

"Well, he doesn't any more! Jillian, get on the phone and call Ann Robertson over at Hub Safe, and tell her to cancel Mr. Charbonnier's line of credit forthwith!"

"Now why does that name ring a bell?" I wondered out loud.

"Because she wrote your mortgage, that's why," said Reed. "Now, getting back to the Financial Narrative, I want to know all about the money, all the way through the marriage. Where it came from, who spent it, what it was spent for. Earnings, unearned income, inheritances, everything."

"Well, I know how to write!" I said brightly. "And speaking of money, how much is all this going to cost?"

"Well, there's my retainer of $7,500," he said, (higher than Ringling & Haycroft's, which didn't surprise me). "You can bring it next week when you deliver the narratives. And after that it's hard to say – maybe $14–15,000 all together."

"Well, what's the most expensive one you've ever done?" I tried again.

"More money than you'll ever have!" he replied with fierce glee. "Second, you are going to write a Personal Narrative, the story of your life with Duncan. I want to know everything. And don't leave anything out!" he snapped, "but you can skip all the sweet stuff about when you were happy."

"Oh, no I can't!"

"I don't need to hear about that!"

"Oh, yes you do; I know how to write!" I bantered again.

"That's about the fourth time you've said that." (Second, but I let it pass). "And you will deliver the narratives early next week, so that I can read them before we meet again on Thursday, at three o'clock. Is that all right with you?"

I got up to leave.

"Now what time are you coming to see me next week?" he quizzed. He knew I hadn't heard a word. "Three o'clock!" he answered in a voice that said, and you will pay attention when I speak from now on.

"Three o'clock," I repeated crisply. ". . . Eastern Standard Time!" I added in my best who said you could have the last word? tone of voice. Later I realized we were still on Daylight time, and Reed must have been grinning at his own gracious restraint in not editing me.

The New Hampshire granite gripped my hand to say good-bye. "Now if your husband gives you any more trouble, you just ask him out for a drink, okay?"

"Okay!"

Back outside, in the September sun, I said, "I've never met anyone like that before in my whole life!"

Shea had never doubted how it would go. "He believed your story."

I nodded. "And he took my case."

And so I went home and wrote for Gabriel. I'd written a lot things in my editorial career, but never about my own life. Would there be chapters, I wondered, watershed events where portions would begin and end? I doubted it. But when I sat down to actually do it – in a forty-eight-hour marathon on the word processor (because that's all the time I had) – chunks and natural divisions rapidly suggested themselves. Events I hadn't recognized in their own time, as the end of one era and the beginning of the next, tumbled forth. Reed must have known this would happen, and in this act he had imposed on me, my strength would start to return.

III

The Easy Keys

Welcome thou kind deceiver!
Thou best of thieves; who, with an easy key
Dost open life, and unperceived by us,
Even steal us from ourselves.

— John Dryden, *All for Love*

My Personal Narrative

Well, Gabriel, the first thirty-five years of my life were unremarkable in every way. The product of a middle-sized, Middle Western town, I admit to being the indulged only daughter of an eight-days-a-week "country doctor" as my father, Asa Larkin, still refers to himself. My mother never functioned normally so my childhood was a little bewildering, but it later became clear that the combination of multiple sclerosis and an organic brain syndrome was responsible for the confusion in our household. Life at home was such that Dad used to go to the emergency room to relax, and I would go to the library to get some peace and quiet. This led to my being dubbed "Bookworm" early on, but a child who has figured out how to survive has usually also found a reason to feel glad inside. And books made me glad, the ones I read, and the ones I wrote. While I was growing up, Dad talked a lot about being a rugged individualist, but even he has never entirely understood that my own opinion of me was always the one that mattered most. And while this trait, over the years, has not always endeared me to lovers and in-laws and more recently lawyers, in the end, I suspect it is part of what has seen me through.

I attended the village schools through 1968, doing well in the subjects I liked and poorly in those I did not – "your basic B+ student" according to Ginny Bartlett, my former French teacher and a close friend to this day. It came down to this: I liked words, hated numbers, and would have flunked chemistry if my high school teacher hadn't taken pity on me. "Ursula, I'm not going to be the person who interferes with your literary career, so I am going to give you a 'C-' instead of the 'F' you deserve. Just promise me one thing: you will never write about chemistry!"

"Oh, it's a promise, Dr. Leo," I had said at the time. Who knew what was ahead?

My algebra teacher, Mr. Eggbert, was no less patronizing: "Ursula, the only math you'll ever need to know is how to count up to twenty-eight, and I guess you can manage that." Another gentlewoman's 'C,' but not to worry, I got my strokes in the word world – for my witty essays, my ghost-written book reports, and being the only student in the school who could consistently out-argue the debate teacher. Did I mind if I got a 26 percentile on the writing sample of the LSAT? Certainly not. Thanks to one of my college writing profs, I had a literary agent in New York before I was twenty-one.

After several years of bouncing around three of the best schools the Midwest had to offer (my family was adamant that I not "go East"), I finally wound up with a Master's Degree in Japanese Studies from the University of Michigan. I went on for an MBA, but rapidly realized this was not a good fit, and strolled in to deliver this message to my accounting professor. "George, I am no longer a going concern. Do us both a favor and please don't call on me for the rest of the term. I am moving to New York in January to seek my fame and fortune."

The Dean gave me a going-away dinner, and I gave him two dozen pots of tulips and hyacinths to be forced the following spring, a good deal for us both. In New York I pursued my dream of working for a Japanese trading company, deliberately disregarding the fact that they weren't hiring *gaijin* females in the 1970s. I have never liked the N-word (No). Later that year, Matsumoto & Co. hired me. And there I met fellow employee, Duncan Charbonnier.

The younger child in another Midwestern family of two children, Duncan never got to spend a lot of time with his father, Jock Charbonnier, the famous pro golfer, as well known to you for the headlines he makes in the gossip columns, as for those he makes in the sports pages. Jock's frequent tournaments took him away from home, but Duncan's mother Elsie, who has never shared Jock's love of sports, kept the home fires burning, shall we say.

Duncan, always a leader, did well in school, the "best and first at everything" his whole life, as he and his family were fond of saying. When he graduated from high school in 1968, Duncan informed his parents that he wanted to be financially independent from them so that he could live a life with no strings attached. He felt his parents interfered to an unwarranted extent in the life of his older brother, Kit, simply because they were paying for Kit's schooling and everything else. Duncan told me that for this reason he turned down an acceptance to Princeton, and decided to attend a small college close to home. He worked his way through, (see Financial Narrative, Gabriel), and also used money he had saved from working summers during high school on the assembly line at Cross Motors. Few Cross Motor execs have ever endured the toil and tedium of being on the line and this experience helped Duncan to be more effective when he joined Cross management in 1976. Duncan eventually earned a Master's Degree in Chinese Studies and moved to New York in the summer of 1974.

As two of the three Americans hired as an experiment in Matsumoto's Corporate Planning Department, Duncan and I were in a position I have always liked: breaking new ground. When there are few rules and no precedents, there are usually opportunities to do a lot of good work. I liked Duncan in the first nanosecond, but had no intention of dating a co-worker. We began dating seriously the following January, but because we both felt it was high risk, spent a lot of time out of town or in places where we would be unlikely to run into fellow employees. And in fact, Matsumoto didn't find out about our relationship until two days before the wedding, and then only because they wanted to send Duncan on a business trip; and one has to have a pretty valid reason to say no to the Japanese.

For Duncan, the move to New York was his first time away from home. Throughout his childhood, his father had been gone on the pro golf circuit, and Elsie, who never felt comfortable in Jock's glittery world, had always made it clear that she preferred Duncan's company to her husband's anyway. As Duncan once put it, "when I came along, I was just what my mother wanted." I accepted all of this at face value. Jock was always pleasant enough to me, and I didn't see that his personal affairs were any of my business. Asa, on the other hand, took a dim view of the Charbonniers from day number one: "Ursula, these people are intellectually dishonest," but I brushed it aside, along with his uncharacteristically uncharitable comment on first meeting Elsie: "Mark my words Ursula, that woman is a closet alcoholic!"

In the summer of 1975, Matsumoto sent Duncan to Japan for three months, and new management came from the Tokyo office. I was fired because they couldn't justify having a woman in management. Matsumoto's financial consultant noticed my absence one day, and asked if I would come work for him. And that is how I came to be employed by the inimitable Teddy Michaelson, former head of Corporate Finance at Orange Brothers, and co-founder of Bishopsgate Associates (named after the debtor's prison in London!), a small investment banking/financial consulting firm which no longer exists. Teddy has since gone on to become a successful novelist (*White Wednesday, The Weaver's Plot,* and *Mr. Green Hasn't Come Yet*).

I knew nothing about finance, so Teddy sent me to night school at NYU. He also sort of let me learn on the job, which is the best way to learn anyhow. The closest I ever came to doing my own deal was in October, 1975, when I had the idea to sell William Paley a chain of greenhouses (this was during the plant craze in the mid-'70s). I had all my facts in order and was set to make my presentation to Jif Pepperell (a close Paley relative), but Duncan Charbonnier proposed that morning (29 October) and I was worthless by the time I got to Black Rock. My mind was on mergers but not acquisitions – and I blew the presentation.

A few months later, just before Christmas, Duncan and I were married at the United Nations Chapel in New York. My grandfather had died suddenly just two weeks before, and in an effort to cheer everyone up, I had announced our engagement when I went back to the Midwest for the funeral. Elsie and my mother immediately began squabbling about wedding plans, and both fathers would not have minded if we'd eloped. Duncan and I decided to head the mothers off at the pass by swiftly planning a very simple wedding, to be attended only by parents, our brothers, my former Pi Phi roommate and her husband, a resident at New York Hospital who agreed to rush through our blood test (at that time, New York had the longest waiting period in the nation!), one friend/witness each from Matsumoto and Bishopsgate, and our accountant friend who urged us to wait until January for tax reasons.

Duncan, who according to Elsie still has the first nickel he ever made, later found a loophole in the tax laws – designed for separated couples – and we paid no penalty for marrying before the New Year. We ended up honeymooning with Duncan's very extended family at a ski resort in Colorado. Ever the good sport and the only non-skier in the group, I did my best to get along with Elsie and fit in with the cousins who were trying out for the U.S. Olympic ski team. But I finally had to draw the line when Elsie tried to make us take the twin beds in hers and Jock's suite.

Shortly after we were married, Elsie asked me not to call her "Mom" and said, "You're not the person I would have picked out for him." I decided to roll right past that and win her over, but I never managed it; in contrast, Jock and I got along well right from the start. As he said in a letter he wrote Duncan just before our wedding, "I want you to know that I couldn't feel more strongly that the match is perfect."

We settled in at Duncan's apartment in the Murray Hill section of the city and continued to work for Matsumoto and Bishopsgate. This might be a good spot to talk about two customs that developed early in the marriage. Custom 1: Sometime in those first weeks, Duncan said he wanted me to keep a daily record of every penny I spent, as he had always done in the little leather daily diaries we have both since used over the years. I didn't like the idea at first, but agreed to do it for a month. To my surprise, I found that it only took a minute each day to record expenses, and that it was a wonderful way to track much more than money. It's remained a habit for me, and a good one; Duncan, on the other hand, not only stopped recording his own expenses, but later became a pain to share the check-book with, because he would never enter withdrawals until the monthly statements came. Although I was always the one who wrote the checks for regular bills, I was continually frustrated in my efforts to have a handle on where we really stood.

Custom 2: We decided early on that on each wedding anniversary and half anniversary we would have a "semiannual summit conference" to clear the decks on the marriage. It was to be a sort of built-in safety check to make sure no issue would slip through the cracks – an opportunity to discuss problems, dreams and plans. We continued to do this through our thirteenth anniversary, but in March of 1989, Duncan admitted that he "hadn't been honest at them for years."

Duncan had never liked New York, and although I adored it, I knew our days there were numbered. He wanted to live in the Northwest, and so in June (1976) we packed up our belongings, put our possessions in storage and drove to Portland to hunt for jobs. Duncan had several dozen interviews, but none panned out.

But on a lark, while still in New York, I had answered an ad from *The Wall Street Journal* to sell commercial real estate in Portland; the firm invited me to interview and offered a job at $35,000 plus commissions, if I passed the next real estate exam. That was good money in those days for someone my age, but the thought of selling real estate did not appeal in any way, so I turned it down, even though Duncan encouraged me to accept the offer so that he could continue to job hunt. And he had already begun to househunt in Portland, knowing that the inheritance from my grandparents' estate would be coming my way later that year. We had been living in a sort of residential motel (with a kitchen), and eroding what capital we had. Duncan felt very discouraged, and we returned to Ann Arbor.

We rented an apartment not far from Jock and Elsie's house. I was home-sick for New York and missed having an exciting job, but I did want to have a baby before I was thirty (I was then twenty-six); and Duncan wanted to get an MBA. Cross Motors, one of the major U.S. auto firms headquartered in the Detroit area, at that time paid all expenses for graduate school, so Duncan found a job at Cross, and began work on an MBA by night. Spencer was born the following August (1977). Duncan's parents moved to South America two months later, where they were to live for the next three years; Jock had been offered a lucrative and glamorous position with an exclusive golf club outside Rio.

Because we now had a baby in an apartment building that didn't allow them, we began looking for a new place to live, and the following April, thanks in large part to the inheritance from my grandparents, we were able to pay cash for a lovely condominium. I was always very reticent about this, because Duncan didn't want anyone to know that we had paid for the house in full. That autumn, we were surprised to learn that I was pregnant again, and Amanda was born the following June (1979). With Cross Motors, night school, two babies and no family support we really had our hands full, but through it all we were a solid team.

I was "all thumbs" with infants having never even done any baby-sitting, but Duncan was a splendid father. He may not have been generous with his money, but I've never known anyone who was more generous with his time – he always nurtured and he cared, even when he was exhausted by other pressing demands from Cross and school. Acquaintances marveled at how consistently kind and thoughtful he was, and several even asked, "Is he really always that nice, even when you're alone?" "Yes, he is," I'd reply. And then they'd say something along the lines of, "Hm . . . too good to be true." I just thought I was incredibly lucky.

When Amanda was ten months old, I became very ill for several months. My Ann Arbor doctors thought I had leukemia or a lymphoma, but Asa's hunch (first case he'd ever encountered of toxoplasmosis – and he made the diagnosis over the phone!) turned out to be right, and we got through that tough time, too. Thinking I was really, really going to die, however, changed my perspective on everything. I have rarely felt ungrateful in the years since.

Duncan completed his MBA in December of 1980, just as his paternal grandmother died, and we had our hands full once again with final exams, two babies with bronchitis, and handling all the funeral-related social obligations at our home in the same week.

Neither of us liked living in Ann Arbor, and we both had always viewed it as a temporary stop while we "punched the tickets" of the MBA, experience in Cross Motor's Finance Group, and starting a family. Because we were reared in what Duncan dubbed "the Midworst," we both wanted to get back to the East Coast. I was itching to go to New York, but Duncan wanted to work for Germane Engineering Corporation (GEC), and that meant Boston. After more than a year of sending résumés to various parts of GEC on his own, he was finally offered a job in 1981, through the efforts of a former Cross Motors co-worker who had moved to GEC the year before.

We moved to New England in 1981. Although Duncan's salary increased enormously, our living standard plummeted due to what I call "the sticker shock" of moving to Massachusetts. We bought a Dutch colonial in Conover, but it was the sort of house where you held your breath and prayed every time you flushed a toilet. We were so poor we didn't drink for a year; in retrospect, maybe I was the only one who didn't drink for a year. And it didn't really matter. We were delighted to be back East. Germane was a wonderful environment – a terrific change from staid, hierarchical Cross Motors; Duncan thrived, and we often talked late into the night: about Duncan's work and where we hoped to be in life – five, ten and twenty years out. The schools were terrific; Spencer and Amanda were stimulated and challenged. We were too poor to go out for dinner on our sixth wedding anniversary, the first that we celebrated in Conover, but Duncan gave me a book to mark the occasion, and in it he wrote: "Six is forever. Love, D."

Most important of all, everyone was in good health.

IV

The Wrong Track

O what a tangled web we weave,
When first we practise to deceive!

— Sir Walter Scott, *Marmion*

In the year that followed, Gabriel, I had reason to consider in a new light Duncan's inscription in my 1981 anniversary present, for that summer, Jock left Duncan's mother. He later told me he'd been unhappy for more than a decade. This was not a surprise. The previous year (after Duncan had moved to Boston, but the kids and I were still in Ann Arbor), I had inadvertently surprised Jock at home (with his latest lady friend, Darcy) when Elsie was out of town. Duncan and I had borrowed money for a month to buy new cars (so we wouldn't have to break our CDs), and in Duncan's family even very short-term loans are paid back with interest. I was delivering our check (on my way to nursery school with a carpool full of kids) the morning that I found them. I decided to behave as if the incident had never happened, with the exception of telling Duncan. Jock later told me that he'd left Elsie because all he'd "ever known from women was coldness and criticism," but that with Darcy it was different. I was still too young – and too happily married – to detect the lack of originality in this comment.

In the spring of 1983, Elsie came to visit us in Boston. Her divorce was very much in progress, and I figured she and Duncan had a lot to discuss, so I didn't think it strange that they were up talking until two in the morning. Duncan's response to his parents' break-up had been anger. Anger at them (how could they do this after thirty-six years?); anger at himself (could he have intervened and prevented it?); and sometimes, it seemed, even anger at me. People told me this was normal, to be loving and patient, and it would pass. By my definition, that meant making *even more* allowances for Elsie.

Spending time with Elsie was never easy for me, but anyone would have to have had compassion for the transition she was going through. I determined to make the visit a good one.

"Would you like Total or Nutrigrain?" I asked brightly when she trudged downstairs the next morning.

And this was her response: "Do you want me to leave your house?"

No. She hasn't just said that, I thought to myself. So I repeated the question. And she repeated her response, adding that she and Duncan had been up fighting half the night, though she didn't say what about. At that point, I did the most positive thing I could think of: shift the focus to Amanda, who was excited about her nursery school graduation festivities scheduled for later that morning, in the Town Meadowland adjacent to our property. But Elsie would have none of it. Her tone became angrier, and her words stronger.

"You have stolen my son!" she declared. "And now I have no one. Jock has gone, and you have Duncan." I still wasn't grasping her meaning.

Then, with a smile on her face, she said "Mark my words, someday this [getting left] is going to happen to you!" She continued in this way, until it was time to take Amanda to school.

Why was she saying these things to me? Later she would tell me this conversation had never taken place, but Amanda heard all of it, curling up to me and snuggling as children do when their world turns dark. I called Duncan at midday to ask what was going on, and he said they'd quarreled the previous night. Sound sleeper that I was, I'd missed all of it. Elsie left on the first plane she could get the next day, and Duncan was so angry he wouldn't drive her to the airport. After the taxi took her away, he shut the door quietly and hugged me for a long time. "She's torn me in two," he said.

"Well, I'll just have to put you back together again!" I grinned up at him.

But Elsie's nasty remark stayed filed in my brain: "Mark my words, someday this [getting left] is going to happen to you!"

And I thought back to that remark Jock had made the previous year during one of our many chats: "Ursula, all I've ever known from women is coldness and criticism, but with Darcy it's different."

As I mused on Elsie's dark prophecy that someday Duncan would leave me, I told myself that ours was not a home filled with coldness and criticism, plus there were our semiannual summit conferences – so how could this ever happen to us? Still, a divorce in a family does inspire one to try a little harder and take nothing for granted.

At about this time, Asa also said something that gave me pause. "Ursula, the most disturbing thing about this whole situation is that your marriage is now in danger."

"Dad, don't be ridiculous. Jock's behavior has nothing to do with Duncan and me."

"Oh, but my dear, it has *everything* to do with you."

Looking back on all this now, Gabriel, I can see that even as 1983 opened, early events were silently laying the foundation for the destruction that would follow. I thought back to Mieko Takashima's New Year's comment, and how I'd so easily brushed aside her superstition.

Then just three weeks later, on Duncan's thirty-third birthday, we had a bad car accident up in New Hampshire. We'd had a number of them in the past two years, but this time I got hurt. The first occurred in Kennebunkport in 1981, about six months after we'd come back East. Duncan was driving forward out of our parking place, but put the car in reverse instead, slammed on the accelerator, and smashed backwards hard into a guard rail. It was as if for a minute he'd lost track of what he was doing, and then the impact slammed him back to reality. Strange, I thought, but brushed it off as something that could happen to anyone.

The following year, on a ski weekend in Vermont with a car full of kids, Duncan drove round a bend in the road and collided with an oncoming van. The bend was narrow and the van wide, he told me over the phone, but when I arrived at the scene, I was puzzled, for the road seemed more than wide enough to have accommodated both vehicles. Just one of those things, I told myself again, and fortunately only the car was hurt.

But the next time, this third time – I was. The driver in front of us, who we later learned was drunk, drove into the car in the oncoming lane. Duncan tried to drive around them, but wasn't fast enough, and my side of the car was hit. Glass fragments shot into my face and hands, their sting blending with the bite of the January wind. My body hurled outward into the car door, and my back would be in agony for the next two years, unless I was swimming or soaking in a hot tub. Dick and Betsy McCall, now far away in Japan, were with us that night, and I remember telling Dick that something about Duncan's reactions had been delayed.

"When you know every inch of someone's body, the way I know Duncan's, you know when they are slowed." But this time Dick brushed it off, saying Duncan had done the best he could. Throughout 1983, I had only the vaguest sense that something wasn't right with Duncan, but it was never anything I could put my finger on.

The children were small and demanding, I was in chronic pain from my back, and Duncan was understandably sad over the break-up of his parents' thirty-six year marriage. Jock had for many years enjoyed the extramarital attentions of several women. What was unusual about his fling with Darcy Kincaid was that he planned to marry her. She wasn't intellectual like Elsie, he told us when he visited in the summer of 1982, but she wasn't fault-finding either.

Duncan often told me that what his dad really wanted and needed was someone intellectual *and* good-looking, but instead had always had to settle for half the equation in one person. "But I have both in you," Duncan would say during those years as he pulled me close.

Initially, I thought with time and all the attention the children and I lavished on him, that Duncan would bounce back. But as the months went by, his anger only deepened. The three of us adored him, and the four of us functioned so well as a unit; I felt that surely in time his heart would heal.

In August of 1983, Jock and Darcy were married in Michigan, and we flew out for the wedding. Although Duncan was still very upset about the divorce, he could see that Darcy was a kind, caring individual (I even heard him tell this to Elsie's ninety year-old mother), and it was obvious that Jock was ecstatic. Darcy encouraged Jock to be more involved with Spencer and Amanda (Jock had not been happy about becoming a grand-father, because it made him feel old; when Spencer one day dubbed him "Uncle Jock," Jock said he'd like to continue being called that, and the name has stuck). But "Uncle" Jock's personality was different with Darcy; he was more demonstrative and outgoing.

Darcy, a Cross Motors flight attendant, had been in Boston shortly before the wedding, and had bravely come to meet us on her own. When she got down on the floor to play with Spencer and Amanda, it seemed to me they might at last have a grandmother of sorts. My mother had always been too ill to interact with them, and Elsie had never shown any interest in the children.

The wedding day was heavy and steamy, and Duncan dripped beneath his suit in the hot Michigan sun. After the reception, when he went to get our car so that we could head to the airport, he didn't return for more than two hours and was angry and out of it when he finally came back. "I had trouble finding the car," he said, and we damn near missed the plane. He was mean, all the way home and on through the night, which was totally out of character for him.

At about this time (1982-1983) Germane Engineering, Duncan's employer, temporarily acquired a minority interest in a company called Scientific Perturbations, based in upstate New York. Duncan was GEC's representative in the deal, and occasionally attended the board meetings. This was how he came to know Leslie Drew, an attorney who worked for SciPerb and was also on their Board. Leslie lived in Westbury at that time, and he and Duncan often found themselves on the same plane.

In 1984, Leslie began telling Duncan about his plan to establish a com-pany to produce scientific software for the then just developing computer-assisted molecular design (CAMD) market. When Duncan and I talked late into the night, he often told me "Leslie stories," and I thought the new business sounded incredibly exciting. One day in the spring of 1985, Leslie phoned Duncan from Genentech and asked him to consider becoming president of the new company. It was to be named Genesis Laboratories.

It was now May, and we were scheduled to move to Geneva the follow-ing month for Germane. But that was not all that was going on in our lives. One night two autumns before – that would have been 1983 – Duncan had come home and after a very pleasant glass of wine, we'd headed off for dinner alone at a nearby restaurant (Conover Crossing, now out of business). The road conditions were good that night. There was no reason to have any problem. Suddenly, Duncan drove off the road and down some railroad tracks. After what seemed like an eternity, but was probably only a minute, Duncan brought the car to a stop. He was confused. Then he sort of popped back to reality, put the car in reverse, and backed up all the way down the tracks until we reached the road. Then, without a word, he drove on to dinner. My repeated demands for an explanation brought silence, that night and over the ensuing year and a half.

Similar episodes occurred during this period. Duncan would become spacey, lose contact with his surroundings, make chewing movements with his mouth and fall down. Once he fell off a ladder in front of the children and crashed into the living room windows. He would lose touch for just a minute or two, and I'd run for the orange juice, thinking he had diabetes, which his father developed at about the same age. The episodes only lasted a minute or two, and then he'd be fine.

At our semiannual summit conference in December of 1984, I said, "Hey, we really need to get you some help." Duncan said he was uncomfortable with the doctor we had (Duncan's objection was that we knew Sam socially, but mine was that Sam's first love was his lab at Mass General and for this problem, whatever it was, I realized we needed a good clinician). I said, "Fine, I'll find you a new doctor." And I spent a long time looking over the next few months before I settled on John Arthur, an internist at Westbury General. In one emphatically memorable sentence, Gary Sabin, a dentist-friend of ours in Conover, had recommended him: "John Arthur is a good person *and I trust his medical judgment!*" Duncan went in to see Arthur for a physical in March, but never kept his promise to tell the doctor about these episodes.

Some time that spring, Hillary Sabin, Gary's wife, told me that she had been with Duncan when he spaced out one evening (at Regina College where the four of us had gone to swim – Gary and I were still down in the locker rooms when her encounter with a spaced-out Duncan had taken place up in the lobby). She told me she was convinced Duncan's problem was substance abuse, because his behavior was identical to her sister's and brother-in-law's, both of whom were cocaine addicts. I dismissed the idea as being ridiculous, because Duncan, who was into healthy food and exercise, was the last person on earth who would ever abuse his body.

But the spacey episodes continued to occur. With our impending move to Switzerland, I was getting nervous, so Gabriel, I did what I often do when I'm nervous – Miss Bookworm went to the library. In fact I went to a number of libraries because I wanted to find out what was going on with Duncan's body. It was probably something metabolic or neurological, I reasoned. When I read about temporal lobe epilepsy (TLE), it seemed to me I had found a perfect fit. This possible explanation also suggested a plausible reason for Duncan's silence about the episodes: people with TLE don't remember what happens to them. When these symptoms appear for the first time in someone Duncan's age, there is a possibility that one is dealing with a condition "secondary" to the epilepsy – usually a brain tumor or other organic brain disease, unless there is a history of head trauma (and Jock has since confirmed there was not). I thought the worst, and not without reason.

Later in May, I went back to see Dr. Arthur myself. I had only met him once, but my impression of him was positive. He seemed smart, careful, conservative – the way I like a doctor to be – and a good listener, some-one who expects the patient to be a partner in making the healthcare relationship work. Most important of all, Duncan had said he liked him.

I began with a description of the railroad track episode, and all the one-car accidents, space-outs, and falls. I listed objective observations (Duncan falls down, loses contact with surroundings) and subjective observations (he's lost his sense of humor; it's like the person is going away). I was scrupulously accurate on my data, but my incorrect interpretation would come back to haunt me: "Look, it's not a marital problem. It's not a psy-chological problem. It's a medical problem!" And definite about wanting a straight answer: "You and I are going to get along a lot better if you don't pull any punches with me. Now what do you think this is?"

The blue-grey eyes met mine and didn't blink. "I think you already know, Mrs. Charbonnier. You tell me."

"No, that's your department. I'm not trying to do your job." I sat back in my chair, resolved to say no more. Ever Asa's daughter, I knew the ground rules.

"Tell me what you think it is," repeated John Arthur.

He's going to make me say it out loud, I thought. "All right. Partial complex epilepsy – with psychomotor attacks."

His body jerked forward, but his eyes hadn't moved from mine. I froze, not knowing if I could talk again, for a minute. Thankfully, he spoke first.

"You're being awfully specific, but you're probably right." I knew it would be poor form to cry in front of him, and it took a lot of effort not to. It was one thing to sit in a library, alone, with *Clinical Neurology* and my worst suspicions, and quite another to hear smart John Arthur say, ". . . but you're probably right."

Then he added that we would have to do an EEG and CT and get Duncan to a neurologist, and it was agreed that I would begin keeping a medical log of Duncan's "seizure episodes," as family members of such patients are advised to do.

"What about driving?" I asked. "Do I have to be concerned about that? I worry about the children. My heart sinks every time they go off in the car with him."

"Let's wait and see what the test results show."

"You know, lately I've been getting mad at him when he falls down and refuses to get help. But I won't get mad at him anymore. Now I have insight."

I waited a few days to tell Duncan I'd been to Arthur, because we were both supposed to have a meeting with Leslie Drew, and I wanted Duncan to have a crack at the Genesis opportunity. Duncan said Leslie also wanted to meet me, but I didn't find out why until Leslie came to our house a few days later.

As part of the new company, Leslie planned to develop a newsletter on protein engineering for the Japanese market; Shinyaku Chemical had already put up the money for it, and Leslie needed a writer. Because of my writing/Japan background, Duncan had said to Leslie, "I think my wife can help you." Duncan knew that I was chomping at the bit to get back in the work force, and he thought this would be a wonderful challenge for me. I wasn't so sure, but in view of what I'd learned at the library, I knew I had to try.

On the way to my next meeting with Leslie (about 1 June) , I said two short prayers as I drove down Route 128: "Oh God, please let Duncan live!" and "Give me this opportunity, and I will make the most of it!" In the years that followed, both of these prayers were to be answered – but, I think you would agree, in most mysterious ways.

V

The Racing Years

You who seek an end of love, love will yield to business:
be busy, and you will be safe.

— Ovid, *Remedia Amoris*

At this point, Gabriel, Leslie Drew's talks with Duncan about assuming the presidency of the new company were put on hold until our family returned from Switzerland. But Leslie said he wanted to see me now, to pursue the idea of a newsletter for the Japanese. He invited me to Genesis's temporary quarters, a one-room, makeshift office behind the funeral parlor in Westbury Center. "We'll be moving into larger quarters this fall," he said. Then we got down to business. I told Leslie right up front that I knew about Japan, and I knew I could write, but that I knew nothing about chemistry and even less about computers. Never to be deterred, in typical Leslie Drew fashion he replied firmly, "You'll learn!" We shook hands and agreed I'd start sometime after our family returned from Switzerland. I hurried home to the children, and announced to Hailey Canfield who was baby-sitting for them, "I got the job!"

I would later learn that Leslie Drew could have talked the flowers off the wallpaper, if he ever put his mind to it. Mercurial, glib, charismatic, Leslie Drew was a high-tech version of P. T. Barnum. Only later did Leslie tell me that over wine at my house two weeks before, he had made up his mind to hire me. What he couldn't know, and would not learn for another four years, is that I was just as determined to get the job, keep the job, and build it into something beyond anything he could have imagined. I knew something was seriously wrong with Duncan, and from the beginning I saw Genesis as an opportunity that could turn into a means of support for me and the children, if I worked hard enough and if the worst happened.

The weekend following Leslie's visit to our home, I told Duncan about my seeing Dr. Arthur, and he was furious, but agreed to return and submit to medical tests that would be conducted by Bruce Pfizer, a Westbury General neurologist. I didn't understand why Duncan was angry. If I'd had his symptoms, I'd have hoped someone cared enough about me to consult a doctor. But he never saw it that way, not once over the next four years.

Well, we went off to Switzerland, Gabriel, but it was not the "Roman Holiday" everyone back home in Conover thought it was. All through the summer, Duncan's symptoms persisted, and I confided in Darcy when they came to visit us in Geneva, but she didn't want Jock to know, and Duncan didn't want anyone to know. I didn't even tell Asa. Gabriel, you can see the medical logs from the Ringling & Haycroft file for the full record of Duncan's seizure episodes, 1985–1989, but a few vignettes from our summer abroad will illustrate the point that the children and I were living with something disturbing and beyond our understanding.

On our way to Switzerland, GEC sent us to England for a week. While Duncan worked, the children and I toured London on our own. On Saturday, Duncan was finally able to join us, and what a happy day we had, starting with a first row view of the changing of the guard at Buckingham Palace (Amanda dropped her beloved Panda bear through the iron gates and upset the ceremony when a sympathetic soldier was charmed into retrieving it for her). Then it was on to lunch at an Indian restaurant (my kids were practically weaned on curry!), and a leisurely afternoon at the British Museum, followed by a trip to a toy store in Oxford Street. I went off to shop down the block, and when I returned, the children brought me to Duncan, who was wandering in a daze on the lower level of the store. He was very confused. "What are we doing here?" he asked me. "Buying toys," I said, realizing it was past time to settle on purchases and head back to our hotel.

More episodes of confusion and inexplicable behavior followed over our summer in Switzerland. One night Duncan returned from a day in München and joined me for a quiet hotel dinner after I'd put the children to bed. When the steward came to take our wine order, Duncan looked back and forth, repeatedly, from the steward to me, and finally asked me in an angry voice, "*What* is that guy's problem?" I gave the steward our wine order in French, hoping his English hadn't been good enough to understand Duncan. Another day Duncan forgot where he'd left the car, and we spent two hours walking the streets of Basel, hunting for it. Often he would be spacey and out of it in the evenings, and sometimes he would break into a sweat and fall down. We were getting used to it, and accepted that this was the way it was going to be.

While the children played and explored during our summer in Europe, I spent the days (and nights) studying, trying to drum some science into my head: proteins, nucleic acids, biochemistry, molecular biology, drug design. For the former lowest "F" in chemistry, it was the intellectual equivalent of trying to climb Mt. Everest with olive oil on my hands and feet. There were no reference points, except for the articles and prepositions in the sentences. So I pretended it was French: I approached my reading as a foreign language, one word at time. One day Duncan came home and found me surrounded by a circle of seven dictionaries, one for biochemistry, one for medicine, and so forth. I really believed that if I worked hard enough, I could make myself understand every word.

Asa was not pleased to hear I was going back to work. "I just don't see how you can neglect your husband and children by doing this." I would hear this a lot from him over the next few years, and it hurt, but I made myself brush it aside. If we were lucky and Duncan came out of this all right, Asa would never have to know what I'd been through. And if Duncan became more ill, then in time Asa would understand what I had done. Certainly under the current circumstances, all the admonitions to "stay home and be a good wife and mother," made no sense whatsoever.

The Duncan I had known and loved was disappearing before my eyes. Looking over my medical log from the summer of 1985, I think you'll agree I had sufficient cause for alarm. I began to hang out at the libraries of the World Health Organization and the Geneva Medical School, trying to learn more about Duncan's symptoms. All that I read remained a perfect match for all that I'd seen. The books said that false negative test results were the norm for people with temporal lobe epilepsy, and that it could be years before concrete proof would appear, and that it might never appear. By August, when everyone in Europe was on vacation, I had both libraries to myself. One day at the Geneva Medical School, I just surrounded myself with neurology books, and hid behind them, and cried.

In the second week of September, we returned to Boston. On our first day home, Duncan's stepsister, Lori Kincaid, who'd recently moved to Conover and been taking care of our house all summer, announced to me that Duncan was behaving in a "slow and confused manner"; and the next day, when I returned home from doing errands, I found Duncan in the kitchen, semi-spacey and acting weird. He kept walking into walls and into the wastebasket, before I finally got him to lie down. After dinner, he fell into a very deep sleep, as he often did after these episodes of confusion.

On our third day home, Lori came over for dinner, and with me watched in sadness as Duncan became increasingly slowed in his actions and sloppy with his food, until he was barely in contact with his surroundings. And then he spilled spaghetti all over Spencer, got up, and staggered up the stairs, his coordination nearly gone. I followed and got him to bed. There was a cold sweat on his forehead. "I'm exhausted," he said, and he fell into a deep sleep for the next twelve hours. When he woke up the next day, he said, "I'm still exhausted."

Several weeks later, he spaced out again, and announced to me and the children that he felt "like I'm somewhere else — as if there are other ways of being," and added that he felt like he "was outside" of what was happening. Another time, we were in a restaurant, and when the waiter came to take our order, Duncan became angry and insisted to the waiter, "Don't you want to know my name?" and the waiter had replied, "Well, I think I know your name, Sir. Let me just check on the reservation list, here. Ah yes, Mr. Charbonnier, is there anything I can get for you?" It was very sad to watch all this at certain times, and totally baffling at others, like the night Duncan spaced out and kept saying, "Are you using razors?" Now what the hell did that mean? I called Arthur.

Dr. Arthur sent Duncan to a second Westbury neurologist, Dr. Richard Thorensen, who repeated the EEG and CT studies. That autumn, just a few months after our return from Switzerland, Duncan began a new job in GEC's newly-established Computer-Integrated Manufacturing (CIM) group, and I went to work for Leslie Drew. Both jobs were new territory, and both were exciting. We were brimming with things to tell each other at the end of every day. But Duncan's symptoms continued, and I continued to record them in my log.

Things continued in this way over the next few years, until one Sunday evening in September of 1987, when Duncan had a particularly bad episode. He behaved in slow motion and was spacey throughout dinner. Afterward, he spoke incoherently and collapsed at the foot of the stairs in front of the children. They helped me carry him up to bed. When I came back down awhile later, they demanded an explanation. Spencer went so far as to say he wanted to discuss Duncan's falling with Dr. Arthur. As it turned out, I had an appointment for a routine check-up a few days later, and agreed to take them with me.

Dr. Arthur could not have been better with them. He gave Spencer, and even little Amanda, a chance to express their concerns. Then he asked them questions and was patient while they answered. He was sensitive to their fears, but at the same time he was honest with them. Spencer, in particular, later said how much he'd liked that. Arthur told the children he would order more tests, and that we would work together to find out what was wrong with their Dad. Though Duncan was again furious that we had been to see Arthur, he did consent to what turned out to be the fourth round of CTs and EEGs.

Altogether, four neurologists had been involved in Duncan's case — Drs. Bruce Pfizer and Richard Thorensen from Westbury General, then Dr. Bruce Landsberg from New England Medical Center downtown, and in this latest 1987 round, Dr. Hugo Schell, a private practitioner in Brandon, "the grand pooh-bah of all neurologists of the greater western Boston suburbs," as I'd heard him laughingly called. "He's the guy they send the really tough cases to, the ones no one else can solve," said John Arthur. Schell ordered a 24-hour EEG; contrast dyes were injected into Duncan's brain; every effort was made to induce a positive test result. The results Schell obtained were again negative. Everything had come back negative, *every time*, which was an enormous relief on one level, but left one big unanswered question on another level — *what* was causing these episodes?

I somehow put this question aside, and the four of us went on with our lives.

But I continued to keep my log, and to feel grateful. Maybe God was giving this family a little reprieve. One evening, during cocktail hour, I had come into the living room, and found Duncan staring out the window at the children, happily playing in the Town Meadowland behind our house. "Oh, if I could only have a little more time with them," I heard him say.

By now I had become expert at holding back my tears and fooling almost everyone. Only Leslie Drew noticed. As he helped me carry a large platter into the dining room one Sunday evening, he was drawn to Ginny Bear, Amanda's favorite large stuffed animal that we kept in a corner high chair. Leslie stopped short, nearly dropping the lamb roast.

"Ursula, why is that bear wearing safety glasses?" he demanded.

"Because, Leslie, life is a dangerous place . . ." I replied. Leave it to Leslie to discern the detail. My words trailed away as I tried to avoid his gaze, but the dark Drew eyes had penetrated my own. No questions, Leslie, I pled in silence. My boss turned away and engaged my husband in small talk. I settled the children in their chairs and poured the wine for dinner. "I hope you're not offended Leslie, we give Spencer and Amanda a taste on special occasions, so that it won't be forbidden fruit when they grow up."

"My mother always did the same thing," said Leslie Drew, eyeing me curiously. "She was French, you know."

Throughout these years, we focused on our work and our family, nurturing and enjoying each other and each other's progress. *Molecular Modelling News* and my situation at Genesis had both got off to bumpy starts, but Duncan, who is a master of diplomacy, coached me every step of the way and taught me how to make my professional life work. He also continued to take on a lot of household responsibilities, and even offered to go to the grocery store and do errands on Saturdays so that I would be free to write. Outsiders marveled at the "team spirit" in our household, and often I did, too. Spencer and Amanda were also doing well: they enjoyed learning, excelled in school and had lots of friends. In the spring of 1988, Spencer won the Principal's Award (Student of the Year) at his school by an unprecedented unanimous vote, and he followed in his dad's footsteps by serving as President of the Student Council. Amanda, too, was thriving.

At about this time, we also decided to put our financial/legal life in order, in case the worst happened. It was the one area of my life I considered untidy, especially in view of Duncan's deteriorating condition. After some prodding on my part, he finally agreed to hire a financial advisor in 1987. One of his good friends at work, Ivy Parrish, referred us to Westbury Financial Ventures, a relatively new and aggressive firm that was producing consistent and wonderful results for its young and growing client base. In years to come, I would learn that WFV founder, Hobart Holliday, lived in Conover, and that his oldest son, Ethan, was in Amanda's grade.

During the 1980s, a number of Germane executives had signed on with Westbury Ventures, and we decided to join them. After initially assigning our case to a series of advisors, Westbury finally matched us up with Rob Stoughton. Young, bright, and easy to work with, Rob and later his brother, Frank, helped us organize all facets of our financial life: a savings plan for Spencer and Amanda's college educations, the revision of our wills and more sophisticated estate planning. I found some relief in these initiatives, for Duncan's seizures were not going away. And I was forever mindful of the third set of neurologist's words to me, "I don't know what this is, Mrs. Charbonnier, but whatever it is, it is just going to get worse." For the sake of the children, I wanted to be sure all our affairs were in order.

Neither Duncan nor I were happy with our Dutch Colonial, and the tiny Cotswold cottage with which we'd both fallen in love in 1981, and not been able to afford in 1983, came on the market again. This time it was to be ours. Rob and Frank helped us cruise through all the paperwork, and set up a special banking relationship for us with Hub Safe Deposit & Trust, a bank that handed out very few mortgages. We moved into Inverary Lane last summer (1988).

Duncan said several times how smart we were to be buying a small house, something that would be just right when the kids were gone in another seven years – what a perfect house this would be in which to be grandparents, and I had no reason to doubt him. In fact, over the years he'd occasionally say he married me because he thought I'd "be a terrific grandmother!" Maybe we really would get to be grandparents someday, I told myself in my more optimistic moments.

But then reality would intrude. The sweats and spaceyness would begin at dinner with the children, along with lip-smacking, cud chewing-like movements. It could not be hidden or denied. Duncan would rock back and forth in his chair in the dining room, in his own world. Next to us, but far from us. One night in May, he finally got up from the table and stumbled up the stairs, saying over and over again that he loved me more than I could know, but that he felt he was "at the edge." Several nights later, it happened again, but this time Duncan became angry, for no reason apparent to the three of us, and stormed out of the house, "to take a long walk," he said.

Years of this behavior had trained Spencer and Amanda to accept it quietly. Amanda said several times that this was "just part of his problem" and added, "You know what, I think we're going to get the answer after he dies." I looked over at my eight year-old daughter and thought, how does she bear it so well?

VI

Hell

Our torments also may in length of time
Become our elements.

— John Milton, *Paradise Lost*

In 1988, Gabriel, just four days before Christmas, everything began to change at Inverary Lane.

For some time, maybe the previous six months to a year, Duncan had urged me to demand a lot more money from Genesis. He felt I was grossly underpaid. I suppose I was, but at the same time I loved the job. I had begun to master parts of it; and then there was that wonderful flexible schedule that made it possible to work without shortchanging the children. I wasn't ready to rock the boat, but Duncan continued to press me to tell Genesis I needed a 50 percent raise that fall or I would have to quit. My publication had a 100 percent renewal rate among those still in the CAMD field, and Duncan said that gave me "plenty of leverage."

I don't like to give ultimatums, but I began to feel he might be right, so I presented my case to Archie McGowan (my boss, who had co-founded the company with Leslie Drew and Frank Morrow), and to my amazement and delight, in mid-December I got the 50 percent raise, which Archie made retroactive to the first November pay period. When I came home and told Duncan, his reaction stunned me: "You're still underpaid, and the only reason you can afford to have a job you love is that I'm supporting you!"

That wasn't all that happened in December. For the first time in four years the travel and excitement related to a major GEC project Duncan led were winding down. Then a headhunter approached him about a terrific job possibility at BBB, another high tech firm, and Duncan seemed really excited, but the interview never materialized. In mid-month, Germane sent Duncan to a "Leadership & Mastery" course, and he told me that from it he learned that he was "doing everything right in [his] professional life, and everything wrong in [his] personal life."

Very abruptly Duncan stopped encouraging my professional growth, and he stopped going to the grocery store and cut back enormously on pitching in around the house. Then he withdrew emotionally and started staying up late, listening to music through earphones, and tuning out the family. Overnight, Mr. Nice Guy, the Team Player, disappeared from our lives, and for the first time Duncan complained about the amount of time I was spending on Genesis work.

He continued to be very unpleasant into January. One morning Duncan announced that his problems would all go away if he just got caffeine and alcohol out of his life. This puzzled me – Duncan had already eliminated caffeine (in tea, coffee and colas) and I'd never seen him abuse alcohol. I called Arthur to tell him what was going on and to get some advice. Privately I worried that we were now starting to see the personality changes of a brain tumor, and I told Arthur about this and Duncan's most serious recent space out episode when our neighbor, Ted Talbot, had come to dinner in November:

"We had a pretty full house that night. Amanda had one overnight guest, Spencer had two, and Ted had brought their large Siberian samoyed. Ted and I were having cocktails in the living room, and I had thought Duncan was chatting with the children in the next room, when Amanda suddenly appeared to say that Duncan was 'acting weird,' and that her friend 'Emily saw it,' and that I must 'do something right now! Emily saw it. I hate this, especially when I have a friend over!'

"At this point, Duncan staggered and stumbled into the living room, and walked into the love seat by the fireplace. Then he backed away and walked into it a few more times. I pulled him aside and took him upstairs. 'Give me five minutes,' he said. Well, he came back down a little later, and we got through dinner, but Duncan behaved strangely the rest of the evening and was unable to conduct an intelligent conversation at dinner. Ted said goodnight at the earliest opportunity."

Arthur listened to all this. "Ursula, I think it's time we got a third party involved, because you and I are getting nowhere. Who could you get to talk to Duncan?"

"Since Duncan's closest friend, Dick McCall, is about to move to Japan, Jock – his father – is the only other person I can think of."

"Well then talk to him, Ursula. Maybe he can make some progress with Duncan."

That night, Duncan came home and poured himself an enormous glass of wine, filling up the whole goblet, something I'd never seen him do before. "I thought you were eliminating alcohol," I said.

"I was on the wrong track," he replied.

My father-in-law was scheduled to pass through Boston a few weeks later, and I invited him over to my office, so that we could chat privately. For the first time, I told him about the many episodes of Duncan's worrisome behavior, from the railroad track episode in 1983 to the present. To my surprise, Jock seemed disbelieving and even a little angry. "I want to see a copy of your log," he said coldly. I had anticipated this request (though not its tone) and had one ready for him. "I also want to talk to your father and Dr. Arthur."

When both of them corroborated my story (I had told Asa what was going on back in 1987, but Asa to his credit never intruded by discussing it with Duncan), Jock said he wanted to take Duncan skiing for five days in Colorado, in March. "I need an extended period to really talk with Duncan and encourage him to get some help. And I promise I'll call you *before* he gets back to Boston, so you'll know what to expect."

But Jock did not phone me until the day *after* Duncan returned home, and this is what he said: "I want you to know, Ursula, that you are a significant part of the cause of Duncan's problem. Unhappiness with you has created his medical symptoms. Furthermore, I intend to call Dr. Arthur back and tell him just that." This struck me as ridiculous. How could anyone be responsible for another person's falling down?

That night, over a beautiful oyster dinner that Duncan had taken great care in preparing, he announced, "I have nothing in common with you but a checkbook and two children."

I paused, forked oyster in mid-air, and stared at Duncan, in burning awareness that he was going to be just as copping-out and accusatory as his father had been on the phone that afternoon.

"*If* we have a marital problem, I would have preferred to hear it from you and not your father! I also don't buy the idea that I am responsible for your falling down."

"I haven't been honest with you for years," Duncan lashed back. "And it's your fault I haven't been honest."

"Well, what should I do while I wait for you to get honest?"

"That's up to you," he replied. "Everything I've done has been according to your agenda – having children, leaving Cross Motors, working for Germane."

History was being revised before my eyes. I hadn't gotten pregnant by myself, and this man had always doted on children – his and everyone else's. "The best dad in the world," friends often said of him. As for Cross Motors, Duncan had never liked the place. He'd spent four years looking for ways to get out, and was thrilled when he finally managed it. Working for Germane had not been my idea, either. I was the woman who was homesick for New York. Yes, Boston had grown on me, but it had not been my first choice. It was home now, and where I wanted to be, but Boston had never been on *my* agenda.

By this time my oysters were drowning in tears, and I couldn't eat. Duncan went on, showing no emotion whatsoever, in a series of comments that made no sense: "I only married you because I was lonely and you were enthusiastic . . . Well, what has sex to do with love? . . . I'm tired of being best and first at everything like I have been my whole life."

I'd had enough and stood up to leave the table, whereupon Duncan shifted into a sweetly conciliatory tone: "You know, I feel really badly about this."

The incongruence of content and tone troubled me. There was something indelibly horrifying about hearing a message of loathing delivered in a loved one's voice of tenderness.

That night I cried myself to sleep, and woke up about 4 a.m., feeling weak, nauseated, and hungry all at the same time. I remember stumbling down to the kitchen and choking down some bouillon, but I felt empty and deserted inside, like a bombed out city from World War II, an emotional Dresden. What on earth had I done to deserve this? And would I ever find out? Where had the person, Duncan, gone? And who was this monster that had taken over his body?

I began thinking what it would take for me to restructure the lives of me and the children under our rapidly deteriorating scenario. I asked Spencer and Amanda what had been missing from their lives, and was struck that their answers matched my own. "Mom, we want vacations, like other families have, dinners with friends, a pet, family outings, more time together, more visits with faraway friends." In short, what many of us think of as a normal, everyday life.

In fact, our little foursome had become increasingly isolated in recent years, but the process had been so gradual that I only now noticed it. Duncan had been critical of a number of acquaintances and regularly discouraged me from inviting people to our home. The previous summer he'd even refused to attend a large family wedding in Pennsylvania, and only years later would I learn he had blamed our absence on me. I went along with all the social withdrawal, in part because I was busy with work, but also because I didn't want Duncan to have a "seizure" episode in front of others, as he had at our dinner with Ted Talbot.

How, I wondered, would I get through the difficult period ahead? I would do it by focusing on the good and positive things in my life: good health, great kids who are team players, and a wonderful job in a growth industry. This was also an opportunity to show the children that we are all responsible for our own lives, for the form and direction they take. "We can't blame others for our problems," I told them. "Our answers lie within ourselves." I hoped I was on the way to finding mine.

But in fact I was still very much on the train. Every morning at eight, before Asa saw his first patient, I would call and recount the previous night's horrors. And every morning he would patiently listen to me and say, "Don't crack. Don't break. Duncan's trying to make you crack. Don't break. Be strong."

Then I would call my dear friend Julie in Connecticut, because there were days when I really thought I must be losing my mind. And she'd give me a different, but equally healthy message. "Look, this is not the Duncan we have all known and loved. But this man is sick, Ursula. You have to see that he's sick. It's not you. You're fine. I promise. You're all right. He's the one with the problem. But you've done all you can for him. Now you have to take care of Spencer and Amanda, and yourself."

In the midst of these confusing weeks, Jock called me again to say he'd finally caught up with Dr. Arthur on the phone, and that our internist had recommended Duncan "go on medication for his seizures." So why wasn't Duncan on medication?, I wondered, the next time I talked to Arthur.

"Your father-in-law never called me," said the doctor, "but if he had, I'd have told him what I told you – that medication would have been my recommendation if things had been unchanged. But I no longer consider Duncan's problem medical."

I called Jock back and gave him hell. I'd had enough of the Charbonniers' "mushroom treatment" ("Feed them shit and keep them in the dark," as Duncan was so fond of saying).

Jock showed no discomfort whatsoever at having been caught in another lie. "You should never have gotten doctors involved in Duncan's situation," he said angrily. "And stay away from doctors now, or you'll just make everything worse."

But staying away from doctors was not to be in the cards. In late March, at a regular check-up, Arthur found a lump in my breast, a big one that we couldn't believe I'd missed; then one night in early April, blood poured out of my body for two straight hours, something that had never happened to me before. Was my good health going too? At that point I finally lost it and screamed at Duncan, "You who have no appreciation of life, get away from me!" When the bleeding finally stopped and I came to bed, Duncan asked if I'd remembered to close the garage door.

Throughout this period, Spencer and Amanda continued to insist that Duncan was "sick," and didn't waver an iota. They said it to me every day. Because Duncan was such a loving, kind husband and father for so long, and because they could see no reason for him to have changed, they didn't waver. "And if he's not sick," said Amanda, "then either he's been a very good actor all these years or he's a very mean man going around messing up other people's lives. But I think Dad is sick, Mom, no matter what Dr. Arthur and Granddad say."

I didn't know what to believe any more. But it was all but impossible to believe what was happening before my eyes. Spencer and Amanda said all of this actually was happening, but as I told Arthur, "If it weren't for my kids, I would think that I was losing my marbles." They matter-of-factly accepted all they saw. Maybe only adults torture themselves with doubts about the unbelievable.

One night I asked Amanda, "Do you remember what life was

like before?"

And she answered, "Everyone was nice. Dad was spacey, but Dad was still kind; and Mom and Spencer were kind too, and they both still are."

As spring progressed, family dinners, formerly a delight of our life together, degenerated into tearful nightmares that left me feeling tired and emotionally battered.

One night Spencer asked Duncan if he could take a dinner tray up to his room because he had so much homework. Duncan said fine, and then just minutes later became angry with Spencer for carrying food up to his room and not joining all of us for dinner. Spencer and Amanda were nonplussed. Well, my son came back and ate at the table, but he was confused. This from a father who has always stressed consistency!

I decided things might improve if I went away for a few days, so I went off to New York to visit friends. While I was gone, the children had their hands full. When I came home, they gave me an earful, telling me that Duncan had been unkind all weekend, "without any reason," and that Ivy Parrish had come over and stayed for three hours, had tea on the patio, then gone off on a walk with Duncan, leaving the children alone.

"They also tried to make us go flying in her airplane," said Spencer, "but we wouldn't go."

I knew that Ivy loved to fly, and that she and Duncan occasionally took short flights to the Cape over their lunch hour. I accepted this, that Ivy and Duncan were good work friends, in the same way that I have friends at work or in other parts of my life, not all of whom are female. But the marital relationship is an exclusive one from my perspective, and Duncan had always claimed to share that view. The children told me that the relationship with Ivy had gone beyond a work friendship. I hated hearing this from my children.

"Mom, I don't like to tell you this, but we felt uncomfortable having Ivy in our house," said Spencer.

"I don't like Ivy either," said Amanda. "She's just trying to get on our good side. Mom, I'm just like a dog – I know bad people when I sniff them."

I relayed the children's comments to Duncan. "Under no circumstances are the children to go flying in her airplane."

"Well, if they change their minds, they will go flying in her airplane, and you'll have nothing to say about it!" he retorted angrily.

Actually, I hadn't even been thinking along the lines that Ivy and Duncan were emotionally involved, but when only a week later I got a similar message from Duncan's secretary, Dot Colton, I could no longer ignore the possibility.

"Ursula, I want to ask you something . . ." she began tentatively. "Have you noticed anything different at home about the way Duncan is behaving? We've noticed changes at work. Can we talk confidentially?"

I felt torn. My first loyalty was to my husband, so I ended the conversation. But then Dot continued it the next time we spoke. "Ursula, it's part of a secretary's job to read faces, and Duncan's face isn't the same . . . He's under tremendous pressure . . . being pulled in different directions . . . He's being more impatient, negative and critical with others, something he's never done before in my presence . . . there is more of a look of strain on his face. Others have noticed it, too. Last week he told a co-worker to 'go slap around' some people in another department . . . You know Duncan doesn't even speak that way. There are just things I think you should know," she summed up, indicating there was much she was leaving unsaid.

I had to listen to all she was telling me, but I didn't dwell on it, because my major concern at that point was the well-being of Spencer and Amanda. Duncan's treatment of them had gone from doting to mean in the space of one season. It had become unacceptable, and I confronted him on it.

"Duncan," I began, "do you think your behavior might be having a negative impact on Spencer and Amanda?"

"Yes, in the short run, but that's not nearly as important as doing the right things for myself," he answered bluffly. "And now that I'm being completely honest about my feelings, Ursula, I'm not going to be having any more seizures."

I relayed this to John Arthur who replied, "Well, we'll just see about that, won't we?"

My patience with Duncan now grew shorter. "Why should we go on living under the same roof if you're not in love with me anymore?" I asked him.

"Well, why not?" he grinned. "A marriage without love was good enough for my parents, it ought to be good enough for you, and there are many reasons to stay together besides love – it's convenient, or for the children. Ursula, why don't you just look on this as living with a college roommate? After all, you didn't love your college roommate."

"I didn't have a marriage certificate with my college roommate. Furthermore Duncan, to stay in a marriage where I am no longer loved would be sending a very unhealthy message to the children. It would also be impossible for me to sleep with you."

"I don't see why," he said.

"Because sex for me means love and a connection with someone."

"Well, for me it doesn't," said Duncan blithely. "I like you, and I respect you, but sex for me means nothing more than that. It certainly doesn't correlate with love."

Now look Gabriel, the person I've lived with for all these years could never have said, felt or thought such a thing. I'm more sure of that than I am of anything I'm seeing or hearing these days. Fourteen years' worth of scrapbook pictures say this can't be happening, but it is. I showed Duncan a candid photo Amanda had taken of us when we were raking leaves, when he'd sneaked up and hugged me.

And this was his reaction: "Oh, that's just a picture of a man hugging a woman. It doesn't mean anything."

"One thing I do know for sure, Duncan, even during these confusing days, a marriage without love is nowhere close to good enough for me."

"That's right," said Amanda, who had been listening from an adjacent room. "And my mom doesn't want to live in a 'darriage' and neither do we!"

"What's a 'darriage'?" asked Duncan.

"It's a divorced marriage, and we don't like it."

"I don't love your mom for many reasons!" Duncan shouted at her, and then with Amanda still in the room, he turned his attention back to me, "I know one thing for sure, you don't give a shit about me! I don't believe you! I don't trust you!"

At this point Spencer walked in, and Duncan turned to both children and threatened, "I'm going to get your mother thrown out of the house and live in it with you. And if you choose to live with your mother, I will see to it that you lose your house, your town, and your school. But if you stay with me, you can keep everything. Your mom is saying bad things about me."

"No, she's not!" said Amanda. "And why are you being so mean to my mom?"

"I told you before – I don't love your mom!"

"We want to stay at Inverary Lane with our mom!"

"Well, I might make that possible," said Duncan, momentarily shifting into a conciliatory tone, followed by a nasty one. "And then again, I might not! I'll have to see."

The three of us then explained that losing our pleasant old home life and the old Duncan/Dad was bad enough, that we shouldn't have to lose our home/school/friends, too, that we liked our lives as they were and wanted to be able to go on with them. Duncan's response was to laugh and make more contradictory statements.

His shifting moods and threats began to terrify me. I had no idea what my rights were and started walking around scared. Afraid to go to a lawyer, as friends were encouraging me to do. And afraid not to. One day at a plant store when I handed the cashier my Visa card, she said, "Address?" and I thought I would suffocate in fear.

The fear was getting harder to hide, and it surfaced in moments that should have been routine. At a regular six month check-up, our dentist Dr. Wally Post said he wanted to talk to me about replacing old fillings. "Some should be done right away, Ursula, but others can wait."

"No," I said, "let's do them all now."

He looked at me quizzically. "Ursula, I've known you for ten years, and it's not like you to encourage doing work that I said could wait a year. Now what's going on?"

I couldn't answer him; I was totally focused on trying not to cry. "Afraid of loss of insurance?" he said, looking me in the eye.

Tears brimmed over the edge, and I nodded. "Come into my office. I want to talk to you." He followed me in and closed the door. "Duncan has been more into himself and different for some time. I noticed it a few years ago – when he had all that work done in 1987, remember?" Tears were now streaming down my face. Still unable to speak, I nodded. "And we'll do all that work now," he said. A veteran of much living himself, Dr. Post knew better than I what lay ahead of me.

That night I tried to reach out to my husband. "Talk to me Duncan. Tell me what it would take to make you happy again, to make you feel fulfilled with life."

"I'm afraid of being judged," he replied.

"I promise not to judge. I'll just listen."

"Well . . . I want to start a school to teach people how to deal effectively with corporate life, because I know how to do it and no one else has ever done such a thing before. And I've also been thinking about going back to school and getting into ecology. That would really make me feel good."

I kept my promise, Gabriel. I didn't say one judgmental word. I also didn't tell Duncan that a whole industry exists that is already devoted to helping people cope with corporate life. It seemed unkind and unnecessary. I never stopped trying to reach out to Duncan. Not even when he said: "A wife, children, a house, cars and a community are not for me."

"What is for you?" I replied.

"A three day canoeing trip in Maine without you," (I did offer to go, even though I'm NOT a camper!) "traveling in South America, starting a company, going back to school, and teaching a course." These replies made no sense to me.

"Where are you Duncan?" I asked.

"I'm at sea . . ." he said.

And I never gave up on looking for a rational explanation, no matter how inappropriate his behavior, such as the night he invited Amanda into our bedroom, and inquired, "Amanda, do you think I'm sick?"

"I just want a normal life Dad, like other kids have. I want to go on vacations and do things as a family."

"You don't really think families have fun on vacations, do you? Amanda, I don't like traveling. And I don't like being with your mom."

"But Mom is nice! Why are you being mean to her?"

"I don't like your mom."

"But why? She loves you, and she's not like other moms who expect jewels and furs and big houses – she just wants someone to be nice to her. She loves you, and she buys you presents."

"I don't care about them," said Duncan.

"But you say you love them, and you wear them! I've been there."

During all this, he contradicted himself about travel — he liked it, he didn't like it, and about loving me — he did, he didn't. Watching the confusion in my nine year-old's eyes brought me to tears.

"Duncan, maybe I can't stop all your behavior from touching the children, but with my last breath I vow I will keep it from damaging them."

Whereupon Amanda broke into the conversation. "Someday is some man going to do to me what you've done to Mom?" Duncan laughed at her. "Dad, I want things to be the way they were."

"Things are going to get better," said Duncan.

I'd heard enough and left to shower. Later in the evening, Amanda said, "Dad lied to me again after you left the room. I don't trust him anymore. He says things to me, Mom, and then says he never said them. Why does he do that?" I hugged her, but I had no answer.

This was heartbreaking to see, Gabriel. We spent more than a decade putting everything we had into making these kids loving, trusting and stable individuals. Now I see that foundation being chipped away at, and it angers me. I sense that we are going to ultimately be okay, but sometimes, like today, I just can't see how.

Throughout these months, there were times when all I could do was say to my children, "I love you guys, and you can count on me." It became my 'party line,' whenever Duncan behaved strangely in front of them. Our whole world was falling apart. But as to why, I was more clueless than my children. And thanks to them, I was about to learn.

Spencer and Amanda brought it up first, one bright April afternoon, in the middle of Conover Center. We had just returned some library books, and were in the parking lot of the Isaiah Jones Tavern, when they hit me with it: "Is our dad on drugs?"

This sent *me* reeling back to the library. There was some irony here, Gabriel. As you know, I produce the world's only newsletter on computer-assisted drug design, and yet I didn't know anything about drugs, except for the ethical, therapeutic kind. Without delay, I immersed myself in books; I called my contacts at the National Institute for Drug Abuse in Bethesda, and they sent me information; and some of the scientists at Genesis, who had already begun to share the children's suspicions, sat me down and told me the hard facts of life about drugs. Here's what they said:

Drugs could keep anti-hypertensive drugs from working (Duncan had been taking medication for high blood pressure since about 1980). Drugs would account for the temporal lobe seizure episodes and the negative test results over the years. Drugs would account for the total personality change, including Duncan's comment that a short-run negative impact on Spencer and Amanda wasn't nearly as important to Duncan as "doing the right things for [himself] now." Drugs would have given Duncan the illusion he is "more in control than ever." Drugs and their expense would also account for the unexplained hundreds of dollars of checks for cash that have been withdrawn from our account (not by me) since the third week of December, when this nightmare escalated. And they would explain the nastiness with which Duncan has treated all of us.

Where had I been all these years? Why didn't I know these things?

"Why should you have known these things?" countered Asa. "You didn't grow up with them."

One morning at breakfast I told a very discouraged Spencer that he must speak to Dr. Arthur or some school counselor about what was happening in our family and his feelings about it. He angrily replied, "I'm never going to talk to anybody about this." Then he missed the bus, which he never does, and told me he was unhappy when I drove him to school.

"Spencer, I know life seems difficult now, and that we don't understand why, but fundamentally *life is good* and someday we will understand."

"Yeah, right, Mom."

"In the meantime, you can always count on me."

My sad son opened the car door. "Well, thanks for the ride, Mom, but we aren't a family anymore – because of the way Dad is."

This made me angry, and I told Duncan he absolutely had to start treating the children better. I wondered how much longer I could put off calling an attorney. If drugs were the cause of all this, I knew I couldn't waste much more time, especially after Spencer and Amanda started making fun of Duncan, his frequent trips to the bathroom, and his chronically runny nose, which they explained was a symptom of cocaine use. How did my children know this? They had learned about it in school.

"Oh, is it noticeable?" Duncan asked them during one of these episodes.

"Yes, it's noticeable!" they replied in tones of disgust.

That did it! I called Arthur on his day-off to explore this possibility, and I never call doctors on their days off. We went through all the symptoms and events, and in the end, here's what Arthur said, "Ursula, there are just five possibilities for Duncan's behavior: he's either a very messed-up individual, has a seizure disorder, has had an emotional disruption, has high blood pressure, or there's drug use. But as I told you before, I no longer consider Duncan's problem medical. You know, in about five years Duncan Charbonnier is going to wake up and say 'where the hell was I?' And what am I going to tell him? That he had a deal all these years and he didn't even know it!"

"But you see bad stuff every day," I responded. "How can you be nice to people who create their own problems?"

"There are many kinds of problems besides medical ones," he said wisely. "But you're all right, Ursula."

"Then how come everything is so wrong?"

"Because Duncan is decompensating. When he says that working all day and coming home to you and the kids is 'an empty life,' you have to realize that the emptiness is actually inside Duncan, and not in the environment."

Asa concurred. "Your doctor is right, Ursula. Although a brain tumor or early Alzheimer's could still be a very remote possibility, I think Duncan's problem is 'functional.'"

"What does that mean, Dad?"

"That there is no physiological or medical basis for his problem. Duncan's brain is affected, I'll grant you that, but the cause is not structural or organic in nature. It's behavioral."

Life may have been crumbling on the home front, but circumstances at Genesis couldn't have been better for me. In my performance review, Archie McGowan pronounced me "outstanding across the board." Then he turned personal. "Ursula, we all know there is a major problem at home (it was a little hard to miss – I was down to ninety pounds and my hair had started to fall out), and I won't pry, but I want you to know that I am here for you in the office, outside the office, whatever you need. This little company cares about you, and we want to help you through this time."

"Keep giving me good work to do," I told him, "and I will be all right. I also need to grow in my career because I may be facing the prospect of bringing up two kids on my own, which I can't do on $30,000 a year."

"That 50 percent raise you got last year was the beginning and not the end of what will be happening to you at Genesis," Archie said.

When I told Duncan about my performance review, he asked "How do you explain the turnaround from your corporate situation of three years ago?"

With sincerity I replied, "You taught me everything I know, and I applied it and put my own twist on all of it, and now I've learned how to do it myself." He truly had taught me how to navigate through corporate waters, and I was grateful.

"I'm happy for you," he said flatly.

It has slowly sunk in that Duncan is doing his best to tear me down and isolate me. Whenever I try to remain happy anyway, it only makes him tear me down more. Duncan says I am "an angry person at many different levels." But I think he must really have been describing himself. No one else thinks I am angry, and most of all, I don't think I'm angry, even with all that is going on around me.

As spring wore on, my weight loss escaped no one's attention, except Duncan's. Even our financial advisor, Rob Stoughton, expressed concern when I stopped by Westbury Ventures. "Whether Duncan is ill or bailing out, I don't care," a friend had warned, "just get a handle on where you stand financially."

But I had only the vaguest idea about where we stood, because Duncan had always kept a tight rein on all the paperwork, and whenever I'd asked for it, he'd put me off. Now I needed to understand these matters for myself. Never again would I trust that part of my life to someone else.

"Are you all right?" Rob said in alarm, as he noted my emaciated state.

"Please – just get me the information," I said, "and try to explain to me what it all means."

He put me into a conference room, and came back a few minutes later, his arms filled with files and notebooks of papers. And then very quietly, very gently he began, "Ursula, none of this is as complicated as it seems. Let me walk you through it . . ." and some time later he ended with, ". . . if you need anything else, please call me. I'm here." He knew.

I have lost my best friend and my world has been through the Cuisinart, but something in me is saying to trust people who extend themselves to me now, because I need help from others in a way I never have before. I don't have the energy to doubt anyone. I may be naïve, but I'm trusting my work world, my physician, our financial advisor who is trying to help me learn, and all other people who extend themselves to me now. I somehow believe I am going to be all right, but right now, today, I just can't see how. I don't know how much more of this I can take without explanation.

Am I dealing with a medical problem, a very messed up individual as Arthur suggested, a midlife crisis or a drug addict? Or none of the above, or all of the above?

By now, Duncan had become increasingly paranoid, a trait I would never have used to describe him before. "You've been controlling my relationship with Dr. Arthur, Ursula, but you're not going to be anymore." This struck me as absurd. How could anyone control John Arthur? He was too good at what he did, and he'd been in the business too long. "And you've embellished my seizures, Ursula. But that won't happen anymore – because I'm going to see a marriage counselor."

"A marriage counselor?" What did that have to do with seizures? "But don't people usually go to a marriage counselor *together*?" I asked.

"No. I'm going alone."

This wasn't the way I thought marriage counselors operated, but what did I know? Perhaps I would ultimately be included.

The "marriage counselor" Duncan visited turned out to be a psychiatrist, part of Westbury General Psychiatry, a practice made up of M.D.s and social workers, taking a team approach. Duncan told me we would next see them together, and then I would have the option to make an appointment for myself to discuss "our problem."

"And just what is 'our problem'?" I asked, still in search of a logical explanation.

"I'm not going to tell you, and if you continue to ask me, I'm going to walk out of here," threatened Duncan.

"Well, when are you planning to tell me?" I persisted.

"When I feel like it, Mommy," he replied in an icy tone.

"I am not your Mommy."

I recounted all this to Asa. "What do you think about our getting involved with psychiatrists?"

It wasn't a branch of medicine for which he had any great respect, but to my surprise he thought it was a good idea. "Ursula, I think you're on the right track now. This time, kid, I think you're going to get some answers."

VII

The First of the Paid Enablers

All seems infected that th' infected spy,
As all looks yellow to the jaundic'd eye.

— Alexander Pope, *Essay on Criticism*

Well, Gabriel, our attempts to work with Wilson Garry Culp and his social worker Irena Cossell were not the positive experiences for which I'd hoped. Duncan saw Culp alone at Westbury General, and then we saw Cossell together the following week. I thought she asked a lot of insipid questions, but I tried to answer them politely and cooperate with the process. I encountered her the next day when I went to see Culp at the hospital, and she apologized "for taking Duncan's side" at our session the day before.

"You don't owe me any apology," I said.

Then she apologized again and said, "Mrs. Charbonnier, I am trying to be sympathetic."

"I'm not here for sympathy, Dr. Cossell; I'm here for enlightenment," I said. But I don't think she grasped my point.

As for my session with Culp, he had been in such a hurry to schedule me that they had squeezed me into a shorter-than-usual appointment in what should have been the lunch hour. I had no idea what to expect, but I hoped the conversation would be a little more content-rich than the previous day's talk with Cossell, which had wasted most of my afternoon. As a GEC employee, maybe Duncan could afford to kill half the week in doctors' offices, but I was in the newsletter business. Deadlines were chronic, and time was precious. I didn't like wasting other people's, and I didn't like anyone wasting mine.

But if seeing Culp was going to bring us closer to the truth, then like Asa, I was all for seeing him. Culp bustled in, only a few minutes late. Short, bespectacled, chubby, something in his manner reminded me of Senator John Tower. He motioned me into a little cube chair diagonal to his, and because we were short on time, he dispensed with the niceties and got right into neurology.

Whenever he finished a sentence, his neck would retrovert into his body, like a turtle's. Then whenever he asked another question, it would jut out again, and he would give a little grunt and pat his tummy, while he waited for my answers. When the silences got a little long, and when I had nothing to say, he stirred uncomfortably in his grey cloth cube chair.

Culp kept insisting that I'd had a conversation with Dr. Schell, the fourth of Duncan's neurologists (actually, a colleague of Landsberg's was the only one of Duncan's neurologists with whom I'd ever talked). This answer frustrated him, but it was the truth.

After several iterations, Dr. Culp changed course. "Well, do you know why your husband's so angry with you?"

"No, I really don't," I replied.

"Well, you go home and just ask him about the night you had dinner with senior people from Germane. You created a scene in a restaurant and argued with everyone at the table about gallium arsenide."

My response to that was, "Well, how could I have an argument about gallium arsenide, if I only have a superficial understanding of the subject?" Software engineers at Genesis (who know the true limits of my understanding of chip technologies) later got a great kick out of the gallium arsenide story.

This was a bit much, even from a psychiatrist in whom my confidence was rapidly waning. Culp must have been referring to a February dinner we'd had out in the country with Ivy Parrish, her husband Ozzie Lowe, a senior engineer at Germane, and another senior GEC couple. I could think of no other 1989 social occasion which came close to Culp's description.

It had been a strange evening though, Culp was right about that. Duncan had told me it was to be a business dinner to discuss a new venture. These people were going to break away from GEC to start a new company that would produce fault-tolerant chips, and they ostensibly wanted Duncan to join them. On several occasions in the days before the dinner, Duncan tried to get out of going, but I had been looking forward to an evening out, and in the end we went.

There was a lot of computer talk at the table, and I had little to contribute, but you can learn a lot by listening. Had we talked about gallium arsenide? I did remember something about it, but only recalled making a comment on an article from Japan that had come across my desk that week. Anyway, the GEC people never did talk about the new business venture, which was supposedly the reason for gathering. And another thing about the dinner that seemed strange: I had felt a little disconnected from our companions, as if they were all in some other world. And I'd had only one glass of wine, instead of my usual two. Someone at Genesis joked about it with me later in the summer: "Ursula, did it ever occur to you that maybe you were the only one at the table who wasn't on drugs?"

No, it hadn't occurred to me, but it did now. The conversation with Culp had grown tedious. I looked at my watch and reminded him that my time was up and his next patient was waiting, but he insisted I stay a little longer. He kept trying to get me to say I was angry. Was I angry about this? Was I angry about that?

And when at last I said, "I am angry that Duncan is angry that I got a physician involved in all this," he seemed pleased, and I was finally allowed to leave. Then I said, "Don't *you* want to see me again?" and he replied, "NO! I don't want to see *you* again!"

Then I asked his receptionist how much all this was costing, and when she told me, I said, "A person would have to be nuts to spend that kind of money on . . ." I'd forgotten I was in a psychiatrist's office, and the people in the waiting room started to stare at me.

She smiled and whispered, "You wouldn't believe the people who come in here!"

"*That* does it!!!" I said, and turned on my heel and walked out, only I wasn't out, I was IN – in Dr. Culp's coat closet, and I burst out laughing, opened the door and said, "Well, I'll never get very far going that way!" and then I really did leave.

I think I tolerated another couple of sessions with Irena Cossell and Duncan. Gabriel, here's a sampling of what I heard at them:

"Ursula gets her way all the time . . . I'm leading my life according to her agenda . . . Something in my interpersonal relationship with Ursula is unclear, but I'm still hoping . . . She made me do all the work . . . Ursula didn't do Christmas last year . . . I'm not having enough input into the lives of my children . . . Ursula forced the children to go to camp . . . I was attracted to Ursula because she was attractive and fun to be with, but she isn't anymore . . . Ursula is so defensive!"

"Yes," agreed Cossell, "you're so defensive!" Now what in God's name was I supposed to say in response to that?

"And how was your sex life, Duncan?" inquired Cossell.

"Oh, I guess it was about average," he replied. Cossell bit her lip and looked sad for me, but I was biting mine to keep from roaring with laughter.

I stayed behind at the third and last session I attended, gave her a copy of the medical logs that I asked her to share with Culp, and said to her, "Look, if you people persist in writing this off as a marital problem, you will be missing the core of the problem!" I could tell this didn't register, and at that point saw no reason to continue going.

Later I would follow up by phone to ask what she and Culp had thought about my epilepsy log, which graphically described incidents from 1985 through 1988, and this was her reply, "We didn't think much of it."

Duncan saw Cossell another time by himself, and he has continued to see Culp.

And here's a postscript to my meeting with Culp. I actually did follow up with Duncan about the gallium arsenide dinner. He said I had argued with people about gallium arsenide that night.

"Well am I for it, or against it?" I asked.

"I couldn't hear you, because I was at the other end of the table," Duncan said (that couldn't have been true, because I was seated in the middle — two rows of three people facing each other), "but after that night, people at GEC started taking bets on how soon we'd be divorced."

The following month on Mother's Day, our across-the-street neighbors, Ted Talbot and his housemate Bud Alden (soon to move from Inverary Lane) saw me in the yard and invited me over to see the progress they'd made on *their* Cotswold cottage. Bud is an architect, and he and Ted had spent the past year redoing their house, which was a mate to ours (designed by the same MIT architecture student in the 1930s). Seeing that I was not my typically cheerful self, Ted brought up the episode that had occurred when he'd come for dinner the previous November. It was the first time he had mentioned it. "Ursula, I thought you handled it so well. You were so sensitive and concerned. And yet you carried on like nothing was wrong."

"What did you think you were looking at?" I asked him, grateful that he had finally brought it up and desperately wanting an opinion from another rational adult.

"Epilepsy or diabetes," he said. "Or maybe he'd had too much to drink."

"No, he'd just had a glass of wine. He'd just gotten home from work before you arrived."

Then Bud spoke. "I think you should know about two other strange incidents I've experienced with Duncan in the past few months."

I was all ears.

"One Saturday morning last winter, I encountered Duncan in the Rover Brothers parking lot in Westbury. He was wandering around talking to himself. I went up and tried to engage him in conversation, but he just stared blankly, walked right on by me, and kept talking to himself.

"Then when I was over at your house a few nights ago (Bud had come over to talk about architectural details in *our* Cotswold), after we'd finished going over things inside, I stepped outside with Duncan to chat about the exterior of the house. That's when he said to me, 'Gee Bud, if you like the outside so much, sometime you ought to come over and let us show you the inside.' Don't you see, Ursula, Duncan had entirely forgotten that we'd just been inside!"

"We think he's ill, Ursula," said Ted. "And we're very concerned about you and the children."

Gabriel, Bud and Ted have agreed to testify or otherwise verify that these episodes with Duncan actually took place. (Take them up on that if you need to. They now live in Stover, and we've stayed in touch.)

Coming so soon after my unproductive encounters with Culp and Cossell, this new information from Bud only increased my sense of urgency to find a logical explanation for Duncan's behavior. Returning home, I tried to talk with him about the inaccurate statements he'd made to Culp and Cossell.

"You cannot go on telling lies about us to all these people," I said.

Duncan replied in a taunting voice, "What are you going to do about it?"

"And how are we going to pay all the psychiatrist's bills?" I wanted to know.

Duncan said I could pay for them, and that I could also start paying for the groceries and mortgage out of my checkbook. "You can pay for all that now!" he said. "I am ready to kill, and I'm going to make you use up all your assets on legal fees!"

"You've changed the rules," I said.

"That's right," said Duncan, with a twisted grin on his face. "I've changed the rules."

I was shocked. "The law won't let you do that, Duncan."

"Well then, Ursula, you don't know the law!"

Now I had little choice but to see an attorney. Friends recommended Sue Sage at Ringling & Haycroft, one of the large firms downtown. I had no better way of finding a lawyer, so I took their recommendation.

I hated this. I still loved Duncan, and I still believed he was ill. But the well-being of Spencer and Amanda would have to be my first concern, a higher priority than that marriage vow I took so seriously (because of my parents' situation). "In sickness and in health, to love and to cherish . . ." How can you cherish someone who is threatening the well-being of your children?

Despite my reluctantly engaging Ringling & Haycroft, I meant it when I told John Arthur that I'd continue to do everything in my power to prevent a divorce. "You are doing the good and right thing," he told me in late May.

And then this letter came in the mail:

31 May 1989

Ms. Ursula L. Charbonnier
1 Inverary Lane
Conover, MA 02100

Dear Ms. Charbonnier:

Your husband, Duncan J. Charbonnier, has consulted me regarding your current marital situation, and asked that I represent him in that matter.

There are issues of property disposition and other similar matters which require disposition and resolution. Both Mr. Charbonnier and I desire that this be accomplished in the most amicable and expeditious manner as possible.

Please have your attorney contact me so that we can discuss this matter and the appropriate actions to be taken to effect a resolution. If you have not engaged an attorney, please advise me of that fact. I will be happy to speak to you to explain what my client intends. I am, however, prohibited from giving you advice, which I am sure you realize.

There do not appear to be any extraordinary circumstances which would preclude an amicable and efficient settlement of all matters between you, and I look forward to being able to effect that result efficiently.

Very truly yours,

Chubb W. McIntyre

I flung the letter across the table. Amicable and efficient? No extraordinary circumstances? What the hell then *do* they call it when a formerly devoted father and husband of thirteen years walks in one night and announces to his family, that "a wife, children, a house, cars, and a community are not for [him]"?

VIII

Seek and Find

O what may man within him hide
though, angel on the outward side!

– William Shakespeare, *Measure for Measure*

The first Friday in June, I came home from work and found a note from Duncan saying he was exhausted and had gone to Maine for the weekend. He left a phone number I didn't recognize, and returned the following Sunday.

A few other observations, Gabriel: Duncan's normally large appetite has decreased, and he himself admitted he'd lost about ten pounds. Duncan and I attended Genesis' fifth birthday party during May at Leslie Drew's place up in Marblehead, and our head chemist told me afterward that Duncan didn't "look like the same man" he'd seen at the Genesis-Merck dinner the previous December. He described Duncan as "gaunt" and "chemically not the same."

In fact, Duncan had developed some strange, new habits: he'd begun putting hot sauces like salsa or hoisin on *all* kinds of food, and one morning when he was fixing a bowl of bananas, and we ran out of milk in the kitchen fridge, and I suggested he grab a new milk carton from the garage fridge, he became annoyed and picked up his glass of orange juice and poured it over the bananas and ate that. He'd also become sloppy. Formerly meticulously neat, Duncan was now throwing things on the floor instead of into wastebaskets, and he was leaving shoes and other items of clothing all over the house. In the bathrooms, he was saving empty Band-Aid boxes, and in one of them I found what I thought was baby powder, and threw it out. The children, based on their own observations and what they've learned in school, continue to suspect drugs.

But when I confronted Duncan about this, he angrily replied, "*You'll never be able to prove it.*" And then, "How many people have you told I was on drugs?"

"A number of people have suggested it to me over the past several years," I replied, now knowing drugs would account for all we've experienced, but that that didn't make drugs the correct explanation. "No one here has stopped caring about you, Duncan."

"What does that have to do with anything? You're mentally ill, Ursula, go hug yourself," and he pushed me away.

Hanging in there with a Duncan who maintained there was no hope wasn't easy, but it still felt like the right thing to do. Like Arthur, I believed in marriage when all was said and done. The doctor, the children, and I believe that I am not Duncan's problem – something else was. And short of physical abuse (and so far there hadn't been any), I wasn't going to quit.

It always seemed to me that Divorce was a debacle on every level – to seek or grant one without a fight would be pure selfishness. Maybe if Duncan saw us hanging in there no matter what, then maybe this family still had a chance, I reasoned. I now believed that Duncan had severe psychological problems and/or a drug problem, and told him so. He was clearly not the wonderful man he'd been for so many years. But the three of us still remembered that terrific guy; I was still in love with him, and I wanted him back.

The third week of June, Duncan and I drove the children to their camp in Maine. He made a lot of wrong turns, and it took an extra hour to arrive. I was glad the children were getting away from the craziness. They would have four weeks of peace. The night we came back from Maine, the two of us had dinner on the patio. Duncan became angry about the lettuce and threw some salad to the ground. I didn't pick it up, at first. I just stared at him. Here was the most civilized man I had ever known, angrily throwing food.

I decided to go back to Ohio for the approaching Fourth of July weekend, and stayed with Ginny Bartlett, my former high school French teacher, who lived down the street from Asa. I was tired, sad and scared, and needed a mom. Ginny was the closest person I had to one. I needed someone to take care of me. And she did.

Although Ginny and I had remained close through the years, I'd kept my concerns about Duncan close to the chest. Apart from the professionals, colleagues at Genesis, and our neighbors Bud and Ted, only Asa, Dick McCall, Julie in Connecticut, and later friends in Illinois, knew.

But as I sat in Ginny's home recounting it, she listened without surprise – as if she knew what I'd say next, what the next event would be, as if she knew my story better than I did. That was my sensation at the time, and I was right. Ginny waited for me to finish. It took a long time.

Then she gave it to me straight: "Ursula," she practically shouted in my face, "Listen to me, and listen carefully. Without doubt, you are dealing with a substance abuser, but *you* are in denial. When you get back to Boston, you have to get help for yourself. I want you to go to Appleton Hall, and GET HELP FOR YOURSELF." Ginny was no stranger to Boston. She'd been born here and worked on Newbury Street, in the years before she'd settled down. She knew about Appleton Hall, that it was one of the finest centers for substance abuse in the nation, and that it was in Beaumont, the town next to Conover.

Ginny didn't stop there. "Sooner or later, Ursula, you are going to start to find empty bottles. I can't tell you when, and I can't tell you where. But you will."

We got that far on the first day. And she hammered away at me for the next three, going through incident, after incident, and explaining them to me through the prism of alcoholism. Those puzzling moments when Duncan hadn't remembered admiring the garish trumpet lithograph, or telling Spencer he could take a dinner tray up to his room or showing Bud Alden the inside of our house – all of them had a context as far as Ginny was concerned. "Those were blackouts, Ursula!"

"Blackouts? But Duncan didn't lose consciousness; he didn't collapse," I protested.

"But he did lose memory of these events," she shouted. "Jesus Christ, Ursula – that's what an *alcoholic* blackout is!" Ginny had spent years working with the illness and the people who had it. She knew what she was hearing. If she said it once, she said it a hundred times that long Fourth of July weekend: "If it looks like a duck, and it walks like a duck, and it talks like a duck, it's a duck."

She told me about something called Al-Anon, a program for the family and friends of alcoholics, and she told me to get into a group. I wasn't a joiner, it wasn't for me, I told her. She'd hear none of it. She talked to me about something called "The Twelve Steps." I didn't want to hear about them. I wanted to find out what was wrong with Duncan. She didn't want to hear about Duncan. She wanted me to face what was wrong with me, and what was wrong with me was that I was being deceived.

"Initially by Duncan," she said, "but now by yourself." I cried. I protested. I slept. I didn't believe her. But she was undeterred. Ginny just kept talking. And listening. And insisting. "YOU ARE IN DENIAL!" she shouted. "Furthermore, I will bet you that Duncan is probably dual-addicted."

"What does that mean?"

"You are dealing with more than alcohol. You are dealing with drugs!"

When it was time to say good-bye, she hugged me and predicted, correctly as it has turned out: "You are going on a great adventure!"

"I don't want to go an adventure!"

"You are going on one, nonetheless. And you are going to be the better for it!"

I went back to Boston with different eyes. Eyes that started watching, and started looking. Actual seeing was still a way off.

My first evening back in Conover, Duncan had a bad seizure. He came into the house from grilling burgers and staggered over to the counter and almost dropped the plate he was carrying. He ate very little and was spacey and weird during our meal. The next night at dinner, he behaved strangely again. He rocked back and forth sideways and was spacey and uncommunicative. Again, he ate very little, then came into the kitchen and hugged me and staggered upstairs. He managed to undress part way and get into bed. Then he fell into a long stupor of a sleep.

I still didn't believe he was an alcoholic, but I did suspect drugs. I decided to call Appleton Hall. And it was very hard for me to do. A psychologist named Dr. Dalton saw me on July 21. I told him everything and gave him the medical logs I'd kept from spring 1985 through December 1988. He said he felt the problem sounded more like a neurological one than one of drug abuse, but that he wanted to read my logs and speak to other members of the team before deciding. When he called back, Dalton suggested I return to see Harry Ballard, a psychiatrist on the team.

I then called Arthur to tell him I'd seen Dalton and would be seeing Ballard next (with the children, who were now home from camp). "This is still your case," I told Arthur, "but I want all of us to work together. I want all of us to be on the same team." He agreed to speak with Ballard before my next appointment on July 31.

I also told Arthur about Duncan's repeated threats not to pay the mortgage and other family expenses, and that he had pushed me away and told me that I was "mentally ill." Arthur said, "Well, we just have a difference of opinion about that, don't we?!" It was a small thing, but this vote of confidence from my internist gave me much-needed strength. He didn't think I was a nutcase. Did he know I'd had dark moments when I doubted all I was seeing and hearing, when I thought I might be losing *my* mind? I think he must have.

The week before we saw Ballard was a case in point. Duncan had come home late after a GEC dinner meeting, and Amanda joined us on the patio, where we were having drinks. Amanda said that she and Spencer and Christa, our children's caretaker, had found a kitten that day at a pet store, and wanted to purchase it the next day. The three of us discussed other items we would need for the kitten. Duncan praised Amanda for organizing this endeavor and agreed she could go ahead the next day. Less than an hour later, when Duncan came into the house and heard us talking about getting the kitten, he became enraged.

"No one consulted me about getting a cat! I want no part of a cat." Then he started arguing with Amanda about who would pay for cat food and kitty litter and vet bills.

This went on until about eleven o'clock, and Amanda was beside herself and in tears. At this point she said to Duncan, "If I could have anything in the world, I would want my old Dad back, the way he was, and if I can't have that, I want a new Dad."

"You may just have that opportunity!" he angrily replied.

Every day brought a new version of hell and a new discovery. Duncan was spending increasing amounts of time in the garage in the evenings, and on one of them, Amanda went outside to watch him. He hadn't realized she was there. When she came back in the house, wondering out loud "what Dad was doing," I'd ungraciously replied, "he's probably out in the garage getting his fix," and there was Duncan glowering at us through the open kitchen window.

One Saturday afternoon, I returned home unexpectedly and found Duncan's briefcase open on our bed. Inside, I found $100 bills loosely rolled up in a plain white envelope. I'd seen lots of empty white envelopes strewn about Duncan's car over the past months, but hadn't thought much of them. And Duncan never carries $100 bills. When I later asked him about this he told me the bills had been "a present from [his] mother," and he accused me (falsely I might add) of having a key to his briefcase. Though my boss, Archie McGowan, had long since recommended I have one. Earlier in the summer, as Archie had gradually learned more about my situation, he'd advised me to "become a total snoop. It's the only way you're going to learn what you're dealing with, Ursula." In recent months, Duncan had been guarding his car like a fortress, locking the glove compartment, and finding all kinds of reasons why we could never use his car if mine was available. He'd also begun to lock his briefcase and had established separate bank accounts, in his name only.

"You've got to get back into that briefcase," said Shea Phillips, the business manager for *Molecular Modelling News*. "And you've got to get into that car." Like my children and the scientists at Genesis, Shea strongly suspected that Duncan was on drugs; and she was increasingly frustrated at my unwillingness to acknowledge it. "You need proof, Ursula. All right. That's the kind of person you are. It's obvious to your French teacher, and your children, and everyone around you what's really going on. But if you need proof, you need proof."

IX

The Beginning of Insight

And ye shall know the truth, and the truth shall make you free.
– John 8:32, *The Bible*

"Proof," and I use the term loosely, was to come sooner than I thought.

The following Monday, July 31, I found a change of address form for a bank account I didn't know we had that had been completed with my signature – in handwriting that was not mine. Although the signature and date did include my distinctive number "7" and letter "U," many of the characteristics of Duncan's own handwriting appeared in the signature: periods that are more like lines than dots and extra curls in the "9" and "C" and "nier" part of "Charbonnier" that I would not have made. When I showed it to Amanda, our resident aficionado of mystery stories, she gave it a withering look and sniffed, "It's not even a very good forgery!" I also discovered that my driver's license was missing, and I had to go to the Registry to get a new one. As it turned out, the Registry was to be my first stop in what would be a very busy day.

My second stop was Appleton Hall, where the children and I were to see Harry Ballard. He was the psychiatrist recommended by Davis Dalton, the psychologist who had seen me earlier in the month. I'd been impressed with Dalton, which gave me hope that Ballard would turn out to be just as solid. Only my second experience with a psychiatrist, this appointment would turn out to be totally different from my session with Wilson Garry Culp.

Where Culp had been accusing and mindlessly provocative, this man was measured and as in search of "truth" (regardless of what it turned out to be), as I was. Culp had focused the conversation on an anger I didn't have; Ballard focused the conversation on the bewilderment I did have. He asked a lot of questions. We only had an hour, but he wanted to hear as much as I could tell him, and he took a lot of notes.

Several times he interrupted to ask me if I'd ever found any empty liquor bottles, and I said no, as I have whenever anyone has asked me that. Ballard, like the others, seemed frustrated that my story did not fit into any neat category: neurological, emotional disorder, alcoholic or drug addict.

"Look, I'm frustrated too," I told him, "but I have to tell my story as it happened and not tailor it to fit your pigeonholes."

"I have to put a diagnosis down for you so that insurance will cover this. What do you want me to put down?"

A doctor had never asked me this before. "Well, I don't know. What do you think you should put down? What's wrong with me?"

Ballard grinned. "Not very much. I'm going to call it 'situational stress disorder.'"

"What does that mean?"

"That means you're going to be fine once you get out of this situation."

"Oh." I couldn't imagine ever being out of this situation. It seemed like it was going to go on forever.

"We still have more to talk about," he said, "and I ran out of time to see the children, but I want to talk with them. Can the three of you come back at the same time next week?"

"Yes. Most of this happened in front of them, Dr. Ballard. They want answers, too."

The third stop of the day was Armstrong Field. Only about ten minutes from Genesis Labs, the non-military portion of Armstrong Field included a private hangar for Germane Engineering. Duncan was scheduled to go to Chicago on a day trip, leaving before breakfast, and getting home in time for dinner. Here was the opportunity to get into the car. Shea and I decided to go that afternoon and find out, once and for all, if anything was hidden in the locked glove compartment.

"Maybe nothing!" I said to Shea.

"Maybe nothing, my foot!" she said disdainfully. "Ursula, what is it going to take for you to admit that you're dealing with an addict?"

"Proof!" I insisted. "You can't just accuse someone of being an addict without proof."

I wondered how we were going to get past the MPs and GEC security people, who guarded all comings and goings on Germane's portion of the Air Force Base. Then divine inspiration struck in the form of the earlier missing license. I smiled up at the MP. "My driver's license is missing, and I think I left it in my husband's car. It's parked at the GEC hangar."

And as I'd hoped, the MP was trained to focus on the detail he didn't like in my story. "You can't drive on a military base without a license!" he said officiously, "but your friend could drive you." Shea and I traded places and in due course located Duncan's car.

A man smoking a cigarette came out of one of the buildings and started watching us. I explained briefly that I was looking for my license – so I couldn't take any photos, even though I had brought my camera. I unlocked the car and pretended to be hunting for the "missing license." After a suitable minute of this, I unlocked the glove box. There was a brown bag inside, twisted shut at the top. Inside was a nearly empty liter of Gordon's Vodka. In the first instant I was too stunned to move. I just stared at it, and heard Ginny Bartlett's voice: "Mark my words Ursula, sooner or later you are going to start to find empty bottles. I can't say where. I can't say when. But you will."

Vodka is the one flavor of alcohol I do not like, so I've never bought it. This was *the first time* I had ever found an empty bottle – yet not four hours earlier I had been in Harry Ballard's office saying I thought alcohol abuse highly unlikely. I felt stupid, betrayed, deceived. I had Shea walk over to the car to look, so that I would have a witness, and somehow held myself together, because the man with the cigarette was still watching us. Now I knew that at the very minimum, I had been dealing with a closet alcoholic all these years – probably since the night of the railroad tracks, maybe even before that.

Shea would tell me later that I fell apart as soon as we got out of Armstrong Field. I had held reality in my hand. I had found the proof I was seeking, and there were no more excuses to make for Duncan's behavior. Back at Genesis, Eliza Pickering, Leslie's secretary, took one look at me and knew. She too had suspected a substance abuse problem. I left it for Shea to explain to her, and I got on the phone. First I called Tony Milton, our close friend and the Executor of both of our wills. Sometime in 1989, I had confided about Duncan's seizure episodes. Now, as he heard about the vodka bottle, he had two immediate reactions:

"Ursula, you have to divide this problem into two parts: getting help for Duncan and getting the financial control out of his hands." I had no idea how to do that, but I remember that's what he said. "I also think you should see your internist as soon as possible and tell him what you found."

Then I called Asa. "Now I know what it is, Dad," I choked into the phone. "It's alcohol. I held the vodka bottle in my hand. He had it locked up in the glove compartment, in a brown bag, twisted around the neck of the bottle. I talked to Tony, and he said to go see Arthur right away. I'm going to try to get in this afternoon, if I can. I'll call you tomorrow."

By coincidence I had another appointment scheduled at Westbury General late that afternoon, a follow-up with the surgeon who had aspirated the lump in my breast. I called Arthur's secretary and she said he'd be willing to see me at the end of the day. By the time I reached his office, I was a human puddle.

When he came in I told him everything: about the $100 bills, the forged signature, the missing driver's license, the vodka bottle, the children's and my suspicions of drugs. I said Duncan was sick and needed help. Arthur

2222

told me again, as he always did, that the law prohibits him from doing any tests for drugs without Duncan's permission and that nothing can be done until Duncan himself wants help.

"Do I just have to wait for a tragedy to happen? What would you do in my place?"

"I don't like to give patients advice, Ursula."

I asked him again, "What would you do if you were in my place? It's my decision, it's my responsibility, but what would *you* do?"

"I'd confront him with what I found; I'd file for divorce; and get him thrown out of the house," he replied.

"But I don't want a divorce. As Spencer said to Duncan several weeks ago, 'Divorce is for quitters, Dad, and we're not quitters.'"

"Well, just because you file for one doesn't mean you have to go through with it," Arthur said.

Thinking of the role the family doctor sometimes played in substance abuse interventions, I said, "I was hoping you could offer me something more practical."

"Look, I've told you before, the law prevents doctors from doing more in situations like yours. I'm sorry Ursula." He hugged me and let me cry.

I now realized that an intervention was not to be. And besides me and the children, who would have come, anyhow? Elsie, who thought Duncan could do no wrong? Or Jock, who'd come right out and said that I was "the cause" of Duncan's falling down? Not Ivy and other Germane employees, who were reportedly "taking bets on how soon we'd be divorced." And not Dick McCall, who was in Japan. Nor our friends in Connecticut, with whom Duncan had stopped communicating. And certainly not Dr. Arthur, who for all his sympathy, had no intention of getting into a situation where he could be sued by Duncan. How about Wilson Garry Culp, the psychiatrist Duncan was still seeing? It seemed unlikely. Culp was encouraging Duncan to put himself first these days – ahead of me, ahead of the children, ahead of all family responsibilities. It didn't take a mental giant to see that an intervention wasn't going to happen. The reality that Duncan was drinking secretly and had been lying about it didn't matter to any of them. Apparently I was the only person who was seriously concerned about that.

There was nothing to do but go home. I thanked Arthur for all the years of standing by our family, and told him that I may have misled him, but never intentionally. He already knew that and refused to let me pay him. There would be no official record of my visit. I went home, still in tears and told Christa and the children what I'd found at Armstrong Field. The next time we saw Dr. Ballard at Appleton Hall, we would at least be able to tell him that we now knew what we were dealing with.

Several days later, Duncan went back to Dr. Arthur's office for a regular blood pressure check, and acted like everything was just fine. He didn't know I'd found the vodka bottle the previous Monday and had gone to Arthur for advice on what to do about it. And, as far as I know, Arthur never told Duncan about my visit or what we discussed.

In addition to feeling stupid, betrayed and deceived, I now felt powerless as well. Much later I would learn that on this day, and with this realization – I had just taken *my first step* toward getting well.

X

The Twilight Zone

O God! that men should put an enemy in their mouths
to steal away their brains; that we should, with joy,
pleasance, revel, and applause, transform ourselves into beasts.
— William Shakespeare, *Othello*

At this point, Gabriel, a few people suggested I get Duncan's rifle out of the house. He'd been unwilling to register it since we moved here in 1981, and while I'd never seen him use it, people kept telling me that an unregistered gun in the house of a suspected substance abuser, who was behaving like Duncan, was not a great idea. In Massachusetts, it was also against the law. I wasn't sure how to approach the police discreetly, which was why I hadn't called them before. Furthermore, I knew they recorded all incoming calls, and I didn't want to be recorded. My objective was to get rid of the gun — not to get Duncan in trouble.

Shea Phillips said she would ask Robert, her longtime friend and Chief of Police in Beaumont, for guidance. As it turned out, Robert was a close friend of Conover's Deputy Chief Avery Boland. Robert called him, and it was arranged that Boland would come to 1 Inverary Lane the next morning, in an unmarked car, and take the gun away.

"Hi, Mrs. Charbonnier. Deputy Chief Avery Boland here. Robert sent me," said the smiling, sandy-haired man, as he extended his hand to me. So this was the Conover Police Department I had been afraid to call. I would be afraid no longer.

"I was surprised you came so quickly," I said, showing him in.

"Actually, it's my *second* call to your neighborhood this week, for the same purpose — to pick up a gun. The other night, only a block away, over on Chandler's Hill, a very prosperous businessman was threatening his wife and daughters and one of the daughter's boyfriends with a gun. I had to take the gun away. The man is an alcoholic and has no memory of the incident."

"So that's why you believed me. My own lawyer doesn't even believe me!" I said.

"Of course I believe you, Mrs. Charbonnier."

"Please call me Ursula."

"Ursula, this sort of thing is more common than many people in Conover care to admit. And for every case the Department knows about, there are probably a dozen we know nothing about. I can't tell you the name of the family over on Chandler's Hill, but I'm sure they're people you know."

Avery's story gave me pause. Spencer had several friends over on Chandler's Hill. "Here's a receipt for the gun," he said. "I want you to send the original to your lawyer and keep a copy for yourself."

"Thanks. Would you like a cup of coffee?" I asked.

"Yes, and I'd also like you to tell me your story – all of it."

And so I did: from the railroad tracks through the "seizure" episodes; the neurologists and repeated medical tests; Duncan's and his father's anger that a physician had ever been involved; Jock's warning that I should stay away from doctors now or I'd make everything worse; the radical behavior changes from December on; the threats to withhold family financial support; the forged signature; the new separate bank accounts; and the vodka bottle I found at Armstrong Field.

Avery listened carefully, occasionally interrupting with a question, and very interested in all I had to say. "Ursula," he said just before he left, "I want you to promise me three things: that you'll talk to your family in Ohio once a day; and that you'll sleep twice as much as you think you need to; and that you'll call us again if you need anything. Remember, we're here to help. May I borrow a photo of Duncan?"

"Why?"

"I want to make copies and circulate it." Beyond that he didn't elaborate.

Two days later, I went to Conover Trust to update Lynne Andersen, our banker, and she, too, was helpful. "Ursula, I suspected there was a problem last spring, because of all the documentation you requested. What I'd like to do now is put a renewable thirty-day watch on your account. The forged signature and missing driver's license concern me also."

I also called Robert to thank him for contacting Avery Boland. He wanted to know how our visit had gone. Then he told me that police departments don't have the resources or even any authority to do more for people in my situation. "And I can tell you from my many years on the Beaumont force, that we see many, many of them."

"Then where can people in my situation go for real help?"

"I don't have a good answer for you," said Robert sadly.

That night when Duncan came home, the glove compartment of his car was locked. I thought if I could get inside, I'd probably find another vodka bottle. I tried to get the children to distract Duncan, but that didn't work. Then he said he'd like to grill dinner (outside) instead of baking it inside. "I'm sure you would," I said, "and I know why." Then I went out to the garage with my camera, unlocked the glove compartment, and started photographing a new vodka bottle that was about one fourth empty. I managed to get in three snapshots before I found him standing over me.

I looked Duncan directly in the eye and said, "I know about your vodka bottles! I was advised to take pictures this time." His eyes blazed. "Excuse me, but I'm going in the house," I said. Then I drove to the home of my neighbor, Jackie Melrose, who was getting the film developed. Ringling & Haycroft said my snapshots don't make an airtight case, but may help, and to photograph everything I can from now on.

Later that evening, the children and I tried to talk to Duncan about acknowledging his drinking problem and getting help. "Do you think you might be having a problem with your drinking? Or do you think you may be an alcoholic?" I began gently, as was suggested in the books Jackie Melrose had brought me from Countway, the Harvard Medical Library where she worked.

And just as all the books said, he denied that he had a drinking problem and turned the conversation around. "I don't have a drinking problem. My problem is you and the marriage. The real problem isn't the vodka bottles; it's that you went looking for them!"

"Why don't you talk to John Arthur, Duncan, or go to Appleton Hall? Go somewhere to get help. The children and I have already been to Appleton Hall. The people there are experienced in this area. Arthur is a good person. Let him try to help you."

Duncan got angry and said he wouldn't discuss anything with me. "You have jumped to a lot of conclusions!" he said.

I suggested Duncan sleep elsewhere that night. I can't imagine ever feeling comfortable around him again. He refused and told me to shut the bedroom door.

"I'm never going to shut our bedroom door again," I replied.

"Why?" he asked.

"Because I no longer feel safe with you." And in that moment, I finally knew that no matter what happens now, short of finding out he has a brain tumor or something truly beyond his control, I will never be able to go back to trusting him again. In all of our marriage, kicking somebody out of a bedroom was not something we ever did. That night Duncan moved Spencer's trundle bed into the den and began sleeping there.

As wonderful as the first fourteen years of knowing Duncan had been, all the love and total trust were behind me now. How right Arthur had been last spring when he told me that things would never be the way they were. But the way they were was the best of life that I have known.

Now my primary concern is the physical, emotional and financial security of Spencer and Amanda. I will probably have to file for divorce in order to protect the family financially. Spencer said that he wants to show Duncan the vodka bottle and ask him to get help. I admire my son's spunk, but a mini-intervention is no job for a child — it's not even a job for an adult without training. So I told Spencer no. I also told him that somehow we are going to survive this mess, that we are going to go on and build a good life for ourselves.

The next day, a Saturday, Duncan had lunch with Tony Milton, and whatever Duncan said about our situation caused Tony to tell me that I "bear a lot of the responsibility for Duncan's abusing his body." When I asked him to explain, he said I should talk to Duncan, that Duncan would tell me. But Duncan refused to tell me. Tony said, "This much is clear Ursula, your marriage is over."

While Duncan was out with Tony, I had taken the children to the Conover Town Pool. There I ran into our family friend, David Madden, a practicing psychiatrist and the Associate Clinical Director of Eastforest Lodge, a facility similar to Appleton Hall. When I told him what was happening in our family, David said that more than a year ago he'd realized Duncan had a drinking problem.

"But how could you tell?" I asked.

"Passivity, flushed face, glassy eyes, smell of aldehydes on Duncan's breath, failure to keep and later to make social commitments, and bringing liquor to Town Green events." Duncan had stood David up for squash games over the past few years, and finally stopped making plans with him altogether.

David was dismayed to hear of our contact with Wilson Garry Culp and Irena Cossell over at Westbury General. "God Ursula, how did you get mixed up with people like that?"

"Our internist sent us to them."

David shook his head, but on hearing of our contact with Appleton Hall and Harry Ballard, he felt much better. "I know him by reputation. Ballard's a good man, extremely competent, and I'd be happy to give him a call, if you'd like. I can provide some perspective from having known your family and interacting with Duncan. I can tell Ballard that you are honest, sane, and an accurate observer." Well, at least somebody thought I was still sane. I gratefully accepted his offer.

The next evening, Sunday, August 6, I came down to the den and tried to give Duncan a small hug while he was at the word processor. Although I could never again reach for him with the feeling of a wife toward a husband, I could still extend my heart to him as a fellow human being. To use Duncan's own words, he was "at sea," and I wanted him back on emotional *terra firma,* so that he could again function as the father of my children.

But Duncan thought I was trying to read what he was writing, and pushed me hard in the neck, and sent me flying across the room. It hurt, and I'll never get close enough for him to do that again. Amanda was in the den when it happened, and said to him, "*What* are you doing?"

What Duncan had been writing turned out to be a letter of explanation to Dr. Arthur, which Duncan says he hand delivered the next morning and followed up with an office visit at about six o'clock that evening. Arthur later confirmed with me that they "discussed Duncan's drinking problem," but when Arthur suggested AA, Duncan said it was "not for him." I've now read enough to know that without AA, Duncan is highly unlikely to remain in recovery, even though he claims to have stopped drinking since he caught me snapping the pictures of the vodka bottle.

Incidentally, Gabriel, Duncan hasn't exhibited *one* withdrawal symptom, and friends who've had firsthand experience with alcoholics – Ginny Bartlett, Joe Butler, a neighbor and minister, Jackie Melrose, John Barnum our cleaning man, and Dr. David Madden – say that the lack of withdrawal symptoms strongly suggests that Duncan is still drinking or else is chemically dependent on something in addition to alcohol.

On August 7, the children and I returned to Appleton Hall to see Harry Ballard, as planned. We told him what I found at Armstrong Field, and that we'd confronted Duncan about it, and asked him to join us in getting help. Ballard and the children discussed alcoholism in general and our situation in particular with candor and a matter-of-factness that made me think well of him. He did not talk down to Spencer and Amanda. Ballard also told me that the neurologist on the Appleton Hall team thought that Duncan had temporal lobe epilepsy in addition to a drinking problem (Amanda agrees, I'm undecided but haven't ruled it out, and Dad, David Madden and John Arthur say there is no TLE problem).

That same day, I told Sue Sage of Ringling & Haycroft that I was ready to file, but she refused to until she got corroboration of my story from Drs. Ballard and Arthur. I regret having bought into this demand; but I wasn't thinking clearly. Knowing that my own father would never have talked to a lawyer in a patient-divorce situation, I shouldn't have authorized her to call Arthur.

Arthur talked to Duncan at six o'clock about alcoholism, and one hour later spoke with Sue Sage and said he had "no proof that Mr. Charbonnier has an alcohol problem or any other kind of problem." Ballard, who never actually saw Duncan, couldn't say Duncan was an alcoholic either.

At that point, my lawyer said, "Ursula, we think that *you* are the troubled one in the Charbonnier family, and we hope that you get well." And she didn't stop there. "Furthermore, we think that you have handled this whole situation poorly by going to doctors behind Duncan's back and getting the police involved – because now Chubb MacIntyre can easily make the case that *you* are the unfit parent!"

I was stunned. My horrors were mounting. I now had a lawyer who didn't believe me, and I hadn't lied to anyone about anything. How could this be happening? Was the whole damn system in denial mode?

The children and I wanted to go back to Appleton Hall with Duncan to work together as a family on the alcoholism, as Harry Ballard had recommended. But Duncan talked with Ballard on the phone in mid-August and said he had no interest in working with him and no interest in working on the drinking problem with Spencer, Amanda, and me. Ballard told me I have to accept that.

John Arthur concurred. "Ursula, this is pretty much out of your hands now."

"When I came to you in 1985, I had no idea we were dealing with an alcohol problem."

"Well, don't beat yourself up too much about that," said Arthur, "because up until about six months ago, neither did I."

"I don't know how I'm going to prevent it, but Spencer and Amanda Charbonnier are *not* going down the tubes!" I vowed to him.

"Look Ursula, I'm no fan of divorce, but the plain truth is you're all better off without him."

"I know," I said sadly.

Duncan moved into Tony's house in Cambridge later in the month. And Tony hasn't spoken to me since, but I can only conclude that either he doesn't understand alcoholism and the denial that accompanies it, and/or as Spencer suggested, Duncan "must have told a very convincing lie."

In the end, Duncan has not fooled his children or his doctor or me. He may still be fooling himself, GEC and the rest of the outside world. His mother, Elsie, wrote me a letter telling me "how sorry" she is about our impending divorce, but she must have had no idea about Duncan's drinking problem, or she wouldn't have chattered about having a pleasant glass of wine somewhere in the first paragraph of her note.

Jock called me over Labor Day weekend (when Duncan officially moved out of the house) to say he and I were "still friends," and it was clear from our conversation that Duncan hadn't been honest with him and Darcy either.

Harry Ballard called me back in late August, shortly before he left on his vacation, to offer his services in case I or the kids wanted help in the future. I thanked him and said I'd call back if we did, and asked him to thank his colleague Dr. Dalton, because they had helped me. I had learned from the time spent with them.

"What are you going to do now?" Ballard asked.

"Go about my life with as much dignity and cheerfulness as I can muster," I replied, because I couldn't think of anything better to say.

Also in late August, my boss Archie McGowan asked me for an update. He was appalled by Sue Sage's attitude and worried about me and the children. "Ursula, if it's all right with you, I want to call Angus MacKenzie, Genesis' General Counsel." I felt like I was dying inside, and was thoroughly frustrated that everything I had done all along the way had only made everything worse. We didn't catch up with Angus until August 29, and he sent me to you, Gabriel.

Duncan now lives at Babylon Village, a condominium development in Conover, just a minute or two down the road from us. Several of the boys in Spencer's Spanish class (who also have alcoholic fathers living there) call it El Rancho Divorcé. I am trying to treat Duncan with as much courtesy as I can – alcoholism is a disease, I keep saying to myself – and even invited him to have lunch with us last weekend. I have no interest in keeping him from the children or in using the children as a weapon. I do worry about their safety, but the legal system can't help me with that, so I'm appealing to a Higher Power.

Spencer and Amanda want to continue to live in Conover, at Inverary Lane, with me. That's what I want too. For all Duncan's frugality during the years of our marriage, Spencer and Amanda tell me that he's not stinting on himself now, and is buying plenty of new household items. I do wonder where the money is coming from.

You said that at the end of this narrative to say some words about why Duncan Charbonnier wants to get out of this marriage. I still don't know, and Spencer and Amanda say they don't know. Last week I asked Duncan why we bought the house on Inverary Lane if he'd been planning to get a divorce; he replied he hadn't been planning to get a divorce. I tried to find out again this past Saturday and asked him, "What could be so bad that you had to rip up four people's lives?"

And in a reply more attacking than informational, he said: "I don't have to tell you, and I may never tell you."

Apparently Culp and Tony Milton know, so I can only conclude that Mr. MacIntyre knows too. Perhaps it's obvious to everyone but me. If you figure it out, please let me know. At this point I think I'm made of Teflon anyhow, so it won't even hurt. A number of people have suggested that perhaps Duncan has simply lost his mind.

This ordeal has been an appalling waste of thousands of dollars, tons of energy and years of my life – and I know I'm not done yet. Please help me to put it behind me as quickly as possible. What Spencer, Amanda, and I want now is to get on with our lives.

Part II

A Story of Survival

XI

On Our Own

The first of earthly blessings, independence.
  — Edward Gibbon, *Autobiography*

"Well, did you get my letter?" he asked in his excited schoolboy voice, different from the futsy-dutsy old man tone of our first conversation.

"Your letter?" I was truly puzzled. Didn't I just see this man last week? Why would he write me a letter? "A letter about what?"

"About your narrative. You have suffered enough for five marriages." Clearly, Gabriel G. Reed was disappointed.

"No, I didn't get your letter. Maybe it will be in the afternoon mail. Here's a *New Yorker* cartoon for your office," I said quickly, wanting, at more than 69.4¢ a second (even I can't talk that fast), to get on with the business at hand. From Ringling & Haycroft I had learned the ground rules for dealing with the "Boys' Club" of Boston Divorce Lawyers: unless you are John Paul Getty or you enjoy throwing money away, small talk with attorneys is a poor (pun intended!) idea. In fact, for last week's little excursion into the Charbonnier Matter, the tab was more than $800 for two lawyers, one paralegal and one secretary – all note takers for Gabriel G. Reed, who at $250 an hour couldn't be bothered to take notes. Not a bad haul for one afternoon's entertainment, and then for the pleasure of the instant "read-play," my narrative which took two non-stop days and nights to churn out, Reed billed me another $500. At least Gabriel reads fast. Duncan's words from last spring to me and the children were coming back to taunt: "I am going to force you to use up all your assets on legal fees, and when I get done, and I don't like the outcome, I am going to quit my job and leave you all with nothing."

Gabriel chuckled when he read the cartoon and handed it to Jillian Frost. "Not now," he grumbled at her. It had a very long caption. "You can read it on your *own* time!" Does the man read minds as well as narratives, I wondered.

"It has been my experience," he began, "that the shorter the marriage, the longer the narrative and the longer the marriage, the shorter the narrative. Once I had one that was seventy-two pages, and they were only married for three days. That . . . was a record."

"Really? Where did mine fall in the equation?" He didn't answer. "Well, she must not have been paying much attention to him!" I added.

Merrill Crosby burst out laughing. A sprightly figure with closely cropped dark hair, she looked vaguely familiar. "Merrill is going to take over from me, on helping Gabriel with your case," explained Jillian Frost. "In two weeks, we want you to come back so that we can update all your financials."

"But I did them for Ringling & Haycroft," I protested, not wanting to pay for the same procedure twice. "Can't we use those?"

"A financial statement with the Conover dump sticker as the fourth largest expenditure is not my idea of a well-done financial statement!" snapped Gabriel over the rims of his glasses. "And you, Miss, are to keep writing your narrative for me. I want continual updates. Is that clear?"

"Yes."

And so I went home and wrote:

Narrative Addendum

Spencer, Amanda and I have now been on our own for close to two months. The weeks have not been without their moments, but we are holding our own and managing better than I might have thought. When Duncan walked out of here over Labor Day weekend, his parting shot to me had been, "You'll never be able to live without me!" I bit my tongue to let him have the last word, but I had the last thought: Watch me. Just watch me!

I quickly edited that to "Just watch *us!*" for Spencer and Amanda have more than risen to the challenges of the past eight weeks. I am fortunate that they are old enough and wise enough to see what has really happened here; otherwise we might have enough raw material to keep two shrinks busy for years. And on that subject, psychiatrist David Madden, who's had a lot of experience in his practice with both children and alcoholics, continues to assure me that both children are fine and show every indication of remaining that way — *because they had such solid foundations.* According to David, the first five years of a child's life are all. Now I'm more at peace than ever with the decision I made to stay home in their early years — even though I know the opportunity cost of not developing a career is going to lower our standard of living for a long time to come.

As far as the children are concerned, Duncan is not spending nearly as much time with them as we would have expected. In the first week or two after moving out, he took them swimming at Regina College in the evenings and made repeated efforts to see them, but as Asa predicted, his interest waned rapidly; now phone calls have dwindled to once or twice a week. Amanda usually sleeps at Duncan's place one night each week and additionally has tea or swims with him one other night; Spencer sees less of him, and says he's so turned off by all he has heard and seen this year, that he doesn't even care. But on some level it has to hurt deeply. I know how it feels to have the parent of the same sex totally drop the ball on you emotionally. Knowing it's because of illness explains the loss, but it doesn't really lessen the pain. I also know from firsthand experience that children can grow up to be fine with just one functioning parent, and I intend to stay functioning. Spencer has told me that he doesn't know one man he looks up to and respects. I think I need to learn a lot more about boys, quickly.

Spencer has also told me that he doesn't see why Amanda and he should have to bear the consequences of their Dad's irresponsible behavior. "After all, we didn't marry him, Mom – you did." I let him blow off some steam and agreed that life sometimes does seem unfair, but I also tried to tell him that we can't control events; we can only control how we react to them. But Spencer wasn't ready to hear this yet, so I backed off.

And something in myself wasn't ready to hear this either. After all, I am the one who chose Duncan – Spencer was right about that. And Duncan's behavior and choices are bringing injury to the three of us, the three who still wanted to be a family. And try as I might, I am a long way from forgiving myself for the pain that my choice of this man for their father is now inflicting upon them.

I am encouraging both children to have dinner with Duncan at least twice a week, but it doesn't usually work out that way. Several times I've asked Duncan, as a courtesy to us, to please firm up weekend plans with the children by Thursday night each week. But he refuses to do this and said the children could just turn him down if he spontaneously invited them anywhere, and he would accept that. It seems to me such an approach will only result in their spending even less time with him.

One Sunday in early September, I had to go into Genesis to do some work. When I came home that afternoon, Amanda told me that Duncan had come over, let himself in, and gone searching in my closets until she interrupted him and told him to stop. I asked him later what he'd been looking for, and he said his "ski clothes," something he *never* kept in my closets anyway. Divorced friends had told me I was a fool not to get the locks changed, and after this episode I decided they were right.

Duncan really has walked out on us and totally abdicated all responsibilities related to home ownership. He hasn't asked if we needed or wanted help. This new tone was pretty well set by the end of August, so I went to Oglethorpe's, the user-friendliest hardware store in Conover, and asked Wally to help me select the basic tools I would need to get started on my own. The Oglethorpe charge, at that point, was still in Duncan's name (I've since taken out my own), and Duncan went bonkers when he got the bill. At first he said he wouldn't pay it, and later he said I could expect it to show up in the final divorce settlement. "Look Duncan, I am not out to take you to the cleaners, but if you want me and the children to have a separate life, you can at least pay for the basic tools and supplies to get us started."

As for upkeep of Inverary Lane, I have blisters on my hands and moments when I think it would be convenient to weigh 150 pounds, but when I get discouraged, I play back the "You'll never be able to live without me" line, and then my batteries get thoroughly recharged and I'm off and running to the next task. I am determined not to let the house go to seed. It would be just like Duncan to say that I can't manage Inverary Lane. I signed up with a new handyman who is willing to let me follow him around and learn how to do some projects myself; I spent some time to find someone who is able to discuss materials, techniques and options in a lucid fashion. And thanks to him I was able to do the repairs on the back walk myself. I am arranging to get the gutters cleaned and the windows washed. Pruning is next, and I am actually looking forward to doing it my way this time around. Duncan's pruning is too timid!

I have also been getting the inside of the house whipped into shape. Ever since we'd moved in, the children have had nothing to sit on in the den, just the cold terra cotta floor. Duncan always said we didn't have the money for furniture (after all, we were "saving for college"). I had a couch delivered the week after he moved out. Duncan had told me to cancel it last summer and get back the down payment we'd made the previous winter, but instead, I paid the remaining balance from my salary. And now the children and their friends have a place to sit.

The most important of the house projects to me, however, was the lighting. We had literally been living in the dark with only about seven or eight lamps (most of which I'd paid for), and few built-in lights. So I had some installed at Inverary Lane, inside and out. People tell me this was a mistake, because Duncan will be entitled to half the increased value in the house that comes from these improvements. But I say we get to enjoy them now, and if we lose the house, there is something to be said for leaving it in better shape than we found it.

In mid-September, I gave a slumber party (actually, a belated birthday party) for Amanda and her friends, and I invited Duncan to come by the next morning, so that he could also play a part in the occasion. When David Madden delivered his daughter Hannah to the party, he stayed to chat for a few minutes. This was about a week and a half after I'd met Reed & Associates, and David said he could see that the fight was back in my spirit. I asked him why I was feeling so good, and having this seemingly paradoxical reaction – after all, my husband had just walked out on me and my kids. David said, "Two reasons, Ursula. One, you've grieved already. Elise and I have seen you really grieve over these past months, and now your grieving is behind you. And two, you've lived with this incredibly angry person for many years. The anger came out in many ways and without realizing it, you accommodated to it. But now it's gone from your daily existence, and you don't have to do it anymore. That's why you feel so good."

Our dentist, Dr. Post, told me virtually the same thing when I was at his office a few weeks later. "How are things going on the home front?" he asked. I told him about finding Duncan's vodka bottles and that Duncan had moved out. "I'm not surprised, Ursula. I tried to drop hints when you were in here last spring but the law prevented me from coming right out and telling you. About two years ago, I smelled liquor on Duncan's breath at an 8 a.m. cleaning, and that, coupled with some gum problems, which Duncan at his age should not have had, led me to conclude there was a drinking problem. Is he in AA?"

"He told our internist it wasn't for him."

"Well, without AA, Duncan's prospects for recovery are not good. Alcohol problems don't just go away. You're lucky to be getting out now," said Dr. Post.

Dr. Arthur, on the other hand, who talked with me several days ago, had a different opinion. "I really believe Duncan has stopped drinking."

"Are you sure we haven't overlooked something organic?" I asked. "When I look over the whole broad sweep of fourteen years, the behavior changes in Duncan are almost impossible to believe."

But Arthur replied, "As far as I'm concerned, this problem is *not* medical."

Having digested the books on alcoholism in Countway – the ones that doctors write for other doctors – I now think that Arthur is the one who is being naïve. I still think Arthur is one whale of a good doctor (my second favorite in the world), but his understanding of alcoholism and alcoholics, like that of most doctors, probably needs deepening.

In early October, Kathy Molloy, a long-time friend from graduate school days, called. I apologized for not returning her calls earlier in the year, but knowing her husband Kevin is a senior engineer at Germane, I hadn't wanted to get into a conversation about our difficulties at home. And owing to Duncan's increasing social withdrawal, our once frequent contact with the Molloys had wound down to almost nothing in recent years.

Kathy, who was now seven months pregnant with Number 2 (I *was* behind on news), had trouble believing all I told her. "But I just saw Tony Milton recently and asked about you guys, and he said you were fine."

"Actually Duncan moved in with Tony in late August, when he left our family, and Tony is no longer speaking to me. He told me I am in large part responsible for Duncan's physical problems. I can't tell you how betrayed that made me feel. Duncan never even liked Tony. He used to say to me, 'Tony is *your* friend.' "

"This makes no sense," said Kathy. "Duncan was always so into his family. Ursula, I've known you for almost twenty years, and something just doesn't add up. Furthermore, Kevin is no fan of Ivy Parrish's. He's locked horns with her on more than one occasion – during all those ridiculous 'touchy-feely' personnel retreats she's so fond of conducting at GEC. Duncan would have to be sick to be mixed up with her.

"And there's something else I should mention to you," Kathy added. "I haven't thought about this for several years, but the spring I was pregnant with Betsy (that would have been 1987), something strange happened that I never told you about – mostly because I didn't know what to make of it.

"I was at the Walden Post Office, on my way to work one morning, and saw Duncan in the parking lot. When I walked over to say hello, he wouldn't talk to me. He was totally spaced out and just kept wandering around the lot. I told Kevin about it, how strange it was. And then I never thought about it again until now. But listening to your story of Duncan's seizures, and his encounter with Bud Alden at Rover Brothers in Westbury . . . well, suddenly the Post Office incident has a context."

"It certainly does," I agreed. "Listen, I wonder if you'd do something for me. I heard through the grapevine that Duncan is 'in transition' at GEC, but I don't know what that means. Do you think you could find out?"

"I'll ask Kevin to make some discreet inquiries and see what we can learn. And we want to start seeing a lot more of you and the children. We've missed you guys."

A week later, Kathy called back. "I found out what 'in transition' means at GEC. It can mean just what it sounds like – between jobs – or it can mean someone's career is on hold while the company figures out what to do with him or her. But it often means someone is involved in an EAP situation."

"What's that?"

"EAP stands for Employee Assistance Plan. That's when a company helps an employee with drug, alcohol or emotional problems. Kevin wasn't able to learn anymore right now, but he said he'd keep his ears open. In the meantime, we want you and the children to join us for Thanksgiving and Christmas."

"But you're having a baby at the end of November."

"The baby is scheduled to arrive *in-between* the holidays. Not to worry!"

I had been wondering how we'd manage our first holiday season on our own. Now I knew: we would be spending it with friends.

At about this time, I also had a business lunch with my neighbor, publisher Ted Talbot. He'd been advising me about the possible acquisition of *Molecular Modelling News* by Harding, Towle & Lamour. When we finished with business he asked about the personal, and he encouraged me to make another attempt to reach Tony Milton.

"Ursula, I've been through an entirely unexpected divorce too, and I know that friendships are among the casualties in the process, that sometimes you are really amazed at the people that you lose. But you shouldn't easily accept losing any friends of long-standing from your life, not without giving them every benefit of the doubt. Try again with Tony," he urged.

I mulled over what Ted had said and finally did call Tony and got his machine. I left a message saying the kids and I were fine and that Duncan still hadn't given us an explanation for his actions, but that my problems with Duncan needn't interfere with our friendship. And I asked him to call me, but I never heard from him.

By early October, Spencer, Amanda and I had slipped into a pretty stable routine of life as a threesome, and a number of people were urging me to take a little time off. The children's caretaker, Christa, without whom we wouldn't be doing so well, seemed to have the kids and the house pretty much under control, and she too was encouraging me to go. Having exhausted every excuse, I allowed them to boot me out the door and went to the Cape for three days, and returned feeling better than I had in a long time. I've decided that travel alone is highly underrated, and I can't wait to do it again!

I've also decided single parenthood is another endeavor that has gotten a bad rap. Since Duncan's departure, there is laughter at our dinner table again, and the house is often filled with other people's children which suits me fine. I miss Duncan's innovative cooking, and I absolutely hate having to do everything fast and race through my days, but "alone and happy," hard as it sometimes is, really is better than "together and sad." Conversations with Spencer and Amanda are as stimulating as ever – bits of ethics, choices, fairness, interspersed with the usual jokes and irreverence, and even Streak Louise, our cat, has grown lippy. I continue to hold my own amid all, even though I am still being routinely harassed by Spencer and Amanda to "go out and find us a new Dad right now!" This is the opposite of the way I was told children in their situation are supposed to feel.

I am very tired when the day comes to an end, and now go to bed even earlier than my children. I used to spend half the night reading or thinking, but now sleep so soundly that I sometimes don't hear the phone that is next to my bed. I have now been through two back-to-school nights solo, plus a neighborhood party and other assorted events without Duncan. Reactions from my fellow Conoverians have ranged from the typical: "Not sweet, kind, gentle Duncan – Ursula, I don't believe this!" (from a man who lives down the street) to "Spencer, does your father have psychiatric problems?" (from a youngster who hangs out with my son).

I have been surprised by the outpouring of support from the neighborood and the schools and the town. People I didn't think even cared about us have been coming out of the woodwork and are just quietly finding ways to do little things that mean a lot (like offering rides to the children and including them on their family outings). Not so long ago, Duncan had me convinced that I had few friends in Conover; now I can see that for a long time, I must have been looking at the world through his misanthropic eyes. Life looks a lot brighter through my own. The increased human contact has made the children aware that other people have problems too, and they are finding that reaching out is a two-way street.

On the lighter side, Amanda remarked to me last week that "this divorce thing isn't so bad Mom." Apparently the "snob squad" at school, (one of whose members is going through a very similar situation with her family) has scooped up Amanda and suddenly my daughter is hanging out with the "in crowd." I teased her the other night about taking care not to become "one of them," and she assured me that one-on-one they were all much nicer than anyone realized.

On the financial front: in mid-October, I came home from work and found an overdraft notice from Conover Trust, indicating the bank had covered the October mortgage check (otherwise it would have bounced). This infuriated me. I had been carefully keeping track of checkbook activity, but Duncan had taken several hundred dollars out of the account via the machine, so I hadn't known about his withdrawals, and that's why we ran out of money. The next morning I went over to Conover Trust to ask my banker what I should do.

"Ursula, if I were you, I'd just drain the account."

"But there isn't much left in it, and Duncan would probably just retaliate by stopping his automatic deposits. What if he does it again?"

A teller who overheard me grinned from across the room, "Oh, I wouldn't worry about that if I were you. Duncan left his bank card in the machine two days ago, and so far he hasn't come back to get it, and if he doesn't come back to get it in three months, I'm going to destroy it!" he said.

My banker was grinning too. "Ursula, I'm sympathetic, but it's up to the lawyers and not the bank to do something about this now."

In the midst of all this stress, my body went into full rebellion mode like it did last April, only this time I was glad to be alone and not have to put up with any sarcastic remarks from Duncan. I called Arthur, who is insisting I go see a gynecologist this time, despite my antipathy toward the subspeciality. "I'll even send you to the person my wife goes to." Oh swell, more doctors, just what I need. Boy will I ever be glad to turn the page on this calendar year! It better be true that "life begins at forty."

These days, Duncan is alternating between bestowing unusual (for him) treats on the children (movies, outings, material extras) and threatening to withhold things that would truly enrich their lives (e.g., oboe lessons for Amanda, Japanese lessons for Spencer, and camp for both children). Last weekend, after first saying he wouldn't pay for them, Duncan told both children it would be up to Chubb MacIntyre whether they could have lessons and attend camp. My children are not amused, and as you can imagine, Mr. MacIntyre is not a very popular fellow at my house.

Amanda spent the night at Duncan's one Friday, and reported that he went into his old routine about how the children could keep Conover and their house if they chose to live with him, but that they would lose everything if they chose to live with me. Amanda cried and got mad (a healthy sign I would say; last spring, she'd merely cried), and then she really let Duncan have it: "I'm living with my mom no matter where she lives."

And according to Amanda Duncan replied, "That's your choice, and you better make it!" Amanda visited him again several days before Halloween. Someone rang the doorbell and ran away, leaving a pumpkin with a signed card on the doorstep. Amanda said the card was from Ivy Parrish. Duncan was pleased with this original gift and the charming manner in which it was delivered.

This past weekend Amanda asked, "Are we going to win the divorce, Mom?"

And I replied, "Amanda, in a divorce there are no winners. Divorce is just like a civil war. Everyone's life gets ripped apart, and there are no winners."

———————

I brought this Narrative Addendum with me when I returned to Gabriel's office in mid-October, along with the list of "Charbonnier Bills Outstanding," he'd requested. At the rate Gabriel was ripping through money, it was plain to see that cash flow would soon dry up.

"Since I assume you expect to continue to be paid promptly, which ones of these do you suggest I not pay?" I asked him at the outset.

He perused my list over the top of his glasses. "Well, don't pay your doctor," he said.

"You can't not pay your doctor," I protested, citing Asa's favorite bumper sticker: "Feel sick? – Call your lawyer!" Reed was not amused.

"Well, you have to eat and heat and pay the electric bill. How about letting the hardware store wait? And start running up finance charges on your credit cards. That's what most people do."

"Well, that's not what I do. I've never paid a finance charge in my life."

"Well then, don't pay your mortgage."

"Don't pay my mortgage! Well, what happens to me if I don't pay my mortgage?" I inquired.

"Well, you are not going to get spanked!" he said jauntily.

"Well, that's a relief! Now seriously, what happens?"

Gabriel never gave me a straight answer, but I assumed he'd been through this at least a thousand times before, and it seemed there was probably something to be said for postponing payment to someone who would wait to be paid (a bank) as opposed to someone who wouldn't wait very long (regular monthly creditors and Gabriel G. Reed, who had already threatened to "throw me to the birds" if I didn't keep up with his capacity to spend my hard-earned money).

"Times are tough and getting tougher in this state," he went on. "Did you see the morning paper? Our bonds just dropped to a B rating."

"That's because you liberal Democrats spend too much," I told him.

"We need to raise taxes. Tsk, tsk. You are a conservative Republican."

"From Ohio," I proclaimed, "but I'm not really that conservative."

"Oh, yes you are!"

"Oh, no I'm not. I'm not even always a Republican." Then I got back to the business at hand. "What should I do about camp deposits? The children want to go back to camp next summer."

"Pay them."

"But they're $600! Where am I going to get the balance?"

"I would pay them now, and take my chances!"

"What are you, a miracle worker? And what about Amanda's braces? Who's going to pay for them? Insurance covers less than half."

"Well, let's wait and see what the judge decides. By the way Merrill, have we picked our judge yet?"

She rummaged through a file. "Not yet."

"I thought you couldn't pick your judges," I said.

"Well, you *can't* pick your judges, and you *can* pick your judges. I like to pick mine," Reed smiled.

"What about the braces?" I persisted.

"Did you have braces when you were a child?" he asked.

"No, I was a borderline case and decided I could do without them." I could hear myself starting to growl at this irrelevant chitchat.

"Well, you look like you did." he said breezily.

"The orthodontist is going to decide whether Amanda needs braces. Not some judge."

"Lighten up, Ursula! Lighten up."

Then he turned to Merrill. "We need a judge, and a court date for temporary support, and we need to schedule a date to depose Mr. Charbonnier."

I was feeling more superfluous by the minute. "It's time for me to go," I said.

"Scoot!" he started to bellow, as he picked up a large metal saber from his desk. "Look what I bought this week," he said, admiring his latest antique acquisition.

"Oh, is it a Toledo blade?" I asked pointedly.

"No!"

"Maybe we could use it on MacIntyre," I ventured. This he enjoyed.

"You know," I continued, "my children have taught the cat to hiss whenever she hears his name! I don't know where they get it from."

"They get it from you!" Then he showed me a hand-sized black rock that he'd overpaid his antique dealer for at the same time he acquired the blade.

"What can I do with this?" he asked.

"Well, you could use it for a paperweight . . ." I ventured, "or maybe you could throw it at one of your obstreperous clients!" And then I left.

The next week did not get off to a banner start. Ted Talbot phoned early one morning to say that Bud had a terrible accident while working in the Abbott Road house and slashed the femoral artery in his right leg with a power saw. After three operations and first thinking the foot would have to be amputated, Bud's surgeons now thought they could save it. "Bud's been on morphine and has weeks of hospital stay, many skin grafts and much physical therapy ahead of him," reported Ted.

Events had also taken a rough turn at Genesis Labs.

CEO Leslie Drew didn't mince words. "The New York publisher who was thinking about acquiring *MM News* has changed his mind. Harding, Towle & Lamour have decided they have no further interest in it. They've concluded that the molecular design market will always be too small."

Why could no one see my vision of where computer-assisted molecular design was really headed?

"Ursula, if you can't triple subscriptions in sixty to ninety days, I am going to make some changes, despite your 100 percent renewal rate."

"Are you going to get rid of the publication?" I asked him point blank.

"No, but we can't go on as we've been. We'll implement some of your proposals in the next thirty days and see what happens."

Was it simply my imagination or was everything around me imploding?

Early November found me back at Westbury General, visiting Bud and meeting the new gynecologist recommended by Arthur. Bud said the doctors couldn't be pinned down about how much time it would take for his leg to heal, but he was just grateful he'd get to keep it. "For the first time in my life, Ursula," said Bud, "I've decided it's no longer imperative to look great on the beach," his way of saying that this is the pits, but he's going to make it.

Then I went downstairs to see Dr. Junius Moropolous, the gynecologist. At first he gave me pause when he looked up at me and said, "And how old are you, Joanne?"

But when I said "My name is Ursula, and I'm thirty-nine," and he laughed too, I knew that we were going to get along. When he was done with the exam, he said, "We're going to have to do a little surgery on you, and try to find out what your body is up to."

From what he said next, I gathered Arthur had briefed him on our family situation. "You know, I get about one a day like you, but you're going to make it, kid," he said punching me gently on the shoulder. "I can tell you're going to make it." His medical manner reminded me of Asa's.

"So what is it?" I asked. "What happens to these guys who wake up one day and suddenly stop wanting to be husbands and fathers?"

Moropoulos stared off into space for a long moment, then looked me squarely in the eye and said, "I think they just get a short circuit." And that was about as adequate an answer as I was going to hear for a long time.

XII

Hardball

Long is the way
And hard, that out of hell leads up to light.

— John Milton, *Paradise Lost*

"You're late! You kept me waiting!" he snapped.

"I am not late — you're early!" I retorted. In fact, I'd been out in his waiting room for ten minutes phoning in some last minute edits for *Molecular Modelling News,* while he was dawdling beneath the Cigar Store Indians with one of his fur-dripping clients.

"You have a real job," he exclaimed.

"Of course I have a real job. How else could I afford to pay your bills?" Something about him brought out the snappy retort in me and made me feel I could fight again. Each time I saw him, his energy made me feel better and better.

"Lost a pound or two," he said disapprovingly, in reference to the surgery he knew I'd had the week before. "Did they scrape your insides out?"

"The problem was caused by my sudden weight loss, and *only* my sudden weight loss, so I'm fine; I'm recovering nicely, Gabriel. The children and Christa took good care of me."

"I need someone like Christa to take care of me. I could use someone like that."

"Really? How old are your children?"

Merrill Crosby looked at Gabriel and laughed. "My children are so old that I have to lie about my age!" he replied.

"Oh, I get it, the sitter's for you."

"That's right," he laughed. "Now give me the next installment of your narrative, and five minutes to read it."

I handed him the pages.

Narrative Addendum

For the first time in awhile that nervous feeling is coming back, and as all the libraries are closed at this hour of the night, I guess that just leaves taking refuge with the Macintosh. I sense the prelims of Divorce 101 are over, and that we are now moving into the "hardball" stage.

Having turned off both kids, Duncan has only one remaining trump card: using money as a weapon – and it is clear to us that he will play it to the hilt. I have just about convinced myself that I can make up for almost everything that has happened to the children, but I cannot financially, overnight, make up for the opportunity costs of staying out of the work force to be their full-time Mom for nine years; and I don't see why Spencer and Amanda should now have to pay the price for my choice.

Duncan's contact with the children remains about the same. He did spend a little more time with Amanda over the past few weeks, and even took her shopping (she's in growth mode again and needs a lot of new clothes!), but he sees little of Spencer. Apparently he invited both children to go to Michigan the day after Christmas for the last week of the year to visit each of his parents. I told the children they were free to do whatever they wanted, but to my surprise first Amanda and later Spencer declined the invitation. Duncan assumed I had something to do with it, according to Amanda, so she said, "Mom, I told a little white lie, and said that you really tried to get us to go, (in fact I really was *neutral*) because you wanted to be alone, but that we still didn't want to go." She meant well, but if I were Duncan, her remark would have made me feel even worse.

Amanda phones Duncan more than Spencer does, and says she often leaves several messages in the evenings, and asks him to return the calls, but that he doesn't 'til the next day.

"Maybe that's because he's traveling on business," I said.

"Or perhaps he doesn't sleep at home every night," said Amanda.

When I hear comments like this, I really try to put my feelings aside, but what's happening to Duncan's relationship with our children is deeply discouraging. During dinner one night in early November, Spencer was tearing Duncan down, and I interrupted him and told him he absolutely must be courteous to and about his father "no matter what."

My son gave me a withering look and replied, "You call *that* a father!" and I who am rarely at a loss for words didn't know what to say, so I said nothing.

I spent the following weekend doing lots of yard work and getting

1 Inverary Lane shipshape. When Duncan came by to pick up Spencer and Amanda on Sunday afternoon, he sat in the car for fifteen minutes and just watched me working away. Duncan then left to take Spencer to a neighboring town where Spencer intends to join the weekend basketball league, but he soon returned, so that Spencer could get the $30 fee from me for joining; Duncan refused to pay it. That same day Amanda reported that Duncan has "a new job in marketing" at another GEC facility in Farboro, but that he did not give her a phone number or any specifics when she inquired. This past week, she said he was involved in something to do with designing Germane's new logo. I still don't know what he's doing.

The first week of November, Shea took me to Westbury General for day surgery. I wasn't even scared when they knocked me out. I have reached a point where the only thing I am afraid of is allowing myself to be afraid. Even though surgery was more of a "show stopper" than I thought it would be, I am okay and in another week or two, they say my body will no longer look like "Joe Palooka won the fight!" Christa and the kids were super post-op, except that Spencer and Amanda made me laugh so hard at dinner that my stitches hurt like the devil.

When I went back to the hospital to get the stitches out, I visited Bud Alden, turning up just as the doctors were removing all his bandages; he was not doing well. He insisted I inspect the leg from all sides, and I felt intensely grateful for a childhood in the hospital with Asa, where I had learned to look at practically anything without flinching. Bud and Ted wanted to know if we would help him out by keeping their samoyed for the weekend of the eleventh and twelfth (and maybe a number of future weekends as well). Duncan reportedly asked Amanda "if Ted was staying over too." Note: overnight guests at 1 Inverary Lane will be restricted to children and quadrupeds until further notice!

On November 9, Genesis Labs had a Board of Directors meeting. The bottom line does not look good, thanks to the non-molecular modelling part of the business which Leslie stubbornly refuses to abandon. So now the new CFO is in radical surgery mode and Archie McGowan says if I can't bring in a lot of advertising revenue (something new for *Molecular Modelling News*) before January, there may well be no publication, despite my 100 percent renewal rate. My response to that was, "I'm gonna go out with a bang, not a whimper," and I was sailing along with the multifront war until I got your news that we really will have to go to court for temporary support before the deposition.

Sorry I lost it on the phone with Merrill this afternoon. My kids brought me back into line when I arrived home tonight. They snatched your letter out of my hand, and took one look at the quote from Chubb MacIntyre that "Mr. Charbonnier doesn't have ten cents left over after he pays her each month," and both kids just hooted for about five minutes. They've seen where Duncan lives, and how much money he's spending on himself these days. Spencer said, "Mom, no judge is going to be dumb enough to believe this." I'm not so confident, though – after all, I've had jury duty and Spencer hasn't!

But what really sent me into dissolve mode this afternoon wasn't all of the above. Sometimes it's the small things that push one over: Amanda called me at work this afternoon after her first oboe lesson and announced, "Mom, I absolutely love the oboe!" and I realized that she's probably going to have to give that up now, just because of the divorce. Whatever Duncan's beef with me is, I still cannot fathom why he is taking out his anger and frustrations (whatever they may be) on the children, by depriving them or threatening to deprive them of these enrichments to their lives that he can well afford. Maybe it's that Duncan knows the hot button for me is the children, and while intellectually I expect him to pound on it, emotionally it is sometimes hard to handle.

Closest friends say Duncan is really just totally out of control and doesn't know what he is doing. They remind me that for many, many years he was a super husband and father, something more than a decade of scrapbooks, my intact if remote memories, and these two neat kids all substantiate. Julie, my friend in Connecticut, continues to believe that sometime in the distant future, Duncan will be his old self again, and though my relationship with him will by then be history, it is important to salvage something he can have with the children. She knows whereof she speaks: her father walked out on her, her absolutely neat mom and seven siblings when he was in his late thirties and was just starting to come to his senses several years later, when he dropped dead from a heart attack.

I have been thinking about how our lives will change after the temporary support hearing on Monday, and wondering how we are going to make it through the winter – not a good season to sell a house (but since I'm ignoring the mortgage, I suppose it's only a matter of time). Maybe I will be a happier camper after I see you guys on Thursday, but at the moment I feel a strong identification with Horace Greeley – you know, the editor of *The New York Tribune* who ran for President and in the course of just one month lost the election, his spouse, his job, his mind and his life!

I have also been thinking a lot about what one of the scientists at Genesis Labs says about the primary law of the jungle not really being "survival of the fittest," but "do not get between a mother she-bear and her cubs." He's right, and that will probably keep me fighting. This entire experience has given me a whole new respect for biology!

———————————

Reed looked up from the narrative. "I've set up a meeting for us with Chubb and Duncan at this office next week. Can you make it Thursday at nine?"

"Yes."

"I'll be seeing you," he said, waving me out.

"You will," I nodded, and left.

XIII

Out of the Frying Pan

Delays have dangerous ends.
William Shakespeare, *Henry VI*

The weather couldn't have been much worse the morning of our first four-way meeting with Duncan and Chubb MacIntyre. Merrill Crosby came bounding down the double staircase and called to me from between the Cigar Store Indians, "Gabriel just phoned from his car and is fuming in snow and a traffic jam on Route 93." In fact, it had taken me two hours to drive into Boston from Conover, normally a twenty-minute ride.

Gabriel was still sputtering when he walked into the office an hour later. One can't have one's lawyer off stride when the opposition is due to arrive any moment. "Here, I have something that will cheer you up," I said, handing him a red envelope. "Something to broaden your antique collection, if not your political horizons!" said the note to which was pinned a "Dewey for President" button.

His irritation melted into a grin of delight. "Are you sure you want me to have this?"

"Yes," I said. "The only thing I ever did with it was to put it on my leaf man, and by the time I have a leaf man again, Massachusetts will be a two-party state, and then it won't be funny anymore!"

"Well, why would it be a two-party state?"

"Well, I don't know. Maybe just for fun!"

"Let's remember why we're here!" he said, shifting back into lawyer-mode. Gabriel had calmed down and was back in control again. "Chubb MacIntyre will be over any minute, Ursula, and he'll try to charm you with his bluff Irish way, but don't be taken in by it." Duncan had already arrived and dived into the bathroom, only to reappear with a very runny nose and a blank, vapid expression.

I let Merrill take care of the introductions with Gabriel, who ushered Duncan into the "mausoleum": a conference room with a mahogany table that could easily have accommodated forty for dinner. I sat down next to Gabriel, who immediately started rummaging in his pockets and glowering at Merrill impatiently.

"What is it?" she finally asked.

"His glasses," I answered. "He needs his glasses." Gabriel sent Merrill off to find them and gazed at me nonplussed.

The meeting wasn't very far along before Gabriel quickly got a clearer slant on The Charbonnier Matter; we could both see that Chubb MacIntyre was as much in the fog as his client. Reed had described MacIntyre accurately, though: tall, corpulent, garbed in traditional power-grey flannel, and full of Irish charm.

Chubb kept insisting my children were much younger than they actually were, while Duncan grinned silently and uncomprehendingly from across the table. Finally, Gabriel could bear it no longer. "Ursula, tell Mr. MacIntyre how old Spencer and Amanda really are!"

"They're ten and twelve, Chubb, and I happen to know, because I was there when they were born!" Chubb was even more surprised a few minutes later when Duncan had no idea what the amount was of his weekly automatic pay deposit, and that I knew it to the penny.

Gabriel had enough. He marched me into his office, closed the door, clapped his hands on my shoulders, and said, "We are not just talking alcohol here. We are talking hard drugs! Chubb told me Duncan wrote a letter to his mother about not wanting a divorce. Do you know anything about that?"

"No," I said. "Gabriel, Duncan Charbonnier had everything – a wife and children who loved him, a nice home, good job – and he threw it all away. Gabriel, why do men do things like that?"

"Because, Ursula, men are stupid! Like that fellow in the poem – I haven't thought about it in a good many years – the one who went home one summer night and put a bullet in his head."

"Richard Cory," I half mumbled to myself.

"You stay here, Ursula." Gabriel left me in his office and over the next two hours moved back and forth between me and the mausoleum to negotiate with Chubb and Duncan. Basically, they were knocking the stuffing out of our living standard, down to something below half of what we now had, and Gabriel implied that once formal child support was set, that's about where the children and I would come out financially.

"But you think you deserve it all, don't you darlin'?" he said on a break.

"Yes!" I said without hesitation, "because I don't think I even did anything bad to anyone!"

Duncan's words were echoing from last spring: "From now on you can pay for the mortgage and the groceries. You can pay for all that now!" I couldn't believe the law would really let him do that to us. I was so naïve. "Well, you get an 'A' in Drama!" I told Gabriel. "Jesus!" I roared in disbelief.

"Please call me Gabriel," he said without skipping a beat, his nose nearly touching mine. For a moment my mind froze, and then my whole body dissolved into laughter. For most clients, this would have been the one moment for Gabriel to exhibit gravity and horror. How then, I wondered, had he known that one sharp puncture of humor was the right thing to do for me. This took nothing away from the outrage of the moment, but the physical act of laugher made it bearable. Over the next several weeks, Gabriel delayed and delayed, very effectively I might add, keeping us out of court for the setting of child support, which enabled me and the children to go on financially for a little while longer. He wanted to get Duncan's deposition done before we went to court, and scheduled it for the fifth of December at this office.

"And be sure to bring an update of your narrative with you," he instructed.

When I arrived on D-Day, as I had come to call it, Gabriel snatched the updated narrative out of my hand and dived into another room for a quick read, barely pausing to say hello.

"Oh, he's in a great mood this morning," I commented to Merrill.

"He's always like that before depositions," she replied. "Come in here and go over some last-minute items with me, while Gabriel reads your narrative."

Narrative Addendum

Well Gabriel, I guess we made a little progress in the last month. You kept us out of court, and I finally found out why Duncan Charbonnier wants to get out of this marriage. Thanks to a friend I have in common with Elsie, I was able to get a line on the current scuttlebutt in Ann Arbor: "Duncan Charbonnier doesn't want a divorce – Ursula does. But life with Ursula is not for Duncan because Ursula is selfish, job-oriented, makes him do all the work, is spreading rumors about his drinking, is always working and has no time for others, and has always placed doing her own thing above the marriage." Elsie bought it all, hook, line and sinker, but the bearer of the tale did not buy any of this, and the good news for me is that I no longer have to wonder if I had amnesia for some terrible deed I might have done.

Life continues to be a challenge on all fronts:

Work: Genesis Labs continues to threaten *Molecular Modelling News,* but I just act like I'm *The New York Times* and I'm going to be there forever: I'm booking authors well into 1991; getting advertising commitments from American vendors; and planting seeds with the Japanese. I've told Archie that my goal in 1990 is to have a bottom line that even the CFO will love!

Domestic: The day before Thanksgiving, Christa announced that after a whirlwind five-week courtship (no wonder your business is booming!) she is going to marry a twenty year-old and move to Germany in the spring. I figured six months is more than enough time to solve almost any problem, but then Christa said she was quitting school (to save money) and would now have to find a full day of work for every day of the week. Translation: unless we can find her a patchwork quilt of morning jobs with others by month's end, she is going to stop working for us in early January. So far I've got her booked for three mornings; three down and two to go!

Children: Well, the grade cards were spectacular, and invitations and understanding from other families continue to pour in, but there is much discontent among the troops about proposed cutbacks in extracurricular life. Or as Spencer Charbonnier humbly announced the other week, "Mom, I am the smartest, funniest, poorest boy in Conover!"

Spencer and Amanda seem to be doing fine, although I suppose that the jury will be out on them for years. Their teachers in and out of school say that if they didn't know what was really going on here, they would never guess there was a problem. I am gradually learning to manage both children (most of the time) with different balances of firmness and wit, although I sometimes have the feeling that I am the one who is actually being managed.

The commands to "find us a new Dad," continue unabated, and only humor saves the day: "Well, do you mind if I get divorced first?"

"YES!"

"All right, I'll get married. What are your requirements?"

"Number 1, NOW, Number 2, NOW, Number 3, see 1 and 2."

"Mom, how about a time out? We think you need to see a movie."

"Sounds great to me." So what did they do, they took me to see *Look Who's Talking,* the one about a baby who's matchmaking for his single mom. Sometimes, you just can't win!

Shortly before Thanksgiving, Amanda had the first of several serious chats with Duncan: "Dad, can't you pay us as much as you want?"

"No, I can't. The judge gives me an amount, and I can't pay any more, because I don't earn any more. Maybe your mother could spend less. She spends all my money on clothing and things for herself, and that's why there isn't enough for you and Spencer." But Amanda knows that's not the case – and as you know, I will have no trouble documenting where the dollars have really gone.

Amanda is furious at the thought of losing her oboe lessons, and has told Duncan that she plans to space them out to once every two weeks, or once every two months if need be, but that she has no intention of giving them up, PERIOD!

Duncan called just after I'd learned that we go to court on December 7 for temporary support. I calmly told him that it doesn't take a mental giant to see that the children and I are not going to make it on half of what he gives us now. With total dispassion he replied that he could get by on it just fine, and didn't see why the three of us couldn't. Later that evening he called Amanda, and for the first time I'm aware of, she really blew her cork at him. I happened to be passing through the room, and when I realized what was going on, I quickly grabbed some paper to take notes:

"Dad, you're making me lose everything I've had since I was two years old, and you don't know how much it hurts. No matter how mad you are at Mom, you should care about me . . . I think you're being unreasonable, and I don't think it's fair. . . . This place is called Earth, and on Earth you need money to get everything. On Earth you need money, and you need love. . . . You're so unlike fathers in other divorced families. They care enough about the kids to give them what they need . . . I know you have the money. You just won't give it to us. I've always loved you, but it just seems greedy and selfish. You don't need half for yourself. Three people, four including Streak, need more than you do. Don't take us to court."

At this point Duncan said something about needing money for himself. "It just doesn't add up, Dad; it seems like you don't care about me. My Mom cares about me, and she gives me what I need. Mom gives me what I need, and you used to. Why are you taking Mom to court on Thursday if you care about me? Why do you even have to do that if you have enough money to live on by yourself?"

Then, to my dismay, in the next part of the conversation she brought up the night Duncan shoved me across the den last August. "You can't deny it because I know the truth, can you? Can you deny it if I saw it? Dad, what I saw is what happened. Mom was wearing her terry robe with the blue bows and dots (I hadn't even remembered what I was wearing that night). If you don't remember Dad, then something's wrong with you. You don't just forget something like that. Did you tell Grand'mère that you walked out on us? Dad, stop laughing . . ."

What followed was this: Duncan said, "Amanda, I won't take orders from you."

"Dad, will you please answer me?"

"No, I won't please answer you, and I'm going to have to say good . . ." At this point Amanda hung up on him. This is a very polite child, and I'd never heard her light into someone like that before. The next time Duncan came to collect Spencer, he and Amanda barely said hello to each other, and he looked very unhappy.

All through the years, Amanda and Duncan had been extremely close, and this was a real departure from their usual way of relating. What I learned from this was that the August night was a bigger deal in her mind than I had previously thought. It's not something that she and I had talked about much. Now she talked to me about it in details that I hadn't remembered, not just what I was wearing, but what we'd had for dinner that night, how I'd come into the room, and all that followed. It saddens me that this is going to be one of her childhood memories of our life together. This is not the way I want to be remembered by my children. And it's not the way I want them to remember Duncan. The last twelve months have been Hell by any standard, but they are still a deviation from all that went on before.

Thanksgiving weekend was spent quietly – counting blessings, seeing friends and catching up on sleep. All three of us are tired. Duncan never approached me about plans for the day, but on Thanksgiving morning, he invited Spencer and Amanda for breakfast at his place; in the afternoon the children and I put the finishing touches on desserts we'd prepared and headed to the Molloy's for a festive Thanksgiving dinner in Walden. It was easy to be with people who'd known us for so long and who knew what was really happening now. Spencer and Amanda played with little Betsy (now two-and-a-half), and Kathy, Kevin and I reminisced about how dear Duncan had been with Betsy when she was a baby, not so many years ago. I was struck by my new ability to accept that there was an old Duncan and now there is the current Duncan, and I could talk about them both side-by-side.

The next day, Duncan took both children out for dinner, and when he came to pick them up, he reeked of Listerine. Duncan had been buying one quart bottles of it in the days before he left Inverary Lane (back when I didn't know the product was nearly 27 percent alcohol). Duncan keeps insisting to both children that he is no longer drinking, but I am not the uninformed person I was last spring, and I have to draw my own conclusions. Over the rest of the holiday weekend I had calls from Duncan's stepmother, Darcy, and her daughter, Lori Kincaid; a lovely, long walk with Elise Priest; and time to do some real cooking, including Bud and Ted's favorite dessert, which I delivered to the hospital Sunday night. Bud is mending slowly – the first of the skin grafts took place last week, and the surgeons found a lot more dead muscle and nerves.

My conversations with Darcy and Lori were not pleasant, and I don't expect to hear from them again for a while. I told Darcy that Duncan had a problem, "and once I'm out of the loop, Darcy, you and Jock will be Duncan's next-of-kin."

And this was her reply, "Jock and I have no responsibility for Duncan. And if Duncan has a problem, and we really doubt he does, it's not *our* problem." One can argue I shouldn't have said this, but in the big, long-run, Duncan's family will now never be able to say that they didn't know or that no one ever told them. Now Duncan's family has the information, and they can do with it what they will.

Duncan can continue to deny to everyone (including himself) that there is any chemical dependency problem, and having always been more clever and convincing than I'll ever be, he will probably pull it off. Spencer and

Amanda now believe Duncan when he tells them (and he does regularly) that he's stopped drinking, but I smelled the Listerine last week. Duncan declares he doesn't use cocaine. But when he arrived at your office two weeks ago, he disappeared into the john for several minutes and came back with a runny nose and amnesia for the ages of his children and the amount of his automatic bank deposit. These are facts, not opinions. I guess the bottom line is that none of this amounts to a hill of beans, even if you could prove it in court, and you probably can't.

None of this will stop us from getting on with life, and we all managed to have some fun this weekend. Amanda, who always has an open ear, heard through the grapevine that the Girl Scouts (she is not one) were sponsoring a very cheap one-day trip to New York, and having inherited the I-love-New-York gene (a double whammy, I might add) she convinced me to sign up, and we went on Saturday. This meant Spencer had to spend two overnights at Duncan's — a first since Duncan moved out last summer. Duncan treated Spencer and two friends to dinner and a Celtics game, and there is nothing Spencer likes better. New York worked its usual magic on me, making me believe that anything is possible. I couldn't do too much for GDP this trip, but there were other dividends: watching Amanda bargain very successfully with two street vendors; having lunch with my dear friend Julie who trained in from Connecticut; and finding that I could look at all the old special places and still feel good, if obsolete, feelings about them.

Julie was great with Amanda. Her father walked out on their family when Julie was just Amanda's age. Julie, who is younger but wiser than I am, told me that a child gets some things from its mother, but some things from its father. "From its father and from his love, a child gets its sense of self-worth. Therefore, it is important to underscore to the children every day that Duncan is not well, not happy, not himself these days, but that he loves them. If they doubt his love," said Julie, "they will ultimately doubt themselves, something you have to make sure never happens." Julie told Amanda to call her anytime, and I know Amanda will.

On the way out of Manhattan, the bus driver gave a minitour. Amanda, who has pretty much known her way around New York from an early age, enjoyed being driven past all the familiar sights, and I looked out the window and experienced a little déjà vu of my Thanksgiving feeling, namely that there was the old Duncan and the new. We rode past the building where Duncan and I had worked, the street corner where we used to meet for secret lunches, the UN Chapel where we were married at just this time of year, and a score more places that had meant something in another life. I could look at everything and really smile. New York is like going to a candy store. And Boston is like coming home for dinner.

Last week, Amanda brought me a little present: a red pencil topped by a computer-shaped eraser — and on the pencil was the message: "ALL

SYSTEMS GO."
   A good way to start the last month of this year I would say.

XIV

Into the Fire

What of the faith and fire within us
Men who march away . . .

— Thomas Hardy, *Men Who March Away*

"I don't like what is happening with your children," said Reed as he came back into the room waving my narrative in his hand. "They're too involved."

"Duncan said and did all of these things in front of them over the past year and a half, and in all the years before that. There's not much I can do about that."

"Well, I still don't like it. Where's Chubb? I want to get started."

"Seth Wright's coming with Duncan instead," said Merrill. "MacIntyre smashed up his Mercedes and broke his hand." She and Reed exchanged a knowing look, and two days later, he would tell me why.

Gabriel placed me at the small desk in the corner next to his, and told me I was to sit poker-faced no matter what was said, jot down all lies and discrepancies, and pass him my notes. He told Duncan to sit in the far diagonal corner by the window, and motioned Wright, who would slouch on his tail bone and chain-smoke over the next five hours, into one of the wing chairs. A professional stenographer, at a cost of hundreds of dollars, would record the session.

After offering the ritual cup of coffee, Gabriel rapidly dispensed with the preliminaries of address, profession, job status and got down to business. "Now tell us, please, Mr. Charbonnier, what had occurred in your marital relationship with Ursula that caused you to take the rather important step of looking for a new place to live?"

"I lost trust in Ursula."

"What happened, sir, that caused you to lose trust in Ursula?"

"She accused me of being an alcoholic, and of being on drugs, and of being an irresponsible father, and of lying and deceiving her." What was I supposed to think of a man who drank vodka secretly out of brown bags locked in his car and who had willingly submitted to thousands of dollars worth of unnecessary neurological tests over the past four years?

This response led Reed into the drinking. "And when did you first address with your internist, Dr. Arthur, the subject of your drinking? Tell us the substance of your conversation with him."

"Last August. I said that I had been drinking too much, and that I needed his help and advice."

Gabriel moved on to other matters, then after a time abruptly began questioning Duncan about his drinking again. "Didn't you tell us that you thought you were drinking too much?"

"I did not say that," replied Duncan. I looked at Reed, who delighted in catching Duncan in this lie, and I felt sick at Duncan's inability to remember what he'd said not an hour before.

Seth Wright's memory was equally poor. "The record will reflect exactly what my client said," Wright protested to Reed.

Reed looked mildly amused, apparently used to dealing with lawyers who were more absent-minded than the witnesses. "What, tell us if you will, were your drinking habits at or around the time you quit?"

"Use of alcohol around dinnertime each day," said Duncan.

"Is that it?"

"Yes."

"Well, did you ever drink before five o'clock in the day, on any day?"

"Yes."

"Before noontime any day?"

"Yes."

"Do you drink hard liquor before noontime?"

"Yes."

"What's the earliest in the morning you ever drank?"

"I don't remember."

"Have you ever done that in front of Ursula? Did you make a point of keeping that a secret from her?"

"I didn't make a point of it, no."

"But you avoided it in her presence?"

"Yes."

So our dentist, Dr. Post, had been right. He really wasn't exaggerating when he said he'd known since 1987. The magnitude of my stupidity bore in on me even more as Duncan continued: this was what was really happening on all those mornings Duncan had insisted on getting breakfast for the children. "You just take your time getting ready for work, Ursula," he used to encourage. "I enjoy having time alone with Spencer and Amanda in the morning before they go to school." Later, Amanda would tell me that Duncan seldom spent time with them at breakfast, and was usually off in another room "doing something." Well, now we knew what.

Later in the deposition, Reed got into the various car accidents preparatory to asking, "Mr. Charbonnier, would you call it an accident that time you drove down the railroad tracks?"

"No."

"You went off the highway and headed down the railroad tracks, right?"

"For about ten feet."

"Ten feet, that's all?"

"I didn't measure, that's my recollection . . . it's hard to recall."

"Okay, and why did you decide to go out to the restaurant down the railroad tracks as opposed to the highway?"

"I was very upset at the time, and I don't know why."

Close to the end of the deposition, Gabriel asked what I thought was a very strange question. I didn't understand why he asked it. Shortly after Duncan complained about how he helped with so many household responsibilities, Gabriel said, "Mr. Charbonnier, what is the most traumatic thing that ever happened to you?"

"Being present at the birth of my two children!" said Duncan in a proud tone.

This threw Gabriel slightly, as if it were the first time he'd gotten this particular response to one of his standard litmus test questions. "Should have tried it without anesthesia!" I wanted to shout, but Gabriel would have shot me on the spot.

"I didn't say 'exciting,' Mr. Charbonnier. I said 'traumatic!'"

"And I answered you," Duncan replied, again inappropriately pleased with himself and his answer.

Even Seth Wright, a bachelor, stirred uncomfortably at this response.

Something in Gabriel's expression disturbed me also, in part because something in Duncan's response had disturbed him. "Had enough!?" I wanted to shout. Maybe his mind heard me.

There were three lawyers in the room with all their meters ticking. The waste of money and time was unconscionable. Gabriel finally put a stop to it in mid-afternoon. Duncan hadn't had much to say about me that was particularly scathing or that I could feel badly about. Did it really make any difference that Duncan admitted he hadn't been honest for years or that his admission of "early morning drinking" was "on the record?" I thought not. Nothing was said that would make a dime's worth of difference to me and the children, but it contributed thousands of dollars to each lawyer's coffers, as Duncan had threatened me it would.

At the end, Reed gave me his paper napkin for a souvenir, which I hung in my office with this caption: "The world's most damned expensive napkin, $2,278 or thereabouts, 12/5/89."

_____

The following Thursday, Pearl Harbor Day 1989, we went to court for temporary support, and then the real fun began. By the time this case was over, I would be as at home in these surroundings as an animal in the forest.

The Probate Court in Cambridge, Massachusetts is a building that looks like it is ashamed of what goes on inside it – and it needs to be. The steps on its east facade are crumbling, the iron gate is caving in, and the orange bricks cast a sickly glow even on sunless days. The lobby teems with lawyers and clients, huddled on benches. It's easy to tell the lawyers. They are the ones who look unconcerned. And why shouldn't they be? Most of them will make close to $1,000 as they wait for a judge, $2,000 if it takes all day. I joined Merrill who was waiting in a corner by the coffee stand. Gabriel arrived in a grumpy state, complaining about his back, grousing about his aching teeth, and popping penicillin. "Have you checked the docket?" he asked Merrill. "Who's our judge?"

"Tracy," she replied.

"Well, it could have been better, and it could have been worse, but it's not bad on the whole," said Gabriel. Then he took Merrill aside, and she came back and said good-bye. Later she would tell me that he yelled at her and sent her back to the office in tears, but to me he said, "I didn't see why you should be double-billed for the morning."

I was not the best company, because I just kept blowing off steam about the irrationality of the whole situation. "What am I doing in this place? Everyone is mad at me," I continued. "My father is furious at me for being in this mess, and says it's all my fault for marrying a psychopath and an alcoholic; my children are angry at what's happening to our lives; and none of us knows why Duncan is doing any of this."

"Well, I'm not mad at you. Look, you didn't invite me to the wedding!" Gabriel smiled. "Come on. I'll buy you a cup of coffee. You know, at the deposition the other day, I realized you're much more intelligent than your husband is."

"Don't call him 'my husband!'"

"Well, what should I call him?"

"Call him 'that person.'"

"Well 'that person' is fine on GEC and what goes on at Germane, but if you get him onto anything else, he just talks. He doesn't really say anything, and he doesn't really make any sense. Do you think you'll ever take him back?"

I couldn't believe he was asking me this after twelve months of total hell and God knows how many thousands of dollars. "Gabriel, do you want to hear something awful? I don't want him back! There's been too much deception for too long. Furthermore, forty year-old wimps, who sit in lawyers' offices at more than $1,000 an hour, and snivel about their tough lives, do not impress me in the least!"

"What are you going to do when this is over? After you're divorced, I mean."

"I don't know, but at least I'll be out of Limbo."

"You'll have opportunity," he said brightly.

"That's my idea of happiness," I replied

"That *my* definition of happiness," he said. "When this is over, you are going to have a whole new life!"

"How do you know?" I grumped back at him. The irrationality of the process and the waste of time and money were closing in on me again. I wanted to be back at the office. I wanted to be thinking about something productive and life-affirming like molecules. "I don't want to be here!"

"Look, here comes Chubb, bandaged hand and all! How's your hand, Chubb? We were all worried about you."

At which point MacIntyre gave us some cock-and-bull story about breaking his hand while unsuccessfully trying to spank his dogs. Not one word about any smashed up Mercedes. When MacIntyre moved on to catch up with Duncan on the other side of the lobby, Reed said, "We really were worried about him. You see, Ursula, Chubb has a drinking problem, just like Duncan. And he's also in denial about it. But all the lawyers know."

"Oh that's just great!" I thought, birds of a feather . . .

"And so does Judge Tracy, who is very active in AA, and I'm telling you this Ursula, so that if you get a chance to bring up alcohol and Appleton Hall when we're in front of the judge, do it. You're intelligent. You'll know what to say. It may get you a little more in child support . . ."

I was beginning to feel out of place again. "Oh, are you an alcoholic too?"

"No, I never drink anymore, but I used to have a drinking problem. So did most of my friends, but they're all dead now. Why don't we go inside and wait our turn?"

This is a bad dream, I thought. A meteorite fell on my head, and I woke up in the company of a bunch of drunks in the Probate Court in Cambridge, but in just a minute, I am really going to wake up and I'll actually be at home in my bed in Conover, and . . .

"Ursula, are you listening to me?"

"Huh?"

"I said I like your suit." Reed was trying to be nice and pull me out of my gloom.

"Thanks. You know, in my place you get a lot of advice: dress up, dress dowdy, but I say, 'be yourself and take your chances.'" Then I looked up at Judge Tracy – white-haired, black-robed, and red-faced.

"Well, I know what he had for breakfast!" I said to Gabriel.

"Not nice, Ursula," he chided in a mock serious tone. "Tracy used to be a lawyer, you know. Not a very good one. Only made about $15,000 a year, until they made him a judge. He was a shining appointment of the King Administration."

"Oh, swell!"

Then Reed launched into a monologue about the court world and his insights on it. A young lawyer was at the bench, and Gabriel started critiquing him. "Don't try 209A," he coached. "Never works. I used to try that one before I knew better."

"Hey, he's young," I protested.

"Does that make me old?" he asked in a suddenly serious tone.

Now it was my turn to cheer him up. "I'd say that you're just right!" I quipped.

"The Lord works in mysterious ways! Are you as nervous as I am?" he grinned.

"Well, you know what they say, 'Don't be nervous, but don't make any mistakes!' "

"Jesus!" he said.

"Please call me Ursula," I said softly.

"You liked that one, didn't you?" he said. This might be a total waste, but at least Reed was amusing company.

"The Charbonnier Matter," someone intoned, and then it was our turn. I followed Gabriel through the swinging gate, and the four of us, Chubb, Duncan, Gabriel and I stood before Judge Tracy. I didn't feel nervous. Just out of place. I was the only one of the five of us who had never had a drinking problem, and they were making all the rules. The rules that were about to change the lives of Spencer and Amanda – and not for the better.

MacIntyre immediately launched into a diatribe about what a bitchy, big spender I was, and I would later learn that just by virtue of being Reed's client, Tracy already had me typecast negatively. The air fairly bristled with Boston class warfare: the poor Irish Judge vs. the wealthy Irish Lawyer vs. *nouveau riche* upstart Mr. Reed from New Hampshire vs. Mr. Duncan fair-haired Charbonnier Germane Senior Executive vs. Mrs. Conover Rich Bitch Charbonnier. I listed us silently as I heard Chubb tell Tracy, "If she were Mrs. Reed, Judge, she wouldn't have these problems."

"Of course I wouldn't have these problems," I wanted to retort, "because Reed wouldn't have been stupid enough to lose someone like me." But I had been coached: Shut up. Be courteous. Don't speak unless spoken too. Wear your black patent leather Catholic girls' school pumps, look demure, and for God's sake don't let them know how smart you are.

Then Tracy, MacIntyre, and Reed launched into a self-congratulatory dialogue about what a great job Reed had done in helping rewrite the child support laws, and how much improved they were. I was trying not to throw up.

As soon as I could manage it, I told the judge in simplified language how Dr. Arthur and I had worried for years that Duncan had epilepsy and possibly a brain tumor, and that only this past summer, we had learned he had been drinking secretly, and the children and I had immediately gone to Appleton Hall for help, and that I didn't see why my children should have to pay the penalty for my ignorance.

Tracy was thrilled to have a fellow-alcoholic before him. His eyes shone, even as Duncan protested, "Judge, I am not an alcoholic, and I don't have any drinking problem."

"Now Mr. Charbonnier, despite what you say, I know from my many years on the bench, that when the family says there's an alcohol problem, there's an alcohol problem. The family always knows." He wandered a bit in what followed, but basically he lectured Duncan about being in denial. "Now is there any hope of you folks getting back together?"

"No," said Duncan, too quickly, I sensed, for the the judge's taste.

"I tried, Your Honor," I said more slowly, after a thoughtful pause. "The children and I went to Appleton Hall several times, and we asked my husband to come back with us and work on the problem as a family, but he refused. All the doctors have told me this is out of my hands now."

"Well, sometimes an alcoholic marriage can be saved, and sometimes it can't." Then he turned to Duncan. "I'm chairing the AA meeting in Stover tonight. Why don't you come, son!"

"Maybe I will," said Duncan ingratiatingly.

I rolled my eyes at Gabriel. I didn't like the way Tracy was lapping this up.

"I didn't do that at all well," I said to Gabriel when we got back out in the hall. "I was too emotional."

"Well, it was an emotional matter. You did just fine. Let's have another cup of coffee and talk about it." He handed me some money. "No cream, one Sweet'n Low, and I'm going to the men's room."

"That's okay, I'll get this one," I said handing him back his money.

Then I ran after him, and caught him just short of the door. "Give me back that money. After thirteen years with Duncan Charbonnier, I promised myself I was never going Dutch again!" He laughed.

When Reed returned, Chubb came over to us, and I broke the rules by trying to talk to him as a human being instead of the opposing counsel. "Look, if you have any influence over this man at all," I implored, referring to Duncan, "get him to AA."

"For all I know, Mrs. Charbonnier, you planted the vodka bottles in his car!" he said coldly. How could he say that to me? What kind of a person did he think I was? I looked at him in total disbelief as he strode away.

"Gabriel, why did you even suggest I tell Judge Tracy the truth? Duncan denied my story, McIntyre tried to impugn it; you were distracted by it; and I didn't help myself or Spencer and Amanda in any way. This whole process is a travesty. The court is in denial, anti-family, and thinks women who stay home to nurture children are complete fools, and it treats them accordingly! What goes on in Probate Court is a sociopath's dream and an honest woman's nightmare!"

"Ursula, this is the best western civilization has to offer," said Gabriel.

"Well, forgive me if I'm not impressed!"

Gabriel put his arm around me to comfort me as we walked out of the courthouse. But I was so mad I marched straight into Cambridge Street and the path of an oncoming truck. Gabriel pulled me out of the way, just in time. "We don't want anything to happen to you."

The support order was handed down several days later, about half of what we'd been used to living on, as Reed had so accurately predicted. Duncan did not pay us the first week's support "forthwith" as the court ordered, and then delayed the following payment, so the children and I went for two weeks in December with no financial support from him whatsoever. The court didn't mind. I was about to learn that millions of fathers don't pay their child support on time, if at all, and that they regularly go unpunished for it.

The message from "the best western civilization has to offer" boiled down to this: if you stay home to be a full-time mom and nurture children, you and your children become vulnerable to getting royally screwed by The System.

Was this the reward for staying home for nine years and for being a loving and faithful wife, partner, and friend? If I had it to do over again, would I stay at home and nurture a family? What a hopeless case I am — of course I would! Maybe the legal system didn't value my contribution, but somehow I still did.

In the nine years I did stay home, whenever people out in the world would ask me what I did, it was my habit to reply that I was "the Curator of National Treasures." Occasionally people got it; more often they would launch into a discussion of art and antiques. To my way of thinking, our children are our national treasures, but it was painfully evident as I stood in Judge Tracy's courtroom that the legal system just doesn't see it that way. Reality was dawning: Duncan really does stand a good chance of getting away with systematically destroying everything I hold dear — family, home, children and a happy, stable way of life.

How, I wondered, was I going to keep my kids happy, trusting, and well-adjusted in a court system that allows their lives to be torn apart?

XV

Implosions

Barbara, The System is the Snow Job!

— A Boston Lawyer, *Private Conversation*

At the Genesis Christmas party the following week, I met Joe Gerard, a Digby Grant client whose first divorce had been done by Reed. Joe was engaged to marry a Genesis documentation specialist. He encouraged me to find another lawyer as he gave me a long lecture about Reed: "Let's just put it this way, Ursula, Reed is no gentleman . . . He's a total sleaze bucket . . . All he cares about is money . . . He's flamboyant and dramatic . . . He brags about his multimillion dollar settlements." I, myself, had heard him do this. "He'll make as much money off you as he can, and then he'll dump you . . . Ursula, you ought to give him lessons in how to be a human being." I didn't want to give anyone lessons in anything. All I wanted to do was get divorced.

And without "using up all my assets on legal fees." So the next time I went to see Reed, I politely suggested, "Please send Merrill out. I don't want to be double-billed."

"Well, someone has to take notes," he protested.

"I know how to take notes," I said in my best Madame Editor tone.

"You're wonderful!" he said. "You are a perfectly lovely client!" So I took the notes, and we had a pretty civilized meeting.

But the warnings about Reed continued to come, the next from dentist Wally Post, a Reed alumnus as well as a Digby Grant "recidivist," or as Dr. Post joked, "I am now shopping for Wife Number 4," as he handed me a newspaper ad for diamond rings, and proceeded to drill.

"Well, you were right about your suspicions of early morning drinking," I told him between drills. "Thanks for tipping us off. Duncan admitted it at the deposition last week."

"I told you before, the dentist is usually among the first to know. You've got a lot on your plate, Ursula, and you're a long way from done. I've been through it — more than once. Did you know Duncan's psychiatrist, Culp, was responsible for the break-up of my second marriage?"

It is unusual to hear one doctor make negative remarks about another, and this was the second time I'd heard a low opinion of Culp; David Madden's assessment had been equally scathing. From what I gathered, Culp was from the school of telling his patients to "act out" all their angry feelings. It didn't matter who got caught in the fall-out.

"There isn't much I haven't seen, Ursula," continued Dr. Post. "You know those forms you have to fill out when you come here and go to the doctor? – single, married, widowed, divorced? I like to put down, 'all of the above!' But you'll come through this. It's going to take some time, but you're going to be all right."

In mid-month, Tony Milton finally returned my call from early October. I was pleasant but cool. He made a number of lame excuses about why it had taken him two-plus months to call me back, and he tried to wriggle out of his August statement that I was in large part responsible for Duncan's abusing his body. "I'd like to come see you and the children at Christmas," he said tentatively. Why did I think he would never turn up?

I also had a call from an old Ann Arbor friend I had in common with Duncan's mother, whose own relationship with Elsie had never been easy. But to be entirely fair, she encouraged me to call Elsie and tell her what had really gone on in our family since the railroad track episode. "Give her a chance to be helpful to you and the children, Ursula. She can't be helpful if she doesn't have the facts." So later that week, I called Elsie.

She was angry when she heard all I had to tell her. "Ursula, this is just another loss for me. This is a nice thing for you to do to me at Christmas. Furthermore, Duncan is not my problem. What did you do wrong, Ursula?"

When I recounted this to David Madden, he said, "This gives you a taste of how she probably treated Duncan as a child. All the rage he is spewing out at you and the children now should more properly have been directed at his mother for never meeting his needs."

I didn't have much time to dwell on Elsie, because my hands were full with my job at Genesis and my new job of trying to be two parents on the time and income of less than one. My biggest challenge lay in comforting Spencer and Amanda, who were understandably unhappy about the impending reality of losing Conover, school, and Inverary Lane. They knew Hub Safe was about to initiate foreclosure proceedings – and that Duncan's behavior had brought us to this disaster. But they were showing remarkable maturity in accepting it all.

Ally Everett, a former school teacher of both children, made some discreet inquiries to the school system on our behalf, and learned there was no way Spencer and Amanda could finish out the year unless we lied (which I wouldn't do) or we could somehow get a Conover address (so people in town were keeping their ears open for house-sitting opportunities for us). A few people offered to take us in, ironically those with the least room and resources – some of whom were real surprises to me. Leslie

Drew told me the foreclosure process in all likelihood would drag out until school ended, so there was no need to panic. The bottom line for the children was that their friends were standing by them. Most of all they were standing by themselves, two continuing, living, non-stop miracles!

Leslie Drew also gave me some new insights into Duncan on the afternoon of the Genesis children's Christmas Party. He invited me into his office to talk, where for the first time I learned that it was *Leslie* who decided not to hire Duncan in 1985, and not the other way around as Duncan had always led me to believe. "What were your feelings about Duncan, Leslie? Why did you decide not to hire him?"

"I always found him stiff and opaque. And in the course of learning more about him, it became clear that Duncan didn't do any real work at Germane. Oh, he knew how to make it appear — inside and outside the organization — like he was one of the doers. People like Duncan can hide and be successful for a long time inside large organizations, but in a place like Genesis, every individual must contribute and do necessary work every single day. In a small company, there is no place for someone like Duncan to hide. I realized early on that Genesis couldn't hire him, and I let negotiations lapse." As I absorbed this new information, my history with Genesis seemed all the more remarkable to me, as did the shock that Duncan had lied to me about this, too.

What did he ever tell the truth about? I now asked myself.

More questions about Duncan's professional competence surfaced during December, when the children and I celebrated Christmas with Kathy and Kevin Molloy in Walden. Baby John had arrived just days after Thanksgiving, *between* the holidays as Kathy had so confidently predicted.

Kevin explained that Duncan had essentially been "put on the shelf" with his new staff job at Germane; it was in no way a promotion, as Duncan had told his mother. In the deposition testimony, Duncan had stated his new position was a lateral move. Who could say which of these stories was true?

Just after Christmas, my bureaucratic hassles with car ownership in Massachusetts began, when I went to Harrington Insurance to process the registration for my station wagon. Both of our cars were in both of our names, which meant both signatures were required for registration; Duncan refused to sign mine. Not wanting to be in trouble with the law, I went to the Conover Police for guidance. Sergeant Pimm said my insurance company could handle it, but Dan Chessman, my insurance agent at Harrington, was frustrated.

"Mrs. Charbonnier, never, in all my years in the insurance business, have I heard a story like yours. I am sure the Registry will not accept your form, unless your husband signs it, too. And what if Mr. Charbonnier has an accident or gets into any trouble with his car, do you realize *you* could be sued? Why? Because your name is on the title and you need *his* permission in order to get your name off his title." No, I hadn't realized any of this. "Here, I want you to use my phone and call your lawyer right now."

Merrill Crosby advised we try to get the registration processed without Duncan's signature. "That's unlikely to work," repeated Dan, but to my surprise and relief, the runner he sent over later in the week managed to get my form processed. "And you won't get in trouble if Duncan doesn't register his car, unless you drive it." The Conover Police corroborated this. The liability that goes with being legally linked to someone who is behaving so self-destructively concerned me greatly. How was I to protect myself, not to mention any innocent third parties Duncan could injure? It was the same question I had asked myself the previous summer, and half a year later, I still had no answer.

The children and I never did hear from Tony Milton over the holidays, but in early January, as was our New Year's custom, I did get a call from Janey Thayer, my close Ann Arbor friend. It was our first conversation in a long while. I'd heard her husband was ill and thought I might be able to help with some research leads from my work, but Janey quickly turned the conversation to me and asked point blank, "Is Duncan an alcoholic?"

"Why are you asking me that?"

"Because what's happened to you, Amanda, and Spencer sounds very much like an alcohol story. My siblings and I have been through this for years with my mother." I had forgotten, but now Janey's stories were coming back to me. "It's been a long haul for our whole family, and it isn't getting any better. I cannot emphasize enough to you that the alcoholic has *an unlimited ability to lie.*"

There was no reason to withhold the truth at that point, and as I recounted my bizarre story, Janey kept saying, "I believe everything you're telling me. I believe everything you're telling me." She had known Duncan since he was a small boy; her husband's family and Jock's had been friends for three generations. "Ursula, people who have been through alcoholism understand and know when they are hearing a true story about it. Please start going to Al-Anon," she urged.

"I can't fit it in. I'm a single mom, with a demanding job, and a hopelessly full schedule."

"All I can tell you is that it has helped me a lot, and it continues to help me. Elsie and Jock are in denial, and you can't do anything about that. But I have confidence in you and the children. Not only will you rebuild your lives, you will make an even better life than you had before. Until Duncan gets help for himself, he will make no progress. But I believe in you, and you are going to be fine."

Her support, understanding, and confidence temporarily boosted my low spirits, which plunged lower, once again, when Duncan did not bring our child support check over until the *end* of the next Saturday. This meant

I couldn't deposit it until Monday and couldn't use the funds until the following Wednesday or Thursday, which was like getting it almost a week late. His true colors had begun to show on every front. He did agree to take Spencer shopping for new dress clothes for his friend Jake's upcoming Bar Mitzvah, but he made a huge stink about paying for them, and made Spencer call me from their shopping expedition to say Duncan wouldn't pay for the clothes. I couldn't believe a father would do that to his own son out in public. All I could think to say was "deduct it from our child support check for the week," which is just what Duncan did. He also made the children pay for the other things they bought, including the gift Spencer needed for Jake. Given his six-figure salary, Duncan's parsimony boggled the mind. I could not fathom what had happened to Duncan's value system or how he could allow his children to suffer in any way.

When he returned Spencer to Inverary Lane, Duncan engaged me in a conversation about our mortgage, which was equally incomprehensible to me. "I have no intention of paying the mortgage ever again," he told me angrily, "and the law won't make me. I told you last spring, you can pay the mortgage from now on." I couldn't believe he really wanted us to lose Inverary Lane, and that he was saying this in the presence of Amanda, who was sitting on a kitchen counter munching Fritos.

"Get real, Duncan. No one with a brain would expect me to pay the mortgage given that you earn four to six times what I do and that the judge set child support at the mortgage plus fifty dollars a week for *everything* else."

"Then you don't know the law, Ursula. That's exactly what will be expected. I'll make no effort to save this house," he continued, "and you are going to be the loser. I'm going to take you back to court and make you use up all your assets on attorneys."

"You can start paying for all these attorneys, Duncan. And if I did have any money, I would spend it on an attorney before I would send it to any bank."

"Did Gabriel Reed advise that?" he demanded. "Did he tell you not to pay the mortgage?"

At that point Amanda, who had been listening, said: "My mom doesn't have to tell you what she discusses with her attorney!"

Duncan looked at us, and said, "I'm going to destroy you!"

"You can't destroy me, Scarecrow! And you are not going to destroy the three of us, no matter what you do. So we'll go live in an apartment and start over – but we will not be destroyed."

He was agitated and started to leave several times, each time turning back into the kitchen and shouting some more. I finally said, "I don't want to talk to you anymore. If you have anything to say to me, you can call Gabriel G. Reed."

When Amanda told Spencer about the conversation, he was unperturbed. "Look Mom, Dad can't destroy us unless he kills us and chops us into little pieces, and he can't do that."

A few days later Asa called, and I recounted what Duncan had said to me and Amanda.

"Ursula, you should report that conversation to the Conover Police, especially the threat about destroying you."

"Dad, I really think he just meant it in a financial sense, not a physical sense."

"Well, it's still a threat!" Asa said.

"It reminded me of what you said last fall, that when Duncan failed to destroy me, that his rage would turn outward and he would commit an antisocial act or that his rage would turn inward and he would destroy himself. So far his rage hasn't turned inward; I just hope he doesn't hurt anyone else."

"Look Ursula, you've done everything humanly possible over the past years to avert a tragedy. You went to your internist, you kept a log, you and the children sought help at Appleton Hall, then you went to lawyers, you've been honest with the police and your insurance agent, you had the gun removed from the house, you've repeatedly told the truth, you even informed Duncan's family. If anything happens now, you cannot blame yourself."

"You know, Shea and others have said Duncan's behavior reminds them of Charles Stuart, the guy who allegedly murdered his pregnant wife."

"And they're right. I've told you before, Duncan is a sociopath. Such people are not treatable. They have character flaws that go undetected by those around them – for years. I still think you should report this to the police."

The following week, when I got back to the office, I learned that top management at Genesis Labs had fired my Business Manager, Shea, as part of a dramatic downsizing that was in the works. Archie McGowan, my boss, invited me in to talk about the company's troubles.

In addition to everything else, the last thing I needed was job insecurity, but acting braver than I felt, I tried to take it philosophically, "You know, Archie, every year or two, I go through this little exercise of listing the ten worst things that have ever happened to me and the ten best. Most of the time the overlap of the two lists turns out to be seven or eight out of ten." I could see he was quickly playing through the same exercise for his own life, and that for him, it was also true.

That night Amanda went with Duncan to the Conover Library after dinner.

"Did you tell him the news about Shea and Genesis?" I asked.

"You don't tell things like that to a person you don't like."

"Don't you like your father?" I asked.

"No." And I felt flat at hearing it.

Our family and finances were in a shambles. And as my dentist had so accurately predicted, I was a long way from being done with all these problems, in large part because of the racket Family Law is, as it is currently practiced in Boston. I was determined to try to stop our financial hemorrhaging the next time I saw Reed.

"Well, Mrs. Charbonnier, what brings you here today?" Gabriel greeted me breezily at our next meeting.

"I am here for a divorce," I snapped. "In case you had forgotten, that is the complete legal and financial breakup of a marriage." Reed grinned. "Please don't invite Merrill in to take notes. You know I can't afford to be double-billed, and I'll be happy to take notes for you."

This time he was not amused. "How dare you come in here and tell me how to practice law? I could have you thrown out, Miss!"

"You don't throw people out for telling the truth!" I said. I think that's the only reason he didn't send me flying into Newbury Street. "Now, when am I going to be divorced, and how much more is this going to cost? When we were at Probate Court last month, you said that you never have enough money – so this financial carnage is going to go on as long as I allow it to. In this motion for court costs that you never filed," I said, showing him the paper in my hand, "you said $14-15,000 dollars, and we are already well beyond that, with no end in sight. Now, please try to be honest with me, Gabriel. I have always been candid with you."

"Look, your lawyers are working hard. It's Chubb and Duncan who are holding up the process. All Duncan cares about is money, and he wants more than is in our offer."

"He isn't acting like a man who wants to get divorced; he's acting like a man who wants to destroy me," I said.

"All right. Now, let's talk about that for a moment. Listen to me. Duncan Charbonnier is a sociopath." Oh swell, now Gabriel was saying it too. "He has no brain, no heart, no feelings – and he is brain-dead for this relationship. He could stand in front of this window, and watch children being run over on Newbury Street, and calmly count up 'eleven bodies.'"

"And be proud of himself for doing it with such efficiency," I added.

"That's right. And this is not a new thing, Ursula. He's been this way for years."

"I'll agree with you that he's been tight with money for years, but I will not agree about your other points: the behavior was an abrupt change. I could cite plenty of examples, but it all comes down to this: I don't believe someone can fake it in and out of bed for fourteen years. I told that to John Arthur, and I'm telling it to you! I really don't understand what happened to Duncan. Maybe he was always a sociopath and an alcoholic and I didn't see it, but when I remember all the tender, consistently sweet behavior, my mind nearly shatters at the contrast – I can't absorb it. But I did not hallucinate the past, and I am not hallucinating the present. I can't help it if they're irreconcilable."

"Come on Ursula, I'm half Scotch, and I'm not nearly as tight as Duncan Charbonnier. Hadn't you noticed that you'd been living without furniture and other basics for years?"

"Well, when you're twenty-five, no one has anything, and you're paying off school loans, and you don't notice things like that. I've been rich and I've been poor, and I'm always the same person. Now what is your plan for resolving this case?"

"Chubb and I are having lunch at my club on Wednesday to discuss it. He told me Duncan is 'having a heart attack' about the mortgage, and Chubb is very angry about something he didn't mention on the phone. Do you know what it might be?"

"Oh great, another $1,000 lunch at the Iroquois Club on Duncan's and my nickel!"

"You're cheap!" he exploded. "All professionals charge for their time, but I will pay for my own food!"

"Can't you guys find a more sporting way to make money?"

"Look Ursula, *The System* is the Snow Job, I'll grant you that, but let me pound this into your head – it isn't going to change. Certainly not in time for this case. Furthermore, you had better get used to being in debt, because you are going to be in debt for a very long time. And I expect you to pay me in full every month, no matter what."

"You know that's impossible. Maybe Judge Tracy hasn't passed second grade math, but you have. Duncan's 'child support,' and I use the term loosely, barely covers the mortgage, and you know it. You also know that when I went into the hospital last fall, I changed the beneficiary on my life insurance to you, so that if anything happened to me, you would be sure to get paid. Now if that doesn't demonstrate good faith, I don't know what does. It is also a fact that my salary is a fraction of Duncan's, and I send more than half of it to you every month. And *you* are the one who told me not to pay the mortgage! You said my first priority had to be to pay you. Now how do you expect me to do that?"

"Take out a bank loan and start eating hamburger helper!" he snarled. "At a minimum this is going to drag on for another six months."

"This is outrageous beyond words!"

"You, Miss, are an extremely impatient person to expect such a speedy divorce, and to expect the world to work in a rational way, because it seldom does!"

"Well, I at least expected the law to be rational, and it isn't."

"Well, don't take it out on me!" he thundered.

"You don't want to know what my children think of the law!" I thundered.

"Oh, yes I do."

"Oh, no you don't."

"I do."

"Very well then. Last night at dinner Spencer said, 'The Law sucks!' I wasn't crazy about his verbiage, but I could hardly argue with his incisiveness. And I almost wish you had been there, because they asked me to explain the difference between illegal and immoral."

"Well, you can go home and tell your children that today I taught you the difference between unlawful and illegal."

"I don't get it. What's the difference?"

"Unlawful is against the law, and ill eagle is a sick bird."

Then The Law is a very sick bird, indeed – I didn't add.

Merrill came in in the middle of all this. "I'm just dropping off papers. I know the meter is ticking, and I won't stay."

"I turned it off awhile ago," Gabriel replied glumly.

"In that case can I stay?"

"No, you can't, because we're having a fight!" I said.

"Gee, maybe you should charge him for your time," she suggested brightly.

"Well, I would, if I could figure out a way to get him to pay for it!" I called after her.

I picked up my mug and started to leave.

"Put your mug down, and listen to me!" said Gabriel, taking it out of my hand.

"Are you afraid I'll throw it at you?" I asked.

He stood behind one of the leather wing chairs and gazed at me. "Duncan told Chubb he went to the AA meeting in Stover that night with the judge."

"I don't believe that," I replied.

"Well, you weren't there, and I wasn't there, but that's what he told Chubb."

"Bull!" I said.

"Well, if he did go," Reed continued, "he went because he was trying to impress and thought it would influence the judge. But the support decision was made right after we left the courtroom, so it wouldn't have made any difference."

"Gabriel, have you ever been in debt?

"Yes, I grew up on a chicken farm in New Hampshire during a very bad economy, and that's about as dirt poor as you can get." I had guessed he'd been poor as a youngster – because of not knowing how to swim, and because of the beautiful, strong hands that hadn't come from pushing a pen in a legal office, and the scrappiness, and his overly-impressed discomfort with his own wealth. I looked at his face, and my first reaction played back to me: in it I thought I saw early . . .

"Pain," I said out loud, "Sometimes I can be a real pain." I shook his hand to leave, "I'm never going to like debt," I said sadly, "and I am never going to like fighting with you. Nothing about getting divorced makes any sense to me at all!"

XVI

Black Holes

Woe unto you, lawyers!
for ye have taken away the key of knowledge:
you did not enter yourselves,
and you hindered those who were entering.

— Luke 11:52, *The Bible*

Two weeks later we were summoned back to court. MacIntyre had filed a contempt charge against me — for not paying the mortgage. I couldn't believe it. How come nobody thought Mr. Duncan Charbonnier ought to be paying the mortgage? *He* was the Germane senior executive who made well over a hundred grand a year; I was the housewife/editor who made a fraction of Duncan's salary. Why were the courts and the bank coming after me? And why weren't the courts and Hub Safe going after Duncan?

Life was unraveling on the Genesis front as well. In mid-January, Leslie lost all operating power at Genesis. Biff Grayson, the largest venture capital partner in the deal, assumed day-to-day management of the company, and several of the scientists were being "pulled back" (venture capitalist euphemism for demoted). Paul Sudo, the tough, hard-driving Frenchman who ran sales at Genesis and had never been a fan of *Molecular Modelling News*, was now going to become my boss. The editorial freedom I had enjoyed for so long seemed near an end. Pressure to turn my publication into a "house organ" began immediately.

All my values were being tested at once. "Integrity is getting to be a very expensive hobby," I said to Rob Stoughton when I went in to Westbury Ventures to have him do my taxes. "There is no hope for me!"

For the first time in years I found myself thinking about Ian Ruddway, the man I didn't marry in the years before I met Duncan. "Ursula," he used to say to me in total exasperation during our many fights, "you are nothing but a rigid, dogmatic, puritanical idealist!"

And then I would hear the words of my Grandpa, and his words kept drowning Ian's out: ". . . because it's the truth, Ursula, and you just have to keep on telling it, no matter what!" The reference was to a story from

Grandpa's boyhood, and a job he'd lost for being honest – a job whose income his fatherless family had depended upon. If they could see me now, I laughed to myself: Grandpa would be cheering me on, and Ian Ruddway would be shaking his head and wrinkling his nose.

Meanwhile, Spencer and Amanda were getting vocal about wanting a full-time mom again, and as much as my work mattered to me, in my heart I have always been and remain a mom first and a writer second, and so it shall be until they leave the nest. I'm too old to be remade. How I longed to be with them and nurture them for a spell and try to make up for all the pain they'd borne in recent years! And yet, if Duncan hauls us back to court and is allowed to give us even less, how will we make it if I don't work? In effect, the law makes it easy for breadwinners to abandon their families in this country. Amanda told Duncan how she and Spencer felt, and he of course was not pleased.

This would all be moot soon anyhow, for my job stood a good chance of being eliminated, and I would not easily or quickly find another, nor would I be able to find affordable childcare on any salary I might make. My bank account was nearly empty, because I was repaying Asa and Gabriel while I still could. I hate debt. Gabriel told me to get used to it, but I never, never shall. Who could have imagined the events of the last year? Leslie gone, present, but in terms of power gone. He changed my life, coming into it just days after I thought I'd learned the cause of Duncan's seizures. And now he was leaving. Dear God, I survived Leslie.

Things were deteriorating on the legal front, as well. When I walked into Gabriel's office in early February, I handed him a check for $1,000 but instead of saying thank you, he yelled at me for not paying his bill in full, and said that Jillian Frost would take it up with me. I also noticed a $1,500 charge that made no sense to me, but rather than tell him about it when he was so angry, I decided to bring it to Jillian's attention, and pulled out a letter from Asa instead.

"I like the handwriting, but I don't want to read it."

"Maybe you should, since it concerns you." In it, Asa acknowledged partial repayment of the loan and indicated he expected the $6,500 balance I still owed him for Gabriel's initial retainer. "He raised chickens during the Depression, too!" I told Gabriel.

This peeved Reed. *"It was later than the Depression!"* He still didn't believe Asa was serious and continued to bully me.

I just calmly repeated that eventually he'd get paid. "I've never let a bill go unpaid in my life. Gabriel, you can bully me 'til the cows come home, but I'm standing firm."

"I'd like to hit you," he snarled.

"Please don't."

"Oh, I might want to, but that doesn't mean I would!"

In the appointment that followed with Jillian, she also bullied me about the money, and didn't even pull back much when it turned out the $1,500 charge was an error, maybe because she didn't know I'd given Gabriel a check for $1,000 – which right there lopped $2,500 off the balance. When they caught up about it later in the afternoon, Gabriel charged out of his office like a mad bull and clomped his arm on my shoulder.

"Hey, I'm not upset about this," I said calmly.

"Well, I am!" he said dramatically. "Find out who did this!" he said to Jillian Frost.

"Are you still going to throw me to the birds?" I asked.

"We'll talk about this in court, next week."

Jillian hadn't been very nice to me upstairs either. "Hey, I invested in marriage, motherhood, and molecular modelling," I told her, "and two out of three have gone belly up."

"Oh well," she'd said snidely, "there's still motherhood!"

In the meantime, a second acquisition possibility for *Molecular Modelling News* had emerged in Europe, and three of the publication's corporate sponsors had also expressed an interest in trying to put a deal together.

I refused to do all the things Paul Sudo had ordered me to do the week before, and then following advice from Ted Talbot, I firmly and politely told Paul what I *would* do for him: "I'll help you find a replacement for me. What are your requirements?"

Sudo waved me away, with a sigh, "You know you can't be replaced."

When I told readers I'd stand in the breadlines before I'd compromise on the integrity of *MM News,* they knew I meant it, and so did Paul Sudo; but on some days, it was still a little hard to tell the "good guys" from the "bad guys." Take Jeff Abbott, the new CEO the venture capitalists hired to replace Leslie Drew. In our first meeting Jeff said, "Will you have lunch with me next week? I like your publication and your philosophy."

Then John Stevens, my editor in Stuttgart, phoned and told me that I was being invited to speak at Elmau III (the third conference on Computational Methods in Chemical Design) in October. "Well, that's great John, but there isn't a snowball's chance in hell that Genesis will send me to Germany. How about if I write a speech, and you deliver it for me?"

Amid all these delightful and amazing incidents, remained the ongoing nightmare that Duncan really did appear to be getting away with "destroying me" in some sense. When Jillian Frost and I left the courthouse after my contempt hearing for not paying the mortgage, she told me the charge against me had been dismissed; this made me wonder if I were losing my mind, because it sure hadn't sounded that way to me, and I'd been standing in the courtroom right next to her. She gave me some legal double talk afterward that made me feel like I couldn't understand English. Sure enough, the following week, confirmation came that what I thought had happened in court was exactly what had happened. For this incorrect interpretation and a botched job, Jillian Frost had "earned" hundreds of dollars in one afternoon.

But more amazing to me than Jillian, was that not one person in The System was calling Duncan's cards – on the mortgage or even his unregistered gun and car. I spoke to the Conover Police about the car again, but it was clear they had no intention of enforcing the law; rather, they were almost amused at my story, despite my insurance agent's ongoing concern. As one policeman put it, "Ursula, we're much too busy to pursue the matter of an unregistered car, but why don't you call Warren Carver over at the Town Hall. He's supposed to enforce the 'unregistered over thirty days' rule." Then I tried the Legal Department of the Registry of Motor Vehicles last week, but they didn't care either: "Mrs. Charbonnier, go back to Probate Court if you're really that concerned about the non-registration of a car with your name on the title." Right, I thought, spend another thousand dollars I don't have. I am slowly getting the message: the laws don't apply to the Duncan Charbonniers of the world. *Time* magazine, in its essay on alleged murderer Charles Stuart, had got it right last week after all, "Evil can wear a three-piece-suit, hold down a responsible job and own a house in the suburbs."

In the midst of all this, Amanda said she wanted to grow up to be a divorce lawyer, which made me feel like I'd been a total flop as a parent, until she explained she wanted to go into the field to get the laws changed, "so that people can't do to their families what Dad is doing to us." Spencer, our resident realist, informed her there was no hope for making a change, but I said maybe Amanda would be successful. In the meantime, the children somehow carried on cheerfully. They continued to filibuster for a new father; and since I was being uncooperative on that score, they've created an imaginary one, named "Theodore."

"Well, what does Theodore look like?" I asked gamely, trying to match them in spirit.

"Never mind," they said, grinning conspiratorially at each other.

Spencer then made another "go get married" speech: "Get on the stick, young lady. There are lots of good men out there – go out and grab one!"

I laughed and said, "Well, who has time to shop?" The sun never sets on my court jesters. Thank God for children, for their insights and their humor.

In late winter, I learned that Merrill Crosby had resigned from Reed's firm. I'd always wished she were my friend, instead of my lawyer, and I accepted when she called to ask me to lunch the following month. New connections seemed to be forming all around me, like a pregnancy of the soul. This is like winter, I thought to myself. Everything seems to be dead on the outside, but new life is taking hold on the inside.

One night David Madden's wife, Elise Priest, called on the spur of the moment. She and her daughter, Hannah, were going to a slide show at First Parish, the grey stone church in the Center of Conover. Someone was giving a lecture in the chapel on the subject of hurricanes. Would Amanda and I like to come, too? That sounded interesting. "Yes, we'll meet you there," I said.

That night, I found many we knew gathered in the chapel. Half of Inverary Lane was there, and everyone was glad to see us. Amanda and Hannah scampered off with friends, and I took a seat in the back, by a cabinet with a little light inside. Above my head, winds squalled past stained glass, as I listened in the dark to the story of the storms. I'm here, God. This is Ursula. The one in tears, over here, in the corner. I'm in a hurricane, too.

How will You find me in this darkness?

XVII

$\mathcal{B}$eacons in the $\mathcal{S}$torm

. . . Not till the hours of light return,
All we have built do we discern.

— Matthew Arnold, *Morality*

After the slide show when the lights came back on, Elise introduced Amanda and me to minister Matthew Hale. He welcomed me with a smile from the heart and offered to show me around: the library, the kitchen, the parish hall, the parlor, the main church – and would Amanda like to ring the bell? She would. "It was cast by Paul Revere and Sons," he said proudly. Then he spoke about the sanctuary's Country Gothic architecture and told me how seashells gathered by nineteenth-century children on an outing formed the floor of a side entrance. I asked about the aisles. "With no center aisle, how *do* you manage weddings?"

"Oh, that's easy," he laughed. "They come down one aisle, and go up the other one! I hope you'll come back again, Ursula, anytime and often."

"I will," I promised. "Thank you. Good night." It was another beginning, a small tugging at the soul, in the nature of a new root.

The next Sunday, to my surprise, Spencer came willingly to First Parish. Apparently his closest friends were there, too. I had promised myself long ago that I would never make my children join anything against their will, or attend a Sunday school, but I had always hoped that they would one day share my view that we are here for reasons beyond ourselves.

"But how can they learn to express that value if you don't show them a way?" a friend had once asked.

"No one showed me. I found it on my own."

"Yes, and look how long it took you."

I couldn't argue with that. Certainly Spencer and Amanda wouldn't be getting any guideposts toward spirituality from Duncan in his present state. His own spiritual emptiness, in a very large sense, had left him vulnerable to having an alcohol problem. Then I remembered John Arthur's description of Duncan: ". . . the emptiness is inside him and not in the environment." That much I knew.

I had also been thinking more about my new role as a single parent. Now I was "the leader" in this family, the one to determine what was needed, and then go make it happen. A storm was teaching me to navigate. Being lost was giving me a direction and a course. I heard Gabriel's voice: "What are you going to do when this is over?" I am going to write and publish *Snow Job*. I am going to save *Molecular Modelling News* or build a new publication. I am going to love a decent human being again, someday, and I am going to build a stable, loving home with him.

I called my old college roommate, who lived in Seattle and had encouraged me to join First Parish when we'd first moved to Conover in 1981. "Let me tell you why you didn't hear from me at Christmas . . ." I began.

She listened quietly and when I was done said, "Please contact the Hales," referring to First Parish's husband-wife ministry team and her friends of many years.

"Actually I've already started going to First Parish, and I've decided to tell Trudy everything."

"You won't regret it, Ursula. Both Hales are first-rate. They'll care. And they'll help you."

The next Sunday I went to First Parish. I was alone, but again surrounded by friends. At my appointment with Trudy Hale that afternoon, I told her everything. She was obviously experienced with alcoholics, and it didn't take her long to grasp all the elements of our current situation. We discussed my spiritual values and my "checkered" spiritual career. She assured me that there is plenty of space for me and someone with my outlook at First Parish. This was the first time in my life I felt a sense of belonging in a place where I would have to make no spiritual compromises. We talked about divorce, and she made the point that in cases where an alcoholic refuses to get help or even admit there is a drinking problem, divorce is often the best and sometimes "the only healthy option." My internist had already told me that, and I understood I was doing the best thing for me and the children by getting out of the marriage.

Then she focused on the practicalities: Did I have a good lawyer? I had an expensive lawyer, but I wasn't sure he was a good lawyer. "There is a man named Jonah McCoy . . ." But I wasn't ready to leave Gabriel yet.

Had I been to Al-Anon yet? And before I could answer, "Here is the name of someone in our church who has been active in Al-Anon for many years. Call her." And I did, but not finding her in, I left a message for a call back.

Amanda, too, felt at home at First Parish, and came with me the next Sunday; most of her friends were there, and she, too, expressed an interest in going occasionally. Where had I been all these years? Home, snuggled up in a cocoon named Duncan. People tell me the children will ultimately and naturally follow my lead, if I'm patient, and let them go at their own pace.

Ally Everett, the children's former school teacher who'd been so great about keeping in touch with us, called me that Sunday evening to see how Spencer and Amanda were doing. "Honestly Ursula, if I didn't know what was going on in your family, I would never be able to guess from seeing the children in school. They seem absolutely fine."

"And I am hell-bent that they are going to stay that way, but since you called, can we talk for a minute about Spencer?" I told her about the essay he had written for English about "The Worst Thing That Had Ever Happened to Me."

"Let's get Mary Francis in the loop for counseling at school," said Ally. "She doesn't normally handle his grade, but I think she would be the best fit. Let me make the contact for you." I agreed she could test the waters with Mary, and if Mary were receptive we would go ahead.

The week before me was to be a busy one, filled with turning points.

On Monday, I had lunch with Frank Morrow, the head scientist at Genesis, and said I sensed that for me the turbulence at the Company had passed, that I had survived the storm, but what happened? "Ursula, you have friends on the Board and at the Company that you don't know about. Our new management likes the publication and all you have to do is to keep making money and do your own thing, and you'll be left alone to be creative and free. If you keep it up, you'll have a tiara around your head at Genesis."

On Tuesday I went to see Gabriel. I had faxed him what I jokingly referred to as "Gabriel's Marching Orders," a concise list of what I wanted in the divorce, with a "let's get the show on the road and get this thing over with" message. I was totally fed up with his expensive delays and wanted to get on with my life.

"Don't you realize that I am the best person in the world for you?" he began, turning on the Reed charm. "You are my most deserving client."

But I wasn't going to be diverted this time. "I came here to talk about 'Gabriel's Marching Orders,' " I said.

"Nobody gives me marching orders!" he roared.

"It had quotation marks around it," I replied calmly.

"*That* is the only thing that saved you!"

Whereupon Chubb MacIntyre called. And when after a few minutes it was apparent that they were rambling on about things unrelated to The Charbonnier Matter, I said "Tick, tick, tick," referring to the meter. Gabriel tried not to laugh, got off the phone, and announced, "You're cheap!"

"I'm not cheap, Gabriel – just sick of people getting rich off of situations like mine!" Why be indirect!

Then he was really steamed. "I'm not going to talk to you about any of the negotiating issues on your list. Have you been to Al-Anon yet?" he said, changing the subject, something lawyers do when they know that you've got them on moral grounds.

"I already told you, it isn't for me!" I'd been diverted – it was too late.

"Don't give me that!"

"Well, I did put in a call to some Al-Anon person the other day, and I'm waiting for a call back."

"Don't tell me about waiting for a call back – I want you in Al-Anon NOW! And I am turning off the meter for this lecture!" he said with a flourish. "You have got to come to understand that Duncan Charbonnier has a disease. This is no different than having cancer, and if he doesn't get some help, he is going to die. Do you hear me? He is going to die."

"Look Gabriel, I believe in free will. Duncan has choices. He doesn't have to drink secretly. He could go to Appleton Hall, he could work with Dr. Arthur, or with me and the kids. He doesn't have to rip up everyone's life. He chooses to." Gabriel looked at me with a mixture of frustration and concern.

"I want you in Al-Anon, is that clear? I'm giving you a kick in the fanny to get to Al-Anon now! You are broken-hearted and broken in spirit. When this is over, I want you whole and happy. I care about you a lot – professionally!" Then he added, "The next time I see you, you better have been to Al-Anon. No more excuses!"

"All right, the next time you see me, I'll have been to Al-Anon. But the fact remains we are making no progress on this divorce. I am running out of money, and I can't keep up with your verbal gymnastics. I am unsophisticated about all this."

I got up to leave. It had been a stalemate of a conversation. "I guess I didn't brighten your day today."

"Well you have before, and you will again!" he said giving me a firm handshake.

That Wednesday, I had my meeting with Mary Francis, the guidance counselor who agreed to work with Spencer. This was my first time dealing with the school on a family issue, and I didn't know what to expect, but in the first minutes I realized that Spencer would be in competent hands. Ally Everett had covered the basics of our story, and I filled in the blanks for Mary. Like Harry Ballard at Appleton Hall, Mary was clinical yet sensitive about alcoholism in a family. Like me, she was all for confronting it head on, and for keeping youngsters informed. We were going to be able to work as team.

"Spencer's English teacher and I have decided we want to keep his essay and this information in a closed loop between us, and not involve the rest of the school."

I thought that made good sense, and decided to share with her what had happened the night before at our house: "Last night Spencer cried in my arms – very atypical twelve year-old behavior – because over the previous weekend, Duncan had told him why he wanted a divorce, but said Spencer couldn't tell me because I'd use it against him in court. Spencer said he was torn between wanting to tell me and not wanting to break his father's confidence."

"Ursula, by doing this, don't you see that Duncan has disempowered Spencer. I am going to talk to Spencer about how he must now take command by throwing the ball back in Duncan's court. Here's what he needs to do. I want to explain the technique to you. It goes like this: 'Dad, why did you give me negative information that I couldn't use in a positive way? What were you thinking of when you did that? Don't do that again.'"

She continued. "Duncan will begin 'layering' more on Spencer, if Spencer doesn't nip this in the bud," she explained. "And you have a role to play here, too, Ursula. You can protect Spencer by firmly telling Duncan that this was no way to talk to a child, and he is not to do it again.

"Another thing Ursula. The Conover Schools don't want to lose Spencer and Amanda. Ally told me about the judge's ordering your house to be sold. We want to find a way to keep you in this community. You're a writer. Maybe we could look into creating a job for you – for example as a writing consultant – so that Spencer and Amanda could go to the Conover Schools for $25 a year if the worst happened, and you were forced to move outside the Town. I'm also going to keep my ears open for a house-sitting situation for you and the children. We want you in this community, and we're going to try to help. And I will start meeting regularly with Spencer, and stay closely in touch with you."

This was far beyond anything I expected in the way of help from the school system. My only contact with the schools had been to teach creative writing through the years on a volunteer basis. I called Ally to thank her for putting us in touch with Mary Francis.

That night, when Duncan came by to get Spencer, I delivered the message as Mary had instructed. "What you said to Spencer the other evening is no way to talk to a child."

"Spencer isn't a child," said Duncan.

"Well, it's no way to talk to any human being!" I replied firmly. "And don't do it again, Duncan."

That Thursday, I had lunch with our new CEO, Jeff Abbott. We seemed to be on the same wavelength about the CAMD business. He was direct in his comments: "Ursula, I want you to stop worrying about your job. I like *Molecular Modelling News* and what it is trying to achieve, and I'll do nothing to compromise it. If anyone gets in your way, just let me know and I'll take care of it. I'm putting the word out for people to leave your publication alone."

The following day, I called John Stevens in Stuttgart and said we'd come into "calmer waters" at Genesis, that Jeff Abbott liked *MM News*. John reiterated the Elmau III invitation and said it was in process.

On Friday, I at last had dinner with Karen Dale, the person from

Al-Anon recommended by Trudy Hale. Karen was also trying to get divorced from a long-time alcoholic, and as she put it, "losing hard-earned money to lawyers, who aren't really earning it."

She told me stories about what alcoholism had done to her family and gave me a lot of Al-Anon literature to take home and read. She described the different kinds of meetings that were available. "We suggest you try more than one, and as many as six, until you find a group that is right for you; they're all so different."

"I'm not even sure I want to go," I said. "First of all, I have *no* spare time. And second of all, I don't see what's to be gained by sitting around talking with a bunch of strangers."

"They won't be strangers for long," assured Karen, "especially when you find out how much you have in common. Alcohol stories are strikingly similar Ursula, and in listening to others' and eventually sharing your own, you'll derive new sources of strength. Getting up the courage to go to that first meeting is hard for everyone. For many people it takes years. And for every person who finally starts going to Al-Anon, there are probably dozens who never get there."

"I've heard there are several different formats," I said tentatively. "Can you tell me about what's available in the area?"

"Here's a little brochure I've brought for you that lists all the meetings in the greater Boston area. They're listed by town, by type, and by day of the week. But you could have gotten this by calling any AA or Al-Anon office listed in the phone book, and they'd have mailed one to you. Conover still doesn't have an Al-Anon group." She opened the booklet to the page for Westbury. "But you can see that there are more than twenty meetings a week in Westbury alone."

"In Westbury alone – that many?!" I said, astonished. "But it's such a small town!"

"It *is* such a small town," agreed Karen, "with a large number of alcoholics in it. And most of them have families, and all of them friends. Westbury's no different from any other town."

"But where do all these people come from? Who are they?"

"Some of them will be people you already know, in some cases people you've known for many years," said Karen. "You'll be surprised who you see there. Everyone goes by first names only, and when you encounter these people in other places, you must never acknowledge them as fellow Al-Anon participants. That's the deal, Ursula. What you see there, stays there. We take that very seriously. You need to know that going in."

"I think I'd like to find a 'steps' meeting," I said, "where participants discuss one of the 'Twelve Steps' each week, and how they apply it in their own lives."

"That's where I went," said Karen, "the Tuesday night meeting in the Congregational Church in Westbury Square."

A few days after our dinner, Karen's son Edmund, a senior at Conover High, called and offered to be available to Spencer, "if Spencer just wants to hang out with a guy. Mrs. Charbonnier, it's hard to find a good male role model when your father is an alcoholic." I was taken aback by his candor. The call had been unexpected, hard for him to make, and I thanked him for it.

In the week that followed, I attended my first Al-Anon meeting. What I found was a motley crew of about thirty nice people; what I got out of it was that all of them had been devastated by the pain of having an alcoholic in their lives, but that all of them were "hard triers" and determined to deal with their pain in a constructive fashion. A lot of the associated pain really is *optional.* I think that's part of what Gabriel had been trying to tell me.

To Elsie Charbonnier I sent the brochure "Is Al-Anon for You?" (if you circled more than three it is). I circled and annotated six, even though Asa and friends in Ann Arbor who know Elsie said she'll just toss it in the wastebasket – because the whole Charbonnier family is in denial mode.

Two nights later I tried another Al-Anon meeting, this one at a nearby hospital extension. It was a newcomers' discussion meeting, and I didn't like it at all. In fact, I left in the middle. One sniveling, rambling man dominated the entire discussion and wouldn't let anyone else get a word in edgewise. And what was he pontificating about? Why controlling, of course! The irony escaped only him. I called Karen Dale. "Your advice about trying different Al-Anon groups was right on target, and like you, I find the Steps Meeting in Westbury Square to be a good fit."

The reality of losing the house was now registering with Spencer and Amanda, and they were very unhappy. They couldn't believe their own father would want them to lose Conover. Here they had support and love from so many sources. I had to do all I could to preserve that.

Still, I told myself, no matter how awfully Duncan was behaving now, he really was a splendid father in their early years; although as I learned in Al-Anon, he was probably splendid, in part, because he was able to control. With my increased salary and the children's incipient adolescence, Duncan probably began to feel he was no longer in control, and that combined with his parents' divorce sent him over the edge. If I had only been more educated at the time, I might have made a difference. According to a fellow-physician friend of Asa's who lives in Westbury, there had certainly been plenty of evidence of Duncan's drinking problem, all around me, all through the years, but mostly things that would have escaped the attention of someone untrained. "Like what?" I asked.

"Look here in your photo albums," she said, as we pored over scrapbook pictures one night after dinner at Inverary Lane. "Duncan looks intoxicated in some of these shots, and many of them are morning photos, Ursula." (I'd always kept the camera close at hand for priceless candids.)

"Notice the passive expression on his face; his unusual stance; the redness of his face compared to everyone else's." As I flipped through the pages, it was hard to believe I could have been so thoroughly uninformed and led myself and Dr. Arthur astray for so many years.

Toward the end of March, Merrill Crosby drove up for lunch with a gift of chocolate for the children from her husband Camden. Now that she was no longer my lawyer, we were seeing more of each other, and under much pleasanter circumstances. I asked her for help and guidance in dealing with Gabriel. "I can talk to almost anyone in the world – even the biggest *prima donna* Nobel Prize-winning scientists, but I find it next to impossible to have a calm and productive conversation with Gabriel Reed. What can I do to make it better?"

"First of all, you have to stop ranting and raving about the legal system and how screwed up it is. He doesn't want to hear it, and he can't do anything about it. But he barks at virtually everyone, and he is impossible to deal with. Most people quit the firm after two or three years because of his temperament. But, he really is *the* smartest divorce lawyer in Boston, and nobody could do a better job. I don't really think he's going to dump you either, if you continue to send him money from every paycheck."

She offered to help me and the children scout for a place to live, through friends who lived in a town near Conover, and said that she and Camden would have me and the children down to visit later in the year. Camden, a Rhode Island neurologist, knew a lot about temporal lobe epilepsy, and this had been a factor in Gabriel's assigning Merrill to my case in the first place.

Later that month, I had an appointment with Dr. Arthur. We talked about the unfortunate condition of my hair – the lower five or six inches of which had started to fall off in chunks. "Ursula, time will take care of it," he reassured. "When the stress passes, the hair will regenerate." We also talked about Duncan's behavior.

"Duncan had a need to put up a front most of the time," said Arthur. "I've told you that before."

"Yes, and only Dr. Jekyll visits your office!'"

Then the subject of AIDS came up. "I'd like to do a test Ursula, and do it now."

"Isn't that a little melodramatic? There's no one in my life now." And I had never been unfaithful to Duncan.

"I think we should find out now, so that you'll be ready for your next relationship." I hadn't even begun to think about a "next" relationship; I was having enough trouble getting out of this one. "If the results are positive," he said, "we redo the test because we get a lot of false positives; and if the second one is positive, we do counseling, but hold off on drugs 'til symptoms appear." Oh, this is great, I thought, now Miss Vanilla gets to have an AIDS test. What did Arthur know about Duncan that I didn't know? In addition to decimating my financial and emotional security, had Duncan jeopardized my health as well? But asking these questions out loud would have been futile, for the law was clear on this point: Duncan's right to confidentiality superseded my right to know.

In parting, I said to Arthur, "You know, what Emerson says about compensation is really true. The kids and I have lost Duncan and we're probably going to lose our house, but we found our community. So many people in Conover have really reached out and helped. People drive the children to their activities and invite them along for family outings. And the kindness just keeps coming."

"I'm keeping my ears open for a house-sitting or rental situation for you and the children too," he said.

When I saw Gabriel at the start of April, he began on a direct note, "If I don't get $10,000 by Friday, I'm off this case!" Then he started drafting a letter to Chubb (which I had the nerve to edit) and to make matters more ridiculous he then asked for my opinion so that we ended up writing it together!

"And fax a copy of this to your financial planner, Rob Stoughton tomorrow. You are not filing your taxes separately. You're just trying to screw Duncan."

"I have no interest in screwing Duncan, financially or otherwise. I just don't want *any* financial or legal connection with someone as dishonest as Duncan is."

"Let's talk about contempt. You have been found guilty of contempt — for not paying your mortgage — and the appeal is to cost $1,500 minimum. Now it's unconstitutional that you were found guilty . . ."

"Oh I'd say it's merely outrageous," I exploded, totally ignoring Merrill Crosby's wise advice. "The legal system in Massachusetts is going to look pretty ridiculous in *Snow Job* to any reader with half a brain. I refuse to go on behaving like this is a rational process. It's sheer lunacy and high time somebody stood up and said so! The next time I'm found in contempt of court, it's going to be for saying or doing something content-rich, not something unconstitutional!"

Then came the tirade about the bill. "I care and worry more about you than you do about me," he said.

"That's not true. I've never let a bill go unpaid in my life and I'm not going to start now. I'll continue to send you half of every paycheck."

"That's not good enough."

"Well, it's the best I can do," I said quietly.

"Well, your best isn't good enough."

I waited while he bullied, but stood tall and faced him squarely through the tirade. "Duncan's intention is not to get divorced, but to destroy, and the legal system is aiding and abetting him every step of the way." This did not go over well.

"I insist that you involve your father financially."

"You just don't seem to get the message, do you? My father is out of the loop, in large part because you are a bottomless pit for money." (Spencer had had it right after all when he said, "Gabriel is a moneygrubber – just like my Dad.")

"You tell your father to come to Boston and have lunch with me. I'll take him over to the Iroquois Club for lunch and explain matters to him."

"And charge him $300 an hour for the pleasure, no doubt! No thanks, Gabriel. I don't want you and my father to ever meet, in part because it would be a toss-up as to who would give whom the first coronary!" At this he grinned.

Then I pressed him, as I always had, to cite potential cost and time for the divorce. He finally said, "another $20-30,000 beyond the $10,000 I want this Friday, and early fall at the soonest. And another thing, you are to hold off on your daughter's braces until Judge Tracy decides."

"Judge Tracy does not impress me with his intellect, and I am not going to waste another $1,000 in court to hear about Duncan making an $850 down payment for braces. I'll pay for them myself if need be!"

"Then it will be gone money, Ursula!"

"I told you before, and I'll tell you again: the orthodontist will decide when my child gets braces, and not some judge in Probate Court!"

The one thing we did agree on was that I continue Duncan's term life insurance policy, which he'd always insisted I pay the premiums on. Then I told Gabriel about the major leak between the bathroom and the kitchen. "Water pours out of the kitchen ceiling every time we take a shower."

"If it's $150, fix it; if it's $1,500 call me."

So I had Bud and Ted's plumber come over to look at the ceiling and paid them $25 to tell me it would probably be a $2,000 job. "We can't be dishonest and hornswoggle the next buyer," I told Caroline O'Malley and she agreed we had to be honest. "Naturally I can't afford to have the repair done." The Lord really does work in mysterious ways I guess! Maybe My Higher Power doesn't want this house sold either!

For sure Spencer and Amanda didn't. Someone came by to see the house when I was at work, and they arranged dirty words on the Scrabble board game in progress which upset the househunters. One of the people reportedly was so horrified, she announced that they didn't need to see the upstairs and were leaving. Then the powder room door became locked, as it sometimes does, and when the other Realtor asked Amanda about it, Amanda said, "My mom usually crawls through the window to fix it." She meant the internal window which is about ten inches wide (I am narrow in the hips), and that coupled with the $2,000 leak did not go over well. The children thought it a great hoot, but of course it was not. "No more obscenities on the Scrabble board, guys," I told them.

After the debacle in Gabriel's office, I went back to Al-Anon, and heard one story after another about how the legal system really does aid, abet and profit(!) from the alcoholics in our society. As I experienced and heard reports about what really goes on, it became harder to respect the behavior of lawyers, judges and the courts. Most people really don't know what happens to the families of alcoholics in court, and I was determined to tell them through *Snow Job*. I don't want other people to experience the hell that Spencer, Amanda, and I have been put through. Yes, there are lawyers like Merrill Crosby, but not enough of them.

The children were bearing this all so well. I didn't have the heart to tell them about Gabriel's dumping me, but they knew some new bad thing had happened and were being very sweet. I was on the phone when Spencer left for school yesterday, and he came up and gave me a huge kiss on the cheek which he never does. And Amanda insisted I read a story she wrote, the theme of which was that you have to hang in there during adversity and keep trying no matter what. I wish Asa could see how strong his grandchildren are and how good-humored. And since I was not cooperating about finding a new stepfather anytime soon, they continued to have conversations with "Theodore" at dinner.

I tried to play along with their little game. "When are you guys gonna tell me what Theodore looks like? How will I recognize him?"

And Spencer and Amanda replied, "He's a little shorter than Dad, very smart, very funny and needs to lose a little weight!"

"Is he funny at breakfast?" I asked, but they didn't tell me. "I need someone who's funny at breakfast!"

Sometime in March, I got a call from Becky-Lee Jackson who runs the children's summer camp up in Maine. "I'm afraid we're going to have to cut back on the time they spend with you this summer, but you know what's going on in our family. The only reason I can send them at all is that my dad's paying for it. I sent back my Christmas present, and told him to send it to you instead. The check should arrive next week."

"Ursula, I want you to call me anytime and please give us the opportunity to extend ourselves to you, Spencer, and Amanda during this time. We're here to help and we care about your children." At dinner, I told the children that Grandad was making camp possible for them this summer, and they launched into long, happy chatter about assorted camp matters, and I just sat back and basked in the glow of their excitement. I was more convinced than ever that continuity and stability would help see them through this mess, and camp was a part of that. Another step in preserving their world.

I went for a long walk with neighbor Jackie Melrose after dinner that night. "You know," she observed, "your only crime was being in the wrong place at the wrong time. If I were you, I'd just sit back and let Duncan and the legal system do it to me now − it would seem logical and freeing somehow. But no matter what happens, remember Jeff and I are always here for you and the children."

Then we talked about Jeff's recent local election victory and their new political life. In Massachusetts, registered Independents can vote in any party primary, and I couldn't resist kidding Jackie, "I actually had fun being a Democrat for five minutes the other morning!"

"Jeff appreciated your support. By the way, he ran into Warren Carver over at the Town Hall and heard you got your car insurance problem temporarily resolved."

"That's right, Warren helped a lot by intervening for the time being, but my agent, Dan Chessman, wants to write a separate policy for me when this mess is over. In fact, I need to call Dan to tell him about Warren's help and a new problem we're about to have with the house insurance policy."

Dan was pleased the next day when I relayed how Duncan's car registration had finally taken place, thanks to the intervention of Conover official Warren Carver, but not so pleased when I told him about the contempt charge against me for not paying the mortgage, the impending foreclosure, and that the judge had ordered our house put up for sale. "My lawyer insists I send half of every paycheck to him, and there's no way I can possibly pay the house insurance bill."

"Ursula, take both insurance bills, the one for the car and the one for the house, and send them to Duncan. Not that I expect him to pay them, but when this mess is over, we still want to do business with you. We do understand your situation and the awful predicament you're in."

"You know, Duncan isn't even concerned about the leaking shower and all the water that's pouring through the ceiling, which isn't exactly going to add value to the sale price of Inverary Lane. And you know what he said when I asked him about it, Dan? 'I don't live here anymore. It's not my problem.' Can you believe that? It's not even in *his* best interest to behave that way."

The kids overheard this last part of my phone conversation with Dan, and I asked Spencer if Duncan seemed in control.

"Mom, he acts like he's in control and has no idea that he really isn't."

"Dad isn't going to get away with what he's doing," added Amanda, "because everyone knows you don't lie, Mom."

At that point I lost it and said, "What you are learning is that people can do what your father is doing and get away with it in the legal system."

"No, Mom, what I am learning is that people who do what Dad does hurt others." Amanda brought me right back down to earth with her on-target words, and with the jumble of crooked teeth that showed whenever my daughter opened her mouth.

It was with this view clearly in mind that I acted against Gabriel's advice, and had Dr. Brixon put on Amanda's braces. I was also candid with Brixon's office about our situation and potential financial difficulty. On the day the braces were installed, Amanda and I encountered Dr. Post in the building which he shared with Brixon. "After you get Amanda settled, why don't you come up to my office and chat? I have a few minutes before my first patient arrives.

"Ursula, you are in a terrible mess. I want you to take the name of my personal lawyer," he said pulling out a card. "Get his opinion on what to do next. Part of your problem is that you are dealing with more than one person in Duncan, and that's making everything more complicated. He has a split personality." Obviously I had taken all the wrong courses in college. To be equipped for the life I was leading, I should have studied pharmacology, psychiatry and law.

When I went to retrieve Amanda from Dr. Brixon's, I ran into our neighbor Karen Britton, who asked me to come by and see her and Bill the following night. Bill, an attorney, had been horrified to hear what was happening to me in the legal system. "Ursula, this isn't the way that the law is supposed to work. You shouldn't have been found in contempt of court for not paying your mortgage, particularly since your attorney was insisting that you pay him first. Why don't you go over and see Max Canfield across the street (another lawyer)? This is really out of my area, but he may be able to give you some good advice."

Then Karen said, "Everything that's happened to you has made me realize how vulnerable all mothers and kids are in the system."

"Well, all is not lost," I said trying to be cheerful. "At least my AIDS test came back negative! If I've got my health and my kids intact, then I've got everything that really matters."

During the stretch from Good Friday to the following Tuesday, I felt like I was being crucified, the worst I had felt since the week before I met Gabriel. Meeting Gabriel had put fight back in my spirit and hope back in my heart, but now all that had imploded too. I felt trapped in a labyrinth of pain with dead ends at every turn. "Duncan is getting away with destroying us," I tearfully told Spencer and Amanda. And then, wonder of wonders, they comforted *me*.

Amanda said, "Mom, if anything happens to you, that's when my real troubles will begin. If I have you, I'll be all right. Tell Dad he can have everything but us." Over the weekend, Amanda wrote a letter to Elsie that recounted in very precise terms much that had happened to us, including Amanda's recollection of the day Duncan had said he was going to destroy us. Duncan told Amanda that what he'd actually said was, "This is going to destroy you," but Amanda told him she remembered very clearly what she heard ("I was sitting on the counter eating Fritos when you said it") and he wasn't going to get away with denying what he'd said to us.

I went to First Parish with both kids on Easter Morning, and listened to Matt Hale talk about how we sometimes "have to spend life to save it." So much waste had taken place in the past few years, and yet I was convinced we were all the while building something new; roots were quietly taking hold.

On Easter afternoon, I went over to the Canfields, as they had asked, to get some legal advice from Max, a tall, quiet-spoken, no-nonsense Vermonter who had his own law firm in Boston. The Canfields had known our family for ten years, and their daughter Hailey had sat for Spencer and Amanda since the toddler years. "We're very concerned and want to help in any way we can," said Lydia Canfield.

Max asked me to tell my story, and he listened very patiently, and paced around a lot before he spoke.

"Ursula," he began, "you are in very serious trouble, on three counts: one, the mortgage/foreclosure problem and the contempt finding; two, Duncan; and three, Gabriel. You, yourself, have done nothing wrong, nor have you done anything to cause your problems," he spoke in calm, measured tones, "but as I see it, you have a number of options – all awful – and you need some guidance in selecting which ones to take next. I'd like you to talk to Victoria Harris, a long-time friend of mine, who is a divorce attorney. I can phone her in the next day or two and make the introduction."

"I'm now totally gun-shy of lawyers and the courts," I said. "I'm afraid to talk to any more lawyers."

"I can understand that. But you have to get away from Gabriel Reed, and you cannot defend yourself in court. Call Victoria this week," he said firmly. I went home feeling totally discouraged.

By Monday, I was exhausted and in total agony, and I told Archie McGowan I was too stressed out to come to work. I'd never done that before. He understood. I also told him about my troubles with Paul Sudo, who the week before had said, "You don't know how to manage anything! That's why you're losing your house!"

"The only reason that I am losing my house, the only reason that my life is unmanageable is that there is an alcoholic in it. My life was never unmanageable before, and it will never be unmanageable again! Get that straight!" I had flashed back at him. And he apologized and backed off.

Asa called and also exploded about what a mess I'd made of my life. "Ursula, you've wasted $15,000 and all you have to show for it is being found guilty of contempt of court, and your house is in foreclosure – great use of funds!" I said calmly that I'd always done my best, and if it wasn't good enough for him, Duncan and Gabriel, that I was retiring and hanging up the phone, which I did.

It turned out to be exactly the right week for a new Al-Anon acquaintance to give me the *One Day at a Time* book for a present. Its daily one-page messages were sometimes the only ballast in my days. Karen Dale had been right. It doesn't take long for bonds to form in Al-Anon, and the stories are surprisingly the same. The names and details vary, but the craziness, the deception, and the convincing cover-ups of the alcoholic – these are common threads.

About half the people in my group were adult children of alcoholics, and I listened hard to their stories, so that I could make sure, if possible, that Spencer and Amanda would never feel the guilt, shame, and pain these people spoke about so poignantly.

Another source of energy were the good wishes and prayers of my friends locally and around the world. I could really feel them pulling for us. Ike Peters, a Wheaton Glass scientist and long-time friend in the molecular modelling business, who knew the alcohol story all too well from the experiences of his own colleagues and family, started calling regularly to listen and offer advice when he thought I needed it.

Cheer also came from a number of unexpected sources.

Gale Parker, Conover's famous photographer, dropped by Inverary Lane to have tea one late afternoon. "Kip Edwin told me about your situation, and you are not alone. The law is torpedoing families across the country. My husband's secretary is going through the same things you are, and she's being treated so poorly by the court system – Brooks and I can hardly believe the terrible things that are happening to her and her children, while her husband is getting off relatively scot-free. And many children in my children's generation have had to go through precisely what Spencer and Amanda are now experiencing. I think that's why the younger generation is so reluctant to enter into marriage. Something must be done," she said.

On another day, while at work, I ran down to the cafeteria for a quick cup of soup – not looking my best – and promptly ran into Art Cleaver, the real estate developer who owned the whole industrial park. We recognized each other from First Parish. "Do you live in Conover?" he asked. I hedged, thinking of our impending homelessness.

"Yes, but my children and I are in terrible trouble," I blurted out. "Could I talk to you sometime?" Being in real estate, maybe he would be able to help us find housing in Conover, I reasoned.

"Let's talk now," he said kindly. "Have lunch with me. And tell me what has happened to you."

With as much dignity and cheer as I could muster, I recounted the bare bones facts of our mess, and said I was from the Midwest and had never let a bill go unpaid in my life and was now facing financial ruin. He grinned.

"I'm from Kansas," he said. "And I came East during the Depression ..."

Then I told him I was from Ohio, and we were off and running on a zillion topics: technology, molecular modelling, mercurial Leslie Drew and how we'd each come to know him, how the industrial park had been started as an Innovation Center, his plans for the 1990s, the Internet connection, and plans for a host of counseling services he had in the works for the whole office park. "I believe that you and your children are going to get your lives back on track and find a way to stay in Conover. Now tell me, who holds your mortgage?"

"Hub Safe Deposit & Trust."

"Now you just keep your chin up," he smiled as we left the cafeteria.

In mid-April, I finally caught up with Victoria Harris. Max Canfield said that Harris, Beane & McCoy had "groaned" when they heard I was working with Gabriel Reed, and wanted to know how I'd "ever gotten mixed up with him." Victoria Harris listened to my story and made these points. "You have been overlawyered, and Reed will probably end up suing you," she began. "I cannot understand why Gabriel Reed ever took your case. It wasn't big enough for him. You weren't his type."

"What do you mean?" I asked.

"I won't explain," she said. "Now here is how a divorce would work with me: the minimum cost would be $3K and the maximum $20K; assets would be split 50-50 and conduct no longer enters into divorce settlements. If you want to talk to me about representing you, you can call back." I didn't see how I could get started with another lawyer. But Max Canfield said I couldn't represent myself, and surely Gabriel would be dropping my case soon.

Later in the week, Lydia Canfield called to follow-up on my contact with Victoria Harris. "We still think you have to get away from Reed, and we are worried that Duncan may become violent. His behavior is so different from everything we'd known about him before." She again talked about the mess in the child welfare system, and how cocaine and alcohol and a rotten legal system peopled by bad judges were making awful decisions that were screwing everything up in Massachusetts. "The system needs overhauling."

"I'm very grateful to you and Max for being concerned and spending so much time with me on Easter. And I want you to know that I know all lawyers aren't bad. Lawyer 2B (I had started to number them!) is coming up from Rhode Island for lunch tomorrow. Would you like to meet her?"

"Yes, please come on by."

We stopped by the Canfields and chatted briefly with Lydia. "When will I see you again?" she asked Merrill.

"At the *Dramatis Personae* Party," I said half-jokingly. Merrill and I had said we really ought to do a potluck dinner and invite everyone who had been in this awful saga.

"When's that going to be?" said Lydia.

"When this is over!" I said, "or when Dad comes to visit in the fall, whichever comes first."

At lunch Merrill turned serious, "I really don't think you should get another lawyer. Gabriel won't sue you if you keep sending him a little money every month. He lambastes nearly everyone, but has always been very kind to Mitzy Dillon in the office – he even paid for her schooling, though hardly anyone knows about that."

Before I could deal with lawyers, there were professional matters which required my attention. The American Chemical Society Show was in Boston in April, and for the first time *Molecular Modelling News* had its own booth at the Exhibition. I marketed Legal Sea Foods lobsters as a promotion for new subscriptions, met long-time phone friends, and went out for a wonderful lunch with Ike Peters, who'd come to town for the ACS Meeting. Instead of our usual conversation about matters scientific, Ike talked to me about his childhood, a saga of alcoholic parents and stepparents. "Ursula, there is life after alcoholism. I promise."

Also during the ACS Show, two Genesis Labs competitors took me for walks around the block to discuss whether the kids and I would consider moving to California or Missouri and working for them. But I said that we loved Boston and that Genesis had been good to me during my time of trouble.

Christa was very ill part of that week, so Spencer and Amanda were on their own, with no way to reach me at my booth, but it never occurred to them to call Duncan for any help. They managed wholly on their own, and Amanda wrote me a note about it that I will always treasure: "We don't know how, but we'll figure it out, and we love you, Mom." This was not my idea of how to raise children, but the Commonwealth of Massachusetts was now calling the shots, and the three of us had to live by its rules.

In the week that followed, I met with my boss Paul Sudo, and he came up with an elegant, logical plan on how the two of us could work better together: more work for me in the short run he said, but I could very quickly see how it would really be less work, or better use of time and as we talked through the mutual advantages, and hammered out what we were going to do, it became clear to both of us that we had come through a bad time and resolved our problem. Then I told him we were about to lose all childcare, and that I might need to work at home more often. "Ursula, I never worry about getting work out of you. Do whatever you need to do, and don't even bother discussing it with me anymore. Come and go as you need to." Nice to be trusted by one's boss again!

Amanda chatted with me that evening and said she "didn't like" Duncan and "wished he would die." I said she shouldn't say that now, because if anything more happened to him, she would feel terrible then or later. I was thinking about all those adult children at Al-Anon, and that I wanted my children to feel good about themselves, now and forever. That wouldn't happen if they harbored bad thoughts about Duncan now.

She also told me that she wanted to tell her pediatrician about our family situation, including the "I'm going to destroy you" incident, but that she wanted me to brief Dr. Early first. I phoned his secretary the next day and told her part of the story and why I'd been reluctant to confide in them. She accepted this information as routinely as if I'd been describing the symptoms of an ear infection or a case of flu. "Mrs. Charbonnier, there is more of this in Conover than you would ever believe. Trust me, we hear it all the time. I've worked with Dr. Early for nearly twenty years, and I know. Now we'd be happy to work you in *before* Amanda's check-up – how's May 3?"

At the very end of April, I went to Matthew and Trudy's for a dessert get-together, and learned more about First Parish, which I had decided to join, even though I didn't know how much longer we'd be in Conover. I told Trudy that I had learned from Al-Anon that having a community in which to express one's spirituality was a component that appeared to be lacking in most alcoholics' lives, and one I didn't want missing in my kids' lives. "I can't do anything about their genes, but I can sure do something about their environment!"

The first week in May, I took Spencer to John Arthur for his physical. Spencer was healthy, growing, and Arthur said doing very, very well given all he had to deal with. "He's healthy as a horse, Ursula!"

"Well, he eats like one," I bantered.

Then Arthur turned serious. "Duncan has turned to stone . . . all my contact with him is superficial." None of this was new for me. I just listened.

That same day, I went to see Dr. Early as Amanda had requested and told him everything about our situation, from the railroad track episode to the present, in about half an hour – a record! He listened carefully and asked a lot of questions. "Are you sure something neurological hasn't been missed? The man I remember was nice, too."

"All the doctors assure me that nothing has been missed, but yes, there's still a shadow of a doubt in my mind too. There always will be until I get a logical explanation – if I ever do."

On May 6, Amanda and I went on the last half of the annual Walk for Hunger with a group from First Parish. I walked most of the way from Brandon to the Boston Common with Matt Hale. We talked a lot about my situation, and Al-Anon, and faith and how it evolved in people in general and in himself specifically, about the books that have influenced him and the one he's writing, and about writing books in general. Matt recounted a lot of Boston church history, pointing out landmarks as we walked past Gabriel's office in Back Bay. With the ACS show behind me, I knew I had to face the matter of what to do about Gabriel G. Reed. Matt urged me to contact Jonah McCoy, the same lawyer Trudy had mentioned in March, and the partner of Victoria Harris, Max Canfield's friend.

"Ursula, I'd be happy to talk with him about your situation. Jonah McCoy is a good man."

XVIII

Jonah McCoy

Let all things be done decently and in order.
— I Corinthians 14:40, *The Bible*

On May 9, after several days of phone tag, Jonah McCoy finally caught up with me. "I know this is awfully short notice," I said, "but I'm in a lot of trouble. Can we meet sometime tomorrow?"

"Why not this afternoon?" he replied. "I'm taking the train home right now. I'll see you at my home office in an hour."

This turned out to be midway between Genesis and Inverary Lane. When I rang, a kindly, white-bearded fellow opened the door, and as I crossed his threshold, my first sensation was of a past life: there had been trouble before, and we had resolved it.

He led me into a cozy book-lined room, and asked for time to read the files I'd brought. On the coffee table were a polemoscope and another gadget. I picked it up and looked inside. "Fractals!" I exclaimed in delight.

"You know what they are?" he looked up, surprised.

"Why, yes. They're very important in the work we . . ." and I was off and running about molecular design. A little voice inside me said, "Shut up Ursula, and let this man read in peace!" I stopped in midsentence. He looked bemused and met my gaze. This is going to be okay, I thought. This lawyer's office is going to be different.

In the hours that followed, we talked about science, the law, substance abuse, my case. "Why do you think people turn to drugs and alcohol?" he asked.

"The short answer is, that nature gives us pain," I said, "and rather than face it, these people choose to anaesthetize themselves."

There were also snatches of poetry in that first meeting – he had been an English major at Yale. Then came law school at Michigan and several years in New York. "We've been in a lot of the same places," I said. "Where do we go from here?"

"Well, we have several options. I can be a mediator for you and Duncan, or I can represent you in a mediation, but I don't usually do divorce. My partner Victoria, with whom you spoke on the phone recently, does divorces."

"I don't see how you can be our mediator," I replied directly, "because there's no way after hearing this story that you can be impartial. And I think you like me too much."

"You're right," he said, being equally direct.

"You might be able to represent me, if Duncan can be convinced to go the mediation route. But if he can't, will you be my divorce lawyer?"

"Yes. If you can tell me what you want. As your lawyer I can outline your options. But as my client, you have to tell me what you want."

"I want you to get me divorced – with my house and my children intact." Then I took out my checkbook. "What is your retainer?"

"I don't take retainers."

"Well, isn't there some fee agreement I need to sign?"

"I don't do fee agreements. I'm just a 'country lawyer.' I can send you a fee memorandum, but I never worry about getting paid. All my clients pay me." This was utterly unbelievable.

"Furthermore, we are going to set a ceiling price on this case, which will change only if we mutually agree." His ceiling was lower than Reed's retainer! The man didn't know what he was getting into; we would quickly pass his "ceiling" given the way Chubb and Duncan operated. But Jonah McCoy would be paid in full if it took the rest of my life.

"Have you ever gone up against Chubb MacIntyre before?" I asked, wondering how much experience he'd had with the Boys' Club of Boston Divorce Lawyers.

"No," he replied with a complete lack of concern.

"Chubb MacIntyre is going to make mincemeat out of us," I said, not even bothering to be remotely diplomatic.

"Nobody is going to make mincemeat out of Jonah and Ursula," he asserted in a very strong and very quiet voice. Well, he's aptly named, I thought. Chubb MacIntyre may swallow Jonah McCoy whole, but he is somehow going to get thrown back up whole and intact.

We had talked for three hours. "Just write out the check for two," he instructed.

"We talked for three hours, and I'm paying you for three hours."

"If you make that check out for one penny more than two hours, I'll rip it up!"

"You know," I said smiling up at my new "country lawyer," "this story needed a hero!"

"This story has many heroes!" said Jonah McCoy. "The first thing you'll need to do, Ursula, is to see Gabriel and get a Withdrawal of Appearance, before I can officially take over the case."

"I've already made an appointment for next week."

"Good. Now go see if you can talk Duncan into mediation. It will save you time, money, and the pain and waste of a court battle."

I drove over to Babylon Village, after first calling to see if it would be okay to come by. Duncan was unfriendly, totally unwilling to discuss mediation, and said, "I'm throwing you out."

"Don't bother, I'm leaving. I'm due at baseball to pick up Spencer, anyway."

Half an hour later, I arrived home in tears and Amanda looked surprised. She said Duncan had just called and reported we'd had "a very friendly conversation and were working everything out." Amanda knew her father had lied, and told him so on the phone the next night. Jonah, to whom I later recounted this, found it fascinating.

On the following Sunday, I formally joined First Parish. If I'd been left to my own devices at an early age, I'd have got there on my own. People and a 1960s taste for Eastern religion had delayed me, but I had found my spiritual path anyhow. And the way it had all happened seemed right in a funny way. It was also Mother's Day. Amanda made a stunning ceramic piece – shades of blue in a shallow bowl studded with starfish. Her ceramics teacher later explained how the design had happened serendipitously, and they had chosen to let it stay. The starfish seemed a fine and fitting symbol – they know how to regenerate when life tears off their points. At eleven o'clock that night, both kids were snuggled on my bed, and not wanting to have them leave, I tuned out the TV and composed my thoughts for the next morning's meetings: one with a team of scientific publishers in from The Netherlands, and the other with Gabriel G. Reed.

I had a long "getting to know you" breakfast with the European publishers at the Government Center Holiday Inn, overlooking the Charles and much of Boston and Cambridge. We talked for a few hours about science, CAMD and the future, and then I drove across town to Gabriel's office.

I was determined to be gentle with Gabriel that morning, and began by telling him I appreciated all he had done, but that the Charbonnier pie was finite and his and Chubb's portions were just getting bigger. "You spend money faster than I make it!" I said simply. "This isn't going to work. But it will always mean a lot that you always believed me."

"I still do," he said quietly. "Your husband is a classic. I know you're going to fire me, so get on with it." He reminded me of a small child wanting to get the whipping over with, but I am not a whipper.

"Gabriel, I spent some time thinking about what I wanted to say to you today, and I'm going to take my time and stick to my 'crib notes' and say it. And then I have about five or six other important things to do today."

"Work is going well, isn't it?" he grinned.

"How *did* you know?" I smiled back at him.

"What are you going to do now?" he asked. "You can't just represent yourself!" And then, "It's Jonah McCoy, isn't it?" I was stunned. I'd told no one but the Hales, and neither, I later found out, had Jonah.

"Do you have my phone bugged?!" I demanded.

"I know what's going on around town," he said proudly. "Jonah McCoy is a good man. How did you find him?"

When I said through my ministers, he thought I said my masters, and I laughed and said, "Not now; now ever!"

"I'll cooperate fully with Jonah, of course and have your files sent over immediately. But you still owe me close to $9,000. And I still want to talk to your father."

"I told you before. I don't want you and my father to ever talk to each other. You both have the same style. You're both shouters, and the two of you would never get along!" He grinned when he heard that. "Nothing has ever been as important to you in this case as getting paid."

"That's not true. The bill and the mortgage have been equal concerns of mine."

But I was firm that most of his actions belied that statement, and asked a few focused questions which underscored my point. "Are you cross-examining me?!" he protested, when I persisted.

I laughed. The very idea amused me. "How could anyone cross-examine you?!"

Then he showed me the new motions that had come in that morning for lowered child support, a psychiatric evaluation of me and a *guardian ad litum* appointment for Spencer and Amanda. "This just proves how we couldn't control events."

"What did I do to deserve this, Gabriel?"

"You made lampshades at Auschwitz," he said with an unbearable lightness, and then in the same breath, "Remember, Ursula, this man wants to destroy you."

"He won't destroy me, Gabriel. Read my lips. He will not destroy me. I am going to live a long time, and I am going to do many things. If I can learn computational chemistry, you can't name anything I can't learn. This is a just a storm, Gabriel, and all storms end someday. My experience with people who want to destroy others is that they ultimately destroy themselves."

"You are a perfectly lovely person, a little uptight at times, but that's understandable." I listened to his criticism. I always do.

"Well, what do you think is going to happen to me?"

"You're a survivor," he said. "You know, I have a needlepoint in my bathroom that says, 'After clouds, sunshine.'"

"Well then, we have similar bathrooms," I said. "The sign in my bathroom says, 'remember the sunshine when the storm seems unending.'" We looked at each other, in another of those we've-both-met-our-match moments. Parting professionally wasn't going to be agony after all; quite the contrary, it was going to be rather a relief.

Jillian Frost came in and inserted herself in our conversation. As soon as I could manage it, I thanked her "for all she had done" and I extended my hand and said "after you leave, I would like to say a few more words to Gabriel," and she got the message and buzzed off.

"I am very concerned about what all this is going to do to your children," he said, referring to the motions that had come from Chubb in the morning mail.

"Well, you don't know them, but my children make *me* look like a total pushover," I said, adding "My children have been brought up to believe in truth, to pursue truth – that truth is important."

"Truth *is* important," he replied.

Then he shook my hand, and it was time to go. I looked him in the eye and patted his shoulder. He walked me out and asked if I had a coat, but I just tugged on my blazer. It was a warm spring day. Of course I didn't have a coat. And then we went through that again – his mind had been elsewhere – and he finally got it. I cocked my head and gave him a peaceful good-bye wave. "Keep smiling!" I said to him, "no matter what!" It had been clean and gentle and honest, all I had wanted it to be.

Merrill came up for lunch the next day, and said under no circumstances to sign any promissory notes that Gabriel would now demand. I told her about Jonah, and we had our usual great time together.

The next day, I dropped off papers at Jonah's house on my way to work. This lawyer and I were going to get along just fine. He liked early morning meetings too, and the prospect of finally getting divorced, without having to miss most of work to do it, looked promising.

Now that he had my files from Reed, we could start redoing my financial statement. "You are to start paying your mortgage immediately," he began. "Not another penny to me until your mortgage is paid up! Now here's how you're going to arrange your finances. You will use all of child support for the mortgage – keep it in a special account for the house. And you and the children are going to start living on your salary, which I want you to place in a separate account."

"We'll never manage it."

"Oh, yes you will. And I'm going to show you how. Get out your calculator." In the midst of all the number crunching, I don't now remember how Oliver Wendell Holmes came up, but there was Jonah, talking to me about reciting "Old Ironsides" at a Memorial Day celebration when he was a six year-old boy in a small Connecticut town. "Aye tear her tattered ensign down, Long has she waved on high . . ." he began.

"And many an eye has danced to see that banner in the sky!" I completed for him.

He looked at me, astonished. "What an amazing memory you have!"

"Well, I like that poem, too!" I smiled. And then it was on to Tennyson and other favorites in common, which made the number-crunching a lot more palatable. In this deadly serious business, there was always going to be an element of fun with Jonah McCoy.

A few weeks later, we had some prepping to do for an early morning meeting with Chubb and Duncan, at Chubb's place. Jonah had me meet him at his fourth floor walkup office across the street from the courthouse in Cambridge. Then we took the T to Wadsworth Place and chatted amiably with Chubb's partner, Candice, before we went into our meeting.

Jonah drove Chubb straight up the wall with his slow, plodding, feelings-oriented approach to negotiation – à la the *Getting to Yes* book. It sucked up three hours of Chubb's time, and the hair on the back of his neck fairly bristled, as I later told Jonah.

Chubb read all the documentation I'd brought from John Arthur, the Conover Schools, and Archie McGowan attesting to the healthiness of the children's and my brains. He said they'd drop the psychiatric evaluation, that he'd never wanted Duncan to do it anyhow. Thanks a lot boys, another two days shot from my job!

Then Duncan argued that we should see a psychologist about parenting (I later tried to arrange the appointment, and Duncan refused to pay for what was his idea, and was impossible about scheduling, so I threw the ball into his court and told him to make arrangements – on his nickel). Jonah later said that just showed "how stupid" Duncan was. I showed Chubb recent pictures of the children and Streak, and a lovely one of the four of us together when Duncan was still his old self. "I call this one, 'the way we were' photo." Chubb looked at them a long time, and didn't hand them back the first time I reached for them.

Then he took a pot shot at Al-Anon. "You've gotten mixed up with these Al-Anon people."

"Chubb, you speak of alcoholism as if there's a stigma attached to it. There isn't. Alcoholism is a disease, and I'm learning a lot about it. There are a lot of adult children of alcoholics in my group."

"Well, your children couldn't possibly remember behavior that occurred years ago."

"You know children just don't forget it when their father falls off a ladder and crashes into the living room windows." I sensed on some level Chubb knew I was for real.

"And how do you propose to deal with the alcoholism?" he asked, baiting me a little.

"With compassion," I replied firmly.

So he tried a new tack. "That letter from your doctor doesn't really say anything." But Chubb is "all bombast," as I told Jonah. He took Arthur's letter and the others as serious enough to drop the psychiatric evaluation.

Later he said, "I hear you're going to get the laws changed," and I smiled back firmly and said, "You haven't heard the last of me, Chubb."

As to the matter of joint vs. sole custody, I openly discussed that the children did not want to be forced to fly in Ivy Parrish's airplane. Then Chubb said I only wanted the house for my own selfish reasons, that the kids had nothing to do with it. I looked away from him and turned my attention to his client. "You know, Duncan, it was bad enough to lose you. Do we have to lose everything else too?"

Duncan said I'd told the children that I was going to get the law changed so that people like him couldn't get married. My children later hooted at that one.

It was raining when Jonah and I walked out of Wadsworth Place three hours later. "Do you mind if we walk back in the rain instead of taking the T?" he asked.

I felt like walking in the rain too after that much time with Chubb and Duncan. "Is your meter ticking?" I asked mischievously.

"No, but that was a good question. Ursula, you need a vacation."

"You're right, but that's not in the cards for a while."

"What would you do on your ideal one?"

I closed my eyes and thought out loud, "Swim, make love, read and eat. Someday, someday when this storm is over, I intend to have one, but I'm not there yet."

Then we talked about judges and marriage and money and divorce and found we don't agree on everything, but that's okay. He did not agree with me that Judge Tracy is "a bozo," and Irena Cossell was a personal friend, so my professional assessment of her did not sit well, but we had an easy rapport and could say anything to each other. We got to know each other so fast, by necessity, or as Jonah told me, "Ursula, last week was pretty intense!"

When we got back to his office, we called Gabriel, who Jonah reported had sent a messenger over on a bike in the rain "with fifty pounds of paper" several days before. Like me, Jonah believes that beneath the avaricious exterior of Gabriel G. Reed lies a decent human being.

Jonah opened with, "Gabriel, I've got one of your greatest admirers sitting next to me here in my office." Then they talked about money, Gabriel's favorite topic, and Jonah explained he wanted all my money to go to the bank for the mortgage, and none to him until I could manage it.

Gabriel made some remark about how he (Gabriel) couldn't operate that way, that he wasn't "Robin Hood and didn't want all the poor people of Boston coming [to him] for help." Clearly, Jonah's arrangement with me, however, had to be causing him some discomfiture, for Jonah explained I'd just gotten paid, and rather than pay him as I'd offered, he'd insisted I send $500 to the bank, that he wasn't worried about Ursula Charbonnier paying him!

"Jonah, don't let her come over here to discuss the bill. If I see her again I am going to melt."

"Gabriel G. Reed doesn't melt!" I told Jonah.

"Charm him, Ursula!" he said with a big grin on his face. "Gabriel G. Reed has met his match! This is fascinating, fascinating."

At the end of May, we received no child support and Dr. Brixon, the orthodontist, said he now wanted *me* to guarantee payment for Amanda's braces because of Duncan's bailing out on the family. "Why aren't you going after Duncan?" I asked. "He makes a lot more money than I do!"

But Dr. Brixon, who was himself divorced, knew exactly how the Massachusetts courts operated. Orthodontists usually go after the mothers, because the courts usually let the fathers out of paying. The children were really seeing Duncan's true colors. Elsie was here for the weekend, and neither Duncan nor Elsie returned the children's phone calls.

Finally I called Duncan myself, and he spoke to me in a kind tone for the first time in many months. He expressed great concern for the well-being of the children specifically and the family in general. "What should I do, Ursula?" he asked in a solicitous tone.

"That's up to you," I replied courteously, "but getting into an AA program might help. Al-Anon has certainly helped me."

Then he turned nasty. "You know, you are the one with the problem. You are the person who is messed up, and you'll see that one day."

"Duncan, I'm not the person in the family who's been drinking vodka for breakfast for years or locking it up in my car. Both children are now talking openly about how we thought for five years you had a seizure disorder, and about your lies and your drinking and your threats to make us lose our house. Even if you don't remember saying these things (maybe because of blackouts), they still happened. Even your own lawyer is starting to figure out that you have a problem. At some point you will have no choice but to face the truth."

Duncan hung up on me, probably because he knew I was on solid ground. Then Jonah told me something Chubb said: "You know, Duncan doesn't even know why he's pursuing this divorce, and I can't argue with all you're telling me, Jonah."

Chubb had also looked at my family pictures a long time, and listened to my persistent, consistent concern about Duncan's well-being since last December. He'd seen the children's grade cards and comments from school counselors and teachers. He knew that Spencer and Amanda were doing splendidly. Our internist corroborated that. And if Chubb was catching on, it would be only a matter of time before others did too.

Over the weekend, I wrote Gabriel a carefully thought out letter about how we might complete our professional relationship and address the matter of the bill.

He instantly wrote back an unusual letter, saying he was without a secretary and would write me a "deserving response" when he could. And would I help him find a new one? It was a sort of "fifth grade boy" reply, noted Jackie Melrose. In my letter to him, I had tried to call us both to a higher standard and say that both of us shared in the responsibility for the mistakes we had made, and now I wanted to look ahead.

XIX

No One Accepts Checks

I'm having trouble with my checks, as well, this week.
— Barbara F. Graham,
Private Communication

And it was in that spirit that I decided to tell Eliza Pickering that I just might know of a job possibility for her, after all. With Leslie Drew out of the picture, life at Genesis just wasn't the same for Eliza. "What happened to wonderful Lynn?" I asked Merrill over lunch the following week, referring to Gabriel's crackerjack secretary.

"Oh, he fired her, as he does everyone eventually, unless they are wise enough to quit first," she replied. So, knowing Eliza's options were few, I called Gabriel's office and said "if he still needed someone, I might be able to help."

Gabriel called back the following week to inquire about Eliza.

"She will keep you on your toes," I replied.

"I don't need someone to keep me on my toes," he snapped. "I need someone to help me practice good law, blah, blah, blah, blah, blah . . ."

"Same thing!" I announced firmly, when he at last came up for air.

"Does she know what we really do here all day?"

"Yes, she learned about it as a child."

This reached Gabriel, who said, "Yes, that's one way to learn about it."

Eliza of course got the job, and when I later recounted this to Jonah he was fascinated and amused. "She'll be perfect for him," I said, "and they'll bring out the best in each other, I have no doubt, and it will be a total toss-up as to who will survive whom – because my nickname for Eliza is 'Young Ironsides.'"

Merrill Crosby later disagreed with this assessment. "She won't last three months. I'll bet lunch at the Vista on it!"

"Oh yes she will, but as a back-up, maybe I ought to find her another job," I said, which was how I came to be speaking with Marietta, Digby Grant's office manager. Without giving away any names, including my own, I explained the situation, and asked if they would interview this candidate if things didn't go well for her at the current place of employment. Marietta was intrigued, "Yes. Call me back if things don't work out for her. And since you won't identify yourself or anyone else in this story, I will call you 'Lady X!'"

That was to be about the last light moment in June.

In the first months of working together, Jonah and I were totally consumed with two matters that had to supersede our work on the divorce: saving 1 Inverary Lane from foreclosure, and figuring out how to clean up the Gabriel G. Reed Matter. They were interconnected. For it was by following Reed's legal advice to pay him and not my mortgage, that I had come to be in far worse legal and financial trouble than the day I'd walked in his door.

As Jonah put it, "Ursula, it's the only thing I can fault you for in this whole mess. What could you have been thinking of when you followed Reed's advice? Didn't you ask him what would happen to you if you didn't pay your mortgage?"

"Well, of course I did!"

"And what did he say?"

"He made a joke of it. He said, 'Well, you are not going to get spanked.' And when I tried again to pin him down about the consequences, he wouldn't answer me."

"Did that seem like good advice to you at the time?"

"It seemed questionable," I admitted, "but this was his zillionth divorce, and I just assumed he knew something I didn't."

"Well, if I ever give you advice that seems questionable, I expect you to call me on it, loud and clear."

As it turned out, Duncan's legal advice hadn't been any more aboveboard than mine, though in it Jonah thought he saw an opening to get the house out of foreclosure. In clear violation of Judge Tracy's December court order that restrained Duncan from "transferring, encumbering, alienating or changing beneficial or legal interest in all marital assets," Duncan had exercised $30,000 of GEC stock options and at the suggestion of the lawyers sent half the proceeds to Chubb and half to Gabriel. In a March letter to Chubb, Gabriel suggested that both lawyers "at a minimum receive a 'retainer' toward counsel fees in the amount of $15,000."

On learning this I'd said to Reed, "Where are the teeth in court orders?" And though at the time he laughed at me, months later he'd covered himself in a letter to Chubb: "I thought it was understood that I would need Ursula's advance approval before Duncan was authorized to sell any Germane stock and apply the proceeds to any attorneys' fees." He said he had never received my approval. "I don't think you should disburse any monies to yourselves until the air is clear on this issue," concluded Reed.

Jonah McCoy didn't waste a moment in springing into action on the mortgage. "From now on you are to send every child support check to the bank," said Jonah. "Then, as soon as possible, I want us to try to get all the money back from both attorneys and send it to Hub Safe Deposit & Trust." At that point Jonah began his daily, unremitting, and intense negotiations with Frank Niccolini, the bank's lawyer. "She is sending every spare penny to you people to stave off foreclosure." And when the bank in turn sent back every check I wrote and then charged me interest for the unpaid mortgage, Jonah was not shy in pointing out their Catch-22 reasoning.

"I will continue to instruct my client to send back the checks to you, that you send back to her! And she's going to keep on doing that 'til you start to accept them!" Jonah would tell Niccolini in their daily, and sometimes hourly talks on Niccolini's car phone. "How can they expect you to pay interest on money they won't accept?!"

"In the meantime," he told me, "we have to get back the proceeds from the illegally sold stock options as soon as possible so that you can catch up on those mortgage payments — even if we have to go back to court to do it!"

And that's just what we had to do. Duncan said he had no intention of trying to save Inverary Lane from foreclosure, and Chubb said he wasn't going to give the money back. Furthermore, neither Duncan nor Chubb took the court order seriously, and they didn't think Judge Tracy would even be concerned about what they'd done. What was my problem, they wanted to know.

Without delay, Jonah had us back in court on June 11. Never one to stand in a courtroom when he could chat with a judge over his desk, Jonah marched upstairs to Tracy's chambers on the second floor. Tracy had high regard for Jonah McCoy, and my stock with the judge rose considerably that day, just because Reed was no longer my attorney. Tracy looked pale and slight to me that morning, maybe even a little unwell. He motioned the four of us into the brown leather chairs that ringed his desk. The usual de rigeur photos of family and bureaucrats covered the walls around us, and I noticed an American flag badly in need of dry cleaning in the far diagonal corner.

Although Gabriel had been invited to attend because we were going to ask the judge to get our money back from him, too, he never showed up. When Chubb flatly refused to give his portion back, I said with great pleasure to the judge, "Your Honor, I can't tell you how refreshing it has been to meet a lawyer (Jonah) who cares more about mothers and children having a roof over their heads than he does about getting paid."

Chubb squirmed slightly, but detectably, in his leather chair, as the judge took this in.

After a certain amount of waffling, Tracy finally said that maybe the stock was sold "without Mrs. Charbonnier's permission" and maybe it shouldn't have been, given his freeze on assets, "but what's done is done," and then without so much as a reprimand to Duncan and Chubb, he turned his attention to Chubb's motions for a psychiatric evaluation of me and the appointment of a *guardian ad litum* for the children, namely someone to represent the children's best interests to the court.

A psychiatric evaluation of me was necessary, Chubb's Motion stated, owing to my "repeated bizarre and aberrant behavior," but of course he and Duncan were not required to say just what that was or even give one substantiating example. Why, I wondered, didn't the court think it was aberrant of Duncan to wander around in parking lots, or drink vodka secretly out of brown bags, or tell his family that he was going to destroy them? But I had already learned the hard way that pointing out double standards to a Massachusetts judge is a good way to get found in contempt of court. As for the letters I had brought from Archie McGowan and Dr. Arthur, firmly attesting to my emotional stability, they were totally disregarded that day.

"Jonah, you write up the orders," said Judge Tracy, and he waved us out. Chubb and Jonah walked away from me to put it all together, and occasionally Jonah would dart back and forth to get edits of the Court Orders from me. This infuriated Chubb. "Why do you have to keep showing her everything?"

"Because she's an editor, and I like Ursula to look at everything," Jonah called cheerily over his shoulder.

"Do you think I need to be psychiatrically evaluated?" I asked him with tears in my eyes.

"Of course not, Ursula. They're just doing this to wear you down."

"I am going to blow this system to Kingdom Come!" I vowed, struggling to keep my angry tears from brimming over the edge. "I am going to make speeches across this Commonwealth until I don't have a larynx left, and I am going to tell people that what goes on in Probate Court is a sociopath's dream and an honest woman's nightmare!"

The only good thing to come out of the session with Tracy was his order that Reed return to me his half of the illegally sold stock option proceeds plus interest. "That will be a good start toward paying off Hub Safe," noted Jonah. As we left the courthouse, Jonah said that while they were writing up the orders, Chubb had referred to Duncan as "that jerk," and a lawyer has to think pretty poorly of his own client to call him a jerk to the opposing attorney. "Ursula, I would never do that to any client."

"Maybe Chubb is starting to get the picture," I remarked.

Across the street, Jonah returned to his office; and I stopped to chat with Seth Wright, Chubb's junior partner, while Toby, who owned the lot next to Jonah's office, retrieved my car. I bantered about how my family had wanted me to become a lawyer, but I'd bombed the LSATs, and we talked a bit about intellectual property law and the series on it I was thinking of doing in *Molecular Modelling News.* Then I made my retreat, though Wright seemed to want to continue talking. I got the impression he was starting to realize that something about his own client just wasn't adding up. They are all in the early stages of getting it, I thought, but insight will come too late to help me and the children.

The week before, at Jonah's urging, I had written the Board of Bar Overseers because Gabriel said he was putting a lien on the $8,940.50 he felt was still owed him. Jonah said, "That was illegal. Ursula, ask the Board to intervene to straighten the matter out." This I immediately did, saying "Your prompt attention to this matter will be greatly appreciated by me and my two children. You see, we are dangerously close to losing our family home, in part because these assets are tied up, and we are not at liberty to apply them to the payment of our mortgage." I added a P.S. in a size 18 font:

"And you haven't heard the half of it! Stay tuned . . ."

Thoroughly fed up and frustrated by all that had taken place, I decided to appeal to Gabriel's splendid sense of humor. It was all I had left. Appeals to rationality, fairness, and decency had failed in and out of the courtroom. On top of all the other nonsense, Reed had sent me a check for more than $2,600 – what amounted to the difference between the proceeds from the illegally sold GEC stock options (about $11,500) and the $8,940.50 Gabriel claimed I still owed him. I couldn't believe he would have the gall to return my own money to me, from Duncan's and my illegally sold options, and actually expect me to accept the check!

"Jonah, I think it's time Gabriel G. Reed received a little care package from me," and I explained what I had in mind: a lot of toy money that said "no value" on each bill, along with a children's book for Bessie, Reed's favorite pet bull, about whom he sometimes spoke with great affection. "Jonah, when you were a little boy, did you ever read the book *Ferdinand*?" I asked, referring to the 1930s classic.

And my "country lawyer" replied, "Ursula, I don't believe this! It was my favorite book. Do you know I still have my *Ferdinand* blanket up at my house in New Hampshire?"

"Then you won't mind?" I grinned.

And the very next day, I filled up an antique Matchbox Cars case with Monopoly money, as they call it in the East, and sent it to Reed's office along with *Ferdinand*, Reed's check torn up in pieces, and this note:

Dear Gabriel:

Enclosed please find payment in full for the value of the legal services rendered. It's all there ($8,940.50) – you earned it! I am also returning your check. We both know this is *not your money* to dispense – not even to me. I'm having trouble with my checks as well this week: Hub Safe's Mortgage Department sent mine back, too. Jonah McCoy wisely suggests I call this chapter of *Snow Job* "No One Accepts Checks." What, do you think?

As ever,

U. L. C.

I can't believe Gabriel didn't hoot privately in his own office, but his public reaction was total fury. Jonah rapidly got a phone call from Chubb, "Guess what Ursula's done now?"

"Oh Chubb," laughed Jonah, "I think I already know!" McCoy's and my popularity with the Boys' Club appeared to be plummeting rapidly.

While all this was going on, my attitude about Inverary Lane was in a chronic state of fluctuation. I loved the house, and the connection to Conover and nearness to Spencer and Amanda's friends which it provided, but when I did the mathematics, I just didn't see how we were going to hang onto it. Jonah, on the other hand, my "cognitive lawyer," as he had come to call himself, couldn't have disagreed more.

"Ursula, despite what your father, and your friends and colleagues at work are telling you, I will do everything in my power to keep you at Inverary Lane. Thanks to the recession, the price of your house is sinking like a stone, and the cost of buying Duncan out is becoming ridiculously low. Furthermore, there will be more than enough money to fix the potential problems." He was referring to the leaking roof and the water that poured through the kitchen ceiling.

"Jonah, I'm an apartment person, and I hate yard work. Given a choice between reading a book and planting a flower, it's a no brainer. In addition to all my other responsibilities, I can't be saddled with home ownership, too."

Closest friends, Asa, and Archie McGowan continued to be of one mind – get out, get out, get out, along with the various Realtors who were scouting for housing for me and the kids. Only my Al-Anon buddies and Jonah were adamant that it made better sense to keep the house.

I skipped my next Al-Anon meeting, and went to Jonah's house instead, to clarify my position on Inverary Lane. "Ursula, I am going to continue to try to change your mind," he persisted patiently. I was very tired, and did not look or speak my best that night. I was feeling rather testy, but Jonah was imperturbable, no matter what I said or did.

Then Jonah and I got into a discussion about mothers putting their children first, and he said he couldn't understand why we do it. "Like when oxygen masks are lowered from airplanes in an emergency, and they always say take care of yourself first, then put a mask on the child, but *every* mother I've ever represented tells me she would do it the other way around. I don't get it. Why?"

"Because our eggs go on," I said. "That's why we're all here, Jonah!" But I could tell he didn't fully understand. Maybe one has to have given birth in order to really get it.

If even warm-hearted Jonah McCoy was puzzled, then Duncan Charbonnier didn't stand a chance of grasping the concept of putting children first. I was beginning to feel like the village idiot shouting "Daylight!" at noon. And I would continue to shout it.

Spencer and Amanda continued to be terrific and bounce right along with each new change in our circumstances. In the week after Christa got married and moved to Germany, I came home from work one evening, and the house smelled gloriously of freshly baked cookies. I watched in amazement as Spencer beamed, spatula in hand, taking the cookies off the baking sheet. He'd cleaned up the whole kitchen, too, and announced proudly, "And I make great omelets, *too!*"

Spencer also continued to filibuster for a stepfather at dinner.

"Well, what are your requirements? What should he be like?" I asked.

"Reliable," was his laconic reply.

"What I hope is that you get a stepfather who can keep you in line verbally!" I bantered back.

"Well, will he ever swear at me?" Spencer asked.

"Probably," I replied.

"Good! Then I'll know he's qualified!" Sometimes you just have to sit back and enjoy your children and say not a word.

Jonah McCoy had now met Amanda and had spoken to Spencer on the phone. "Now I understand why you say both children are verbal handfuls!" he laughed with me one morning.

The week after school ended, I drove Spencer and Amanda up to their camp in Maine. I didn't speed, didn't make any wrong turns, and got there in record time. Maybe all these years Duncan was the one who couldn't read maps and got mixed up and projected all that onto me. Our neighbor Patrice Paulsen, who bought Bud and Ted's old house, accompanied me. A psychologist for the Commonwealth of Massachusetts, she told me, "Ursula, if you hadn't confided in me, I never would have guessed what you've all been through. Any good psychologist is going to quickly realize you three are fine," she said referring to our upcoming appointments with the *guardian ad litum*. "You have nothing to worry about except for the senseless waste of time and money that Duncan and the system are putting you through. Duncan, being as smooth as he is, may very well fool the psychiatrist, but you personally have nothing to be concerned about. Hey, you reared these kids over the past year on your own, and you did a good job. And certainly you're not clinically depressed or suicidal!"

I must be doing something right, I reasoned, despite Duncan's remarks to *g.a.l.* Gavin Roberts that Spencer and Amanda are "having a lot of trouble dealing with the separation and the divorce." That was at our first session with him together at his office, a set of sparsely furnished rooms on the first floor of an old house in Beaumont Center. It was right around the corner from the Beaumont Police Station (where I visited Chief Malone after the session).

In person, Gavin Roberts was about like he'd been on the phone – relaxed, self-confident, a good listener, a good questioner, reasonable, and obviously a lover of children in general. He seemed to know his business. I didn't know if he would see through Duncan's facade, but I felt certain he was going to believe me, and that he would give Spencer and Amanda his best efforts.

Duncan tried to do another end run on me at Roberts' office. "Dr. Roberts, I think we need ongoing family therapy with you. Instead of being the children's *g.a.l.*, I'd like you to sign all of us up for group therapy. We can find another *g.a.l.*"

I immediately put a firm stop to that. "No, we signed up for you to be our *g.a.l.* That's what I agreed to because you came so highly recommended by Jonah. So will you PLEASE, be our *g.a.l.*? We need to take one step at a time," I said to him and Duncan, "first the *g.a.l.* process; later we can talk about ongoing therapy, though I'll tell you right up front that Spencer, Amanda, and I probably won't go for it – unless it, like this, is court-ordered. But John Arthur, our family internist, has already told me he doesn't think the children and I need it."

I also brought Dr. Roberts the letters from John Arthur, Archie McGowan, and the Conover Schools. "And there's something I'd like you to do for me," I said. "Would you please contact Harry Ballard at Appleton Hall and David Madden at Eastforest Lodge to learn everything you can about our situation? Here are their numbers."

Roberts promised he would, and scheduled appointments for Duncan and me to return separately the following week, and for the children to meet with him after they returned from camp. Then we got into billing issues, and fortunately after the Appleton Hall experience, I knew enough to see to it that the children and I were not listed as the patients – Duncan was. It would be his insurance, his record, and I was to settle the difference directly with Duncan, who despite his experience, was too unsophisticated to grasp the significance of these arrangements.

Toward the end of the month, Eliza took me out for a great hot dog lunch at the Conover Dairy Joy, just as she was beginning to work for Reed.

"We're probably going to end up suing you," she told me, "but if worse comes to worst, I'll delete you from his database and he'll forget he ever knew you. The man hates technology!"

I chuckled. Part of the method in my madness of sending Eliza to Gabriel was that I felt she would get him "automated."

"By the way Ursula, what was in that 'care package' you sent Gabriel the other day? He wouldn't let any of us see it."

"It's personal," I said, "and if he ever asks you what was in the box, I want you to be able to say honestly that you didn't know."

As it turned out, my effort to be discreet was entirely unnecessary, because Gabriel rapidly blabbed what was in the box to people all over town. Julia Holliday's psychiatrist had even heard about it!

XX

And So To Court

If it isn't fresh, it isn't legal!
— Legal Sea Foods Slogan

"She's known Gabriel G. Reed for twenty years, and she hates his guts," said Julia Holliday, the Conover Caterer, in reference to Dr. Dahlia Sutherland, her psychiatrist at the Governor Chandler Clinic in Brookway. "And she thought the toy money was priceless — no pun intended — the perfect thing to do to Mr. Greed," continued Julia, as I walked into the kitchen of the manse on Pigeon Place. It, too, was up for sale — thanks to the order of a Probate Court judge. "Here, have some gazpacho. I just made it this afternoon."

"How can you cook at a time like this?" I implored, gratefully accepting the first homemade soup I'd tasted in I'm embarrassed to tell you how long. During my happy years with Duncan, I'd made soup from scratch once a week, and nearly everything else too, and while we hadn't quite degenerated to the TV dinner stage over at Inverary Lane, the cuisine had become very simple.

"I keep telling you, it's my therapy," said the petite blond Conover caterer.

In happier days, Julia had presided over a thriving catering business that she ran from the sprawling Holliday kitchen, but now if she earned much money at all, the court would cut her child support payments which, proportionately, were even more of a joke than mine: Hobart, the founder of wildly successful Westbury Financial Ventures (of which Duncan and I were clients), had a salary plus bonus of half a million plus a year, yet was required to pay less than ten percent of that for the support of his four boys, the oldest of whom was Amanda's age. Often he didn't pay them at all. The courts in Massachusetts don't intervene until two payments are missed, if then. And even when Hobart did meet his child support obligations, the payment didn't come close to covering the mortgage, so Julia's house was in foreclosure, too. Because Hobart's firm had set up a special banking relationship for us at Hub Safe, we even had the same bankers:

Richard Rapp, the kindly foreclosure officer who was cheering for the Conover wives to save their houses, and Frank Niccolini, the chain-smoking bank attorney whom Jonah phoned continually!

"Ursula, can you believe the bank's lawyers are coming after *me* for the money and not Hobart! Me, a housewife with four little boys. Meanwhile, Hobart's still out driving his Porsche and jet-setting all over the country with his new girlfriend Pansy, and I'm being forced to file for bankruptcy. You know, when we went before Judge Tracy in the spring, he told me that *I* was going to have to adjust to a lower standard of living, but he didn't say a word to Hobe about adjusting his. Right in the courtroom, Tracy said, 'Mrs. Holliday, your cultural background is such that you feel you're entitled, but there are certain things you're going to have to learn to live without, and you're going to have to step down in your lifestyle.' Ursula, people just don't believe this unless they've been there like you have."

"I know. The moms in Conover have no idea how vulnerable they are. I'm starting to think that being a full-time nurturer of children is the most dangerous job in Massachusetts!" And I wasn't joking.

But I was marveling. For despite her unremitting travails, here was Julia hard at work simultaneously preparing five totally different entreés for five different clients – to bring in a little more income to support her boys. That she had to deliver them in two hours phased her not a whit, and my distracting presence wasn't slowing her down at all.

"Do you remember the old days," she said cheerily, "when Ethan and Amanda went to Mrs. Volt's nursery school together, and my biggest problem was who was going to explain how to get around Conover to the newest Italian au pair?"

"Tony used to help you out with that, didn't he?" I said, referring to the proprietor of Firenze Frames in Conover Center.

"Yes. I used to have him over here for seven-course dinners, while he translated all my instructions into Italian. So what's the latest for you? Dahlia Sutherland told me Reed was really steamed about the toy money and is probably taking you back to court."

"Word travels fast! Jonah and I are going to court – next week. Gabriel's filed a Motion for Reconsideration with Tracy about having to return the proceeds from the illegally sold stock options. We intend to tell Tracy that I need the money released so I can send it to Hub Safe Deposit & Trust to stave off foreclosure."

"How do you psych yourself up for court, Ursula? I can't bear to go over to that depressing place."

"Well, if you really want to know . . . I blast Cole Porter tunes all the way to Cambridge, and I sing at the top of my lungs! Of course, I write my own words."

"You don't."

"I do."

And so it was on the morning of June 25, that I found myself stuck in a traffic jam on Memorial Drive – SINGING! – between iterations of the Serenity Prayer, as the traffic thickened (something I could not change), and it looked as though I might be late to court.

And before I knew it, I had arrived at Cambridge Street. "Hi, Ursula!" greeted Toby and Steve, the attendants in the lot next to Jonah's, across the street from the courthouse. "How long today?" they asked cheerily, for they are getting to know me.

"You know how it is with court," I replied.

"Going up to see Jonah, first?" Then after me he called, "Hey Ursula, be sure to spell my name right in the book. Have ya got it?"

"Yes, I've got it! T-O-B-Y."

I can tell they like Jonah. I jogged up to his fourth floor, and he greeted me as is becoming his habit, "Hi . . . Are we going to win this morning?"

I grinned back at my "cognitive lawyer," as Jonah continued to refer to himself, and nodded vigorously, "Yes, we're going to win this morning!!!"

Minutes later, inside the courthouse, I saw a figure pacing with his back to us in the darkened hall fifty yards away. "There's Gabriel," I said to Jonah, who was dumbfounded because there was no way on earth to see who the figure was. He looked at me thoroughly baffled, and I said, "The reason I know it's Gabriel is that he walks like no one else."

"Are you sure?" said Jonah who followed me down the long hallway, and was amazed to see that it really was Gabriel. I didn't say this out loud, but Gabriel has a unique way of moving – he sort of lumbers along like a wise, old elephant. I would know that walk anywhere. And when he wears a grey suit as he was that morning, well, you can almost hear Gabriel's trumpet.

As I put out my hand, he whirled around and snarled coldly, "*I don't want to shake your hand!*" I was dumbfounded. "How dare you impugn my hon-ah?" he charged.

"*What* are you talking about?"

"How dare you impugn my hon-ah by writing to the Board of Bar Overseers!"

"Gabriel, I'll take full responsibility for that. It was my idea," said Jonah.

Then he started yelling at Jonah. "I'm even more angry at you than I am at her! You know that is the worst thing you can do to a lawyer," bellowed Reed.

But I didn't know. I really didn't know. Gabriel might not have conducted this case in an honorable way, but I'll never forget that he could have thrown me out the first day, and he didn't. I was still grateful for that.

I turned this over in my mind, as I heard Jonah reply, "Gabriel, you have no right to put a lien on her house, and you know it." Jonah was polite, but firm, about the lien business.

I didn't want to hurt Gabriel, even though I didn't think he'd done right by me as a client, and I hated hearing him roar at kind, good-hearted Jonah. The two lawyers continued to argue with each other, and I did my best to tune them out. I hoisted myself up into one of the high window enclaves, outside the first-floor courtrooms, and sat on the sill and immersed myself in Catlow's notes on electronic structure calculations in solids.

The week before, this eminent British scientist had visited Genesis, and we'd hatched plans about doing a Materials Design issue in the January '91 issue of *Molecular Modelling News*. Then, wanting to get even farther away from the moment, I started daydreaming about the speech I'd been invited to give in the Bavarian Alps in October, at the upcoming Elmau conference.

Gabriel continued to shout, and Jonah continued to insist in a courteous, firm, and quiet tone that Gabriel's behavior was unacceptable.

Jonah walked away first. "Ursula, is he always like that?!"

"It's just Gabriel's unusual way of saying 'Hello, I'm here!' Let me try to talk to him by myself. Give us a little time alone."

"That's fine with me. I'm going to go see about our meeting with Judge Tracy."

Jonah walked away, and from across the narrow corridor, Gabriel looked over at me out of the corner of his eye. "Gabriel . . ."

"You shouldn't talk to me without your lawyer present!"

He saw me stifle a laugh, as I rolled right over that. "Come on Gabriel, we're both smart people; let's figure it out."

The electronic structure calculations slipped from my lap to the floor, and Gabriel walked over to pick them up. I was still scrunched up on the window sill, which meant my knees were at about the level of his shoulders, and he had to look up to talk to me. "I'm not going to let a *little person* like you bring *me* down. And I am not amused by this toy money, Ursula. I have brought it in this satchel to show to Judge Tracy."

This struck me as simultaneously amusing and pathetic.

"I don't know anything about lawyers and courtrooms. Gabriel, nothing in my experience has prepared me for any of this. I just keep on listening to lawyers, and I just keep getting into more trouble; it doesn't matter who they are. And you are probably charging me for this morning."

"Jonah probably doesn't care if he ever gets paid."

"Oh, yes he does," I said, "and he will. It's not people like me who don't pay their bills; my dad always says it's the rich people who don't pay."

This struck a chord in Gabriel. "Your father's right," he agreed, and feeling himself softening, he got mad again.

"You know, my dad has been known to accept payment in strawberry preserves, or to wait a long time, and I think the way he and McCoy do business is pretty healthy, but I'm not going to tell you how to run your law practice." Then I tried another tack. "Well, did you at least like the book?"

"I didn't open it," he said in a hurt tone.

"Well then, give it back to me if you don't want it."

"*No!*"

"It's *Ferdinand*, and was written in the 1930s. Did you ever read it?"

"No . . ." he said and stormed away.

Then Jonah came back, and led me up to Tracy's chambers on the second floor, and left me to wait outside with Jimmie, Judge Tracy's Court Officer.

"Jimmie, does Judge Tracy have a good sense of humor?"

"Pretty good. Why?"

"Well, I played a little prank on Mr. Reed. You see, I sent him close to $9,000 of toy money for the value of the legal services rendered, and now he's brought it to Judge Tracy's chambers to . . ."

"You sent Reed toy money?" he laughed.

"Well, he earned it!" I said firmly.

"Tell me how you got McCoy for your lawyer." From Jimmie's tone, it was obvious that he thought highly of Jonah.

"Through my ministers," I replied.

"Ministers!" he said, waving his hand. "They're the worst kind of people."

I wasn't sure if he was joking, so I asked "What sort of people do you like, Jimmie?"

"Baseball players, especially Lou Gehrig."

This gave me an opportunity to say something about *Molecular Modelling News* and the research that some of my readers are doing on the disease that killed Jimmie's baseball hero, and how I try to spend my life on productive things.

Jimmie starting to ask me questions about molecules, when Jonah came out and said I had to come in. "But I'm talking to Jimmie," I protested, "about molecules!"

"Ursula, get in here!"

They seated me between Gabriel who was fuming, and Jonah who was relaxed, and across from Judge Tracy who was somewhat bemused.

"Mrs. Charbonnier, this has gotten entirely out of hand."

And I said, "You're right, Your Honor," because for once he was.

Then he said reporting Gabriel to the Board of Bar Overseers was the worst thing I could have done, like reporting a judge to . . . some similar group (I must get the name for Julia Holliday, sometime) . . . and that maybe sending the toy money was "a little unprofessional."

I had predetermined to nip that one in the bud, looked him squarely in the eye, and said, "Your Honor, it was simply a personal jest in keeping with our usual repartée. Mr. Reed and I have always had a great sense of humor with each other. I had no intention to offend Mr. Reed or this Court." And that was the end of that.

"My concern, Judge," I went on, "is that I haven't received from Reed much *value* for the legal services rendered."

"How much have you paid him already, Mrs. Charbonnier?"

"More than $13,000 Your Honor, and I think you will agree that I am in far worse legal and financial trouble than the day I walked in his door."

Tracy could relate to that simple statement. "Well, it's a little unusual for you to offer a lien on the sale of your house as payment for Mr. Reed . . ." (Jonah had suggested this tactic, and I slipped in that the house was being priced at a tremendous loss already), "but if you are willing to abide by the Fee Dispute Committee decision, then I think Mr. Reed should return all the money to you now so that you can send it to the bank. Is that all right with you, Mr. Reed?"

Mr. Reed was now thoroughly pissed off, and replied in a very quiet rumble of a grumble, "Yes."

Then, while we were sitting there, Jonah wrote up the order and I showed it to Reed, saying, "Is this okay with you?" and he waved me away like the dullard I was who didn't understand court procedure at all, and said, "We'll do this later. Outside."

"Oh," I said.

Then Judge Tracy walked across the room to dismiss us and looked directly at me and said, "I just want to wish you good luck."

I marched across the room, grabbed his hand and shook it and said fervently but jauntily, "Thank you, Your Honor. I could use some. You see, I haven't had any in such a very long time."

This registered with Tracy, whom Jonah assures me is our Judge forever for the duration of The Charbonnier Matter. I could see Jonah was thrilled. Outside of chambers, he said, "Do you realize you got everything you wanted?"

"Well, I'd expected the judge to agree with us, but I also expect Reed will delay in sending the money back to us. I'll catch up with you downstairs, Jonah. I want to say good-bye to Gabriel."

Then I walked over to Gabriel and reached for his hand, but he pulled it back. Then I reached for it again, just as another man walked by, and Gabriel grabbed him and said, "I'll buy you a cup of coffee."

Not to be deterred, I looked directly at the other fellow pushed him gently away, and said, "He'll buy you a cup of coffee in two minutes when he's done talking to me," whereupon the gentleman walked downstairs, leaving us alone, which displeased Gabriel enormously. Stuck with my presence for yet another minute, he fumed and sputtered about *Ferdinand,* which I was still suggesting he would enjoy reading. "In another time, in another place, if we weren't . . . I can't enjoy it now."

"Well, you will when you calm down!" I asserted. As we walked down the stairs together, the heavy satchel of toy money bumped between us. I followed him over to the coffee stand. "Be good to Eliza. I have sent you a gem. And *if* you behave yourself, this one just might last! Now I'm not leaving this courthouse until you give me a decent handshake."

"I already shook your hand," he said as he offered another limp, unacceptable one.

"*I want* – a real handshake!" Then he broke into a grin and grasped my hand firmly in the old way. *"Now that's – a real handshake!"* I nodded, patting him on the shoulder. "See you around!"

The fellow for whom he was buying coffee stopped me, *"Who are you?"* he demanded. I didn't answer him. *"You* are a total delight!"

"I am not a total delight – I am a total mess!"

"No, you are a total delight!"

It was obvious that we were not communicating. "Is Reed your lawyer?" he asked pointing to Gabriel.

"Well, he was my lawyer, but he's not my lawyer. He's my ex-lawyer, where's McCoy? Ohhh . . . it's complicated. My New Year's resolution was to get the liars, alcoholics, shrinks, bean-counters and lawyers out of my life, but so far I just can't seem to get rid of the lawyers."

"Lawyers and men, you mean!" he boomed. This made no sense.

"Who are you?" I asked him.

He grinned, "I'm a lawyer."

"I'm getting out of here. Where's McCoy?"

"Well, I don't know, but if he's waiting for you, he can't have gone far!"

I looked around and there was McCoy, waiting for me, pleased as punch at the way the morning had gone. Jonah later told me that when he was in court the next day, Jimmie had come up to him and asked about me, "Who was she? She was a really nice lady."

And Jonah said, "That was Ursula Charbonnier. She is a really nice lady, and she's fun to represent because . . ." What it boiled down to was my "keep going" attitude.

A few days later, Julia Holliday called with an uproariously funny and true story about what her boys – the little hellions – did to Cornwallis, Hobart's lawyer, when they were all out to dinner at Legal Sea Foods. Julia and the boys had only been seated for a moment, in a little alcove next to another family's table.

"The boys hadn't even had time to misbehave," she recounted, "when the man at the next table insisted on being moved. I looked up and it was Cornwallis, and we'd just been in court a few days earlier, when Tracy lectured me about lowering my living standard.

"Well, the waitress moved him, but after the meal, when I went up to pay the bill, the boys disappeared. They apparently descended on Cornwallis and his family and Ezra mooned him, and all four boys starting prancing around the table, shouting, 'You fucking asshole, we're losing our house because of you. You bastard!'

"Cornwallis begged for help. 'Waitress, waitress . . . help . . . help!' What do you think about that, Ursula?"

"I think . . . if it isn't fresh, it isn't legal!!!" I bantered, but inside I felt deeply troubled by this episode. What kind of a country were we turning into? And why did a grown man like Cornwallis feel no remorse whatsoever at the role he was playing in rendering four children homeless?

These thoughts were still swimming through my mind when I went back to see *g.a.l.* Gavin Roberts in Beaumont alone later in the month, and he scheduled another session with just me during the first week of July. Jonah says this is unusual, but I wasn't afraid.

I brought along a copy of the "Personal Narrative" and the installments that I wrote for Gabriel last fall. "Here," I said handing the sheaf of papers to Dr. Roberts. "This will help you understand exactly what happened to me and the children. I stopped sharing it with my lawyer once the court system got into it, but as you can see, I didn't stop writing about all that was happening to us. Writing about it is not only a release, but maybe a way to potentially help others who are living through the same kind of court-ordered insanity. I'm turning the narrative into a book when this whole thing is over; I'm calling it *Snow Job*."

This fascinated Roberts. "I'm going to read it," he said.

"Well, it's a page-turner, and that's my view of whatever they try to do to me next – it's just another chapter in *Snow Job*. That's what I tell Jonah."

"I love the title," said Gavin Roberts, and then I sat patiently while he explained it to me. "You know, Ursula, it works on so many different levels. Did you realize that 'snow' is a slang expression for 'cocaine'?"

"John Arthur loves the title too," I said. "It even works on a third level – one of my neighbors pronounces it *Snow Jobe* – (you know, long 'o') like the Biblical character." Then I elaborated on what I'd meant by "the integrity issue" when Roberts and I had met with Duncan the week before. I also told him that I intend to remain "clinical and matter of fact" in my dealings with my children. Then he said he wanted to know more about my assessment of their emotions at given times over the past year.

"I've told you before, I can't (and won't) speak for them about their feelings. You must get that directly from Spencer and Amanda, except insofar as I've noted their feelings to specific events in my narrative."

Roberts said he and John Arthur had a phone appointment for later in the morning, and I prayed that Arthur would be forthcoming this time – not the balanced, impartial good doctor because of fears of suit by Duncan. I knew it was important to Arthur to fulfill his physician-obligation to maintain the confidences of both his patients. As Asa's daughter, I understood that. But as Spencer and Amanda's mother, I wasn't always so in sympathy with his philosophy. This was one of those times.

As the month wound down, Ginny Bartlett, my high school French teacher, called several times to say I was in her prayers. Gabriel still hadn't sent back all the money, just part of it, but McCoy said he'll have to because Judge Tracy won't back down this time. But I knew Gabriel. When he saw something he liked, he hit it! At the end of June, my former attorney fired off a letter to me (typed by ep – namely, Eliza Pickering), saying that he was filing a "friendly suit" against me for the balance of the bill.

"Friendly suit!" Now there was an oxymoron if ever I heard one!

XXI

Bulldog Meets Tenacity

It is not, what a lawyer tells me I may do;
but what humanity, reason, and justice, tell me I ought to do.
— Edmund Burke,
Speech on Conciliation with America

By early July and after some legal maneuvering, Gabriel finally sent Jonah my portion of the proceeds from Duncan's illegally sold stock options. Gabriel wrote that it was to be held in escrow until I accepted service of his "friendly suit" against me in the Boston Municipal Court. The lesson was sinking in for me: when lawyers make all the rules, this sort of behavior is not only acceptable — it's legal!

For a woman who was only trying to get divorced with her home and her children intact, my legal life was getting more complicated by the week. "Jonah, I was just trying to get divorced from an alcoholic in denial. And now I have to deal with a foreclosure mess, a new lawsuit from Reed, and a Fee Dispute before the Boston Bar! How can this be happening to a plain old Conover wife, mom, and writer who has never lied, cheated, or stolen? I don't get it. If you'd been dealt my deck, what would you have done differently?"

"I've told you before Ursula, and I'll tell you again," said my patient and cognitive lawyer. "I would have done everything the same way you did, with the exception of not taking Reed's advice about not paying the mortgage. *That* is the only thing I fault you for. And though it doesn't seem like it to you now, I can assure you we are moving inexorably toward the divorce, toward an orderly climax."

"Where do I sign up for an orderly dénouement?" I replied. "And by the way, the Boston Bar hasn't responded to the letter I sent about initiating a Fee Dispute."

"Keep after them, Ursula. Eventually, they will respond."

In the meantime, Gabriel G. Reed had written to me that in view of my help in finding Eliza, he would be willing to knock several thousand dollars off my bill, equal to the amount of a "finder's fee." He also spoke to Jonah about it over the phone, saying "Offers of compromise should be respected."

So I wrote back to Gabriel, to point out the obvious: "The matter of a 'finder's fee' for Eliza is entirely unrelated to any fee dispute between us," because I hadn't done it for the money. "I did it because I thought you and Eliza would bring out the best in each other and be one whale of a good team. If all of this were up to me, you and I would forget any finder's fee, and any fee dispute, and both 'fold our tents' to borrow one of your favorite expressions. I'm not sure I know how to fold a tent, but maybe this would be a good time to learn." This left Gabriel G. Reed unmoved.

By mid-July, the Boston Bar's Fee Dispute Liason, attorney Wallis Lee, caught up with me by phone. The BBA's response to my letter had been lost in the mail because it was incompletely addressed, and she would send another. I told Wallis about Reed's filing a "friendly suit" against me in Boston Municipal Court, at which point she said the Bar, under such circumstances, wouldn't think of touching my case until the "friendly suit" was resolved!

In effect, Reed had done an end run on us: he had made the return of the escrowed money contingent upon resolving the Fee Dispute before the Boston Bar. Then he'd gone ahead and filed the suit in Municipal Court, knowing full well that the Muni Court action would result in the Bar's refusing to hear the Fee Dispute case.

After the brush-off I'd gotten from the Board of Bar Overseers about Reed's treatment of me, I was in no mood to have the same thing happen again with the Boston Bar. "Look, don't you have any honest people over there?" I asked Wallis Lee in total exasperation. "When this whole mess is behind me, I'm going to write a book that tells the whole world how law is practiced in Boston!"

"Well, if you're writing a book," said Wallis Lee, "I'm going to give you someone really special. You and Mr. Heyward Cutting are going to get along just fine."

She sounded sincere. Maybe there was someone honest over at the Boston Bar after all. McCoy couldn't be the only honest lawyer in Boston, and it was unfair to indict an entire profession based on the conduct of Sue Sage, Gabriel G. Reed, and Chubb MacIntyre. In our first phone conversation, I told Cutting that Jonah and I were concerned about the Bar's not hearing my case because of Reed's suit against me in Boston Municipal Court.

Totally undaunted, Heyward Cutting, without skipping a beat, replied, "That's no problem, Ursula. Simply have Jonah McCoy file a 'Motion to Stay Proceedings' in the Boston Municipal Court, until the Fee Dispute is concluded."

"That's an end run on Reed's end run! Brilliant." I told Jonah. "Now why didn't I think of that?"

"Ursula, I'm a lawyer. Why didn't *I* think of that?"

And by the third week of July, Jonah had filed the Stay, which meant Heyward and I could now proceed with the Fee Dispute. In our subsequent phone conversations, Heyward Cutting was consistently self-confident and reassuring: "Well, I'm your lawyer now, and I'm going to defend you." And, "You must never let anyone yell at you again."

When I told him about Reed's remark that he wasn't going to let a little person like me bring him down, Heyward Cutting laughed. "It doesn't matter if he's a big person and you're a little person, or if you're a little person and he's a big person — eat shit, Gabriel!"

I liked this man's attitude.

"Ursula, I'm going to be gone the month of August, but before I go, I want you to write two narratives for me: first, a 'What Happened' Narrative. I want to know everything that's happened to you, what brought you to Reed in the first place. Second, I want you to write a 'Life as Gabriel's Client' Narrative, the key events in your client-lawyer relationship. Can you do that?"

"Why yes, I know how to write narratives for lawyers!" I replied archly.

Wallis Lee was right. Heyward Cutting and I were going to get along beautifully. And from their several phone conversations about the Stay and the Fee Dispute, Jonah liked him, too. This was a good sign, but before I wrote my narratives for Cutting, I did some more checking around town, and without exception, the same word came up again and again to describe the man. And that word was "honest." Heyward Cutting did volunteer work with the Boston and Massachusetts Bars, to defend people like me, because he didn't like the negative impact that some lawyers' behavior was having on his profession. And neither did I. The lawyers I'd grown up with in Ohio were ethical, and so were the judges, who were elected by and accountable to the people. Most of them were horrified at what was happening to the children and me in the Massachusetts legal system.

So along with the narratives, I sent Heyward Cutting:

An Optional Memo:
Mrs. Charbonnier Blows Off Steam

Spencer, Amanda, their friends (they went public with all this when Judge Tracy ordered us to put our house up for sale) and I have learned a lot about the legal system. We are not the only Conover family in this boat. The Police Department knows who all of us are, and I occasionally get phone calls from townspeople who say, "I have a great scene for *Snow Job* for you," and then launch into another outrageous and true story about what happened in court or the attorney's office that day. I could tell you stories that are *much worse* than mine, and I intend to write about them, once I get a chance to come up for air.

And yet I know there are decent people in the legal profession. Jonah McCoy is one of them, and it seems to me that lawyers with high standards of ethical conduct would have an interest in getting things cleaned up. I refuse to accept that nothing can be done.

It has been a revelation to me the extent to which Duncan and people like him can (with malice aforethought) use the legal system as a weapon. I've been shocked to find that what I now call "the premeditated financial murder of a family" is not only legal, but the legal system "aids and abets it every step of the way." At least that has been our experience.

Several lawyers have also told me that as far as the Probate Court is concerned, "conduct is irrelevant." I'm telling you flat out that that is an illusion of the legal system. What if I reared my children with such low standards? If children walked into the family home and said, "I'm going to destroy you," would parents say, "Fine, go ahead, dear, conduct is irrelevant."? Yet the breadwinner in a family can walk in and say that, and it's okay. A whole generation of children and their nurturers, across this land, are becoming economically disenfranchised by the strokes of judges' pens, and our society is paying dearly for it. As I told McCoy, lawyers and judges will have to live in that world, too. And the social fallout from what the legal system is doing to families is going to be geometric.

In June, Chubb MacIntyre, who knows how I feel about all this, taunted me with this comment: "Ursula, I hear *you're* going to get the laws changed!" And I replied, "You haven't heard the last of me, Chubb!"

Because you work with the Boston and Massachusetts Bars, I'm hoping you'll know of some lawyers who are as outraged as I am by a system that takes houses from children and redistributes a hefty percentage of family assets to rapacious divorce lawyers. If you do know of any individuals who have the energy and vision to do something about all this, I'd like to team up with them. How about putting me in touch?

My cover memo to Heyward had begun: "I'd like to tell you the whole story, but I can't because it's way too long, so we're going to go with the 'expurgated version.' If you ever want to read the unexpurgated version, I'll give you a copy of *Snow Job* after it's published. Then again, maybe I'll turn this story into a 'soap' and call it 'All My Lawyers.' You're Number 4!"

It wasn't long before Heyward Cutting called back. "Do you know you gave me exactly what I wanted! The Narratives were perfect, and I loved the memo, 'Mrs. Charbonnier Blows Off Steam.' As for the toy money, anyone would have to think that was pretty funny. Clearly, we have a strong case against Reed. We'll meet to discuss all this when I get back in September, but I am concerned about one thing that can't wait. I want you to take Reed off your life insurance as beneficiary – and do it immediately, Ursula."

"All right. I'll do it today, Heyward. See you in September. And thanks."

While Number 4 was away, the nonsense continued to roll on. It had been a year since I'd discovered Duncan's locked-up vodka bottles, and as the first of The Twelve Steps put it, I was still powerless over alcohol, and my life continued to be unmanageable. For how many more months or years would the consequences of Duncan's drinking continue to affect the children's and my lives? Someone in Al-Anon told me to see "A Star is Born," the 1930s film about alcoholism. Near the end of the film, the grandmother tells her granddaughter, the widow of the alcoholic, "Tragedy, if we meet it when it comes to us, will leave us bigger than it found us." I'll, pardon the expression, drink to that.

Julia Holliday's troubles were also worsening. In addition to making sure she lost the house, Hobart was now intent on seeing to it that she lost custody of Ethan, Enoch, Evan, and Ezra. "I'm going to destroy you," he told her, "and The Law will help me do it!"

"Jesus, Ursula," she said to me on the phone one afternoon, "now he's using the same lines as Duncan! Can you believe this! A child custody suit. I'm having to get letters from the schools and our doctors, just like you did! And Hobart is also insisting on a *guardian ad litum*. My kids are so sick of this. They just want to have normal lives – go to soccer, go to school, play with their friends, and live in their house. Isn't there anything I can do to stop this insane process?"

"What about your new attorney, the famous Robert P. Rhana, the one who trained with Reed? What's he going to do about all this?" I asked. Julia had recently fired her first attorney, the infamous Sandy Straps, for her total ineptitude.

"Rhana's going to fight the child custody case – for another sixty grand, minimum. Now where, I ask you, am I going to get that kind of money? My family can't loan me much more, and all of this is having a terrible impact on my father's health. Five years of staying home making fucking organic baby food," said my friend the Conover caterer. "This is not my idea of a great return on investment."

"Nor would it have been Grandfather's," I said. "If my grandparents could see what Duncan's done to us after I turned over my whole inheritance to him for our first house, they'd die all over again. This man had no mortgage for years because of me, and do you know what he said? 'I owe you nothing for those years, because I paid your rent during the years you stayed home to take care of the children in our subsequent house!'

"Now, if in 1975, Duncan had said, 'Will you marry me; pay for two-thirds of our first house so that we'll have no mortgage for years (but don't tell anyone); give me all your time, money, love, and energy; bear my children; pay for the furniture and everyone's clothes; put your career on hold and manage our household for fifteen years; and, by the way I intend to terminate this arrangement when you're forty, at which time, you can pay for all your expenses and most of the children's out of your low salary – I am sure I would have said, 'No, actually Duncan, I think I can pass that one up!'"

Julia Holliday laughed. "Sometimes it's so hard to keep going, when all these irrational things keep happening, and there's no end in sight!"

"I know, but there's no other choice."

"But what do you when you feel powerless, when all of the lawyers and shrinks and paid enablers just keep getting richer, while you and your kids keep getting poorer?"

"I tell the truth and hope it will start to register with some of them. I make sure the *guardian ad litum* talks to the school guidance counselor, and that both of them talk to all the doctors. I figure that ups the odds that the truth will come out."

"But you know how good these guys are at ignoring the discrepancies, as long as there's a buck to be made."

"Maybe for awhile," I said. "But not forever. Duncan still thinks he's putting one over on Gavin Roberts, but he isn't. Roberts told David Madden that 'Custody is not an issue in the Charbonnier case.'"

"Just think what we are doing for Gross Domestic Product, Ursula!" she teased.

"Julia, *you and I* are America's leading experts on Gross Domestic Products!" And then I got off the phone, glad that we were both in good spirits again.

A few weeks later, I drove down to Providence for a weekend visit with Merrill Crosby, Lawyer Number 2B, and Camden, her husband the neurologist. We went to a lovely Art Fair in Wickford, had a delicious lobster dinner and a terrific tour of historic Providence. We also stayed up late into the night going over Duncan's symptoms and my legal case.

"You know," said Camden, "I think the ending of *Snow Job* ought to be that you go through all this hell with the legal system and the medical profession, and lose all this time and money, and in the end, years later, your diagnosis of TLE turns out to be the right one."

"Nice literary twist, Camden," I commented. "That's what Harry Ballard thinks really is the case."

Camden continued. "But it doesn't really matter if Duncan has TLE or a midlife crisis or a substance abuse problem. What you have to do now is look out for yourself and your kids."

That night, I went to sleep thinking about these new friends, the amazing pathway that had led me to them, and I wondered again at Emerson's message in "Compensation": "For everything you lose, you gain something."

One night the smoke/burglar alarm went off while I was baking cookies, and within minutes the police were at my door and neighbors, too. One of them said, "We want you to know that we are always watching out for you, since Duncan left, and the three of you are alone now." And there I stood, passing out cookies to the police and Inverary Lane crew. I thought of all the families who continued to include my children and drive them to activities now that we weren't able to afford childcare. And I thought of my neighbors, the Melroses, who continued to say, "call us at any hour of the day or night," and the Canfields, who had spent Easter afternoon trying to help me sort out my legal and financial troubles. Superficially my life looked like it had taken a turn for the worse, but on balance, I was an extraordinarily fortunate person – because I had friends.

And Eliza Pickering was one of them. On what would have been the thirtieth day of her employment, Gabriel G. Reed fired her in a very cowardly, cruel fashion.

It was time to renew my telephone acquaintance with Marietta over at Grant and Burgoyne. "This is Lady X, remember me?" She did. And in early August, it became official: Eliza was interviewed by Digby Grant and hired on the spot. Digby phoned Gabriel while Eliza was sitting right in his office, and Gabriel basically gave her a glowing reference and said he'd fired her because he, Gabriel, was "such a miserable person" to work for. "You know what an s.o.b. I can be, Digby!" In fact, Digby did know, because years ago he and Judge Beauzeau had worked for Reed and ended up suing him successfully when the partnership broke up.

At about this time, Amanda had her first appointment with Gavin

Roberts, and was very forthcoming about Duncan's behavior and our going to see Harry Ballard at Appleton Hall for help about the drinking problem.

"Your father says he's stopped drinking for almost a year. Don't you believe him, Amanda?" asked Roberts.

"Well, maybe he has and maybe he hasn't. I don't know. But I've been to Appleton Hall, and I've talked to Dr. Ballard, and I know there's more to recovery than just stopping drinking. If you really want to get well, you have to go get help for yourself." Out of the mouths of babes! And again, I had reason to be grateful for Ballard's candor.

Amanda reported that her one complaint about Roberts was that he kept trying to get her to say that she was upset about the divorce, and "on the fourth time, Mom, I finally decided to say that I was, just to get him off my back."

In a separate appointment, Duncan took Spencer to see Gavin Roberts.

"How did it go, Spencer?" I asked him that evening. "What did you think of Dr. Roberts?"

"Well Mom, to tell you the truth, I found him slow, and he asked a lot of dumb questions, like, 'Do you get along with your mother?' and he blinked a lot," at which point Spencer launched into a terrific imitation of Gavin Roberts that doubled us up in laughter at the dinner table.

Then Amanda chimed in, "So dear, would you like to tell me more about the sitch-uuuu-aaaa-shun?"

Without my court jesters, the entire *g.a.l.* process would have been unbearable. "How much longer is this nonsense going to go on?" I asked Jonah.

"I still see more footdragging by Duncan and Chubb," said Jonah, "but not much more. We must focus on saving the house and getting the divorce final this fall."

And on that note, a little later in August, Jonah and I drove downtown to see Richard Rapp at Hub Safe Deposit & Trust. Jonah had decided that *in person* we would deliver the check for the mortgage balance and the bank attorney's fees. We had come up with the money thanks to a loan from Asa and recovery of all the illegally sold stock option proceeds that Chubb had sent to Reed last spring. Jonah had really done the impossible: gotten money back from Reed, so that we could put it to the productive use of saving 1 Inverary Lane. He had already told Reed that he'd accept no legal fees from me until my mortgage was paid up.

"*You* are an amazing lawyer, Jonah," I marveled, as we pulled into a parking place in front of Hub Safe Deposit & Trust. "Could you imagine Gabriel G. Reed escorting me to Hub Safe to pay off a mortgage with money that could have been used to pay his legal fees? You realize, of course, that you are setting a very poor example for all the G-Reed-y lawyers in Boston," I teased.

Richard Rapp, the mortgage loan officer assigned to my case, knew we were coming and spent some time talking to us. "The Bank doesn't really want your house either, Mrs. Charbonnier." It was obvious he was a nice man, who didn't really want to put Spencer and Amanda and me out of our home. I looked at the pictures of his children in the space above his desk, and sensed that unlike Duncan, this man treasured life and his family.

"You know," I told him, "I'd never even paid a late charge on a credit card bill before all this happened to me. You can check my record, it's true."

"I believe you, Mrs. Charbonnier, otherwise we'd have never loaned you the money for your property. Hub Safe does very few mortgages. You have to have an impeccable credit record for us to even consider dealing with you."

"But what's a person supposed to do when the primary breadwinner decides he doesn't want to support his family anymore?"

"I don't have a good answer for that."

Later in the summer, I spoke with his associate, Steve Palmer, who told me, "Look, we don't like going after mothers and children for mortgage payments, but the courts don't give us much choice. In many cases, child support often doesn't even equal a family's mortgage payment. The courts are just passing the problem along to the banks."

"Can't the judges add?" I asked him.

"They go by a formula, and financial obligations like mortgage payments are not taken into account. They don't care if your mortgage is $1 a month or $10,000 a month. There is no linkage between a breadwinner's financial obligations and the support he or she, by law, owes his or her family."

"So families just slip through the cracks, is that it? And the bank and the nurturers of children are left holding the bag?"

"Look, even in cases where the breadwinners are ordered by the courts to pay the mortgage, they often don't, and the Massachusetts courts do nothing about enforcement. Hub Safe has to go after someone for the bad loan, so we have to go after the persons living in the house, and in most cases that means mothers and children. I don't like the system either."

"Would you be willing to be interviewed when I write more about this, after my case is over?"

"Yes. Absolutely. Come back and see me! And good luck to you, Mrs. Charbonnier. I'm personally cheering for you."

Richard Rapp was cheering for us too. He had started sending me "good luck" messages in the correspondence and faxes related to the mortgage mess.

Maybe Jonah was right about our proceeding toward an orderly climax. Now the mortgage was up-to-date, and for the first time in months, things were stabilizing at Genesis, and I was making great progress in raising money for my trip to Germany in October. Even though Paul Sudo had said the company wouldn't pay for my trip, on a lark, I'd said, "Well, what if I can raise the money?"

"Okay," he'd said, no doubt certain I could not.

But the second week of August, Jane Burns called from IBM's Paris office to say IBM Europe would back my trip to Elmau. I had now raised four times the amount needed for my trip, so it looked like I was going to get to go. Frank and Archie were thrilled (having never doubted I could do it), and Genesis was continuing to be one hundred percent understanding about all the time I was spending out of the office with lawyers and courtroom gymnastics and the *guardian ad litum* and other assorted legal maneuvers designed to wear me down.

With my company, my town, and my children behind me, I couldn't fail, I told myself in the darkest moments of doubt. And then, in the moments when I felt stronger, I would say to Jonah, "Someone ought to tell Chubb MacIntyre he's picking on the wrong woman. Ms. Tenacity has no intention of giving up, because I know what I'm fighting for − my home and my children's world!"

Heyward Cutting returned just after Labor Day, and called to set up an appointment for us to discuss our case and talk strategy. "Well, if you are an early riser . . ." I was going to offer a breakfast meeting since we were both busy people.

"I'm not," he interrupted. "I'm in a lot of carpools, and I don't know which one I'm going to draw that day. Ten is the earliest we could meet."

I am typically not crazy about people who like to start work in the middle of the day, but for participating parents, I am always glad to make exceptions. "How wonderful that you drive your children in the mornings," I told him, "Duncan used do that, and I loved it, the way that he was so involved with the children."

"Well, I don't want to end up like him," said Heyward Cutting.

"You won't, Heyward," I reassured. "I think very few people do. Now when and where do you want to meet?"

"How's the fourteenth? And I want us to meet someplace private."

"The fourteenth is fine, but why can't we meet in a restaurant?"

"We can't meet in a restaurant, or any public place, because we are going to say very nasty things about very nasty people. We clearly have a malpractice case. And I want to be sure no one overhears us."

To me this seemed unduly cautious, but as Heyward lived in Brandon, a town adjacent to Conover, it seemed reasonable that we meet at my house, so I invited him over for morning coffee.

On September 14, in the late morning, Heyward Cutting appeared at Inverary Lane. He was not what I expected. Paul Bunyan was the first thing I thought of, because he reminded me more of a lumberjack than an attorney. "Don't trip over the cords," I cautioned him, referring to the cables that lay in tangles across our terra cotta floor. "They're a lawsuit waiting to happen!"

A tall blond-bearded man with thick glasses and narrow shoulders, Heyward Cutting strode right in, said yes to coffee, made himself at home, and got straight down to business, mincing no words. "I'm informal; I'm direct," he began. "I'm going to say nasty things." It was a reprise of our recent phone conversation.

"Well, there isn't much an editor doesn't hear in the course of a day," I said. "Nothing you say will bother me."

"Let's begin by talking about those Fee Agreements you feel might obligate you to owing Reed thousands of dollars beyond what he originally estimated. I want you to know that I spent three years writing the language in those Fee Agreements, and I argued over every word. It's my language. I made it and I can break it. This is going to be fun."

"I don't know how you can say that. Nothing about this Fee Dispute is 'fun.'"

"From your position, I can understand why that's true. Maybe you and I have a very different idea of fun. I'll tell you right at the outset that I'm just like a bulldog," he continued. "Once I get my hands on something, I never let go of it!"

I sensed he enjoyed words and language as much as I did. "In that case, Wallis Lee was right. You and I *are* going to get along just fine. You see, my nickname is Tenacity! And I like the idea of your being a 'bulldog' because the concept works on at least three levels."

"What are you talking about?" he asked.

"Once you get your hands on something, you never let go of it, just like a bulldog. Did you know that in British slang, the word 'bulldog' means the enforcer, and you are trying to enforce the rules, in this case."

For a flash his face transformed into pure pleasure, in recognition of how he saw himself and wanted to be seen by others. This man was probably dynamite in a courtroom, most in his element when he was saving or avenging.

"And," I continued, "the bulldog's claim to fame is being a rat catcher."

"I didn't know that."

"Well, it is, and I think you will agree that we have some very big rats to catch in this case. From what I hear, you're a very good rat catcher."

"Who told you that?"

"I don't have to say, but after what I've been through with attorneys, I wasn't about to talk with you until I had you checked out." I wasn't mincing my words either.

"What did you learn?" he probed.

"I don't have to tell you."

"I want to know."

"You can't cross-examine me, but I will tell you this: if someone had said those things about me, I should be proud *and* pleased."

At which point Heyward relaxed.

"Let's talk about the fees. I see the more than $2,000 of errors you pointed out, and I agree with you about the thousands of dollars for note-takers and other questionable charges . . ." he began.

"And why," I interrupted, "does Reed charge a minimum of .2 hours for phone calls, even if they only lasted one minute?"

"Well, that's customary," said Cutting. "After all, it takes five minutes to think about the client's case, and a few minutes for the phone call, and another five minutes to get back into whatever you were doing before the phone call came, so that's .2 hours."

"That's sheer laziness," I said firmly. "It doesn't take me .2 hours to deal with every phone call I get in the course of a day. I can flip in and out of conversations and activities a lot more rapidly than that."

"Well then, you're highly unusual," he said. "Ursula, do you think you'd be able to take all these bills and arrange them in some kind of a table for me by date, by person, and by activity – such as Preparation of Facts, etc.?"

"You mean, like a sort of Fee Matrix?"

"Yes, exactly. Could you do that? It would be very compelling to show something like that in a Fee Dispute. It would be very effective."

"Sure. It will take some time, but I'll do it for you this weekend. With a computer, it will be easy."

"Now tell me more about your relationship with Reed," said Cutting. "Did the two of you get along?"

I grinned, recalling some of the repartée. "Reed likes to spar, and I know how to spar back. I can hold my own with Reed."

"But did he make you cry? I want to know if he ever made you cry?"

I couldn't imagine why that would even matter, but I answered. "A few times, but I never cried in front of him. I always waited 'til I got outside and back to my car. It was the irrationality of it all that got to me. And the unjustness." Which made me stop and wonder what this man was doing here, when he might have been back in his office racking up $500 an hour. "Why do you do volunteer work for the Bar?" I asked, suddenly.

"Because a lot of people need a lawyer, to defend themselves against lawyers, and the behavior of some lawyers is having a very negative impact on the whole profession. Also, I became a lawyer because I couldn't afford one."

"Before all this happened to me, Heyward, I didn't know there were lawyers like MacIntyre and Reed and Ringling & Haycroft, taking advantage of people in situations like mine. I grew up watching Perry Mason, and assumed most lawyers had high standards of ethical conduct. Anyway, it's occurred to me that most of the scientists I write for are as ignorant and naïve about lawyers and the law as I was, so I'm planning to do a series on intellectual property in *Molecular Modelling News* next year. I don't want what happened to me and my children to happen to my industry. Do you know any lawyers who might want to write for it?"

He suggested some Boston and Massachusetts Bar leads, then getting back to the Fee Dispute, I asked, "How long 'til we can get this resolved? I'm trying to get the liars, alcoholics, shrinks, bean-counters, and lawyers out of my life before the year ends! And I'm trying to get divorced, and I still have to get psychiatrically evaluated, and in the middle of all that, I'm supposed to go to Germany to give a speech about *Molecular Modelling News!* What do I do now, God?"

"You go to Germany, and you give a great speech! Look, it's going to take some time to get a panel convened before the Bar. And some people might not want to serve on it because it's a case involving Reed."

"But Reed said this had to be done forthwith, otherwise the Stay of Proceedings in Muni Court is off."

"Reed has nothing to say about this. The Bar will do this as soon as it can, so you can stop worrying about Reed. Send me the Fee Matrix next week, and we'll go from there."

It was time to say good-bye. "Things couldn't be much worse for you," he said, walking out to the car.

"Oh, yes they could, Heyward. I could be sick or . . ."

"How can you still smile?" he interrupted.

"Because it hurts more if I don't."

"How did it go?" Jonah asked later that day.

"Number 4 is a piece of work!" I replied. "Heyward Cutting thinks we have a strong case against Reed, and so do I."

XXII

Marathon Mode

Like an unbodied joy whose race is just begun.
– Percy Bysshe Shelley, *To a Skylark*

On September 17, I was back in court to fight for the very roof over our heads. Although the mortgage arrearage had been paid in full and Jonah said that Caroline could remove the "For Sale" sign, Duncan was insisting that Inverary Lane remain on the market. He wanted the house sold so that he could get his assets out of it immediately. But to Spencer and Amanda, he was telling a very different story.

"Dad, can't you get the house off the market for us, since Mom has paid the mortgage? Can't you just say the house is off the market?"

"No, I can't do that. The judge won't let me. The judge is the one who decides," said Duncan, who was now trying to pin the rap on Tracy.

Which meant I was going to spend hundreds more on court that morning so that the judge could officially "decide." When I got up to his fourth-floor office that morning, Jonah greeted me with his now classic opening line. "Well, Ursula," he asked in a rousing voice, "are we going to win today?!"

"Yes, we're going to win today!" I said waving my fist in the air, "because if we don't, I will never be able to go home and look my children in the eye again!"

Minutes later, Jonah and I were seated in Tracy's courtroom. "Don't look now, but here they come," I said to Jonah. "Chubb MacIntyre has grown fat off the vices of the day," I added irreverently.

"Ursula, maybe he can't help it if he has a fat body," said Jonah.

"Jonah, I wasn't speaking about his body. I was speaking of his bank account. The plain fact is Boston judges and lawyers can make more money from destroying the lives of innocent moms and children than they can from going after real criminals! I repeat, Chubb MacIntyre has grown fat off the vices of the day."

"God bless this Commonwealth and this Honorable Court!" called an officer, opening the morning session. Well someone has to – I thought to myself.

As we waited our turn, I studied the parade of frightened and despairing citizens ahead of us, and I studied Tracy. Intently. When you go into a courtroom, it isn't enough to bring your brain. You must be like an animal in the forest, listening for the unexpected and watching for your opening, for a chance to take possession of your moment and run with it. "The cardinal rule of communication," I said to Jonah, is "Know Thy Audience!'"

"The Charbonnier Matter . . ." someone said, and Jonah nudged me. It was our turn to step forward.

Wasting no time, Tracy started in about the children as soon as Chubb said they weren't spending enough time with Duncan. This was typical courtroom shenanigans from my perspective, and it never failed to amaze me: in one breath Chubb and the judge would feign concern about the well-being of Spencer and Amanda, painting Duncan as a concerned father, and in the next Chubb would argue that the children should lose Inverary Lane, because Duncan wanted his equity out of the house now. Chubb saw no inconsistency in this, and neither did the judge.

"My children are thriving by any standard," I told Tracy in a firm, clear voice. And I had my letters from John Arthur and Mary Frances, plus the top-notch grade cards to prove it, which I handed to the judge. "As for Duncan's seeing the children," I said, "he can have them on any and every holiday – and he knows it!"

"Is that true, Mr. Charbonnier?" asked Judge Tracy.

"Yes," agreed Duncan.

Chubb was not happy at the speed, content, and tone of his client's response and quickly shifted the subject to keeping the house on the market.

"Your Honor, she doesn't make very much money," he said, "and no bank is going to loan her the funds to pay off this mortgage. She says her father is out of the loop. So, how is she going to raise the money to buy this house? We want to know her plan."

"What is your plan, Mrs. Charbonnier?" asked Judge Tracy.

Jonah started to answer for me, not very effectively, and Chubb smiled, coming in for the kill. "We want to hear her plan, directly from her," crooned MacIntyre, all but inviting Tracy to interrupt Jonah.

"Jonah," broke in the judge, "Mrs. Charbonnier is a nice, smart lady. We want to hear it from her. How do you intend to raise the money? We want to know your plan today, right now." Tracy peered down at me over the tops of his glasses, and Duncan and Chubb smiled smugly, sniffing victory before I could even respond. Jonah was silent and probably hoping for a miracle.

Oh God, what do I say now? I wondered silently. And then the words came, and I knew exactly what to do. I stood tall, head held high, jutted out my chin, looked Tracy squarely in the eye, and after a suitable moment of silence, I said in my best Katharine Hepburn voice, "Your Honor, I can't look you in the eye today and honestly give you an answer to that question, but I can tell you this: in Al-Anon, we learn to live one day at a time, and *that's* the way I'm living these days!"

A hush fell over the proceedings. We had just punctured Chubb MacIntyre's balloon.

"That's a good way to live, Mrs. Charbonnier," said Judge Tracy, immediately picking up on my allusion to Al-Anon. "I think we'll give you a little surcease and take that house off the market!"

The first thing I felt was Jonah's elbow in my ribs, and under his breath he was ordering, "Don't smile, Ursula. Not one smile until we get out of this courthouse and back in my office." I struggled to compose my face into a very serious expression, and forced myself to say not a word.

Five minutes later, safely back in Jonah's office, I let out a whoop and gave him a big hug, "I love my lawyer!" I exclaimed. "Now I can go home and look my children in the eye!"

"My God, you have such presence in a courtroom!" I heard him say. It occurred to me how much Gabriel would have enjoyed the moment, and I found myself wishing he had been in court for it. Would Chubb tell him, I wondered. Probably not. Lawyers don't talk about losing, even to a common enemy. Especially to a common enemy.

"Now can I go home and pull that 'For Sale' sign out of the ground?"

"Yes, Ursula!"

I took a break from Genesis in the midafternoon, so that the children and some of their friends could help me uproot the Century 21 sign, and we took a spectacular photo of Amanda grimacing in front of the sign with Streak Louise in her arms. In my mind, the caption on that shining September day will forever be, "We almost lost our house, but we found our community." Neighbors and parents who cared about children savored the victory with us. More than one person, expressed a "there but for you, go I" feeling about what had happened to the children and me.

Then I scooted back to work. It was getting to the point where I was only at Genesis in my "spare time," when I wasn't in court, or seeing attorneys, or getting appraisals, or taking care of the children. Archie McGowan and Paul Sudo said you couldn't tell it by my work. Somehow, *Molecular Modelling News* kept getting longer and better and more complex. I had no idea how all the work was getting done, but somehow it was. Wonderful unsolicited articles were trickling in from all over the world. And unexpected phone calls came, offering scoops for publication.

On my way back from work that day, the gates came down and I heard the whistle blow as the B & M passed through Hastings Green. When the gates lifted and the train pulled away, there on the other side of the tracks capsuled in a ray of late afternoon sunshine stood Jonah McCoy. Caught by the amazing, magical coincidence of the moment, I tooted the horn and waved at my cognitive lawyer. "Great day in court!" I called to him, as the other commuters turned to look at us.

"Stop right there!" he called back, and ambled over to reminisce about the glory of the morning.

"Guess where I'm headed?" I smiled. "On my way to Julia Holliday's to plan the *Dramatis Personae* dinner party menu. Dad arrives in two weeks, and we intend to throw a great party in his honor. He's looking forward to meeting the cast!"

When I arrived at Pigeon Place, the kitchen was teeming with pots, pans, and cuisine in varying stages of preparation.

"I can't believe you are in as much trouble as I am, and you can still cook so elaborately – and make it look easy," I marveled.

"Look, it's no different than your going to work every day. Writing about molecules relaxes you, and cooking for dinner parties relaxes me. It's my therapy. Now, I really can't decide which recipe to use for the coulibiac," she said, plunging into the work before us. "And I don't know how far ahead we can make it, and all my consultants are out of town, and there's no one to call."

Struggling to match my friend in spirit, I suggested we call up Julia Child. "After all, she lives in the Boston area, too!" I said.

"You can't just call up Julia Child," she protested. "Who do you think you are?"

"When you're used to talking to Nobel Laureates all day, calling up Julia Child is a piece of cake!" I bantered, dialing directory assistance for her number.

Moments later, her voice said hello from the other end of the line.

"Hello, is this Julia?" I asked.

"No, this is Stephanie," said the voice.

"Well, Stephanie, we have a cooking question, and wondered if you might help us . . ." And in due course, all of our coulibiac questions were answered.

Then Julia Holliday launched into her latest travails with home and the legal system. "It's a good thing you weren't here yesterday. The septic system backed up. We had shit coming out of every orifice of this house. It isn't enough that Hobart is trying to destroy us, driving around town in his Porsche with Pansy, jet-setting all over creation, and Enoch and Evan are back in the hospital. Now the house is acting out!

"And on the lawyer front, here's the latest from Robert P. Rhana. He's no longer representing me. You want to know what he said to me, Ursula? 'Honey, I thought you had a pot of gold, but I guess I was mistaken. You can't afford me. I'm off this case!' That's after $25,000 and I'm still not getting any child support – me, a mom with four little boys!"

"Well don't even bother with the Board of Bar Overseers, Julia," I said. "I can assure you that they won't be sympathetic."

"I already know that. My new lawyer told me."

"Your new lawyer. You move fast. Who's your new lawyer?"

"Jeannie Curtin. She ran into Rhana in court yesterday, and she said, 'Bob, how much are you earning today?' and he replied that he was 'getting 60K for a five-day trial.' And Jeannie said, 'I'm ashamed to share the same profession with you. How can you do this to people?' and he said 'Jeannie, it's just a numbers game. Get with it.' 'It's not just numbers,' she said, 'it's people and children. It's real lives, Rob.'"

"I don't think it registered, Julia."

Asa arrived the last week of September, just after I put the October issue of *Molecular Modelling News* to bed. For three days, we forgot about courtrooms, and alcoholics, and irrationality, and I showed him my world. At Genesis Labs, the scientists demoed our modelling software for him, and showed him how to dock one molecule with another in the effort to design new drugs. For an internist who remembered practicing medicine in the pre-penicillin era, it was a thrill. "This is very exciting, but it's beyond me," said Asa.

"It is exciting," agreed the scientist, "and we have Ursula to help us tell the whole world about it."

Then I introduced him to Archie McGowan, who had been like an in-house father at Genesis, during all I had been through over the past two years. "She has been a shining example to all of us," McGowan told Asa. "She continues to keep going and do good work, no matter what is going on around her. I'm sorry I can't be with you at dinner tomorrow night, but by coincidence, I'm attending my son's wedding in your hometown. In fact, I'm headed to the airport right now."

While we were at Genesis, I got a return call from Dahlia Sutherland, the psychiatrist that Chubb had selected to evaluate me. We'd been having trouble coordinating schedules. The only time she could see me was in late morning, which meant my losing half a day of work, and I couldn't afford to lose any more time away from the job. Early mornings and late afternoons were unacceptable times to meet, she told me. As Asa sat next to my desk, she canceled yet another appointment we'd arranged, and informed me her *only* free time to meet with me in October would be just before I was to leave for Germany. At that point I ran out of patience and "lost it" on the phone.

"Look, I can't waste any more time with court-appointed psychiatrists and *guardians ad litum* . . . and running around getting letters from my doctor and employer and the schools saying that my children and I are normal, fully functioning people. I've had enough! I'm not the alcoholic who's been hiding vodka bottles in my glove box, and running around faking epileptic seizures, and having unnecessary CTs and EEGs with four neurologists for the past four years. *I* am just a plain old Conover mom who wants to rear my children, get up and go to work every day, and get on with my life. I'm not putting up with any more of this nonsense. And

I'm not wasting any more of my time or my company's time with people like you. Is that clear? And furthermore, I am too well to come!" Asa just shook his head.

Then I immediately phoned my cognitive lawyer. "Jonah, don't get mad at me," I began, "but I just blew up at the court-appointed shrink!"

Jonah McCoy laughed. "Good Ursula, that just shows how healthy you are!"

"Then you're not mad at me?" I said. This was hard to believe, even from mellow Jonah McCoy.

"No, I'm not mad at you. Now when am I going to get to meet your pop? I want to meet your pop!" It was the third time he had asked. "I can't make it to your dinner party tomorrow night, but could I bike over in the morning after my Finance Committee meeting at the Town Hall?"

And that was how Jonah McCoy and Asa came to be seated on my patio the following day, sipping pink lemonade in the sunshine, chatting about life, and reflecting on the current messy state of my legal affairs. In the midst of it all, Celia Blaine, the wife of my UK Editor, phoned from England.

An antiquarian librarian, she had just located several more rare books we'd been trying to find as a thank-you gift for Heyward Cutting. The Boston Bar might not let me pay him for helping me out of my mess with Reed, but Celia and I were determined to find a series of books he'd mentioned he wanted. "I would gladly pay $100 a book," he'd said in reference to them, on the morning he'd come by for coffee. But once our case was over, he was going to get as many as we could find "on the house," (and I meant that literally, because I felt certain Heyward Cutting was going to be successful in getting the lien taken off 1 Inverary Lane). The particular books he wanted were hard to find in America because the author was British, and circa World War I.

"Celia just found three more *Bulldog Drummond* books in England for Number 4!" I announced triumphantly to Jonah as I returned to the patio. Asa had lost track of "All My Lawyers," but Jonah was enjoying all the humor we could extract from my otherwise very serious situation, and he had been following the book search with as much delight as my treks to toy stores for Reed's monopoly money.

That night at the party, 1 Inverary Lane glowed with the warmth of many friendships, some of which had been forged only because of my horrendous legal and financial mess. "For everything we lose, we gain something," Emerson played in my head throughout the evening, as I introduced Asa to our guests. The little stone cottage, so recently snatched from the foreclosing jaws of Hub Safe and the equity-extracting hands of Duncan and Chubb, glowed like a gem in the autumn night. I had gone out to the garage to get more wine, and from across the lawn, the lights I'd been advised not to install shone softly in every room. All the red and yellow hibiscus were in bloom beneath the stained-glass windows in the den, as if to say they liked this spot too. And I could see Amanda moving among the guests with hors d'oeuvres that the Melroses had brought.

Jeff and Jackie Melrose stood before the windows, chatting with Merrill Crosby, Lawyer Number 2B. That evening, Asa renewed his acquaintance with Kathy Molloy, whom he hadn't seen since our grad school days, nearly twenty years before, and he got to meet Kevin. He spent some time with Caroline O'Malley, who had come with Ted Talbot and Bud, who was now almost totally mended from the Abbott Road accident of the autumn before.

Elise and David Madden were with us, and David spent some time comparing notes with Asa and Camden Crosby about the overlapping symptoms of alcoholism and temporal lobe epilepsy. Asa liked David Madden, later describing him as "a centered shrink, something one seldom finds."

Eliza Pickering also spent some time with Asa and assured him she would take good care of Spencer and Amanda when I went to Germany the following month; and she and Shea Phillips regaled him with Genesis Lab stories. Trudy Hale made an exception and came to the party even though she was still preparing her sermon for the following morning. Matthew was performing a wedding ceremony on Nantucket, but we would see him the next day at First Parish. Trudy and my father chatted about pastoral care in hospitals, a subject near and dear to Asa's heart, and his wish for a fund the Sisters had established in his name at St. Anselms's back in Ainstree. Julia Holliday, intrepid Conover caterer, ran roughshod over the kitchen, and made dinner for thirty-something look easy. The coulibiac – her first – was a success, thanks to consulting input from Stephanie Child. Asa returned home, with a stronger sense of my world and all I was fighting for.

October began the following Monday, and Jonah and I were to be in crash mode for the rest of the autumn. "You are going to have a very busy fall," he said with characteristic understatement.

"Really?" I responded, bemused. "Jonah, I would kill for a backrub and a nap. I am starting to run out of gas!"

"Well, I can't help you with either one, and you're not allowed to run out of gas, because we're not done yet."

Two nights before I was scheduled to fly to Germany, I was still at the office, late, writing my speech. There hadn't been a spare minute to work on it in the previous two weeks. Paul Sudo was working late too. At ten o'clock, he came out of his office and looked over some of the transparencies I was planning to use in my presentation. I apologized for writing it at the eleventh hour, and that it would have no time for internal review. "It's okay," he said leafing through the materials. "Hey, Ursula, this is good." I was getting used to and getting better at doing *everything* on the fly. But I still didn't like it.

At last, the speech was done, but I was too keyed up to go home, so I stayed a little longer after Paul left and cleaned out my Rolodex. Nearly everything in my life was out of control, but I could damn well keep my closets, and my files, and even my Rolodex in order. I was rapidly sorting cards into "keep" and "cut" and "change address" piles until I came to a card under R: Ian Ruddway. I took it out to throw it away. I hadn't seen him since 1983, and then only briefly over a breakfast at the St. Regis in New York with my chickenpoxed children! My hand froze over the wastebasket. Ahhh, what the heck, I'll keep it, I said to myself, putting the card back in the Rolodex.

The following Sunday, at four o'clock in the morning, I was sitting in the quiet Paris airport, waiting for my connecting flight to Munich and reflecting on the joy of putting as many miles as possible between me and the Boston legal system. For a week, I would be with rational scientists and away from telephones and fax machines, and motions, and filings, and courtrooms. And so why, I asked myself, was I thinking of a lawyer?

Not one of my Boston lawyers, but the lawyer I had loved in the years before I'd met Duncan. The missing lines to a poem I had never given him suddenly and inexplicably threaded like tape through my head. The poem had been missing from my writing files for many years, and when I'd tried to reconstruct it, several lines had remained lost to me. The other twenty-five lines had been intact.

Now the missing pieces played for me: ". . . Chase me into a cold, black night, and then take away the cold. Lure my heart into your labyrinth, play with my spirit on your endless paths, 'til I am lost beyond limit, under the moon's eye . . ." I grabbed a pencil, quickly scribbled the words into my Filofax, thought no more of it, and boarded the plane to Munich, where Phil Vines, a computational chemist, was to meet me. We would motor on to Schloss Elmau.

John Stevens, the *Molecular Modelling News* editor based in Stuttgart, and an Elmau organizer, had predicted the week ahead would delight me in a way nothing ever had before, and he was right.

The Schloss was a yellow stucco castle set in the heart of the Bavarian Alps, not far from Garmisch-Partenkirchen. The days were unusually warm for mid-October, the nights cool and the leaves in the forest were turning. The scientists were on my time clock: rise very early, work hard all morning, play in the afternoon, work hard late into the night, party and then sleep briefly. I was in heaven. Nobody here thought I was overly energetic or intense. I met many people who'd been phone friends since 1985. It was a week of camaraderie and laughter and leading-edge science.

The Schloss was built in a rectangle with a central courtyard, and my cozy room looked over it and beyond into the mountains. I would later learn that the family who built the Schloss and owned it through most of this century had a son who had been married to a close friend of the Production Manager for *Molecular Modelling News*. The family had managed to hang onto the Schloss even through the war years.

There were many staircases and many passageways, at once charming and confusing, and it was easy to lose one's way initially. Hundreds of scientists were in attendance, and we had taken over the entire castle for the week. Three times each day we shared meals in a large dining hall, family style, at tables of ten, and we gathered for lectures in the grand ballroom on the first floor. Twice each day – in midmorning and mid-afternoon – we would break for coffee on the terrace below that over-looked the mountains. Following afternoon coffee, we would head off for walks on the mountain trails, or go off in small groups for excursions in the surrounding countryside. Each evening before dinner, we gathered in the cozy wood-paneled bar to discuss the science presented that day and where our afternoons had taken us.

One afternoon, I got lost in the woods with Ross Eden, a Cray Research scientist, and was actually able to understand part of the answer from a stranger Ross and I met, when I asked in my rudimentary German, "Wo ist Schloss Elmau?" This, after only three days of doing Berlitz in the car in the week before I'd left Boston. Other afternoons would take us to nearby castles or to shops in Garmisch-Partenkirchen.

At Elmau, it was customary to dress for dinner in the evenings, after which we would head to poster sessions and coffee in the lounge by the terrace, and meander through the exhibits, where hardware and software vendors had come to show their wares. One evening, I had coffee with Jack Cooke, the President of a Genesis competitor, and we chatted about patenting software, an issue both of us felt loomed on the horizon. But it was early. A lot of people in our industry weren't worrying about this yet, and they would soon be caught sleeping, we both felt. I told him of my desire to do a series on intellectual property law in *Molecular Modelling News,* and he encouraged me to proceed.

And so our days at Elmau passed. My speech was on Monday, the first full day of the meeting, and I would moderate a hardware panel discussion the following day. I had never done any of this before, and to my delight, it all came easily. More than that, it was fun! I could do this forever, I thought, if only someone would let me.

On the third day, just after the hardware session, a fellow from Concave Computers, one of the vendors that sponsored my trip, offered to take me to Italy for dinner. "Great," I said, "I've never been to Italy."

"Well, it's the German part of Italy," he explained, "no one speaks Italian and they don't use lira. And it is very beautiful. It's more like Germany, except that the town where I am going to take you has flowers and fountains and palm trees."

Right – palm trees in the middle of October! But I went, thinking it would be fun. There was a strike by truckers near Innsbruck, so we would have to take the beautiful backroads.

This would lengthen our journey, but there was much to talk about: advances in molecular modelling, life in Boston and Frankfurt, the joys of parenting – we had a total of four children. And the time passed pleasantly. Then about three-quarters of an hour out of Bavaria, high somewhere in the Austrian Tyrol, the executive from Concave Computers suddenly announced, "My wife thinks I'm an alcoholic."

Oh my God, I thought, how am I going to explain my death? I surveyed the deep caverns below us, and the darkening skies not so far above us, and the little signs every few kilometers that said, "KEHRE."

It seemed best to remain calm as we climbed ever higher on the one-lane twisting roads, even though not all four wheels of the car were always on the road, when we negotiated the tight turns. For a moment, I transported myself back to the Tuesday night Al-Anon meetings in Westbury: "God, grant me the serenity to accept the things I cannot change, the courage to change the things I can, and the wisdom to know the difference." The present moment definitely called for serenity. I could panic, or I could sit back and enjoy the view. If I died, I'd never get to tell anyone how much fun I was having, and if I lived, I wanted it to be a good memory.

"Rudy, what does 'kehre' mean?" I asked.

"Oh it's these tight, winding curves. We call them hairpin turns in German."

"Oh," I said, "that's what we call them in English too. Why does your wife think you're an alcoholic?" I ventured.

And after I listened to him for awhile, and realized that even the oncoming darkness wasn't slowing his speed, I decided to tell him my story, which did slow him down, but only a little.

The trip to Merano took about twice as long as I had thought, but the evening was worth it. Indeed, there were flowers, and fountains, and palm trees, high up in these mountains, and the air did smell of summer. We traversed the hilly streets, paused in the various shops still open late into the evening, and stopped for dinner in a quiet restaurant that Rudy had remembered from another visit. My gracious guide, who in fact did take his designated driver position seriously, had only one glass of wine with dinner, and the Coca-Colas, which followed totally infuriated the Italians. Then we went home the long way on two-lane roads, and got back to the Schloss in time to disco until 2 a.m.

The next day I had a different sort of adventure. In the afternoon, when it was time for play, John Stevens arranged for a cogwheel train to take a group of us to the top of the Zugspitze for lunch. This was the highest point in Germany, but you have to go to Austria to get there. We were standing out on the lawn of the Schloss, gathering for rides to the train station in Garmisch, when I literally bumped into a tall man with a beard.

He was Rob Richardson, the famous crystallographer, and co-author of the Richardson and Rice classic, *How Proteins Work* – the very book Gary Sabin had loaned me back in 1985, the summer that we went to Switzerland. It had been the first book I read as I plunged into learning about proteins and molecular modelling. Even more amazing, six months before my trip to Germany, something about Richardson had crossed my desk, and I had sent him a belated thank-you note for writing *How Proteins Work,* and told him how much the book had helped "turn me on" to a whole new (for me) world, and opened a new era in my life. I figure it's never too late to write a thank-you note. In the note, I had included a copy of *Molecular Modelling News,* to show Richardson what I had done with some of the knowledge and enthusiasm I'd gained from reading his book.

"Oh, you're Rob Richardson," I said, excusing myself for bumping into him. "I'm Ursula Charbonnier."

"Are you the person who wrote to me last spring?" he asked, to my surprise, making the link.

"Why, yes," I said.

"And did I write back to you?"

"Why, no," I said, "but you probably get a lot of fan mail. It was a really terrific book."

"But it's so old," he said. "It's been out of date for years."

"Well, it's still a classic," I said, "and the writing is so clear, that the subject is understandable and comes alive – that is, to a newcomer with a good dictionary or two!" I added.

He laughed. And then he regaled us with entertaining stories about Linus Pauling and a firsthand account of how he had met his collaborator Irving Rice, and how they first got the idea to write *How Proteins Work.*

We rode the train to a switching point, then boarded trams that took us to the top of the Zugspitze. The view over Germany and Austria was spectacular, hard grey rocks against cobalt skies. At the top was a tiny dining spot with several tables. Richardson came over and had lunch with me. I learned we shared a common quirk, a fondness for obsolete technology: he collected typewriters, and I collected slide rules. The clouds moved quickly as we talked, giving sharply alternating views of intense clarity and thick fog. "If anyone had told me five years ago, when I was carrying that tattered book around Switzerland, that in 1990, I'd be sitting on top of the Zupspitze having lunch with you, I *never* would have believed it!" I said. "Things like this aren't supposed to happen to the lowest 'F' in chemistry!"

I came home to find all had rolled along smoothly in my absence. *Molecular Modelling News* would come out on time, despite my trip and court-ordered distractions; the children and Eliza had fared well in my absence. And there were scores of messages on my voice mail, but only one I'll mention here. It had come on the day I was giving my speech. "Hello

Ursula Charbonnier, this is Ian Ruddway. I was just cleaning my Rolodex, and came to your card, and wondered if the number was still good. Obviously it still is. Please give me a call when you can." I listened to the message two more times to make certain I wasn't losing my mind. No. This wasn't happening after the Paris airport and cleaning my own Rolodex. Oh, yes it was. Why now? I thought. I am not equipped to deal with him now.

Shortly after I returned from Germany, Jonah shared nuggets from Gavin Roberts' *g.a.l.* report with me: "Duncan needs to overcome the kids' perception of him as dishonest." Now, how is he supposed to do that, without *becoming* honest himself, I wondered. Roberts noted that Spencer was "distanced and somewhat cynical." Well, who wouldn't be after what we'd witnessed over the past two years? And that Amanda felt "betrayed about the alcoholism and the epilepsy." Guess what, experts? So did I! Despite all this, Roberts concluded he was impressed by Duncan's "genuineness" and "commitment toward (his) kids." This left me wondering what the legal system would think of me if my behavior had been identical to Duncan's over the past five years. Might anyone have suggested that I was an unfit mother? I rather thought so. I doubt they would have been impressed with my "genuineness" and "commitment" toward my children!

After we finished with *g.a.l.* business, Jonah walked me out to my car, and I turned our conversation to a more pleasant matter, for I had come home from Germany ready to move ahead with an intellectual property series for the readers of *MM News*.

"Jonah, do you know any patent attorneys?"

"Why, yes. You ought to talk to Larry Finch. He lives right around the corner from you and belongs to First Parish."

Two days later, in this most improbable autumn of my life, I went to church and there was Larry Finch – ushering. At the conclusion of the morning coffee hour, wasting no time, I introduced myself and told him what I needed: a lawyer who would be interested in helping me with a series of law articles for molecular modellers. "Here is my card," I said.

He smiled. "Send me your publication first thing tomorrow morning."

When I checked my voice mail the next morning, a message from one of Finch's associates awaited me. Her name was Elspeth Antioche, and she wanted to talk about *Molecular Modelling News*. Three days later, we met for dinner, and the rest is history. Elspeth was the first lawyer I'd met who knew anything about CAMD. I didn't have to explain very much. Elspeth had several science degrees in addition to an MBA and a JD, but she would need to spend a lot of time educating me about the law. She didn't mind. She'd just finished writing a book on licensing software, and was about to start another. Larry Finch had known she was looking for an editorial opportunity. *Molecular Modelling News* would be perfect.

We met for dinner at the Vista, and I brought a rather random and sort of shotgun approach to a smorgasbord of legal issues that I felt were troubling CAMD scientists. We tinkered with the list and came up with about a dozen tentative titles for a series on "CAMD and The Law." Would she be interested in writing a monthly "Law Briefs" column for us, in addition to co-coordinating the Series? She would. I would name her our first Law Editor. I told Elspeth I wanted to move in these directions because of what was happening in my own life. "You see, scientists are in an analogous state of ignorance and naïveté when it comes to the law, and if they don't become educated, some of them will get in as much trouble as I and my children." Or as I would say to my readers in a future Letter From The Editor: "If we become educated, we may have an opportunity to shape the law, and if we choose to remain ignorant, the law will most surely shape us."

"Do you think Jonah McCoy would talk to me about prospects for mediation in patent law disputes?" she asked.

"I'll find out," I said.

Jonah McCoy was pleased at the rapid turn of events that had grown in one short week from the casual question in his driveway. "Yes, tell Elspeth to call me." He had also become friendly with Merrill Crosby, Lawyer 2B, who was taking one of his mediation courses at a nearby college, and would shortly become the first mediator in the State of Rhode Island.

"We're getting there," said Jonah McCoy. "Do you realize your Pre-Trial is in less than a week? When are we going to write it? Looks like Sunday evening is the only time we both have available," he said when we next compared schedules.

"How did you know I wanted to help you write it?" I grinned.

"Oh, I just guessed," he said.

"Do you mind if we fight over every word?" I laughed. "I want to produce a document that I won't mind showing to my grandchildren."

"We'll work on it together, Ursula. And it will be something we can both be proud of."

XXIII

Let It Snow

One day at a time.
— Al-Anon Slogan

When Jonah and I arrived at court on the morning of October 29, (ironically the fifteenth anniversary of Duncan's marriage proposal to me) and saw Duncan's Pre-Trial Memorandum, we were more pleased than ever at the scrupulous care we had taken in writing mine. The day before, Jonah had asked me what I contributed to the marriage. "All my love, all my time, all my money, and all my energy," I had replied. The next morning, up on the second floor of the Probate Court building, I would read in graphic detail just how poor an investment I had made:

The Wife, throughout the marriage, insisted on keeping her income separate from the Husband's, treating her income as discretionary (only she had the discretion) and using the Husband's income to pay the family expenses, as he was 'the man.'" Apparently Duncan neglected to tell Chubb that throughout the marriage I had paid for most household items, presents for family and friends, all childcare, and most family clothing, including Duncan's, because *we* "were saving for college." And Duncan's taste in clothing had never been cheap. Not a word about the $800 Louis suit I had bought for him, or the winter coat he was wearing that very day, which I'd purchased at Paul Stuart in New York. *I* didn't even have a warm winter coat for myself. Duncan's Pre-Trial Memorandum spoke of my "unbridled spending," and stated that all family "expenses were paid from the Husband's income."

Jesus, Jonah, this is beyond belief! Did you see the parts about how I was only working only for my 'own personal fulfillment' or how we went to Westbury for financial planning at *Duncan's* insistence? And, it says here that Duncan expects to inherit nothing from his family, and that my family gave us gifts during the marriage of $509,000. All news to me! He also neglected to mention that I paid for two-thirds of our first home, and he consequently had no mortgage for years! Well, I'm telling the judge."

Frank Stoughton of Westbury Financial Ventures, a lawyer himself as well as our financial advisor, would later read Duncan's Pre-Trial and be horrified. "Ursula, this says you only came to us to save for college after 'repeated pleas' from Duncan. Rob and I discussed how it was *you* who initiated the process. We discussed it in this very room – several times in front of Duncan. And this part about buying Inverary Lane at *your* insistence. It just wasn't so. Rob and I spent weeks working with Duncan on the bridge loan, and setting up your special banking relationship with Hub Safe. If I weren't holding this in my hand and reading it with my own eyes, I'd find it hard to believe that Duncan Charbonnier could say these things."

Well, believe it Frank!" I said. "You *are* holding it in your hand, and you *are* reading it with your own eyes. Pretty soon, I won't be able to afford you, and there won't be any money left to manage anyhow after the lawyers get done with us."

There will be someday, Ursula. You are going to do well in this life. Molecular modelling has a bright future, and so have you. In the meantime, I'll continue to help you with your taxes and financial planning, for as long as you want me to."

But here was the part of the Pre-Trial that stung: ". . . the Wife delegated virtually all homemaking and parental responsibilities to the Husband, the children, her cleaning lady and child care assistant. The Wife had effectively resigned as wife and mother."

"Jonah, we have *no* childcare; our 'cleaning lady' for the past six years has been a *man* – John Barnum will get a laugh out of that one. And just who does the court think has been taking care of the house and the children, on a greatly reduced income, since Duncan moved out in August of 1989 and it is now nearly November of 1990? Will somebody please tell me that, Jonah!"

But before Jonah could reply, Jimmie came over to say that Judge Tracy had our records and was waiting in his chambers to see both lawyers. Jonah and Chubb stayed with the judge for some time, and then Duncan and I were called in to join them.

Tracy, in a nutshell, told us that although neither of us was satisfied with what we'd walk away with, we'd better go outside, make some adjustments, and settle the matter, because neither of us could expect anything better from him if this case went to trial. "Fifteen years is long enough to divide the assets fifty-fifty, and that's what I'm going to do unless you work out some other division between yourselves."

"But Your Honor, I paid for two-thirds of our first house with my whole inheritance from my grandparents, and this man had no mortgage for years," I protested.

"That was your choice Mrs. Charbonnier," said Judge Tracy.

"But Your Honor, I stayed home for ten years to nurture everyone. What about the opportunity cost of not building my career. Shouldn't I be compensated for that?"

"That was your choice, Mrs. Charbonnier."

"But Your Honor, Duncan Charbonnier makes four times as much money as I do – six if you count his stock options! Why do I have to pay half the children's unreimbursed medical costs?"

"Because that's equality, Mrs. Charbonnier."

"Your Honor," said Jonah, "Mrs. Charbonnier, it seems to me, has raised a valid point about the opportunity costs of developing her career which were incurred by staying home to take care of her family."

"Well, Jonah, it depends on the circumstances. Take my marriage, for example. We've been married forty years and have four children. My wife took care of the family, and recognizing her contribution as a homemaker would be the most important thing if we got divorced, because she's never worked. I'd pay her about half of my income as alimony to recognize that. But this case is different. Mrs. Charbonnier works, so the assets balance. This is a fairness court, not a win-lose court. Now she could elect to have some portion of the weekly child support check adjusted as alimony," suggested Tracy.

But I would have none of it. Alimony and child support were a zero-sum game in Massachusetts. The net effect of what they were suggesting was lowered child support. Furthermore, alimony was taxable, and child support wasn't. With this plan there would be even less money for the children each week. And I didn't want alimony from Duncan anyway. "No thanks, Your Honor," I said speaking for myself. "I don't want a penny of alimony from Duncan Charbonnier."

"Well, why not? You're entitled to it."

"It's a matter of personal ethics, Your Honor."

"Mrs. Charbonnier, I've told you before that conduct is irrelevant. Ethics have nothing to do with this case."

For once, you've said something I can agree with, I thought.

He continued. "And this is not a sexist court, though I know many people think it is. Take for instance the fellow who came barging into my chambers last week. He was so angry he wanted to beat me up, and Jimmie had to restrain him. He was mad because I said his daughter was healthy enough to get a job and go to work." I thought judges weren't supposed to discuss other cases in front of us, but nobody else seemed to have an objection, so I kept still.

He went on. "It was another divorce case, and she and her husband had had some kind of a kinky sex life, I guess, you know, with chains and things; they had some kind of a funny little sex light . . . I don't know. Anyway, so she had to put up with a little spanking during sex now and then. Big deal! Well, she claimed she was so traumatized by it, that she needed to be under the regular care of a psychiatrist and was unable to hold a job. But I said she had to work. And her father was mad about that." He giggled, obviously enjoying the story. Then he abruptly switched back to The Charbonnier Matter. "Now you folks go out and try to settle this case today," and he waved us away.

"Jonah, if my grandparents could see what the laws of Massachusetts are doing to me and my children, they would die all over again!" I said as we left Tracy's chambers.

Chubb and Duncan went to sit at one table, and Jonah and I spread out at another. Over the next six hours, the lawyers would trundle back and forth between us with various proposals for negotiation. Early on, Chubb took Jonah aside, and he returned to me with a worried look on his face.

"What is it?" I asked.

"Well, it's something I hadn't heard of before, and we'll have to check it out, but Chubb says if we don't get you divorced by December 31, you're going to lose all medical insurance coverage from Germane Engineering."

"But how can that be?" I asked. "You told me it was a state law that divorced spouses do not lose medical coverage."

"That's just the problem, Ursula. It is a state law, but Germane has decided to become a self-insurer as of 1991, thereby depriving all spouses of the benefits of the state statute applying. I wonder if Cile Hicks knows about this. It was her legislation, passed a decade ago, that was supposed to protect people like you."

"Well, I'll call her office and find out," I volunteered. "I will also call the editors I know at *The Wall Street Journal* to make sure GEC gets some publicity about what they're doing."

Chubb came over to us with another proposal. "Can they really take away my medical insurance, just like that?" I asked him.

"That's what they're saying. Look, I'm not happy about this either Mrs. Charbonnier. I have three GEC wives for clients, one of whom has terminal cancer, and they're going to cut her off as of January 1. To tell you the truth, it disgusts me that a company would do this to innocent people."

"Yeah, and I know what GEC spends on its marketing campaigns," I chimed in.

"Ursula, if Chubb hadn't told us, we wouldn't have known," reminded Jonah.

"So what will happen?" I asked Chubb. "Is GEC just assuming it will take years to thrash it out in the courts, and in the meantime they'll save lots of money?"

"Something like that. Look, I only told you about it because I was trying to help." I looked at Chubb MacIntyre for a long moment. He was speaking to me with respect for the first time. Jonah walked away, and Chubb stayed with me to expand on his legal perspective on this unexpected turn of events. His concern seemed genuine. Clearly, he was disturbed by what GEC was doing. I started adding up moments: he'd told Jonah that Duncan was a "jerk" who didn't even know why he was divorcing me; he'd spent a long time looking at "the way we were" photo in his office last spring; and though he'd lost on Inverary Lane during our last volley in court, I could tell he'd liked the way I'd fought. A friend of Julia Holliday's knew Chubb and his wife, and said they were decent people. Maybe they were.

Chubb walked away, and Jonah came back. "My God, I couldn't believe it, you and Chubb MacIntyre, actually having a civil conversation. That's why I got out of the way."

"Hey, Jonah. Chubb's no fool. He's started to catch on to Duncan Charbonnier."

But be that as it may, Chubb MacIntyre didn't give an inch the rest of the day, professional negotiator that he was. The four of us worked straight through the lunch hour, and kept at it until close to four in the afternoon. What it came down to was this: Duncan wasn't interested in paying for camp, or for braces, or the children's home, or their clothing (not that he ever had!) or for any of the things that were part of their previously normal existence.

"What about college?" I asked.

"It's not fair that the children have college *and* life insurance if I die," said Duncan. "It should be one or the other, if anything happens to me."

After seven hours of wrangling at the courthouse, I was having trouble keeping back the tears of outrage and frustration. I was exasperated with all of them: with Duncan, whose lies were still a long way from catching up with him; with Chubb, who knew exactly what he was doing to me and the children, and had no regard for Duncan except how much money he could make off him; and even a little bit with Jonah, for acting like all of this was normal operating procedure.

"Where's your sense of moral outrage, Jonah?" I asked. "You know everything there is to know about me. I've kept nothing from you. If I were your daughter instead of your client, how would you feel about what is happening to me and the children?" Then I trudged downstairs to get away from them all.

The Probate Court lobby is a quiet place in the late afternoon. Gone are the teeming masses that huddle in the halls on weekday mornings. I leaned against a pillar and just let the tears come. It was immoral. It was wrong. It was unfair. And here was the worst part – it was legal. An old conversation with Duncan played back to me: "You can't just abandon your family and leave the mortgage and all your obligations to me," I'd told him. "The law won't let you do that."

"Well then, you don't know the law, Ursula!" Duncan had replied scornfully. "I'm going to destroy you, and the law will help me do it."

I heard footsteps, and saw Jimmie walking toward me. He started to smile, but then he saw the tears, and stopped.

"Jimmie, do you know what a *Snow Job* is?"

"You mean, the kind of *Snow Job* that goes on around this place?" he asked.

"Yes, Jimmie."

"Yeah, I know what a *Snow Job* is!"

That night Duncan called the children. He spoke to Amanda first. "I'll tell you the real reason I'm divorcing your mother," he began, "but it will just be our little secret."

"Oh no it won't be just 'our little secret,'" said my infuriated daughter, "because first I'm going to tell my brother, and then I'm going to tell my mother. Don't you think they have a right to know?"

"In that case, I'm not going to tell you. Put Spencer on."

Against what I thought would be the advice of every expert on the face of the earth, I had let both children look at Duncan's Pre-Trial Memorandum when I got home that night. And I had let them read mine the night before. My attitude from the beginning of our ordeal had been: share the facts, expose the truth to the light of day, and let the chips fall where they may. People like Duncan got away with their behavior in large part because so many court-appointed paid enablers protected them.

"Dad, how could you say these things about Mom?" asked Spencer, referring to Duncan's synopsis of our marriage.

"Oh, it's all my lawyer's fault," said Duncan. "My lawyer made me exaggerate!"

"Well, Spencer," I said to my son, "if my lawyer had made me exaggerate, I'd have told him to go straight to hell!"

Then I got on the phone. "Duncan, it doesn't matter what you take away from me. You can take anything you want, except the children. But what you have done will follow you wherever you go. You will never be able to escape from the truth." He hung up on me.

When I told Jonah the next day, he said, "Ursula, how can you put these children through the meat grinder?"

"Jonah, they've been in the meat grinder for two years, but now the truth is bringing them out of the meat grinder."

For the first time in all the time we'd known each other, Jonah McCoy was angry. In a very quiet voice he said, "Ursula, I am going to very gently hang up the phone on you, and then I am going to call you back in about thirty seconds."

When the phone didn't ring, I looked at my watch. Agony. Ninety seconds later it was my cognitive lawyer. "Okay, I can talk to you now," and then he went on with legal business.

Two days later Jonah called again. "Ursula, I had a long talk with your father last night. Asa thinks you did the right thing by letting the children see the Pre-Trial Memoranda."

"He does?" I was surprised. Although we had a strong relationship, Asa rarely agreed with me on anything.

"And you know how wise I think your father is and how much I like and respect him. Asa is Wisdom. I don't know, Ursula. Maybe you two are right."

"Hey, Jonah, I don't have all the answers either, but I say when in doubt, go with the truth. One thing about the truth, Jonah – it ages well."

What I didn't tell him about the truth, but would have pounded into my head as November progressed, was just how unbelievable it can really be.

After some backing and forthing about perhaps taking the children to Ann Arbor for Thanksgiving – I'd told the children they were always free to spend their holidays wherever and with whomever they wished – Duncan decided to stay in Massachusetts and invite Elsie to come East. Spencer and Amanda had dinner with them the day after Thanksgiving, and Elsie gave Amanda a porno catalogue, saying, "There are some fun things in here for you, dear!"

Amanda brought it home and showed it to me. Perhaps this selection of things entertained Elsie, but it didn't do much for my eleven year-old daughter: there were crotch hooks for golfers; condo-mint candies; "safe sex to go" condoms in Chinese food containers; and large penises protruding from men's underwear labeled, "contents larger than they appear," to name just a few of the offerings. I figured Elsie was entitled to indulge her own tastes, but saw no reason she had to expose Amanda to them.

"The *guardian ad litum* is really going to enjoy your mother's porno catalogue," I told Duncan when he called later that evening.

"What are you talking about?" he demanded.

"Oh, why don't you just ask your mother. It even had her name on the mailing label." I was more amused than anything else. After all, Duncan had spent a year trying to paint *me* as an unfit parent.

Five minutes later Elsie was on the line. "Duncan has gone out. We're alone. Now we can really talk," she said, as she pressed the conference button on Duncan's phone.

I didn't want to really talk. "Look, Elsie," I said, when she started pleading ignorance at the contents of the catalogue, "surely the former National Standards Chairman of Gamma Delta ought to be able to do better than that!"

"Maybe you should fix her up with Tracy!" commented an Al-Anon friend the following Tuesday.

"With Tracy? Why? I don't get it."

"I used to be his neighbor, and during his drinking days, he used to bring home prostitutes and want his wife to watch while they had sex. And Agatha Tracy is a nice woman, Ursula. She was furious, and used to complain to us about it! Old Joe was really wild during his drinking days. He's calmed down a lot since then."

"Oh, I don't know," I said, thinking about the story he'd told last time we were in his chambers. "Jesus, can't they find people with higher standards of conduct to be judges in Massachusetts?"

The next time I saw Jonah, I chatted with him about Elsie's catalogue, and Tracy's alleged custom. "I was afraid you were going to pick up on that story he told in chambers, and put it in your book, Ursula. The fact of the matter is, he'd already told it to me and Chubb before you and Duncan ever came in the room."

"Then surely you noticed, Jonah, that he enjoyed the story so much that he had to tell it twice."

"I don't like to hear what you're telling me Ursula, but I have to listen to you. I have to listen to you." He looked a little sad.

"Jonah, it's okay with me if Joe Tracy has the kinkiest sex life in the world. I just don't want him in a position where he can make important decisions about me and my children."

"Then let's get this case settled, so that he won't be able to."

XXIV

Christmas Present

For nothing can be sole or whole that has not been rent.
— G. B. Yeats, *Crazy Jane Talks with the Bishop*

"Ursula, I am still determined to get you divorced by winter," maintained Jonah McCoy, referring to thirty days of unsuccessful attempts to communicate with Chubb via Susan, the secretary at Candice & MacIntyre.

The note he'd penned on the November bill said it all:

> Dear Ursula — Not too bad. Only $450 for a whole month of saying "Good morning, Susan, will you have Chubb call me today, please?" — Jonah

This might have been funny if we weren't talking about real wasted time and money. Jonah's wasted time. And my wasted money. It was enough to make me start dreaming about "Socialized Law" and an era where this sort of nonsense would no longer be tolerated in the American legal system. Even though the waste was unconscionable from my perspective, it didn't take a mental giant to understand Chubb's strategy: Let the clock wind down to December 31, and then negotiate tough. He and Duncan knew they had me over a barrel about the medical insurance, which Jonah was insisting that I save at all costs.

After several more rounds of "escape and evade," Jonah finally arranged a meeting for Probate Court on December 20. Chubb didn't stay long. The remaining sticking points were all the things Duncan no longer wanted to pay for, including ongoing care from a psychologist, which he still insisted all of us required, and a visitation schedule for Amanda and Spencer. It was obvious that I would probably lose on all the money issues, but I was damned if I was going to compromise on my kids.

On the money side, Duncan didn't want to pay for camp ("Camp is a joke, Ursula."), and he wanted to prune his life insurance down to one-ninth of what he now carried. "But that's only enough for four years of child support!" I protested, "and Amanda is only eleven years old! What

202 Snow Job

if you die?"

"Then you can use the money we've set aside for college for child support. If I die, it's not fair to expect child support and college! I told you that the last time we had this conversation." Was this the same man who only three years ago had insisted we have enough life insurance so that I would always be able to stay home and take care of the children if anything happened to him?

Duncan also wanted to discontinue child support when the children were seventeen-and-a-half years old – in the middle of their senior years of high school. And he wanted the children to see Gavin Roberts on an ongoing basis (with my footing half the bill, of course). To preserve my medical insurance, my cognitive lawyer was urging me to compromise on nearly everything, but when it came to the well-being of Spencer and Amanda, I had to draw the line.

"Ursula, you are going to have to work out a visitation schedule with Duncan. There is always a visitation schedule in a contested divorce."

"No," I said. "The children and I want no schedule. They want total freedom to decide where and with whom they will spend their time. For all we know, a point may arrive when they decide they can't stand me, and that they want to spend all their holidays with Duncan, or even live with him. They ought to have the freedom to choose. And this business about all of us needing psychological counseling is a lot of swill. The kids and I are up to here with paid enablers, Jonah. We just want to get on with our lives. I have neither the time, the money, the patience, nor the inclination to spend any more on paid enablers. If the court orders it, and we have no choice, that's one thing. But I'll be damned if I'll voluntarily sign anything that agrees to ongoing counseling. I will not sign away my children's rights. I promised them. And you can relay that to Chubb."

Chubb was not pleased. "Then this case is going to go to trial, Mrs. Charbonnier, and it will cost you another six months and another $40,000!" he bristled. "And I intend to depose you."

Go ahead and depose me, I thought to myself. Rip Duncan off for another three grand. But you won't learn a goddamn thing. I am squeaky clean!

"Chubb probably hasn't met an honest woman in so long that he wouldn't know one if he saw one," I remarked to Jonah.

"He's just doing his job, Ursula."

"And I'm just doing mine."

"There's nothing more I can do for you here. I'm going back to my office. And Chubb has to leave, too, so you and Duncan can stay and try to settle this case yourselves. Come back across the street and see me when you're done, and in the meantime you can call me if anything comes up that I can help with."

Duncan and I "negotiated" for about an hour, got nowhere, and in short order I was back across the street with Jonah. "We're going to try again this afternoon. I've set up another four-way meeting for us over at Candice & MacIntyre."

"Forget it, Jonah, I'm not coming. There is nothing to talk about. I'm not giving an inch on my kids. Have you got that?!"

"Ursula, do you understand my concept of divorce?" he said in exasperation.

"Jonah, do you understand my concept of marriage? Now I'm going back to *my* office, because I'd like to get some work done today, too! You know, Jonah, you're the only lawyer in Boston who could have put up with me!"

"That's probably true," he said. I could see that my cognitive lawyer was not happy with me, but I knew that my friend, Jonah McCoy, totally understood my position. Spencer and Amanda weren't just names in one of his legal files. He knew them, and he knew me. And he knew Conover and our world. I think that's what made dealing with me in that moment so hard for him.

Seeing no end in sight, I went back to Genesis. I wanted to talk to Archie McGowan, certain he would be able to calm me down, but he'd left for a holiday vacation. Well, Paul Sudo said I could always talk to him, but he was gone on a business trip. Most of the office had left for Christmas. Then I started to cry, and I couldn't stop. Tears poured out of my eyes and nose – it was water, water everywhere, until I heard a quiet voice saying, "Would you like to talk?"

It was cool, poker-faced Vladimir Siegfried, Genesis' Chief Financial Officer, and t-h-e last person in the company I would ever have chosen to discuss my personal life with, a man who prior to this moment, usually talked to me through gritted teeth, when he talked to me at all. "Why don't you take a few minutes to pull yourself together, and come see me in my office?" he said gently.

"You don't have time to talk to me," I protested, trying to give us both an out.

"We all have to make time, at times like this," he said. It was a quiet, calm voice, even if it was Vladimir Siegfried's voice, and I was grateful for it. When I went in to see him awhile later, I unloaded all my frustration about Duncan's deception, alcoholic denial, greedy lawyers, and the outrageous legal system. I don't even remember what Vladimir said to me. But I do remember that he was kind and constructive, and that I felt better when I left.

In the middle of that afternoon, my phone rang. "Ursula, you're not going to believe this, but a miracle has just occurred." It was Jonah McCoy. "Seth Wright called to say he's settled the case with Duncan. And we're getting nearly everything we wanted. Duncan has signed the papers. Seth wants us to meet him at Candice & MacIntyre tonight, so that you can initial the agreement. How would you like to get divorced tomorrow morning?"

"I'd love to," I said. "If it's possible. What about the children?"

"Wright told Duncan that, in effect, he couldn't force his children to do anything, and he'd be making a big mistake if he tried, and to sign the agreement."

"So what's the visitation schedule?"

"Something you'll find completely acceptable. The agreement calls for the children to make a schedule with Duncan, as agreed between the parties, as soon as they go with him to see Gavin Roberts, again, as agreed between the parties."

"I got lost in the legalese. What does that mean in English, Jonah?"

"It means that the ball is in the children's court, just as you wanted it to be. There will be no visitation schedule unless they make one, and if they never agree to meet with Duncan and Gavin Roberts to make a schedule, then there'll never be one."

"Are you sure that's what it means?"

"Yes, Ursula."

"What didn't we get that we wanted?"

"Duncan isn't going to pay for half of Amanda's braces. I'll explain it to you tonight. Now can you meet me at my office at six o'clock? We'll go over everything then, and meet Seth Wright at Wadsworth Place after that."

Five hours later, Jonah and I were racing through the December night toward that orderly climax he'd promised me so many months ago. Jonah alternately winced and marveled as I blitzed through the streets like a veteran of foreign rush hour wars. "And Duncan said you didn't know how to drive in Boston?!" laughed my cognitive lawyer.

"That's because Duncan didn't know my formula: Think like a cow — drive like an anarchist!"

Jonah McCoy laughed. "Would you like to know Duncan's reason for not paying for Amanda's braces?" he asked with a touch of mischievousness.

Conover's user-friendly hardware store flashed to my mind. "Oh, let me guess, Jonah. The Oglethorpe bill."

"That's right!" he said. "How did you know?"

"Oh, I just took a wild guess. Is Duncan Charbonnier an asshole?" I asked.

"No, Ursula. Duncan Charbonnier is a *total* asshole!"

I screeched to a halt in front of Wadsworth Place. "Let's go!" I said, bounding out of the car.

"Ursula, you can't park here."

"Why not?" I snapped.

"Because of all these little red and white signs," said my cognitive lawyer.

"All right. I'll be law-abiding," I conceded, "and park in the garage around the corner."

Minutes later, we strode into Wadsworth Place. "What floor are you going to?" asked the night watchman.

"Thirty-five," I said, finding it hard to believe that this moment had come.

You remembered, Jonah McCoy smiled silently at me as the elevator went up. Yes I remembered, I smiled back at him. When we'd been here last June, my house was in foreclosure, and it was by no means clear that I would retain custody of Spencer and Amanda. "Get me divorced with my house and my children intact," I had said to him on our first day. By God, you did it, I thought to myself. Against all odds, you did it. Maybe once in a lifetime, a woman meets a knight in shining armor, and I was looking at mine. In the past two years my children and I had experienced much that was evil in the Massachusetts system of justice. But the fundamental goodness, in this one human being, had more than counterbalanced it. Gabriel G. Reed may have put the fight back in my spirit, but Jonah McCoy had put the trust back in my soul.

The law offices were deserted except for Seth Wright and Senior Partner Paul Candice, who paused for a little small talk with Jonah. Then Wright motioned us into a paneled conference room, where our voices were absorbed by all the thick carpeting and mahogany and leather. I hadn't seen Seth since that morning last summer when we'd had a short discussion about intellectual property law and software, in Toby and Steve's parking lot. "Thank you for preserving my children's freedom," I said directly in the first moment.

"It was the only thing that made sense," he said. "Given their ages — and their wishes."

I sat across from the long wall of glass that separated us from the chill Boston night, and listened carefully while the two lawyers made some final adjustments to the agreement. Then the room was hushed and still, like an empty cathedral after vespers. Only the rustle of papers and strokes of my pen broke the silence as I initialed every page in quadruplicate.

"Would you like some coffee?" Wright asked, after I'd finished.

"Yes," I said, following him into the kitchen. Though we were all tired from the long and painful battle, we could now sit and trade war stories from our opposing perspectives. I might have captioned what followed, "drinking with the enemy," except that Seth Wright was not my enemy. In the eleventh hour, he had turned out to be another hero, sparing me and my children another six months of financial and emotional carnage. Maybe he and MacIntyre realized who and what I was, and perhaps they had even begun to see through their client. Jonah mentioned that Duncan's unwillingness to pay for his daughter's braces had rankled with MacIntyre and Wright, as well.

Seth Wright was curious about how I had come to have so many lawyers, and how I had met Jonah. "I went to law school with Merrill Crosby, you know," he said referring to Lawyer 2B.

"As a matter of fact, I did know. She and Camden became good friends with me after she left Reed's firm. Camden was a great help with the neurological component of this case," I said, recalling my misattribution of Duncan's alcoholic blackouts to temporal lobe epilepsy. "They had me down to Rhode Island for a weekend this summer, and Merrill has taken a mediation course from Jonah. She's going to open a mediation practice in Providence next year." Wright looked surprised. "They've even come to know the children. It's an interesting way to meet people," I summed up.

"And Ursula and I are practically neighbors in Conover," Jonah chimed in. "We both go to the same church. Our ministers sent her to me."

"How did you get mixed up with Reed?" asked Seth Wright.

"Well, after Ringling & Haycroft didn't believe my story, Angus MacKenzie, who is General Counsel to my company, sent me to Reed." We were all getting pretty loosened up by that point. "Jonah," I said with a twinkle in my eye, "should I tell Seth about the toy money?"

"Why not?" laughed my cognitive lawyer. And so I did, amazed that MacIntyre hadn't told him about it already. It is interesting what lawyers tell and do not tell their partners.

"You sent Reed Monopoly money?" Seth Wright was beside himself with laugher. "And he took you to Judge Tracy with it?!" More laughter. A lot more laughter.

"Yes, for the first month of this relationship, Jonah had to put up with Ursula's perverted sense of humor!"

"Ursula, should I tell him about the Ferdinand blanket?" asked Jonah, suddenly warming to the turn the conversation had taken.

"Yes, Jonah, tell him about the Ferdinand blanket!"

"Should I tell him about *Snow Job,* Jonah?"

"Tell him about *Snow Job,* Ursula!"

When we finally left the offices of Candice & MacIntyre late in the evening, Seth Wright asked, "Who do you think should play my part in the movie?"

"Well, I wasn't even going to put you in the book," I said, "but now I guess I have to. I don't know, who would you like to play your part in the movie?"

"Maybe Robert De Niro!" he exclaimed, as we left him smiling into space, gazing into the stars.

"I don't believe this Jonah," I said when we were safely out of earshot in the elevator. "Am I hallucinating or did we just leave Seth Wright muttering to himself about who should play his part in the movie of *Snow Job!?*"

"You're not hallucinating," said my cognitive lawyer. "But this whole evening has been very hard to believe."

"Jonah, in the space of a few short hours, how did we go from Chubb's threat of six more months of nonsense to signing a divorce agreement this evening? What happened?"

"I'm not sure we'll ever know. But it's possible Chubb was starting to get tired of this case and Duncan Charbonnier. What do you think happened?"

"I agree with you. MacIntyre probably realized I wasn't going to give an inch on the kids and that there wasn't much more money to be made, and he said, 'Seth, crumb the table!'" And I made a crumbing motion with my hand.

Back outside, as we headed for the parking structure against the bracing December wind, Jonah McCoy said, "Where's your coat? Why aren't you wearing a coat?"

"I don't have a winter coat."

"Here, borrow mine."

"That's okay. We're almost to the car. I only had enough money for one coat in 1987, and I spent it on Duncan Charbonnier. I told Reed last year that there were only two material possessions in the world that I wanted for myself: a winter coat and a laser printer. And now it's going to be a long time before I get either one."

"I want you to go out and buy a coat, Ursula."

"Wouldn't you rather get paid first?"

"Not until you buy a coat!"

"I'll think about it," I said.

"Now, I want to talk to you about tomorrow. It's going to be a very emotional day for you, and not an entirely happy one. You'll have mixed emotions. You've been under a lot of pressure for a long time, and when all the energy of that pressure is released," he placed his hand on the top of my head, to make his point and then let it fly into the air, "well, don't be surprised if it takes a while to feel normal again. Despite what you think, Ursula, it's going to take some time. You will not be completely happy tomorrow."

"Nonsense, Jonah. I shall be radiant!"

And I was. The reflection in the door of Probate Court the next morning showed a smiling dark-haired woman whose ankle-length winter white skirt whipped and swirled in the wind. The bright sun made a winter coat unnecessary. My navy snowflake cardigan would do nicely on this clear and shining December day.

Jonah spotted Duncan from across the courthouse lobby. "Look at him, Ursula. Duncan looks like a zombie! He has no affect whatsoever. He's like a stone."

"That's exactly how Dr. Arthur describes him," I said. "Gabriel used to call him 'Scarecrow,' but to me he looks more like a department store mannequin."

"Hi, Jimmie," I waved as Jonah and I jogged up to the second floor.

"The molecule lady! Gosh, you look a lot happier than the last time I saw you," he said.

"I am! I'm getting divorced today! This is the last day you'll see me here!"

"Well, congratulations!"

"Thanks, Jimmie!"

"You do look radiant," said Jonah after Jimmie walked away.

"Jonah, I am even happier than the day I got married – because I am better than I've ever been!"

"You remind me of a line from Yeats," said Jonah. "'. . . nothing can be sole or whole that has not been rent.' It's from 'Crazy Jane Talks with the Bishop,' and nobody can say that Ursula Charbonnier hasn't been rent. You've been torn apart, but you've survived, and now you are going to go on and be all right. I'm not so sure about Duncan, though."

MacIntyre came up to us as we sat down at one of the tables to wait to be called into Tracy's chambers. "It's great that we could settle this case before the end of the year," said Jonah. "I'm glad we got it done."

"Me and thee!" said Chubb. "And we saved your medical insurance," he said turning to me.

"Gee, Chubb's practically acting like he's on our side. Is he?"

"After what's gone on in this case the past few days, you tell me, Ursula. Now I want to explain to you what's going to happen when we get into Tracy's chambers. You're going to be sworn in, and I'm going to ask you a long series of questions like, Did you marry Duncan Charbonnier on such and such a date, and do you have two children named Spencer and Amanda, etc., and you just keep saying yes to all my questions, and then at the end I'll ask if you consider this a fair and reasonable agreement and you'll say yes again, and then Judge Tracy will divorce you."

"But I can't do that, Jonah," I said, "because this is *not* a fair and reasonable agreement." For a split second, I thought my cognitive lawyer was going to lose it in the middle of Probate Court. "But I will say yes if you make just one small change."

"Do you want to get divorced today or don't you?" snapped Jonah McCoy.

"It's just a small edit. All I want you to say is, 'Do you consider this a fair and reasonable agreement *by the current laws of this Commonwealth?*' And then I'll say 'yes.' And we'll be all done. Are you going to miss fighting with me about words?" I added.

"Ursula, if you don't say yes to all my questions you two are not going to get divorced today." He was looking across the tables at Duncan. "You two married each other for looks," he said suddenly.

"No Jonah, if I had married for looks, I would have married 'Huey Valentine' (which Jonah knew was my nickname for Ian Ruddway) – the most exquisite man in the world."

Then Jimmie said it was time to go in. First the lawyers spoke with Tracy for a few minutes, and then Duncan and I were invited to join them.

"Well, I got to be a father in this case," said Judge Tracy as he spoke glowingly about how Duncan had gone to AA with him. I rolled my eyes at Jonah, and made a concerted effort not to throw up. So much for judicial impartiality.

Then Jonah started asking me all the questions, as we'd rehearsed outside. And after a long litany of yesses, he came to the end. "Mrs. Charbonnier, do you consider this a fair and reasonable agreement?"

I looked at him, and bit my tongue. Neither of us said a word. When I was pretty sure no one was going to give an inch, he raised one eyebrow and added, ". . . I mean . . . do you consider this a fair and reasonable agreement by the current laws of this Commonwealth?"

"Yes! Yes, I do!" I said in a very loud, clear voice, and smiled dazzlingly at my cognitive lawyer. It went right over Duncan's and Tracy's heads, but Chubb MacIntyre looked over and got our meaning. I smiled at him, and thought of last June: You haven't heard the last of me, Chubb.

It should have been over, but then Judge Tracy and Chubb launched into a tasteless account of how one of Malcolm Rohrschach's clients had recently committed suicide by bailing out in his plane over his ex-wife's house. That way, both he and the plane could crash into the property. Chubb had been the lawyer for the ex-wife. "You know, I just called up Malcolm and said, 'Sometimes, don't you just hate the business we're in?'"

Right I thought, you guys hate it all the way to the bank, but what I actually said was, "Well, Chubb, in your business I suppose there isn't much you haven't seen or heard over the years."

Then everyone got up and Duncan and the lawyers all shook hands. Duncan walked out of the room first. As he passed, I said the only two positive words I could think of with any sincerity, "Merry Christmas."

Jonah followed him out, and Tracy turned his attention to the next Matter. Chubb came over and looked at me for a long moment over the top of the tall leather chair. In his expression I saw an odd mixture of kindness and regret. He formed his hand into a loose fist and gently brushed it across my cheek four or five times, as if to say, I know, Mrs. Charbonnier . . . I finally figured it out . . . And I'm sorry.

I met his gaze with silence and thought, Thanks, Chubb. Thanks for not making it worse than it was. I had sensed an element of mercy in the miracle that happened yesterday. Now I was sure it had come from Chubb.

As Jonah and I walked downstairs, he recounted what Tracy had said to both lawyers before I walked into chambers: "Mrs. Charbonnier threw that nice man out of her house."

"Then it's a damn good thing this case never went to trial, because we know whose side Tracy was on. The judge got hosed, Jonah!"

And this time Jonah didn't argue with me. "I'm not stupid, Jonah. I know exactly what happened to me."

Conduct may be irrelevant in Massachusetts, but Truth is ineluctable everywhere.

Part III

A Canticle of Dawn

XXV

A New Chapter

The cares that infest the day
Shall fold their tents, like the Arabs,
And as silently steal away.

— Henry Wadsworth Longfellow,
The Day is Done

Back out in the lobby, Jonah gave me a big hug. It was over. We'd done it. I strode out into the now windless morning to collect my car from Toby and Steve. "You won't be seeing me again for a long time," I told them.

"But you'll come back to sign the book, won't you?" they asked.

"Of course I will," I smiled. "Merry Christmas!"

It was the first day of winter, and the first day of my whole new life. As holiday carols played, my car fairly sailed down Memorial Drive. Where were all those mixed feelings that Jonah had predicted? They just weren't there. At the next red light, I sat very still, trying hard to detect the faintest twinge of regret, of sadness or of loss. But all I could feel was joy and the fresh lightness that follows the birth of a baby, when the labor is suddenly ended. Today I was holding new life in my arms, and that life was my life. Now I would be free to fill it with all that mattered to me: family, home, molecules, writing, friends, community. I had done my best, and I could live with that.

As I sped west, an autumn conversation with our CEO Jeff Abbott played back to me: "Ursula, do you know what the single most important factor is for people being mentally healthy after a prolonged traumatic experience?"

"No, Jeff."

"That they didn't go through it alone."

Jeff was right. We didn't go through it alone. I'd been up past midnight most of the week making jars and jars of fudge sauce and cocktail pecans for the many, many people who had helped us through the past two years, and I would spend the next two days delivering them, with the first stop being that grey stone oasis of peace in Conover Center.

"It's over!" I called to Trudy Hale as I walked into First Parish.

"It's over? It's really done?" she asked incredulously, hugging me.

"Yes! I've just come from court with Jonah! Merry Christmas, Trudy!"

"Do you and the children have any plans for Christmas?"

"No," I said, in a rapid emotional downshift that tried in five seconds to transition from post-courtroom euphoria to the peace of Christmas.

"Then won't you and the children join Matthew and me at our home for Christmas dinner? We like to gather at about four o'clock in the afternoon," she said, settling it.

The second thing I did was to send our Christmas photo and a short note to Gabriel G. Reed:

Dear Gabriel —

You are looking at a picture of survivors. Two years to the day after it began, the storm is finally over. Thank you for giving me the boot to get into Al-Anon. You said you wanted me to be whole and happy. I am. In the eleventh hour, Seth Wright turned out to be the hero. A plot only God could have written! Merry Christmas.

– U. L. C.
21 December 1990

Then I went back to Genesis. People kept leaving bottles of champagne by my desk, and Paul Sudo took me aside and said, "Now you can really put all of this behind you; and you can go forward and make the last half of your life wonderful. Ursula, you are a strong and salty woman! Duncan may have taken all your money, but you can work hard, you can always get money. He never killed your spirit. Nobody can kill that!"

"True," I agreed. "If you lose that, then you have nothing."

And there was plenty of spirit at 1 Inverary Lane. For Spencer, and Amanda, and me, this was our first Christmas since 1987 that would be free of agony, and in it I discovered keener sensations than I had known in years past: the majesty and spectacle of light in darkness at the Christmas Eve candle service as our nation stood poised on the brink of war in the Middle East; the warm crush of carolers gathered at the edge of the Town Green to sing together in a cold, black night; and a profound pleasure in reconnecting with friends across the globe via the first holiday missive of my new life.

Remembering Trudy Hale's advice to "be silent no longer," my holiday letter told our story in simple but direct language that ended by looking forward:

Despite what I have experienced in recent years, I more than ever believe in marriage and that nurturing children is the most important job I will ever do. Spencer, Amanda, and I continue to believe that we will someday find a kind and honest man with whom to share our lives again, but 'til then we are standing on our own — with serenity — most days. And that is my holiday wish for each of you: that you will stand with serenity in 1991, a year that promises to demand much from us all.

XXVI

Loose Ends

People wish to be settled:
only as far as they are unsettled is there any hope for them.

– Ralph Waldo Emerson, *Circles*

But I think I knew, even as I wrote those words, that serenity was still a long way off for me, that perhaps another year or two would pass before my life would again feel manageable. It takes time to recover from the first misstep, to admit that "we were powerless over alcohol, that our lives had become unmanageable." All of my affairs – my finances, my home, my children, my emotions – all were in disarray, and I felt spent in more ways than financial from the long and pounding battle.

Life was still layers of confusion swirling amid layers of apparent order. Jackie Melrose spoke wisely through the long winter. "Ursula needs to be patient with Ursula. Give yourself time. Give yourself space. You've been on an emotional and physical treadmill. You've been running on adrenalin. Look at what you've accomplished. But now you have to learn how to relax. Start swimming again."

As 1991 dawned, we received a lot of wishes for a Happy New Year, *". . . And we really mean it!"* was appended to many of them. Within weeks the United States was at war in the Middle East. One war over, and flash! –another so quickly begun. There had been no time to come up for air. Mel Walsingham had left for active duty in Saudi Arabia the month before, and Christa was on her way back to Massachusetts from Germany.

The first week of the New Year, I got a sweet note from Jonah: "Dear Ursula, I cannot resist writing you on my first day back in the office . . ."

No, we had not become addicted to this case, but there were loose ends to tie up: education and insurance trusts to set up for the children's benefit, and the deed to Inverary Lane and the title to my car to be put in my name only. We met at Jonah's home office the following week to begin the mopping-up process. "Come in. Come in. It's cold out there, isn't it?" said Jonah McCoy.

"Well, it's not as cold as it used to be," I grinned. "Jonah, I took you at

your word, and I went out and bought a new coat. What do you think?"
I pirouetted.

"Good choice!" he said approvingly.

"You know, Jonah, after what I've been through and knowing what I now know about the law, I don't think I even want to share so much as a gasoline credit card with anyone again."

"After what Duncan put you through, that's understandable, Ursula."

In early January, Paul Sudo announced his resignation from Genesis; Vladimir Siegfried was to be my new boss. I felt an urgent need to begin *Snow Job*, and asked Vladimir for three extra weeks of vacation, in addition to the three I already had coming. "For years I haven't even been able to use up all my vacation time, and now I am asking you for three extra weeks off to write."

"Yes," he said without hesitation. "Ursula, you earned it." I began working three weeks out of each month, and taking the fourth to write. On one of the writing days in late January, Lydia Canfield appeared at my door. "I've brought you a belated Christmas present," she said over tea. "Here are three more of the books you've been seeking for Heyward Cutting."

I had, in fact, sent him a huge box of *Bulldog Drummond* books at Christmas from the batch Frank Blaine hand-carried from London in December. But Celia hadn't been able to locate the first book in the series, and now here it was, in Lydia's box! "Oh, this is wonderful. I'll send them to Heyward as soon as we resolve things with Gabriel! And Lydia, look at these hilarious Salada Tea Bags I found for him at Al-Anon." The tag lines said: "The Best Things in Life Are Fees," and "Rich Lawyers Have Many Fat Liens."

Before I could phone him, Heyward called me. "I was just talking about you yesterday," I said. "You'll never guess what came my way!"

"You found more *Bulldog* books!"

"Hey, do 'All My Lawyers' have my house bugged?" I said, only half in jest.

"I have news for you, too," he said, sounding just as excited as I. "Listen to this, Ursula. Reed has agreed to drop the lien on your house, the lawsuit in Muni Court, the Fee Dispute before the Boston Bar and the remaining balance on your bill, if you will sign a document that says you will not use his real name or the firm's or any reasonably identified references thereto in *Snow Job*, or in any publication you author or contribute to, or in any appearances you make as a public speaker."

"Why is he doing that?" I asked.

"Maybe he owes me a favor," said Heyward Cutting a little mysteriously.

"What exactly does that mean, Heyward?"

"It means things like you don't put his office on a street that looks like Paris, and you don't say he's a short, fat man with a black mustache, and so forth."

"Something about this just doesn't add up, Heyward."

"You're right Ursula, something about this just doesn't add up, but the nice thing about winning is that you never have to explain why," said Number 4 in an I-don't-want-to-discuss-this-any-further tone of voice. Over the past year, I had spent enough time around lawyers to know when to shut up.

"Well Heyward, as you know, I have no interest in smearing Reed. I am only out to smear The System, so I'll have no trouble signing such a document – and sticking by it. Besides, it says on the first page of *Snow Job* that 'the names have been changed to protect the guilty . . .'"

Sometime that winter, Ginny Bartlett, my former French teacher, called to wish me well. "Ursula, you got off the train of addiction, and you and the children will ultimately be fine. You got off at your station – at Inverary Lane. I told you two years ago, that there were four and only four possible outcomes to alcoholism: insanity, incarceration, death, or recovery. You and the children chose recovery. Your ride is over. But Duncan Charbonnier still rides that train, and who can say where his ride will end? Trust me, you and the children are going to be all right."

But I didn't feel all right. Maybe now I was having that delayed reaction Jonah predicted. I felt overwhelmed. Owing Jonah money was keeping me awake at night; my Ohio, anti-debt roots were torturing me! We were having trouble paying our bills, and every time I turned around, something at Inverary Lane was breaking or getting lost or needing to be replaced. I got a bad cough, and it didn't go away. I was the kind of tired that sleep wasn't fixing. What ever happened to high-energy Ursula? After two months of hacking, I called John Arthur for some antibiotics, but they brought no relief. And then after weeks of skimming along with *Snow Job*, I found myself suddenly "blocked."

"This rarely happens to me," I complained to Jackie Melrose one day.

"Ursula needs to be patient with Ursula," said my stalwart friend, repeating her advice from early winter.

"But *how* to get unblocked?" I asked again.

"Well, I have an idea; in fact, you might have a little fun with it."

"What is it?"

"Why not write a fantasy chapter? Most of your story is about reality."

"Well, what would happen in the fantasy chapter?" I asked, feeling totally unimaginative.

"Everyone would get his or her just desserts! Take all the loose ends and tie them up in a neat, funny little package," said Jackie Melrose. "Now go home and fantasize about that, and bring me your chapter at the end of the day! And Ursula . . ."

"Yes?"

"Have some fun with it. Play!"

And I did.

"I couldn't put it down!" exclaimed Jackie Melrose on the phone the next evening. You certainly got my attention, Ursula. I wouldn't even talk to Jeff until I'd finished your fantasy chapter!"

"Well, you were right," I said. "*After* I played with it, I really was able to pick up and write again. It was a very freeing exercise. Of course, I wouldn't want any of those things to happen in real life, but the exercise opened up new ways of thinking, and now I feel fresh again and very ready for spring!"

XXVII

Opening Lines

> The trumpet of a prophecy! O, Wind,
> If Winter comes, can Spring be far behind?
>
> — Percy Bysshe Shelley,
> *Ode to the West Wind*

The new season was to hold some amazing moments for me. In mid-March, Genesis sent me to Cincinnati on a business trip. The American Physical Society was holding its Annual Meeting, and world-renowned Uzi Landman, Genesis's new Materials Science Advisor, was having a press conference. When I arrived at the airport, I thought I was stepping into a taxi, but instead I walked into a mirror. My taxi driver was upset; she seemed on the verge of tears. "What's the matter?" I asked.

"Oh, you'll never believe my story," she said. I couldn't even see her face, but I can still hear her voice.

Between coughs, I asked again, "What's the matter?"

"Well," she started, "I was married to the nicest man in the world, and we had a little girl, and about two years ago I found out he was an alcoholic, and I've been through hell with the legal system since then, and sometimes we don't get any child support, and next week my house is being foreclosed on, and I'm sure you don't believe any of this." She was crying softly.

I leaned forward. "I do believe you," I said quietly. "I believe every word you're telling me, because I've just been through a lot of the same things."

"You?" she said, turning around, looking at me in total disbelief.

I may have appeared to be a totally pulled-together businesswoman on that spring morning in Cincinnati, in fact I know I did . . . until I told her about Duncan Charbonnier and some of what the children and I had been through. "So the courts are as bad to mothers and children in Ohio as they are in Massachusetts?" I asked.

"If what you're saying is true, they are," she said.

"I'm writing a book about this. It's called *Snow Job,* but I don't know if anyone will read it."

"I'd read it," she said. Then she laughed. "I like the title!"

It was good to hear her laugh. "What's your name?" I asked.

"Amanda Dennis," she said.

"Amanda is my daughter's name. Look, have you been to Al-Anon?" I found myself asking her.

"It's not for me."

"Well, think about it again," I said, trying not to be pushy, but hoping she would reconsider. "You know, for a long time I didn't think it was for me either, but someone convinced me to give it a try, and I can tell you that it's helped a lot." Jesus, Gabriel would never believe this. "May I have your card?"

"Sure." It said: Amanda Dennis, Diamond Taxi Co.

"If anyone publishes *Snow Job,* maybe you can give me another ride from the airport when I come back to Cincinnati. Good luck to you – next week and beyond. I hope a miracle happens, and that you somehow find a way to save your house."

But I wasn't as strong as I tried to sound. Two nights later, Ike Peters, the Wheaton Glass scientist who was also in town for the APS Meeting, took me out to a four-star restaurant for dinner, and spent what amounted to more than 50 percent of one child support check on our meal! The waiters brought huge portions, and I kept wishing I could transport a "doggie bag" home to Spencer and Amanda, and all the hungry children in America who would have been glad to have all this food we couldn't eat. The waste and the expense made it hard for me to enjoy dinner, and I hoped Ike had no idea how I was feeling. He was being very kind, dear friend that he was. He knew I appreciated good food, and that I loved the entertaining science stories he always told. "Ursula, I thought you needed some pampering," he said as we walked back to our hotels.

"I did, Ike. It's been a special evening." But I suspect he did know how I felt. In addition to being a world-class scientist, Ike Peters was also a pretty sensitive human being who had been through some tough times himself.

"You remain my shining example of storm survival," I said in the thank-you note I put in the outgoing mail.

In the incoming mail, I found a large information packet, addressed to me, from a support group network at Westbury General. Maybe I needed some outside help, after all. I decided to take this little postal hint and call the hospital, but I couldn't decide which category was right for me; and neither could the psychologists who were screening the calls. The first one rejected me for the General Loss and Bereavement Group, because I didn't match on the issues other group members had. Then, even though I had all the characteristics of a candidate for the "Young Widowed – Loss and Bereavement Group," the next psychologist decided I couldn't be admitted to that one, because I was divorced: "You know, you'd be perfect for this group, except that your husband is still alive. But look, I have another idea, I know this might sound a little strange, but I'm starting a new support group for women whose husbands have recently declared themselves gay. Would you like to join that one?"

"Well, uh, that part of the marriage was just fine, so uh, no thank you," I said. "I probably wouldn't have much to contribute. Thank you very much. But, if you reconsider about letting me into one of the other groups, please call me back. I really could use some support, you know."

I recounted this to one of the scientists at work who had known Duncan for the past six years. "Rejected from two support groups in one day, Frank, can you believe that! Now that's rejection!!"

"No problem, Ursula," he replied dryly, "We'll just shoot Duncan, and then you can join the Young Widowed and Bereaved!"

"But Frank, here I am reaching out for help, and the best Westbury General psychologists can offer me is 'Women Whose Husbands Have Recently Declared Themselves Gay.' I mean, what if I'd been really desperate and at the edge? You'd think they could find swifter people to screen the calls over there!"

Frank smiled. "Well, at least you're starting to feel better – even without a support group. I notice that cough has just about disappeared."

Frank was right. I was feeling better in some ways, and I was making progress on some fronts: I had some repairs done at Inverary Lane; I was able to send Jonah a little more money; the first installment of the Law Series Elspeth Antioche and I had planned last October was published in *Molecular Modelling News,* and it got rave reviews from readers; First Parish invited me to join the Senior Church Committee, and it felt good to be able to start to give something back. Slowly, in separate small steps, life was turning around.

Then, on the first day of April, Vladimir Siegfried called me into his office. "This won't take long," he said in a voice which made me wonder if I was about to be fired. "It is my great pleasure to inform you that effective immediately, you have a 25 percent raise!" I kept waiting for him to add, "April Fool!" and when he didn't I said "Thank you" and went back to work.

We are going to survive, I smiled to myself.

Then the phone rang. It was to be a heart-thumping afternoon. "Ursula Charbonnier," I answered breezily.

"Ian Ruddway," he said just as breezily. "How are you?"

"I'm great," I blurted out, "I just got a 25 percent raise!"

"That's wonderful! Congratulations! Listen, I'm going to be in Boston on business the first and second of May. Which night are you having dinner with me?" Not *will* you have dinner with me, as most people would have put it, but typical Ian Ruddway – *which night* are you having dinner with me. He said it as a directive, not a question. As if it were his right.

"Well now, let's have a look at the calendar . . . I think the first is probably better," I replied in my calmest tone, feeling I would surely die if he made me wait until the second. "Shall I put it on the calendar?" I added nonchalantly.

"*Yes!*" said Ian Ruddway in his usual definitive tone.

That afternoon, I went home feeling about the same age as my son Spencer, which was to say – approximately thirteen and three-quarters! *Whoooooeeee!*

XXVIII

Putting Off the Ritz

One of the pleasures of middle age is to find out
that one WAS right, and that one was much righter
than one knew at say 17 or 23.

— Ezra Pound, *ABC of Reading*

From the beginning, there were indications that not all would be smooth. With us it never was, but in the age of voice mail and fax, Ian and I were communicating better than ever, just not always interactively. "Dinner at the Ritz" was destined to hang in the balance until the last possible moment, because Ian Ruddway, for the first time in his legal life, was called to jury duty; over a period of weeks he was ordered to report to court each morning to see if he'd be chosen, and naturally, on the day he was to fly to Boston, he was chosen.

Phone calls flew back and forth. God bless voice mail: *If* he could get here, he'd be staying at the Ritz. Where and when could we meet? "Let's keep it easy," I said by return voice mail, "I'll meet you at the Ritz, but I'll leave the time to you. How nice to be doing this in the age of the answering machine!" I added, alluding to our pathetic and frequent history of missing each other by phone, two decades before. This unfortunate pattern seemed destined to continue, but now there would at least be voice trails.

By late afternoon, circumstances were still unclear, and when I could bear it no longer, I called his secretary. "Are you the dinner at the Ritz?" she asked without waiting for me to identify myself.

"Yes."

"He just called from the courthouse. He's on his way to LaGuardia."

Soon the phone rang again. "Hi. I'm at the airport. I think I can make the last shuttle."

"Well, don't miss that plane," I said with all the coolness I could muster.

"I won't," he said in a tone that matched my own.

I knew I was in trouble the minute he stepped off the elevator. Or as I would tell Jonah McCoy the next morning, "Jesus, he looks even better at

forty-seven than he did at twenty-nine! How can that be possible, Jonah?"
My cognitive lawyer grinned at me and said nothing.

The evening before I had waited for Ian's elevator to come down with
my eyes shut, remembering our last good-bye: 1983, the St. Regis Hotel,
New York. Amanda and Spencer, ages three and five, not quite recovered
from chickenpox. After morning coffee I had kissed him good-bye and
gotten into the elevator, framed by Spencer and Amanda, each child holding a hand. Our eyes met. The doors closed.

1991. The doors opened. Both of us garbed in navy. I kissed Ian hello
as if we'd seen each other only yesterday. My lips brushed metal, and I
wondered if he'd been mugged in the Park. "How do you like my braces?"
he asked.

"My first thought was that someone had hurt you."

"No, it's my jaw; it's receding, and that has made the teeth turn inward.
The braces are to bring them back into line. I should have done something about this years ago. Now it's going to take twice as long to fix."

This made me smile inwardly. Obviously his orthodontist hadn't told
him the clinical term for his condition, "characterizing," and this amused
me, because my nickname for him had always been "The Character." In
the old days, I had even called him Character instead of Ian. So *now* he's
characterizing! I thought. Interesting timing, and he was obviously uncomfortable about it. To divert him from his self-consciousness about the braces,
I decided to move up several inches.

"I always knew you'd look terrific with grey hair," I bantered as he led
me into the dining room.

"Hey, c'mon, there isn't that much of it!" he said in that "watch it!" tone
I'd always loved.

"Well, after all, we are middle-aged! Did you bring the pictures of Cam?"
I asked.

"Yes!"

"Does she have you whipped into shape yet?"

"No. We have fashion fights. And let me tell you about the only time
she ever had a temper tantrum with me," and he was off and running
about life with a delightful-sounding three year-old.

"And how did you handle the tantrum?" I asked, "With laughter?"

"*No!* – with brute force – I wrestled her into her overalls!" I laughed out
loud, resisting the temptation to add that my memories of him only covered the reverse operation. And then I knew he was in trouble too.
"Cheers!" he said, grazing my hand, raising his glass, looking into my
eyes, and promptly spilling his Dubonnet all over the place.

"To better times," I edited after they'd brought him a new one. He didn't
have to say a word. A recent veteran of domestic wars, I knew pain when
I saw it, and beneath that exquisite face lay pain. Four eyes reconnected in
the orbit of greens and browns, sown so long ago.

He began with the perfunctory questions, the sort one asks after a long absence: How were my parents, how was my brother. But what he really wanted to tell me about was *his* family, and their present challenges. Each of us had a parent in a final, but agonizingly prolonged stage of neurological illness. We adored our children. Both of us were working terribly hard at our demanding jobs.

I told him a little about Genesis, and how all that had happened with *Molecular Modelling News* had been a consequence of my mistaken premise that Duncan was seriously ill, with epilepsy and possibly a brain tumor.

"I started out thinking, 'Ursula, your husband is seriously ill. Learn chemistry and save the family,' but you know what happened instead, Ian? Somewhere along the line, I fell in love with the subject. You ought to come over to Genesis some time, and let us give you a demo."

"I don't want to see a demo," said Ian Ruddway, "unless you'll stand naked in front of the screen for it."

Same old Ian, I thought. "Well, for that you'd have to buy your own Silicon Graphics, and you probably can't afford one," I said.

"You're probably right," smiled Ian Ruddway, Esquire. "My braces hurt," he said. "They were adjusted yesterday. It isn't pain, exactly, but it's uncomfortable."

"I know," I said sympathetically. "I never actually had them myself, but Amanda has explained it to me. The two of you could compare notes."

A third party listening might have found this conversation hard to follow, because of the jumping from subject to subject and the parts that were omitted. But I could still read between his lines: banter alternating with serious stuff, a trait we'd always shared, that I'd since learned drove others up the wall. I'll bet he still isn't even aware of that, I thought.

"Are you very hungry?" I asked. "What did you have for lunch?"

"I grabbed a hot dog at the courthouse, so yes, I'm very hungry. Shall we start with a Caesar Salad? What do you think you want for dinner?"

"Anything that used to swim," I replied.

I can't believe I'm in this moment, I thought, sneaking a long look at him from behind my menu. I cannot believe that this day has come. And why does it feel like we've never been apart? He's slipped right back in like we've been having dinner together for twenty years. How can this be so easy? I wondered, as I gazed at the alabaster planes of his face, angled and made for splitting light.

He must have been thinking of light as well. "It seems so strange to be eating dinner in daylight," he remarked.

"You often work late," I said.

"Yes," he said, in a voice that indicated further questions were unnecessary.

"Tell me about jury duty."

And he was off and running again, this time teaching me new words like *"voir dire,"* and telling me about the parts of the process that had surprised him. His impressions tumbled out in the speech patterns that matched my own. He wanted to tell me everything, and I wanted to hear it all. I always learned things from him, no matter how mundane the subject. More than that, I always enjoyed learning new things from him.

"Will you split a veggie with me?" I asked. "I like everything."

"Asparagus," he said, when the waiter returned.

"One plate or two, Sir?"

"One!" affirmed Ian Ruddway in a tone more policy statement than polite response. He remembers, I thought. Blast it all, he remembers asparagus. He remembers everything. And he is laughing at me, and I am laughing back.

"Here, I've brought you something for Cam," I said reaching into my bag. It was *Make Way for Ducklings,* the children's classic from Ian's own era, and the story's setting was just beyond the window where we were dining.

"It's a good story," he said. "It has all the right . . ."

". . . elements," I said.

"Yes."

We chattered about our children. I started to tell him a story about Spencer and Amanda, but he quickly interrupted me. "You told me that one before," he said, refilling my wine glass.

I was nonplussed.

". . . at breakfast in 1983."

"Oh, I guess I forgot . . ."

"That's okay," he said smiling, delighting in catching me. "Go on. I want to hear it again." He remembers more details than I do, I thought. This isn't just happening to me. It's like this for him too.

"Tell me more about Cam," I said. "What does she like to do?"

"Well, she goes to school, and she has her play dates. She likes to watch videos, but I restrict them. We argued about it just as I was leaving. Oh, and Ursula, she's great at hailing taxis. You should see her hail a taxi!"

"But what is she interested in?" I asked again.

"How the hell should I know!" he said irritably. I had touched a nerve. I was surprised to learn he was a much stricter parent than I, regularly censoring television and arguing about clothing, two things I rarely did. I guess I'd been lucky on that score. Duncan and I had been pretty much in accord about such things when Spencer and Amanda were very young. Parenting with Ian would have been a battle royale, I thought. Glad I missed it after all!

"You should go to boxing fights," he said, jumping to his television and sports-related legal work. This would have enthralled Spencer, our resident sports junkie, but it was totally unimpressive to me.

"I prefer pillow fights!" I said, as we talked on, fully and easily. Can a conversation be described as luxuriant? I think so, for after all these years, conversing with Ian remained for me like diving into a mountain of soft pillows and thoroughly enjoying every bounce.

"Ian, I am from the school of two and through, but thank you anyway," I said, the next time he reached for the wine bottle. "I am the designated driver tonight."

And then he asked me about the alcoholism and what had happened with Duncan. "It's too much to tell over dinner, and I don't want to talk about all of it tonight. Here, the beginning of it is in this holiday letter I mailed out at Christmas. You can take a copy and read it later. There's a picture of me and the children, too."

He stared at the children for a long stretch of moments. "You're right," he said, "they don't look like you."

"Well, Spencer has Duncan's features, but my colors, and Amanda looks just like Duncan except that she has dark eyes, my ears, and my lips, and the same mind. Of course, nobody got that terrific red hair, but maybe the next generation . . ." I trailed off, remembering the man in my scrapbooks and memories, the one who would never come back. Dr. Wally Post's words played again in my mind, "Ursula, you are dealing with more than one person."

Then I pulled myself together. "I wish you had known Duncan before," I said. "He was *so wonderful.*"

Ian must have realized I was wandering, and brought me back. "Look, you don't have to tell me everything tonight, but I want to know what happened to you. You're even thinner than I remember. But you look wonderful. I want to know, what happened . . . are you all right?" He had reached for my hand, and stroked it as he spoke. The magic is still here, I thought. "Are you all right now?"

"Annealed is the word," I said. "I've been melted and cooled and melted and cooled, many times. I'll tell you a little . . ." I began, and finished up with, "The bottom line is this, when you uncover alcoholism, run don't walk. I don't ever want to be under the control of an alcoholic again. What they say in Al-Anon is true – when you are controlled by an alcoholic, your life really *does* become unmanageable."

Then he asked about the children. "The jury is going to be out for years on that one, Ian, but the doctors and school counselors insist that the first five years of a child's life are all, and Spencer and Amanda couldn't have had a better foundation. So it's a good thing this didn't happen to them in the first five years, and I am glad it didn't happen to them at the end of their childhood."

"Well, for sure not in the first five years."

"There is no good time for this to happen, for children's lives to be torn apart, but maybe the middle *was* the best, because I still have a stretch of years to give them a stable life before they go off on their own. There's still time to rebuild."

"You know, Ursula, we won't know for years how they really are."

"Ian, here's how I see it, and this is what I tell them: 'I get up every day and paste a smile on my face and go to work, and I expect you to do the same!' And they have. They are living miracles as far as I'm concerned."

"You are unbelievable!" he said.

"Everything I am telling you is true. And *Snow Job* is just the tip of the iceberg! What is going on in Boston legal circles is a national disgrace. It's all in my book. And you should see me in court, Ian. I'm great in court!"

"Ursula, I don't *ever* want to see you in a courtroom. Now eat your asparagus! You ordered it!" He misses his three year-old, I thought. "What about the pictures of Cam you promised to bring? Let's have a look at them."

"They're in my room, you can look at them after dinner," he smiled, trying again to top off my wine.

"*You* can bring them down to the lobby," I smiled back at him, putting my hand over my glass.

"Some dessert?" interrupted the waiter, handing us menus.

"Yes!" said Ian Ruddway. "Ursula, you don't eat enough dessert. Now what are you going to have?"

"I want chocolate mousse!" I replied with great enthusiasm.

"Well, it isn't on the menu," he said scanning, "but if you want chocolate, you can have the profiteroles."

"They won't be as good as mine," I said remembering our 1983 discussion about my custom of making my own croissants, and I went off to powder my nose.

When I returned he gestured to my place and said, "I ordered vanilla ice cream for you, because I knew that was what you would want. Now eat your ice cream!"

"And did you get me coffee with caffeine in it?" I couldn't resist asking.

"I did, even though I think you have too much of it!"

This delighted me, and would continue to delight me despite my daughter's disapproval: "Really Mom, how boring. Why would you be interested in a man who knew exactly what you wanted for dessert?" Why indeed my darling daughter!

After he'd polished off his crème brûlée, Ian Ruddway excused himself for a minute, and I did not miss this opportunity to divest the table of my wine glass: "Please make this disappear before he comes back," I said to the understanding waiter, obviously an old hand at these 'ply her with wine' encounters.

But we were not fast enough, and Ian Ruddway was swiftly upon us. "What happened to your wine?" he demanded in his toughest cross-examination tone.

"Maybe I drank it . . ." I laughed defiantly.

"Like hell you did! Time to go," said Ian Ruddway, guiding me away from the table.

"Sometimes, you are so full of shit," I said with great affection, as he led me to the elevator.

Here we go, I thought. He didn't ask my permission, just punched the button to the floor of his room. The man knew I was a sucker for children. "Excuse me, Sir, I just want to turn down the bed," said a hotel staffer as we neared his door. "I'll just be a minute." I don't know how I'll do this, I thought, but I will. Being forced to watch him turn down the bed, and knowing we were not going to be in it, was a test of strength for both of us, I think.

"Where are the pictures of Cam?" I said crisply, deliberately steering Ian's attention to the only reason I had come up with him.

"How tall are you?" he asked, abruptly changing the subject, taking control of the conversation, and deliberately delaying in his lawyerly way.

"I'm 5'5". Now where are the pictures?"

"You are not 5'5"," he argued back, chin out, looking me squarely in the eye. "You're 5'6"!"

I don't believe this, I thought, somewhat irritated and feeling as manipulated as a juror. "Ian," I said in mild exasperation, "I am 5'5", I have always been 5'5", and *don't tell me how tall I am!!!* Now where are the pictures?"

Attorney Ruddway smiled in triumph. "In my briefcase, here," he said handing me an envelope.

I slowly took out three photos. A little girl with the solemn expression of a wise, old soul looked back at me from the snapshots. Her grey coat matched her eyes. I studied the photos for a long moment, as he had mine, and then I said the first word that came: "thoughtful. It is a thoughtful face."

"Cam is a piece of work!" he said proudly.

"She has a thoughtful face," I repeated.

Having seen what I had come for, I put the pictures down and moved toward the door, but Ian quickly scooped his arms around me, and pulled me down hard into his lap on the couch. I pushed to get away, but then he held me even more firmly and forced me to be still.

"I . . . am . . . just . . . going . . . to . . . hold . . . you," he said in a slow, steady voice, spacing out the words for emphasis. When I tried again to struggle against him, he said, "I want to talk about the past, Ursula. I am going to hold you, and we are going to talk about these things."

No, I thought. We can't do that. We can't talk about our past. But he was determined to make me face this, just as he had made me face other things twenty years before. Damn you, Ian Ruddway, and bless you, Ian Ruddway. "Well, can you do that?" I asked. "Are you really able to *just* hold me?"

"Yes!" And after that I relaxed, and Ian held me more loosely. He cradled my head in his arm, as he used to do in the Ann Arbor and New York days, and I snuggled into his lap and let all the old feelings stir. They flickered over me, the way sunshine plays with branches on a breezy autumn day. This is October, and I am in Ian Ruddway's arms, I told myself. It's only May outside this room. Yes, you still give me that "all systems go" feeling, I thought to myself, but I am not going to do anything about it tonight. Not that that would matter in the grand scheme of things. Long ago I had accepted that the sense of ownership would remain. Nothing would ever change that. Not time, not space, not marriages, not children. Whatever this is, I thought, why does it continue to have a life of its own?

"You are still the most exciting person I have ever met!" he said.

"So are you!" I whispered.

"And you deserve to be hugged. Ursula, I wasn't equipped to deal with you twenty years ago."

"I wasn't equipped to deal with you, either. And you used to frighten me." Was I really admitting this out loud? "You used to frighten me because you were so . . . implacable. But you don't frighten me anymore."

He listened, and after we'd both thought about what we'd said for a minute, he went on. "Ursula, I didn't know what to do with you in those days. I got you off to such a bad start. I'm sorry for that. I remember the first moment I ever saw you. I looked at you and thought to myself, I want to . . ."

And I listened to his words, the ones I might have used if I'd been brave enough to say them. The conversation that followed was more revealing than sex. Is this torture or pleasure? I wondered, twisting in his arms. "Ursula, twenty years ago, I was prepared for anything, anything but what I found . . ."

"I have always been true to myself," I interrupted him. "I wanted to be in love the first time, and I was." And then, ". . . I am sorry for certain things too."

"You? What do you have to be sorry about?"

"Oh, I remember a certain moment when I said . . ."

"Oh that . . ." he said, his voice trailing away into a painful episode we both remembered. "But you were completely justified . . ."

"Well, that's not the point," I said. "The point is I'm sorry I said it. And I apologize." And the hurt I had carried around inside me for nearly twenty years evaporated. We nestled in each others' arms and talked about our missteps and our regrets. "Ian, I never expected to be able to have this conversation with you." I reached up and stroked the alabaster planes and traced lazily over the smile that framed his face. This is pain transformed into pleasure, I thought, which is an even higher form of pleasure.

"What went wrong with your marriage?" he asked.

"Ian, I still don't know. But this is what my lawyers say: Number 2 says

Duncan is stupid; Number 4 says he's nuts; and Number 3, who knows me better than any of the others, says that Duncan couldn't deal with my high energy level."

"Well, I have a high energy level," said Ian Ruddway brightly. "How many lawyers were there, altogether I mean?"

"Four, just the ones I already told you about, and that was quite enough for me, thank you! It's all in *Snow Job*. I explain all of it in the book. I am sitting on the miniseries of the decade, Ian Ruddway, *and I know it!*"

But Ian's mind was still on Duncan. Given our correspondence over the past winter, I had assumed he was coming to Boston for *Snow Job*. Now I realized he had come for me. *"Something WAS missing,"* he insisted.

I looked at this man who knew me better in some ways than any other, and I thought about this. Maybe something had been missing, but I didn't know what it was. I had done my best, and I could live with that. I was at peace about that part of the Duncan story. Maybe it showed.

"You look great!" he said suddenly, pulling me more tightly into his arms.

"I am great!" I said. When I am in your arms, I am great, Ian Ruddway, I thought, remembering another poem I'd never given him: "With each new mile I've grown more sure, more fleet, but all that I have done is to complete the orbit we had sown so long ago . . ."

"And you smell so good!" And then, "How many men have you slept with besides your husband and me?"

"That's my business," I said.

"How many? *I want to know.*"

"That's not your business," I repeated, "and besides, it's a small number." This was ridiculous, and why did it matter now? After all these years, what possible difference could it make?

"How many?" he persisted.

"These questions are none of your business, but all right, cross-examine?!" I said. He nodded. "One," I said, "he was just a friend. In fact, we're still friends, and from it I learned that I have to be in love."

"Well, I wasn't in love twenty years ago," he announced.

This did not offend me. Well, maybe you're having a delayed reaction! I repressed! "Look Ian, I'll tell you now what I knew then. You weren't happy with *where you were* twenty years ago, so there was no way you could be happy with me."

"You're right. I wasn't happy." And then he blurted it out, what he had left unsaid at dinner: "Ursula, I love my daughter, but I don't like my wife."

He's not really saying this, I thought. "What don't you like about her?"

"We don't work as a team."

"Ian, why did you marry her?"

"I was the right age. It was the right time. She wanted to."

Now, it was my turn. "How many times have you cheated on your wife?" Would he wriggle out, I wondered, or would he give me a straight answer?

"Once, but you did, too!"

"No, *that* was years ago, before Duncan. I was never unfaithful to Duncan."

". . . she left me . . . for a long time," he continued. "It didn't mean anything."

"She left you?" I was incredulous. Was the woman nuts? How could anyone leave someone like this?

And then he hastened to add, "And if I'd been married to you, it never would have happened."

You're damn right it wouldn't have happened, I thought. "How many women have you slept with all together?"

"Maybe twenty or thirty, I can't remember."

This made my skin creep, and I shuddered in disgust. "But I was the only . . ."

"Yes. You're not like other people," he added. "You never were. Even twenty years ago, you weren't doing what other people were doing."

"I'm still not," I said, "but you're not like other people either. You never were."

"That's right," he said. "And there hasn't been anyone in your life since Duncan left?"

"No one."

"But . . . what do you do? I mean . . ."

"Well," I said impishly, "*someone* is going to have a lot of pent-up demand to deal with — but he'll be equal to it!"

"Pent-up demand!"

I didn't need a Ph.D. or a law degree to tell what was coming next. "Look Ian, I don't want to fight with you."

"Ursula, I haven't even begun to fight with you!"

Now what in God's name was I supposed to say to that? "And I am not here to tease you."

"You're inhibited!"

"I am not inhibited when I am 'at home.'"

"You're shaking," he said, holding me with concern for the first time.

"Am I?" I hadn't noticed. "Ian, I think it's time for me to go. I've stayed too long as it is."

"Wait. I have to go the bathroom. Then I'll walk you down."

I had to go too. "Well, I'm after you!" I called jauntily, which caused Ian Ruddway to turn at the door, and give me an "Oh, really?" look. "I mean, "I'm next," I hastened to add. "I mean . . . oh, never mind!" and I waved him away.

Minutes later, he pulled me into his arms and tried again. "Ursula, this is probably your last chance to get oral sex from someone with braces!"

At this, all of me dissolved into laughter. Oh well, I guess you can't blame a fellow for trying. "You know," he said, "we should go away for about four days and just make love!"

"Look, Ian, if both of us were free, it would be a different story. But I can't do this. I can't do this to your family, and I won't do this to myself. If circumstances were different . . . then, yes."

"Yes?"

"Yes . . . in a heartbeat! You are just like Huey Valentine!" I added.

This caught him off balance, just as I intended. Lawyers like to think they have a monopoly on that, but they don't. "Huey Valentine is a character in *The Bumbling Bee,* one of my books," I explained, diverting him. "He's you. I named him after Dewey Ballantine — and he is a bad guy until the last two chapters. It takes place in the District of Column Bee. I finished that one in 1984!" Mr. Ruddway was now just enough unraveled to allow me out of the room gracefully, figuring the remark was so outrageous that it was probably true, which it was.

"All right," he conceded. "But I am taking you down to the lobby."

In the elevator, he looked me squarely in the eye, and I looked back. I always do. "Ian, I give this romance an 'I' for Incomplete."

"So do I."

"I forgot to call ahead for the car, so why don't we just say good-night now and . . ."

"No, I will wait with you for the car." Then he made some awkward remark about seeing me again — on his terms of course. "Look Ian, that's not what I want. That's not my vision for my life. God knows I have my problems, but lack of clarity isn't one of them. I've never wanted anything exotic; I just want a plain old life, with one special person in it, the same thing I've always wanted, and what I had with Duncan for many years . . . or what I thought I had."

"That's not what most people want," he said.

"Well, it's what I want, and I can't be the only person in the world who feels that way."

Parting was not smooth; it never was. For two reasonably articulate people, we had never quite mastered saying good-bye, and I cried most of the way home on the Mass Pike. Inverary Lane was hushed when I came in — children gone to bed, even the cat was quiet. "Well, Streak Louise," I called to her, "I seem to have blown it with Ian Ruddway once again." Our normally aloof cat mewed sympathetically and rubbed her face against my hand.

I looked at the clock. Midnight. This is ridiculous, I thought, sitting down on my bed. I am forty-one, not fourteen. I picked up the phone and dialed the Ritz. He answered on the first ring. I didn't even say hello. "Ian, dinner was nice, but I don't feel good. If you're still free could you meet me at the Swan Boats tomorrow afternoon? Say around three?"

"*Yes!*" he said, in that "Ursula, get down here!" tone that no one had dared use on me in years.

XXIX

Freedom Trails

We also should walk in newness of life.
— Romans 6:4, *The Bible*

Early the next morning, after Jonah and I had finished with legal matters, I asked for a little personal advice from my cognitive lawyer. "Jonah, over the past year we've talked a lot about what makes relationships fall apart. Now I want to ask you a very different question: what makes something work?"

"Acknowledging the other person," he said.

Acknowledging the other person or as Webster put it, "To admit to be true or as stated. To confess. To recognize the authority or claims of. To recognize and answer. To express thanks for. To state that one has received. To admit or affirm as genuine." Ian and I had begun to do these things last night. We would go further that afternoon, in a chilly Public Garden, which was nonetheless in bloom.

Spring likes to take its time in Boston. The day was damp and grey, and wind whipped at the fairyland of blossoms that surrounded the Swan Boats. My coral linen suit was more in accord with my spirits than the thermometer as I shivered across the Common and Charles Street toward a waiting Ian Ruddway.

Never had I worried about finding him in a crowd or large place. I had always been able to do it by instinct. Would the old system work, as it had always done? I wanted to find out and started down a path at random. Within seconds the familiar force pulled me back and sent me down another. I followed it. And at the end was Ian Ruddway, sitting on a bench reading a book. *It still works*, I smiled to myself. The green eyes homed in on me over the tortoise-shell reading glasses that rimmed his face.

"Have you ever walked the Freedom Trail?" he greeted, waving a book.

"Parts of it," I answered, "but someday I want to do it all."

"Did you sleep last night?" he said half in irritation, half in resignation.

"I slept from twelve to three; I soul-searched from three to six; and I've been with lawyers since breakfast!"

"Oh, your divorce lawyers or your intellectual property lawyers?" he asked archly.

"Both!" I answered. And now you, I added silently. Now you, Ian Ruddway, the most challenging and exasperating of "All My Lawyers."

"I want to apologize about last night," he began. "I had too much to drink. I got wimpy on hugging. I got too aggressive."

Wimpy on hugging. What an interesting way to put it. "You were fine," I assured him, referring to the proper way we had, in fact, both conducted ourselves.

"And, Ursula, if you think it was easy . . ."

Tell the truth, said the little voice inside; tell him the part you're not saying. "It was a great act of will for me, too," I added, completing the thought for both of us.

That settled, he shifted gears. "It's not fair for me to involve you in my familial problems."

"You're right," I agreed, "It's not fair." I wanted him to know I recognized our respective needs for space, that I didn't want the total immersion of twenty years ago, but that I could still be there for him. "Ian look, I cared then. I care now. I probably always will care."

"Shall we walk?" he asked.

"Yes."

And we talked. Mostly light, bantering stuff. About the trees. Ian loved trees, had always been intrigued by trees, and he had to stop and examine many of them closely. I was used to this. And about the Swan Boats, he'd been reading up on their history; I'd been reading up on the fiftieth anniversary of the book, *Make Way for Ducklings,* and the visit of its author to the Public Garden the previous weekend. About his lovely room at the Ritz: "It doesn't have a great view," he groused.

"Well, who goes to the Ritz to look out the window?" I grinned at him, and he grinned back.

"Hey, be careful!" he called as I balanced in my spectator pumps on the edge of the boat pond. "You'll fall in and ruin your suit!"

I'll bet that's how he talks to Cam, I thought. "Well, I might, but then I should enjoy being fished out by you!"

"Well, I don't think it's very deep anyway, but you're so light!"

Which made me turn serious. "Ian, I'm not saying what I came to say."

"Why not?"

"Sometimes even writers and editors have trouble finding the right words . . ." I confessed, and then I was able to begin. "I want to tell you what I liked about last night: . . . You know exactly how to hold me . . . it felt so good to have that conversation with you, or, the beginning of a conversation with you, about the past . . . you have always made me face things, and no one else has ever done that. I think that's because everyone else has always been afraid."

"Let's sit down and have some of that juice you brought," he said. "Shall I open them? What kind is it?"

"I don't know. Whatever was on the top shelf." This was not the carefully planned Ursula he remembered from twenty years ago. "Have you ever had anything like this before?" He knew exactly what I meant.

"No."

"What drives this relationship? Why does it endure?"

"I'm not wise enough to know," he said humbly. Nor was this the man with all the answers I remembered.

Children scampered by as we talked. Some of them paused to smile and say hello to us, as children often used to whenever I was with Ian in the New York and Ann Arbor days. Several were getting a little too active for their caretaker, and she moved in to punish them, unjustly I thought. "We all have such different ways of doing it," I said.

"Yes," said Ian.

"I hate what children have to put up with!" And I could tell he did, too.

"Did I tell you last night that my wife has lost her job . . . after twenty-five years . . . just like that?"

"No, when did it happen?"

"About six weeks ago, and she made a lot of money. We depended on her income. If she doesn't find something soon, we're going to have serious financial problems."

"But wasn't she really good at what she did?"

"Yes, but that didn't matter. A new person came in, he wanted to bring in his own people; he was within his rights."

"But doesn't she have friends and contacts at the other . . ."

"Yes, but no one is calling her back. I think she's really going to have a hard time, Ursula. And her father is dying too."

"You know, one of the things that's helped me during this crisis was to expand roles, because time chips away at your roles, and you have to keep building new ones. When your parents die, you stop being a daughter; when your husband leaves, you stop being a wife. And so I'm taking on new roles: building *Molecular Modelling News,* serving on a church committee, doing more in Al-Anon, working to get the laws changed in Massachusetts, writing two books. And in the course of all that, my world is getting larger and more wonderful. Does that make any sense to you at all?"

"It seems logical," he said.

"It sounds like your wife is losing a lot of her roles, but all at once," I continued. "Try to be good to her during this time. She is going to need you." Say it now Ursula. Say it now. Asking him is the only way you're going to find out. "Ian, do you think you've done your best with your marriage?"

"No," he said, matching my directness. "I could do better."

"Well then, go home and do better," I said. "Go home, and do your best! And I'll be cheering for you. And in the same breath I will tell you that if you do your best, and you still can't make your marriage work – then I see no reason why we can't reclaim our relationship. But we must both be free to do so."

"I think you're right," he said quietly.

I watched him draw inward to think. Could he know how much I wanted him? That I wanted him so much, I saw no happy resolution for us unless he went home to work out his life on his own? Not so different from twenty years ago, I knew *we* couldn't be happy until he was happy. It was *our* only chance, and it would take a long time, if it ever happened at all. And there was little reason to think it would.

"You know," I continued, " practically everything bad has already happened to me. I've been left, I've been fired, I've been divorced, I've been financially ruined, and I've been told I might be dying – and I'm still here. Nothing scares me anymore. It is very strange to be walking about the Earth, and not to feel afraid." And then I asked him the hard one: "What do you think you want for the *rest* of your life? Do you know?"

"That's a real good question. When I was in law school at Ann Arbor, I took a Family Law course." He stared off into space, very far away from me. "Ursula, divorce is war."

"And I wasn't about to argue with him," I would later tell Jonah, who corrected me: "Ursula, if you are ever lucky enough to have that conversation with Ian Ruddway again, tell him that sometimes, divorce can be peace." But I would never do that. Ian had to sort this out on his own, without any external pressure from me. The park bench was starting to feel confining. I wanted to get up and walk. We could do no more today.

He knew it, too. "This afternoon was a good idea," he said, as we strolled toward the parking garage.

"Everything is going to be all right," I assured him, "if I just live long enough. You're a good person," I said, patting him on the shoulder, ". . . and life is precious."

"You're a good person, too," he said, pulling me into his arms to say good-bye. Then there were kisses, like all the good-bye kisses that had gone before them: anything but good-bye.

"How did it go in the Public Garden?" asked Jonah a few weeks later.

"Oh, fine I guess, but it wasn't easy, Jonah. Either I'll never hear from him again, or he'll probably call me up in about five years and say, 'Ursula, I got divorced yesterday. What time are we having dinner tomorrow night?'"

"Sounds like a very confused fellow," said my cognitive lawyer. "Doesn't sound like a man of action. Does the pleasure outweigh the pain?"

"Yes . . . but it's so hard, Jonah."

"Well, as long as the pleasure outweighs the pain, continue to see him

Ursula – but on your terms. Until Ian straightens out his life, he should just be another name in your Rolodex," said my cognitive lawyer protectively.

None of this stopped spring from unfolding, and a lot of my energy remained focused on tying up the loose ends of my life. Many people had told me that the mopping-up process would take a long time, a year or more, and they were right.

On the legal front, Duncan and Chubb were still dawdling on the trusts for the children which were supposed to have been done in February. And then there was my car. Without my knowledge, Duncan had changed the registration of my car from Conover to Farboro, and also neglected to inform me about the excise tax bills for it that the Registry kept sending to his house. Only when my name was placed on a Sheriff's List did I learn about all this, and by then I had racked up fines for ignoring the unpaid tax bills. Straightening this out sucked up another two days of time from Genesis.

"Being a law-abiding citizen in Massachusetts is getting to be a full-time job!" I said in exasperation to the top gun at the Registry, and he agreed that The System had shown a lot of irrationality in my case. But he could do nothing about it, except try to plug this loophole for the future, which he promised to do. Nevertheless, current law was clear: I would have to pay the excise tax and all fines on back taxes to the City of Farboro, and then go to my own Town Hall for a credit when the Conover tax bill arrived. Of course Duncan was in no trouble whatsoever for what he had done. Outraged, I fired off a check and letter to the Town Hall in Farboro, summing up with: ". . . let the record show that neither I, nor my car, have *ever* resided in your City!"

And then there was also the matter of Gabriel G. Reed. Although Heyward had earlier reported that Reed would drop the suit in Muni Court, the fee dispute before the Boston Bar, the lien on my house, and the balance of my bill, in exchange for my not using his real name in any books I wrote or public speaking engagements I accepted, all the paperwork was slow to arrive. This was causing Asa no end of worry, and Merrill Crosby agreed he was right to be concerned. When the paperwork eventually did turn up, I took it down to Tony in Conover Center to get the Release Form framed, along with a cartoon I had been saving for Gabriel.

The cartoon showed a pining cow, with a broken heart bubble above her head, gazing longingly at her bull, who in turn was gazing longingly at a wooden cow out in a field. The caption read: "Can't you see that she's nothing but plywood?" I told Tony I wanted to frame this and send it to Gabriel with a note:

Dear Gabriel — We started with a cartoon, and I am glad that we are able to end with one. Enclosed please find some companions for 'Infidelity' on the wall behind your desk.
After clouds, sunshine! — U. L. C.

It was to be my final peace offering, which Jonah heartily approved.

When I went to Firenze Frames to pick it up, Tony apologized for the cost overrun. "Oh well, Tony," I said philosophically, taking out my checkbook, "after thirteen grand, what's another $40?"

"That sounds like what happened to me," called a woman from the other side of his shop. "I had to buy my GEC stock at $200 and sell it for $59."

"Yeah, well look who's running it!" I said.

"You're telling me!" she replied, taking the conversation more seriously than I had intended. "I took the package and ran. Until recently, I was a writer there for fifteen years, and I know *all* the senior management. My husband is still there."

"Well, my former husband is too, and I know just what you mean."

"Do you live in Conover?" she asked. "Hey, what's your name?"

"Yes, over on Inverary Lane. I'm Ursula Charbonnier."

"Oh my God, Duncan Charbonnier's wife!"

"Ex-wife," I corrected.

"You can't believe what an asshole he is," she said. "You can't believe the stupid things that come out of his mouth at meetings. He makes no sense, and the amazing part is that nobody ever seems to notice. The only reason he gets away with it, is that he is *so good-looking!*"

"Well, what do you think of Sebastian Black?" I asked, referring to the senior VP who shepherded Duncan's operation.

"Oh, he's an even bigger asshole!" she said.

I'm on a roll, I thought. I'll go ahead and ask her. "And what do you think of Ivy Parrish?"

"Processor TWERP!" she chortled.

Tony's mouth was hanging open. I just shrugged my shoulders. What next, I thought. "We should have lunch sometime!" she said as she left the shop.

It was just another of several indications that I wasn't the only one who was catching on to Duncan. In late spring, Genesis hired a new receptionist, who had worked in Duncan and Ivy's group the summer that he left our family. "Something strange was definitely going on in Duncan's group that summer," she said.

Then, for the first time in several years, we got another call for Duncan Charbonnier the Potter. "Oh, he lives in Farboro now," I said obligingly. "Let me give you his number."

A picture was starting to emerge, and there was plenty wrong with it!

"Someday the pieces will come together," said Jackie Melrose when I recounted these things, "but maybe not for years, Ursula. And when they do, the puzzle will all make sense. There is more to come," said my stalwart friend.

But that wasn't so important now. What mattered to me was that we had survived, and it was time to say thank you to the people who had helped us through the storm: by chairing an Al-Anon meeting; by educating CAMD scientists about intellectual property law; by working hard to get the laws changed in Massachusetts so that this couldn't happen to more innocent nurturers and their children; and by reaching out to people like Julia Holliday, who were still very much in the hell of it all.

In June, I went to a lecture and panel discussion on "Divorce and Substance Abuse" at a nursing school in Framingham. Psychiatrists, social workers, and lawyers spoke from their respective viewpoints, and this was what they said: "The substance abuser will do *anything* to protect his addiction, including destroying his family. Addiction is a way to survive. The addict lives a life of extremes, looking for answers externally in order to survive internally. He is always seeking to fit in, to find the right way to behave, to be a part of something, to feel normal, and in the course of that, he skips his own needs. His denial will persist, even when confronted with irrefutable evidence."

I had lived it all, but most of the people in the large audience were where I had been two years before: at the very beginning of learning about court-induced poverty, judicial indifference to children's needs, and just how clever the substance abuser can be at fooling every decision-maker in The System.

"Speak out," I urged them, in a reprise of Trudy Hale's 1990 advice to me. "Tell your friends and neighbors you are in trouble and why. Be explicit. And they will respond by reaching out to you. Substance abusers can only get away with their behavior when everyone around them remains silent. Be silent no longer! Tell people what is really happening to you."

Shortly thereafter, I attended an organizing meeting for the first Massachusetts chapter of ACES (Association for Children for the Enforcement of Support), at St. Paul's Episcopal Church in Conover. Here I learned that roughly two-thirds of fathers are delinquent in paying child support, and that Massachusetts is one of the only states in the country without an ACES chapter, according to Annabella Janeway, a Conover lawyer who had been working for years on the child support problem.

"Why don't they just get networked?" I asked her. "For openers, why not create linkage between the IRS and the child support enforcers? With effective use of computers, Massachusetts ought to be able to track these people." Or as a software engineer I knew had so inelegantly put it, "If the Probate Court system were computerized, these guys wouldn't be able to hide their slop!"

Then the meeting turned to a discussion of some of the rotten behavior of the most famous and expensive divorce lawyers in Boston. You couldn't go anywhere without hearing about them: the Dirty Dozen, as most people called them, the Boys' Club, as I referred to them. And Reed's name was usually at the top of the list. "Hey, he isn't so bad once you scrape away the barnacles," I said.

"Yeah, but who has time to scrape away that many barnacles?" said Annabella, in a "you can't be serious!?" tone. Apparently Jonah and I were about the only people in Boston who saw any redeeming qualities whatsoever in Gabriel G. Reed.

Her attitude reminded me of something Robert P. Rhana, Julia's attorney, had said to me one day at the courthouse in Cambridge: "Gabriel G. Reed is going to have the biggest funeral in the history of Boston, because everyone is going to want to make sure that he's really dead!"

The more I was learning about the attitudes of lawyers toward The System and toward each other, the more I realized that there were other points in The System where change and healing might occur more readily. Al-Anon was one of those places for me. Or as a member of the Westbury chapter had put it, "Those of us who suffer with the disease of substance abuse in our homes never have to be alone again. We can walk into one of these rooms, in many countries in the world, and find people who can understand and help."

Later that spring, I chaired a meeting for the first time. That night, we were on Step Eleven which had been discussed at my very first Al-Anon meeting : "Sought through prayer and meditation to improve our conscious contact with God as we understood Him, praying only for knowledge of His will for us and the power to carry that out." The first time I heard those words, they had been a new concept for me; now they were an integral part of my life.

I underscored this transformation as I opened the meeting: "The first night I walked into this room, fourteen long months ago, my house was in foreclosure, my job was in jeopardy, my financial life was in ruins, and I was struggling to preserve my children's world. Today, these troubles are behind me, in large part because of what I've learned in this room, from all of you."

I talked about the control, the isolation, the distortions, and the blame which had gradually come to permeate our family life, in all its familiar forms: projection ("You can't read a map, Ursula." "You don't know how to balance a checkbook."); rationalization ("I only drank because you made me crazy. I only drank because I was unhappy with you."); and denial ("You have jumped to a lot of conclusions. The problem isn't the vodka bottles; it's that you went looking for them.").

And about "how circumstances come together," how in midlife, I had finally learned to receive: "special friends from the past are coming back into my life; *Molecular Modelling News* is flourishing against all odds; and my analytical nature is being tempered by faith. So how am I doing? Trust is a character defect that I am struggling to retain, and these days, when people ask me how I am, I just smile and say, 'I'm a beta test site for one day at a time!'"

A week later I had the unexpected opportunity to relay some of this to Dr. Harry Ballard when Julia Holliday checked herself into Appleton Hall. Ballard was now Julia's doctor too! It felt odd to be back on these hospital grounds, two summers later, amid the tall trees and brick buildings – this time as clear-headed visitor, not bewildered wife and mother. I looked for Julia in a dormitory with a dozen other patients and was directed to a small sitting room on the first floor, where she was waiting for me.

"Ursula, I've reached the end of my rope; I cannot go on. Hobart is taking splashy trips with his girlfriend Pansy, and driving a new sports car (actually Duncan had one too!), and the children and I are barely making it on child support – *when* Hobart feels like paying it. And God knows where we're going to live if Hobart has his way."

It was all true. Hub Safe had foreclosed on the Pigeon Place house the month before. I had attended the Public Auction in May, and watched as the bank bought it back (along with the second and third mortgage that Hobart had conned Julia into signing in her name only) for a fraction of its old market value. Julia had been forced to declare personal bankruptcy. Hub Safe planned to evict her and the four boys later in the summer, and they had no place to go.

"The high priority we claim to place on children and nurturing is not translated into reality by the Probate Court system in Massachusetts, is it, Ursula?"

"No, my friend. But the people of Massachusetts are going to do something about that. I'm having lunch with someone next week, Julia, someone who is determined to make a difference in The System."

"Who is it?"

"His name is Dan Pace. He's a software engineer, and he's been through hell with The System, too. It isn't only women who get screwed in Probate Court. Pace has some innovative ideas about how to marshal resources, computational and human, to clean things up in the Commonwealth. I heard him speak at a meeting last week, and he was very balanced and articulate."

"I just can't deal with anything new right now. You understand, Ursula. I'm just totally strung out."

"Just focus on getting strong, Julia, one day at a time, and then let's get you through the next court dates. When does Hub Safe take you back to court?"

"Early August. It's in Land Court, not Probate."

"Is Jeannie Curtin representing you?"

"No, she's still doing the divorce, but we had to get *another* lawyer."

"What about Martin?" I asked, referring to her bankruptcy attorney.

"He only does bankruptcy. This is for the eviction. I had to get someone else for Land Court. His name's Sherman Franklin. He's a small town lawyer in Westbury. He specializes in this sort of thing."

"But how will you pay him?" I asked.

"He's willing to wait, like Jonah."

An attendant came in. "Time for Mrs. Holliday's therapy."

"Get well, my friend," I said giving her a good-bye hug. "I still have that dream, Julia: that one day the Governor will invite us to the State House and say, 'Mrs. Charbonnier, Mrs. Holliday, conduct is no longer irrelevant in Massachusetts!' I'll let you know how things go with Dan Pace."

After some negotiating over our very busy schedules, Pace and I finally arranged to meet at an Uno's in Framingham for lunch one Sunday. I was reluctant about committing my energies to any political group, and asked a lot of questions. Yes, there were rotten judges and lawyers in The System, but were they going to be careful to not "throw away the baby with the bath water?" Were they going to be balanced? Was the group going to push for the election of judges?

"I'm from Ohio," I told Pace, "where judges are elected, accountable to the people. That doesn't mean there aren't some bad ones on the bench, but it does mean that The People have continual opportunities to throw them out."

"You're right that judges can act in Massachusetts with no fear of reprisal by the electorate," agreed Pace, "And yes, that's something we plan to address. The questions we need to focus on are: Are they acting within their jurisdiction? Are they performing judicial acts, or are they depriving citizens of their constitutional rights? Ursula, did you know that a lot of children in the Commonwealth aren't even being taught the Bill of Rights anymore? The younger members of my political group never learned about it in school!"

No, I hadn't known.

"Another concern I have is that the people at the last meeting just wanted to focus on divorce reform, and I'm more interested in general reform of the legal system in Massachusetts," said Pace.

"Well, what I'm interested in is making the premeditated financial murder of a family in Massachusetts as illegal as their premeditated physical murder. Most of all, I'd also like to fix it so that lawyers can't get rich off of situations like mine!"

"A lot of our people agree with you about that, so we've decided to split into two groups: one focused on divorce reform, and another focused on more general reform of the legal system."

"Well, I'll be happy to lend my writing and editing efforts to that second group, but it needs a name."

"Do you have any suggestions about that?"

"I think that it should be short and memorable, and more importantly, something positive, not something that's anti-lawyer or anti-anything. Something like . . ." I was thinking out loud. "How about JOLT?!" I said all at once.

"What would that stand for?"

"Oh, something like 'Join Our Legal . . .'" and for a moment I got stuck, and then it came. "'Join Our Legal Transformation,' what do you think of that?" I asked.

"I like it."

"And for a logo you could have a jolt of electricity going through a tipped scales of justice. Maybe that jolt could even unblind Justice's eye, and she could finally see what's really going on around her!"

"That's just what I was thinking," he said. "I'll bring it up, and see if we can get it adopted."

That was one of my first tentative steps toward change on a larger level, but concerns closer to home continued to take up most of my attention. The following weekend, Duncan turned up at Inverary Lane, and came into the house to pick up Spencer. "You still haven't given these children an honest explanation for what has happened in their lives," I said. "The truth will follow you wherever you go; you will never escape from the truth."

"Nobody cares about what I did, Ursula, except you."

"That's where you're wrong. Our children care, and someday you're going to have to get honest and tell them why you did this to our family."

"Well, I'll tell you now," he said. "I don't like you. In fact, I've hated you for years."

"Well, I don't hate you," I replied.

"I only drank because you made me crazy," said Duncan.

"Did you notice that he was smiling when he said that?" Amanda remarked later.

"Why did you go to four neurologists over all the years, knowing that the three of us were worried sick every time you had a CT or an EEG? How could you watch me study computational chemistry, knowing I only worked so hard because I thought you were seriously ill? And then tell people I only went back to work for my own pleasure? How could you waste the time of all those doctors, knowing that truly sick people needed them?"

"I was afraid I would lose my children if I didn't go to the neurologists," he said. "And that's exactly what happened."

"Lose his children," as if they were just another piece of property. The phrase sickened me. This interchange with Duncan only underscored Dr. Arthur's point: "Ursula, you are dealing with a very sick individual." Fortunately, I no longer had to deal with him on a regular basis. He was still using money as a weapon, making life as financially miserable for the three of us as the law would allow, but all other aspects of life were good and getting better with every passing month.

In August, life took an interesting turn. With the semiannual American Chemical Society Show only weeks away, Jeff Abbott announced that Genesis was going to merge with one of our rivals in California: Molecular Innovations, Inc. Their strength in the materials sciences would complement ours in the life sciences. Earlier in the year, MII had merged with another molecular modelling software house in Cambridge, England. With the three companies combined into one, the resulting company would span the globe. We were about to become tri-coastal!

The announcement of the merger at the American Chemical Society Show in New York in late August caused a flurry of media excitement in our field. There was a press conference and a champagne reception in the Penthouse of the Hilton. It was a magical, intensive week that would mark a turning point in the history of CAMD as an industry. There was much to look forward to, and as I rode the train home from New York, I dreamed about things to come. I could see a future again, and it looked bright.

I shared the long ride home with a kind man who had been at a securities convention in New York. Not the Wall Street variety of securities, as I had first thought, but the protection/burglar alarm type of securities. His name was Tim Gannon, and he'd been a state trooper in Massachusetts during the early years of his career.

He commented on the lack of security which had in part been responsible for the dreadful subway accident which had taken place during our week in New York. An intoxicated engineer, running a late night train on the Lexington Line, had ended up killing a lot of people and doing horrendous damage to the train tunnels beneath the city. In the aftermath of the tragedy, it was learned that the accident could have been prevented at many points along the way, if those who knew about the engineer's drinking habits and his condition that night had intervened.

"Alcoholics are having a devastating impact at all levels of our society," I told Tim Gannon, "and there is an incredible degree of tolerance for the havoc which they wreak in all our lives." Then I told him parts of our story.

"But, don't you think it's an illness?" he asked.

"Do we let blind people drive on 128?" I replied tersely. "I don't mean to sound uncharitable, Tim, but why do we let alcoholics drive the legal system? I'm all for tolerance, but not when that tolerance compounds the problem – for the alcoholic and everyone whose life he touches."

In the week after the merger announcement, Leslie Drew turned up at Genesis for what was to be his last Board of Directors meeting. After years of burning up venture capital and leading us down product development paths that ended in failure, Leslie was resigning from the Board as he had from the presidency. Duncan's 1985 prediction had turned out to be true: "Ursula, you'll be at Genesis long after Archie and Leslie are gone. You will be the last one left." Actually, two scientists – Frank Morrow and Venkatachalam – and I *were* the last ones left from the original crew. It was hard to believe. Frank Morrow chuckled when I mentioned Duncan's long-ago comment, "Well, he got one thing right, Ursula!"

After the meeting, I ran into Leslie Drew as he waited for the elevator. Very much out of character, he showered me with praise for *Molecular Modelling News*. "You know Ursula, if you keep this up, you just might get rich doing this!"

"I would settle for getting out of debt to the lawyers!" I said.

"Yes, well you shouldn't have had so many of them," beamed Leslie Drew, Esquire.

In September, Regina College reopened, and I started swimming again. This was our first "normal" autumn in three years, and I'll admit it, I was reveling in my re-acquired normalcy. That September, I was enormously grateful for the formerly tiniest of things: time to read a newspaper, time to cook for my family, time to write, and most of all for what Jonah kiddingly referred to as "l w/out l" – his code for "life without lawyers." It was one of his fondest wishes for me, and I was almost there, he and Ian Ruddway notwithstanding!

One morning, I found an amusing voice mail message from Jonah at my office. Paperwork from The Reed Matter had finally reached him, and my cognitive lawyer was actually singing on my answering machine: "Or press one for further options. Ta Dum de Dum . . . Your attachment has been dischahhhhged, so we'll see if *Banker & Tradesman* publishes *that,* and you get calls from all of your friends saying 'Oh, I'm so glad to see that the attachment on your house by that mean man has been – dischahhhged!' . . . We think alike . . . Call me, whenever you're ready, to talk about Trusts . . . Glad to hear you're thriving."

"Hi Jonah, I got your great message," I said by return voice mail. "I didn't know you could sing! Is an early morning okay?"

"Sure!" said my cognitive lawyer, later that day. "How about 6 a.m.?"

"You're testing me, Jonah. Someday I am going to scare you and say 'yes!' "

"7:30?" laughed Jonah McCoy. "Next Tuesday?"

"Done!" I said.

And the following Tuesday, we cruised through the legal business rapidly, which left a little time to chat about life. Life was going well for us both. I told him about my latest round of phone tag with Ian, still unresolved. "He called. I couldn't talk, and he sounded pretty annoyed. Then I called back, and he couldn't talk. When I got home that night, I learned he'd talked to Amanda in the middle of the day, when he thought he'd get the answering machine, just like when I was in New York for the ACS, and had deliberately called him when I knew I'd get his machine. And now I've left three phone messages for him, and haven't heard a word."

"This is going nowhere, Ursula," said my cognitive lawyer.

"I know . . . two people who desperately want to talk to each other . . . and don't know how."

"Ursula, do you know what you want?" asked Jonah.

"Yes, I've given it a lot of thought." And then, very slowly, "I . . . want . . . to . . . try . . . again."

What I didn't say was this: I want to find out what would happen if – what would happen if we both tried again and this time I did my best. Now it looked as if I would never get to.

Deep in my heart, I had a feeling that something momentous was happening in his life. The feeling had begun in mid-September, the day before he called Amanda. It was instinct, madness maybe, but gut, raw instinct, and I had promised myself never to doubt my instincts again when it came to Ian Ruddway. Time and "the way circumstances come together," as the Al-Anon book put it, proved my instincts about Ian had been right all along, right from the start. Now I was finally old enough, experienced enough, and confident enough to trust those instincts.

"Something is happening," I told Hailey Canfield. "Something is happening. I know it. But what?"

Days later, I opened *The New York Times,* to find part of my answer was on the front page of the Business Section. More articles were to follow through the fall. In a nutshell: Matsumoto, my Japanese employer of sixteen years ago, and another Japanese conglomerate were negotiating to buy a significant share of Ian's company. All the more amazing, the head of the Intellectual Property Department, at the Japanese conglomerate, was the author of an article I was planning to publish in the Law Series of *Molecular Modelling News.* Ian was in the thick of it; and from the sidelines, two threads of my past and two threads of my present were being rewoven into the tapestry that was my life. The article explained why three individuals, (Ian; the lawyer at the Japanese conglomerate; and my old boss from Matsumoto) weren't returning my calls in recent weeks: they were all very busy – negotiating with each other! I shared the *Times* articles with a delighted Jackie Melrose. "Just hold on Ursula," she encouraged. "It's all going to be all right."

XXX

First Things

De Nile isn't just a river in Africa.
– Al-Anon Slogan

While Ian was off in Asia cutting deals, there was plenty to occupy me right here at home in Conover. *Home.* A word on which I meditated frequently these days. How fragile was "home" as an idea and an entity in 1991 American life! In Conover alone, I knew of close to a dozen moms struggling to prevent court-induced homelessness. Julia, like most of the others, had small children and no place to go. And the year before, but for the grace of God and Jonah McCoy – Spencer, Amanda, and I would have lost Inverary Lane. Never mind that my neighbor Bill Britton, a lawyer, had said, "Ursula, this isn't the way the legal system is supposed to operate." In fact, this was the way the legal system *was* operating. "Wake up, America!" I wanted to shout. Why doesn't *The Conover Gazette* tell people what's really going on in Conover! I wanted to tell every nurturer of children in the Commonwealth just how unprotected she/he really was.

Since summer, Julia and some of the other moms had been in and out of courtrooms, fighting to postpone their evictions. Hobart had told both Julia and their *guardian ad litum* that his strategy was to get Hub Safe to evict Julia and the boys, so that he could commence another child custody suit – on the grounds that Julia could not provide adequate shelter for the children.

To the uninitiated, this might sound preposterous, but a friend of mine from Connecticut had just lived through the above scenario. After the courts awarded her only $200 a month in child support, she and her children became homeless; then her ex-spouse, a well-to-do architect who had run off with their son's second grade teacher, sued for custody of the children, in the same court that had said he did not have to pay for braces for his son's teeth. That the architect and his mistress made frequent pleasure trips to the Caribbean was as irrelevant to the court as the architect's new sports car. The bottom line was that the child would have to do without.

If the case in Connecticut were anything to judge by, the Conover moms were not going to have an easy time of it. The legal gymnastics and the fees that accompanied them in Land Court made what I had experienced in Probate look like mere calisthenics. One morning, after a session at the Westbury District Court where Julia had not fared well, I confronted Mortimer Hives, one of Hub Safe's attorneys. "You're a father with children. How can you do this, Mr. Hives? How can you put innocent mothers and children out in the street, particularly when the father is a wealthy and successful businessman?"

"*Oy, evay!* I don't like this," said Mortimer Hives, a petite man with fire engine red socks. "I'm just doing my job. I don't make the laws. I'm just trying to protect my client's million-dollar investment."

"Your client, Hub Safe, doesn't need these children's home, Mr. Hives. I know the people in your Foreclosure Department. I went through this last year, and came this close to being homeless myself, and my ex-spouse, who has a six-figure income, is a senior executive at Germane Engineering. Well, in the course of my foreclosure proceedings, I had the pleasure of meeting Richard Rapp, a very fine person I might add, in *your* Foreclosure Department. And this is what he told me, 'Mrs. Charbonnier, our bank doesn't want your house either,' so don't tell me the bank wants Julia Holliday's house. Richard Rapp used to send me 'Good luck' notes, *and he meant it!*"

Mortimer Hives twisted uncomfortably and tugged at his necktie. Feeling certain he was reacting to more than the lack of ventilation in the Westbury District Court, I continued. "We all pay the price of court-induced homelessness, Mr. Hives. Maybe not directly. But we all pay. Homeless children grow up to be angry adults. And children who have been told by the law that conduct is irrelevant, grow up to believe that conduct is irrelevant. And they will behave accordingly. You and I will have to live in that world, too."

"You're making Mr. Hives uncomfortable," interrupted Sherman Franklin, Julia's eviction attorney.

"I hope I make him uncomfortable. I hope I make him uncomfortable enough to think about what he's doing, and whether it really makes good sense. When Julia offered to use most of child support to pay rent to Hub Safe for the house on Pigeon Place, they should have accepted her offer. It would have been cheaper for the bank than to pay legal feels to Mr. Hives, and it would have been better for those little boys not to be evicted from their home."

"You make Mortimer Hives nervous," Julia said to me after we left the courthouse.

"I don't want to make him nervous, Julia. I want to make him think. Doesn't anyone in the system remember how to think?"

This was "Marathon Mode" times a thousand, and Julia was now bankrupt, exhausted, ill, down to ninety pounds, but somehow still fighting, thanks to the support of a Twelve Step Program. Her doctor, a colleague of John Arthur's, was appalled at what was happening to her and the boys, just as John Arthur had been appalled the previous year, in his conversations with Spencer and me. But the physicians were not only powerless to stop the economic violence that underlay their patients' ills. They could be sued if they even tried, and so they kept silent and did only what The Law of The Land allowed: they wrote prescriptions, offered us sympathy, and wished us better times.

Hobart Holliday's messages on Julia's answering machine spoke for themselves: "Julia, you better hear clearly . . . be prepared for another custody suit, be prepared for a continual fight. *You'll lose* . . . I'm going to ruin your life," in a reprise of Duncan's words to Amanda and me: "I'm going to destroy you."

"But he didn't destroy us," I told Julia. "He galvanized us." I wanted to shout: "Fight, Julia, Fight!" but instead I appeared at her door one Sunday noontime and gently said, "Come on, I am taking you out to lunch."

"Ursula, you don't have the money to go out to lunch!" she protested.

"Come on," I said, refusing to take no for an answer. "A picnic for two is waiting in the back of my station wagon, and it took a lot of courage to cook for The Conover Caterer! We are off to the Town Green."

"Now could you ask for a prettier setting?" I said as we spread the blanket under a golden maple across from the Town Hall. Children gamboled in the warm September sun, chasing dogs and Frisbees gone astray. I gazed over at the Tiffany window above the entrance to First Parish that faces the Post Road: Mary Magdalene in a garden, during a time of trouble.

"Here, open this," I said. "This isn't just a picnic. This is our first meeting to discuss *The Snow Job Cookbook*. We're going to get ourselves out of debt, and we are going to have a whole new life, just like Gabriel said. Now how does this sound: *The Snow Job Cookbook: Eating Your Way Through Mid-Life Re-Birth?* I'm going to write it, and you're going to test the recipes. I know how to write and make babies; you know how to cook and make babies. Massachusetts has proved, beyond a shadow of a doubt, that it's not safe to make babies and stay home and nurture them, so we're going to find another way to survive: by writing and cooking and encouraging others."

As Julia unwrapped the Flair pen, I continued. "I am getting recipes from a lot of the characters in *Snow Job* – even Duncan's lawyer is sending me a recipe. But I'm not a cook. I need you to test them, to tinker with them. You make them taste good, and I'll make them funny. For example, what do you think about a drink called 'The Jock Trap'? Or 'Fruit of the Doomed Quartet: Affidavit Apples, *Pro Se* Peaches, Preparation of Facts Pears, and Pleading Plums?'"

Julia Holliday laughed, the first laugh I had heard from her in a long time. "Hey, a Higher Power deals the cards, but *we* play the hand Julia, and we're gonna say that in our book! Now I have an idea for a drink called Poison Ivy, named after Ivy Parrish, but I can't decide what to put in it . . ."

"How about Chartreuse and vodka?" advised my culinary friend. "And the tag line could be, 'This would even turn an alcoholic off!'"

Now it was my turn to laugh.

"Well, maybe if you give me just a few recipes at a time," said Julia tentatively, "I could test them, but I'm still in this mess, fighting with all the courts and lawyers, and trying not to get thrown out in the street . . . oh all right, go ahead and get the recipes. It's a great idea."

The following day I called Heyward Cutting for a recipe, and for the first time ever, his secretary put me right through.

"Did I do something wrong? Am I late with something?" he asked with concern.

"No, Heyward," I laughed, "You're perfect. I was just calling to tell you about the companion book I'm writing for *Snow Job,* and to ask you to contribute."

As I elaborated on the project, Heyward interrupted, "Hey, I have a great idea. Why don't you include a recipe for 'Lawyers' Brains'?"

I had to agree. It *was* a great idea. "By the way Heyward, I know that when we met you said you didn't want to be in *Snow Job,* but there's no way I can tell this story without you in it. It's important for readers to know that there are honest lawyers in Boston. And I've called the chapter where we meet, 'Bulldog Meets Tenacity.'"

"Oh, I love it. Yes, go ahead Ursula. It's fine with me."

"Well, thanks. I did want to get your permission, because I am grateful for all you've done."

"I'm grateful for all the books you sent, and it was fun for me. I especially enjoyed the toy money."

"It was the perfect joke to play on Mr. Greed, wasn't it?!"

"That's just the problem. It *was* the perfect joke to play on Mr. Greed. You've got the man's number, Ursula, and he doesn't like it."

"Well, thanks to you, I won't have to dial it anymore! You really did do a great job. I want people to know it."

"What happened to you and your children *never* should have happened."

"So I've been told, but I also know that the same thing is happening to a lot of other people in the Commonwealth, and the Board of Bar Overseers is refusing to address most of their complaints. The betrayal I experienced from Duncan was nothing compared to the betrayal I experienced from The Legal System.

"In my ideal world, Heyward – Reed and MacIntyre would say to someone like Duncan: 'If you want to get divorced I can help you with that, but if you want to destroy another person, find someone else. That isn't what the law was made for, and that isn't the kind of lawyer I want to be.'"

Heyward listened patiently and with good humor as he always did when I blew off steam about The System. "I agree with all that you're saying, Ursula. Maybe I should let you use my real name in the book," Heyward Cutting said kiddingly. "But seriously, I almost always get back more than I give in the cases that are volunteer work for the Boston Bar. I thoroughly enjoyed working with you, and I will send you a recipe!"

My quest for more recipes led me to some amusing conversations. Tony over at Firenze Frames promised to send his wife's Tiramisu, and Mr. Italo the tailor offered Broccoli di Rappa. Yes, this book would have a "Barbershop Quartet" even though Conover only had three barbers; we would even up the score with a recipe for Braciole from Anthony at Salon d'Auguste, the man who had kept my hair looking good throughout the crisis, even when it was only an inch long at the top! Recipes started to appear in the mailbox at Inverary Lane: from the Town Library, from the schools, from Oglethorpe's, from all over Conover. Phil Vines told a few scientists and computer vendors about *The Snow Job Cookbook,* and then recipes started arriving at Molecular Innovations by fax — from all over the world!

Gavin Roberts, the *guardian ad litum,* was initially cautious. "Well, is Jonah sending you a recipe?"

"Oh, he gave me a great one for chocolate cake!" I replied.

Then I could almost hear the smile in his voice on the other end of the line. "Ursula, did I ever tell you that I used to be a caterer before I got into psychology?" revealed Gavin Roberts.

"No, I would have remembered that."

"Well, I have a great corn, feta, and red pepper salad I could send you."

"Oh good, I'll put that in the 'Mild Support' Chapter!"

Dr. John Arthur was also amused. "Well, I don't cook much, but if you'll leave me your outline, I'll see what I can do. What kind of recipe would you like?"

"Oh, we have all categories. You can send me anything, but I should be surprised if you sent me an egg recipe!" I said with a twinkle in my eye that did not go undetected. "You know we're even going to have a recipe for Lawyers' Brains," I continued. "I'm calling it 'Les Cervelles d'Avocats' because it sounds much more elegant in French, and my editorial comment is going to be, 'They will do for your arteries what they are doing for The System.'"

John Arthur, never a fan of lawyers, cracked up in laughter.

"I am trying to turn tragedy into humor," I explained. "And I have to get out of the debt Duncan plunged me into and start to make more money, or we're going to lose the house in a few years. The heart has healed faster than the pocketbook."

John Arthur grinned as he listened to my heart. "That heart did heal nicely, Ursula. And you deserve it!"

"Yes, it really did. You know, Duncan's lawyer even sent me a recipe, and offered to let me use his real name."

"Oh, they'll do anything for business!" said Dr. Arthur.

"By the way," I said turning serious, "did I tell you that I found a neurologist up in Canada who is doing molecular modelling on potential drugs for epilepsy?"

"No."

"Well, he's writing my December cover story on 'Applications of Quantum Pharmacology to Epilepsy.' IBM and several pharmaceutical firms are funding his research. Anyway, when I finally found him, I said 'I've been looking for you for six years,' and he said, 'Oh, I've only been doing this for four!' Anyway, if you're interested I'll send you my December issue. I've met so many interesting people as a result of this mess. And I'm starting to work politically to try to get the laws changed. It should be safer to be a Mom in Massachusetts."

"Yes, it should be," agreed John Arthur sadly.

While I was at the doctor's I got some rather surprising news. "You're 5'6"!" announced Sally, John Arthur's nurse, when she measured me. "But I've always been 5'5"," I protested, in a reprise of my conversation with Ian Ruddway. "It couldn't be possible. I'm forty-one. People don't grow an inch when they're forty-one."

"Well, you did," said Sally in partial disbelief herself, because she had been measuring me for years.

I went home and measured myself – carefully. Actually, I was a tad over 5'6". "Ursula, there must be a mistake", said Jackie Melrose. "I'm 5'6", and I've always been taller than you." So her daughter, Casey, measured us, very carefully, and announced, "Mom, Mrs. Charbonnier is just a little taller than you are!"

"Well, Ursula, that fits right in with everything else you've done this year!" laughed Jackie Melrose.

I couldn't wait to tell Ian Ruddway, but I would have to. And to think that I had heard it from him first, as I'd heard some of the most important things in my life from him first. Lately I'd felt taller, but had written it off as my imagination. But, this made it official – I really *was* taller, and medical science could not explain it.

Why had Ian always known things about me before I knew them about myself? Maybe there was more to come, but I could wait for it. There was so much more to do before we'd be ready for each other, if we ever were, and before I'd be ready for anyone at all. Like straightening myself out, I admitted in my few quiet moments alone.

For even as I was trying to help Julia Holliday and others fight to preserve their children's homes, I was still grappling with the concept of "home" in my own heart. Would I ever feel "at home" again? Why did I feel like forces beyond my control were shaping my life and propelling me toward a new "home"? Momentous changes were afoot in publishing and in Japan, and in the emerging knowledge-value industries of which CAMD was a part. Turbulence was ahead, and who and where would I be when the turbulence subsided? I no longer questioned my own survival. I knew I would handle whatever life dealt, but I still liked my old values, even if reality had tried to beat them to a pulp.

My experience with the legal system had left a scar. Would I ever again be able to carve out a relationship of trust with a man in a system where moral law and legal law clashed so violently? In a system that condoned, when it should have condemned, what Duncan had done to me and the children? And what Hobart was doing to Julia and their little boys? How were men and women ever to feel safe with each other? As the Clarence Thomas-Anita Hill saga played itself out on television and in the papers, a co-worker put it this way: "Sexual harassment and violence are okay in America if they're done by men and done in private. What can't be proved is allowable. Congress said so. The Constitution says so."

Published studies said that American women were in more danger at home than they were on the streets. Certainly that had been true in my case, in the case of Miss Vanilla. My children were getting a lot of messages from the law, and I didn't like any of them. These thoughts troubled me and people around me throughout the autumn. Sometimes we tried to joke them away.

One day at work, scientists newly attuned to sexual harassment in the workplace (and neither I nor anyone I knew had ever experienced such problems at Genesis) bantered lightly about the pros and cons of high-performance polymers for breast implants. "You can prove them by 'hands-on' experience," kidded one scientist. "The modulus of elasticity is different – hey, I know what a siloxane polymer feels like, and nobody can make it like Mother Nature!" said another. "In layman's terms, don't violate the 'look and feel,'" chimed in a third, in a jointly conspiratorial paean to our new collectively heightened consciousness.

At night, in a bed where no one had laughed for three years, I wrestled with myself. The best, healthiest message I could send my children would be to trust and love again, to take a chance and build a good life with another person, to show them that it could be done. I read a lot of Father Greeley that autumn, and wondered where I would find a partner who relished play – physical and intellectual play – as much as I did. One energetic team player to go, please!

It made it worse and not better that men ten years my junior had started to ask me out. "I want someone in the range of fifty with a high energy level," I would tell my friends. "I'm not doing midlife crisis twice. I flunked it the first time!" I wanted to write my Higher Power a memo: "Send me no wimps, God! I am tired of men with flabby bodies, flabby minds, and flabby ethics."

And then I would drift off to sleep, but never far away from all that troubled me. "To sleep, perchance to dream . . ." And sometimes the dreams took me to courthouses: I was the village idiot crying "Daylight!" at noon, the woman in a courtroom pounding on invisible glass walls, and shouting through soundproof air, during testimonies about money and possessions. "What about the children?" I would shout into the black hole of courtroom reality. Black holes ultimately crash in on themselves, and one day this rotten system would too, but too late for mothers in Massachusetts, and too late for Julia Holliday.

One night, in a dream, the Holliday boys crashed through those glass walls, and raced wildly from courtroom to courtroom in Cambridge, blasting away with machine guns trained on the Probate judges. There were screams and blood, and then silence, and then something even more horrifying: rivulets of blood re-configuring into dollar signs. "Why did you kill the judges, boys?" asked the largest of the dollar signs. And the whole courthouse turned into an echo chamber, while the bloody dollar signs chased Ethan, Enoch, Evan, and Ezra through the halls and into and out of every courtroom. "Why . . . boys?" "Why . . . boys?" "Why . . . boys?"

Then came their answer, in the echo chamber of my mind: "Because conduct is irrelevant . . . conduct is irrelevant . . . conduct is irrelevant . . . conduct is irrelevant . . ." And then I woke up, safe at home in my bed in Conover, but everything was not all right. This wasn't a bad dream. This was real life in 1991 Massachusetts.

I couldn't get away from it in the daytime either. One afternoon, when I reprimanded Spencer about his behavior, I heard the same refrain. "Conduct is irrelevant, Mom. I learned that from Judge Tracy." Is this really what our children were learning? A bomb had been set in the office of Amanda's school and destroyed a lot of property. Spencer bragged that everyone but the police knew who had done it. "The police are clueless," he said derisively. "And even if they find out, what will happen? A slap on the wrist, a little community service, big deal – conduct is irrelevant!"

When I recounted this to Jonah, he became angry. "Ursula, I don't want to hear about this. Just because conduct is irrelevant in a divorce case, that has no bearing on children's behavior. There is no connection. I'm getting angry just hearing this from you!"

I bit my tongue and said nothing more, but my cognitive lawyer was kidding himself and a lot of other people if he saw no connection between what went on in court and what was happening to the youngsters of America. *The New York Times* ran an article about why 40 percent of America's children were living below the poverty line. Two of the major reasons cited were dropout breadwinners and a substance-abusing parent, and our little family had lived through both.

In the same quarter, *Science* magazine ran a well-structured article on

"America's Children: Economic Perspectives and Policy Options" that correctly identified the sources of children's well-being and graphically described their lamentable decline, but failed to pinpoint the major underlying cause for the U.S. decline in goods and services to children: *a legal system that (a) rewards breadwinners for walking out on their families, and (b) devalues the important job of nurturing the next generation.* And I didn't stop there in the letter that I sent to the Editor:

> The plain fact of the matter is that today in America, it is no longer 'safe' to stay home and nurture children. To do so, a nurturer risks potential homelessness, loss of medical insurance, and dramatic declines in income and standard of living for oneself as well as one's children.
>
> Having recently walked through this piece of reality, I can offer the following responses to the authors' question, "How can government change the public's values and lifestyles without intruding on what many claim are fundamental individual rights?"
>
> Although I have numerous recommendations for positive changes in the legal system that would benefit children, I mention only several here:
>
> 1) **Dramatically increase child support** to more closely resemble the former living standard of the children and the children's primary nurturer. This will enable people to nurture children, and it will deter breadwinners from bailing out on their family responsibilities, which they now do with relative impunity.
>
> 2) **Computerize the enforcement of child support** at the state and national levels, and put some teeth in the law! There is something seriously wrong with a society in which after divorce, the former breadwinner's standard of living rises by 73 percent and the nurturer's and the children's declines by 42 percent. I've lived it, and I know.
>
> 3) **Strive to preserve the family home for the nurturer and the children.** In particular, make this a higher priority than transferring a hefty percentage of family assets to rapacious divorce lawyers.
>
> 4) **Pass legislation stating that preservation of the family home supersedes payments to divorce lawyers.** In Massachusetts, divorce lawyers frequently get away with instructing their clients: "Don't pay your mortgage." Neither the Boston Bar nor the Board of Bar Overseers are offended by such attorneys'

conduct. To make matters worse, divorce lawyers on opposite sides of a case often work in tandem to get judges to freeze family assets, and then these same lawyers subsequently ask judges to channel those assets to them for payment of legal fees! This all too frequent practice, at least in Massachusetts, is another factor that diverts assets from preservation of children's homes.

5) **Pass legislation stating that preservation of the family home must take precedence over the primary bread-winner's experiencing an increase in his/her standard of living.** Loss of the family home (or even the threat of it) seriously destabilizes children on many levels. This is particularly hard to explain to one's children when they see that the former breadwinner is now better off materially than when he/she was supporting the family.

6) **Rid the legal system of the illusion that conduct is irrelevant.** "No fault" divorce encourages people to behave irresponsibly. Your article speaks of holding parents responsible for their children's antisocial acts. Let us begin by making parents responsible for their own antisocial acts.

> Ursula L. Charbonnier
> Editor, *Molecular Modelling News*
> Westbury, MA

Jonah was not pleased with my letter. "How could you say these things Ursula, especially that fourth point in your letter?!? Those things don't happen."

"Well, they're exactly what happened in my case, Jonah, and you know it!"

"Your case was an exception!"

But it wasn't an exception. Someone showed me a T-shirt that said, "The Probate Court is in contempt of nurturers!" and I couldn't have put it better myself, for a nation that fails to protect its nurturers, fails to protect its children and fails to foster its own future.

Ike Peters, the Wheaton Glass scientist who had treated me to the beautiful dinner in Cincinnati the previous spring, called to check in and patiently listened to my lament for the next generation. "Ursula, I think you ought to go back and read *Candide,*" he said.

"Why, what's the message?"

"The message is to tend your own garden. You can't save the world, and you can't change The System. But you can get your own life back in order, in fact you're well on the way to that."

"You mean, 'Think globally, act locally!'"

"Yes," said my scientific friend.

In fact, Jackie Melrose sported that slogan on a bumper sticker on her car, and the message zoomed in on me again as I pulled into her driveway at the end of the day to pick up Amanda.

I told her about Ike's phone call. "We were talking about your bumper sticker this afternoon," I said half-kiddingly.

Jackie Melrose smiled a wise smile. "You know, Jeff met someone at a meeting this morning, someone I think you should call. Have you heard of Devon Carmody?"

"No, who is he?"

"She," corrected Jackie, "is Conover's Substance Abuse Prevention Coordinator."

"Our what?"

"Several years ago, just about the time Duncan started to change and things began unraveling at home for you, Conover hired someone to help the town learn about and deal with alcohol and drug abuse. There's been a lot about it in *The Conover Gazette,* and Devon's done a lot of programs in the schools."

"I didn't know anything about it or her," I said. "I've let all my subscriptions lapse, haven't read a *Conover Gazette* in three years, and I haven't been involved with the schools since all the upheaval started."

"Jeff told her about you, and said she had to meet you. Why don't you give her a call? Here's her number."

I decided to check it out with Julia Holliday. With four boys in the school system, she knew a lot more about what was going on than I did. "So Julia," I said next time I saw her, "tell me what the schools do about substance abuse prevention. Tell me about Devon Carmody, and what she's doing here. Jackie Melrose thinks I should call her."

"I think you should too. Ethan came home just yesterday, talking about a program Devon had done in the morning for his grade, and here's what he told me: 'Mom, they just brought in some messed-up person in a wheelchair and said that this is what will happen to you if you abuse substances. Why don't they tell kids what's really going in families – what's happening to us and the Charbonniers and others?' That's Ethan's assessment of what the schools are doing about substance abuse. They haven't really taken off the gloves yet, Ursula. These children see the devastating effects of substance abuse in their own families, but the problem is still being presented as something that happens somewhere else to someone else. A lot of people in the school system are still in denial about what's really happening. But Devon's trying to break through that denial. She's a good person, and she knows the territory, because she's in recovery herself. That's part of why the Town hired her. Call her. Together, the two of you might come up with something."

"All right, I'll call her this afternoon."

But when I got back to the office, I found a message from Devon on my voice mail: "Hi, this is Devon Carmody, Conover's Substance Abuse Prevention Coordinator. I met Jeff Melrose at a coffee this morning, and he suggested we talk. Please give me a call."

The following week we had lunch at Ted's Place, in Conover Center. Devon wanted to hear my story. And I wanted to learn about the programs she'd been establishing in the schools during the years I'd been focused on fighting for survival. Our respective stories tumbled out, and thanks to two years in Al-Anon, I understood all the vocabulary. We had read the same books, lived through the same agonies: one of us as addict, the other as unwitting co-dependent.

"You know, you're one out of ten, Ursula."

"One out of ten?" I asked blankly. "I don't get it."

"Only one in ten women leaves an alcoholic husband, but nine out of ten men leave an alcoholic wife. Did you know that?"

"No. But there's a lot I don't know about all this, for instance, what's going on in the Town. Can you bring me up to speed on what the schools are doing on substance abuse? I feel so out of touch," I apologized. "About the only contact I've had with the schools in the past three years was to ask Mary Francis, the guidance counselor, to coordinate writing letters for the Court on how Spencer and Amanda were doing. A far cry from the days when I loved to come in and work with children on their writing!"

"Well, fighting for survival can be a full-time job," said Devon. "I've been in recovery myself, for a number of years now, and I understand."

After she told me about some of the programs she'd put in place in the schools, I peppered her with questions. I mentioned Ethan Holliday's reaction to the latest program.

"We have to tread lightly," said Devon, "a lot of people in Conover are still in denial about what's going on in their own lives. But you have to remember, Ursula, that we've made a lot of progress already. Conover is pretty advanced compared to many other places in the country, just by virtue of even having a program and a substance abuse prevention coordinator in the community. That doesn't mean we don't have a long way to go. I agree with what Ethan said. But a lot of people aren't even ready to acknowledge that they have a problem, or that a family member has a problem. Look at what happened in your own life," she said very gently.

"But I really did think Duncan had epilepsy," I countered. "As soon as I found the first hidden bottle, I admitted the reality. I was crying in my doctor's office within hours, the kids and I went to Appleton . . ."

"And how long did it take you to get to Al-Anon?" asked Devon.

"Seven more months, but I didn't think it was for me," I protested.

"And what finally got you there?" she probed again, having already heard the answer not a quarter of an hour before.

"My lawyer gave me a 'kick in the fanny.' All right, I get your point," I conceded. "It isn't going to happen overnight in Conover, or anywhere else. But I still have more questions. Is there an Al-A-Teen Program in the Middle and High Schools?"

"We've tried. No one will come."

"Why not?"

"Would Spencer and Amanda come if we resurrected one?" she said, throwing the ball squarely back in my court.

"No," I said, "because they don't want to talk about it. It's normal for teenagers not to want to draw attention to themselves."

"And most other teenagers feel the same way."

"All right, I see what you're saying. It parallels what Ginny Bartlett, my high school French teacher, the first person who woke me up to Duncan's drinking problem, told me about Al-A-Teen not working in the Ohio schools where she'd tried them. But she did tell me something that may be helpful to you: it's the elementary school children who are just bursting to talk to someone about what's happening at home. Is there a program for them in the Conover elementary schools?"

"Not now, I don't think so. We could look into it, but we'll have to tread lightly. We're talking about a problem that exists in one out of three or four families in Conover, and it's one that many of them don't want to admit," said Devon.

"Well then, that brings me to an idea I've had since 1989, for a 'one-stop shopping' resource for the families of substance abusers in denial – a place in our town where people could go for referrals and be directed to truly ethical lawyers, savvy financial advisors, and clergy and physicians who are sophisticated about alcohol and drug abuse. The way things are now, help is so fragmented. You go to a doctor for the medical part, a financial advisor for the financial part, clergy for the spiritual part, therapists for the emotional part, the police for protection and to get unregistered guns out of the house, and lawyers – often more than one – for the legal part. It takes a long time to find these resources, and some of them are more interested in making money than in truly helping the family. People need *one place* where they can go to begin to get their lives back in order, whether they chose to remain in or to extricate themselves from a substance abusing situation."

I had the concept and the language for the vision down, but no idea about how to get it through the system and turn it into reality. I hoped Devon would know how to do that part. "Do you think we could set something like that up in Conover?"

"Tell me more about how it would work."

"Well, initially, I'd like it to be a networking service, as I said – putting people in touch with real help. Later, it could grow into a lecture series. I have a lot of ideas for topics: 'How to Interact With Your Family Physician When There is a Substance Abuser in Denial in the Family,' or 'How to Find an Ethical Attorney,' or 'Protecting Family Assets and How to Put Your Financial Life in Order,' and how about, 'What to Expect When You Go to Probate Court With a Substance Abuser in Denial.' I could go on, but that gives you an idea. The Police could even come one evening and explain what people's rights are and what to expect from 'The Law' when an alcoholic becomes physically abusive in the home. In other words, *practical* approaches to the behind-closed-doors problems that families really face."

"You know, this idea could fit in nicely with a series I'm putting together for *The Conover Gazette*. Would you be willing to talk to Steve Mitchell, the *Gazette* reporter who covers Conover?"

"Sure. And I'd be happy to help with any writing you need done, for the series or anything related to substance abuse prevention for the town."

"I just had another idea. How far along are you on *Snow Job*?"

"About two-thirds done, and it's only in first draft. Why?"

"I was thinking that as part of my series, maybe *The Conover Gazette* could publish one of your chapters and an interview about you and what you've been through, and we could use that as a lead-in to a story on this new organization we want to set up."

"Do you really think they'd publish a chapter?"

"Why not ask them? Look, call Steve Mitchell. Explain what we have in mind and ask if he'd be interested. And while you're at it, why not submit a chapter directly to Artemis Blaine? She's the publisher for all the local *Town Gazettes*, including Conover's."

"All right. It's worth a try. Actually, it would mean a lot to have *The Conover Gazette* be the first to publish part of the book, since so much of it takes place right here in Conover. Now what about our new networking group; it needs a name. We have to call it something, and it needs to be short and memorable. I was thinking that I'd like to call it Conover CARES. Something modular, so that if it catches on, other towns could use it. You know, Westbury CARES, Beaumont CARES, and so forth, but I haven't figured out completely what the acronym would stand for . . . something like Comprehensive Abuse-Related . . . and then I get stuck. I can't finish it."

"Well, let's think about what it would do, and write down ideas," suggested Devon.

"I wish I had a thesaurus and dictionary with me. Hey, want to go to the Library, and finish the name there?"

And there, in the middle of the old Conover Library, we finished the name: Comprehensive Abuse-Related Referral and Educational Services – CARES! "Cares is also a synonym for afflictions or troubles," I said.

"Now all we have to do is get a first meeting of core people," said Devon.

"Hey, that's not going to be so easy!" Devon looked at me. "But we'll do it," I hastened to add. "We'll just somehow coordinate the schedules of the Chief of Police, frantically busy Jonah McCoy, my Al-Anon sponsor, Julia Holliday, a representative of the Conover clergy . . ."

Devon finished the sentence for me: "you, me, and Davis Fenway, Conover family therapist *par excellence!*"

"You mean *the* Davis Fenway. Would he come?" I asked in surprise.

"Yes, I think he will. He's done a lot of work with me already."

"Really?" I hadn't known. "Well then, that's how we'll get Jonah to the meeting. He's been wanting to meet Davis Fenway for years!"

Over the next several weeks, there were lots of phone calls, negotiations over schedules, and just as I was wondering if we would ever get to square one with Conover CARES, Devon called. "Congratulations!"

"Congratulations? What?" I said, puzzled.

"Congratulations, we've got a meeting – 5 p.m. on the sixth at the Pace House."

XXXI

Conover Cares

Not "where does the tragedy come from?" But "where does it lead?"
— Harold S. Kushner,
When Bad Things Happen to Good People

"Everyone can come: Davis Fenway, Jonah McCoy, Skip Jensen on behalf of all the clergy, the Chief of Police, Ann McMahon, Julia Holliday — *and* the District Attorney's Office in Cambridge found out about our meeting and is sending two representatives! Conover CARES is on its way!" exclaimed Devon.

It was hard to believe that all of these busy, busy people had agreed to be in one place all at the same time to learn about Conover CARES. We would need the knowledge and experience of each of them if this new organization were ever to get off the ground, yet Jonah and Davis and even Skip Jensen had said they could only commit to this first meeting. They didn't have time to be involved on an ongoing basis. But we never looked on this as an impediment.

"You just get them there," I told Devon, "and Conover CARES will take care of the rest." But what I really meant was, we have just this *one* opportunity to make our point, to tap into the concern that each of them had for issues surrounding substance abuse.

The respect people had for their own tight schedules and for each other's was evidenced by everyone's arriving on time at the Pace House. Devon opened that first meeting. "I'd like to start by having each of you introduce yourselves, tell why you are here, what your interest is in substance abuse, and what each of you could share with the group."

In less than an hour, we gained pieces of very different perspectives from the divorce/mediation attorney, the minister, two recovering addicts, the spouse of one alcoholic and the former spouse of another, the family therapist, and the District Attorney's office. What it boiled down to was this: people either had a significant percentage of clients dealing with the emotional/social/financial fallout of substance abuse or they were dealing with it in their own lives.

Then Devon said, "And now Ursula Charbonnier is going to tell you her story, which was our impetus for starting Conover CARES."

I smiled at Jonah McCoy and began:

"Several years ago, I was in a lot of trouble: struggling to cope with a substance abuse situation in our home; frightened about the options before me; and frustrated that I had no place to go for *real* help.

"I felt stunned and unbelieving at what I was seeing before my very eyes. I was confused over the dramatic change in a loved one and the upheaval at home; thoroughly uninformed/uneducated about substance abuse; frightened about what would happen to me and my children; afraid that no one would believe my story (owing to the public persona of the abuser); uncertain about where to go for help and who to trust (could I really trust the schools or the Conover Police Department?); and frustrated that whatever help I did find was fragmented."

What was needed, I told them, was a *one-stop shopping referral and education service.* I explained that I'd promised myself that once the kids and I got our lives straightened out, I would see if Conover were interested in establishing one. I gave them my ideas about how we, as a community, could reach out and help other families in trouble.

"People who are dealing with a substance abuse problem in the family have a lot of concerns. They may need:

• protection (approaching police departments, 'safe houses');
• legal advice (finding an ethical lawyer, what to expect from the Probate Court System);
• financial advice (restructuring family finances, dealing effectively with mortgagors if loss of the family home is likely);
• spiritual guidance (tapping in to local clergy, AA, Al-Anon);
• medical advice (dealing effectively with physicians who are often caught between the needs of the abuser and the needs of the family);
• emotional advice (finding competent family therapists);
• educational assistance (making the most of resources like Appleton Hall, the Conover Schools, and CADEAC – Conover's Alcohol and Drug Education Advisory Council)."

Then I told them that our family was fine now, in large part because of the *community* support we received from the police, the schools, local clergy, Al-Anon members, and friends/professionals who lived and/or worked in Conover, but that finding all these people and then sorting them all out was more time-consuming, expensive, and emotionally draining than it needed to be. Perhaps we could devise a more effective approach, as drug and alcohol abuse remained a problem in Conover – for one in three or four families. I continued:

"A community problem merits a community response. Abuse can only thrive in silence. Giving people a 'safe' place or forum where they can break the silence is a critical first step in helping families, regardless of whether people choose to remain in or to extricate themselves from an abusive situation.

"Working together, we as a community could establish comprehensive referral and educational services for substance-abused families. Toward that end, I'd like to hear your ideas about how we as a community could extend ourselves to families in trouble and offer them concrete help – and hope."

Skip Jensen, of the Methodist Church, spoke first. "We in the clergy deal with this problem all the time, on an ongoing basis, and there are many resources out there for the abuser, but so often, for the people around the abuser, there is nothing. These people just slip through the cracks, and they need as much help as the alcoholic or drug addict."

Then the brainstorming began. A network of referrals was a good beginning, but could we also think about a lecture series for the community, and maybe even add a telephone hotline, where people in immediate trouble could call in confidence?

Davis Fenway summed it all up at the end. "What you're all talking about, if I'm understanding this correctly, is a *warm hand* and a *warm voice* at the end of the phone, to help people who are in trouble. Information, though helpful, by itself is cold and sterile. But a warm hand to go with the information – now that's different. I like the idea. I know at the beginning I said that I didn't have time to be involved on an ongoing basis, but I've changed my mind. I want to be part of this."

"So do I," said Jonah McCoy when we spoke the next day.

The next step for Conover CARES was preparation of a questionnaire, by Devon, Davis and me, to collect initial information for the database that would serve as the basis for the Conover CARES Network. But happiness over the "chemistry" of our first meeting was soon punctured by news from Devon: "Now I'm not going into panic mode," she began, and then quietly explained that Conover's Finance Committee was aggressively pruning the budget and her job was on the block. "Will you speak up for the importance of continuing the position?"

"Yes, of course I will," I said without thinking about all the other commitments on my plate. "When and where?"

"At their next meeting — Tuesday night at eight, the Conover Town Hall. Davis Fenway is going to say a few words, and so will Jeff Melrose from the Board of Selectmen, and the Conover Chief of Police, and certain parents and teachers who have worked with me over the past year and a half."

I didn't know how I was going to fit the meeting in. I'd been up all week with deadlines, was exhausted, and wouldn't have time to prepare any remarks. I'd never been to a Finance Committee meeting and knew next to nothing about the town political establishment that was either going to cut Devon's position entirely, or at best, trim it back to half-time for another stretch of months, then cut it.

When I walked into the packed room of about a hundred people, I was astonished to find that most of the Committee of twelve, seated at the table up front, were members of First Parish. I had expected to be speaking to a committee of strangers, unmovable finance types, who weren't going to give an inch on the budget. Instead I would be speaking to people I had coffee with every Sunday, many of whom knew well what the children and I had been through in recent years.

I sat down next to Ann McMahon, my Al-Anon sponsor. "I'm so glad *you're* going to speak," she said. Well you wouldn't be, I thought, if you knew how tired I am and that I haven't a clue as to what I'm going to say. I looked around at the audience – Our Town. From his chair near the front, Jeff Melrose nodded to me with a New England glint of encouragement in his eye that said, Speak up Ursula. Tell them what it's like. Help them understand why this is important. Instead, I wanted to go home and sleep my first sleep in four nights. I made a silent last-minute appeal to my Higher Power: Couldn't you find someone else? Then, as various Finance Committee members spoke about hard economic times and budget concerns, I felt even less articulate. Comatose Ursula is going to be no match for this, I thought. Then Devon said a few words about how perhaps hearing a firsthand story would help the Committee and turned over the floor to me.

I stood up and looked at the room of expectant faces. I was unprepared, exhausted, with a head empty of words. I began to ramble, then stopped.

"Let me start over," I said. "In 1987 I knew one thing about substance abuse: that it was something that happened in other people's families and that it had nothing to do with me or my life. In 1988 I found out I was wrong . . ." Suddenly, I was off and running. I was connecting with the audience, but when the Chairman tried to cut me off, I realized I had spoken too long.

"One more thing," I said firmly, holding up one hand. "This is a community problem – and therefore it merits a community response! Thank you." And I sat down, exhausted, wondering if I had made any sense at all.

Devon called the following week. "Did you hear the news?"

"No."

"The position is being funded for another *year.*"

"But that's *even longer* than the longest time period they were considering. That's great, Devon!" I said.

"Now we have to get to work on Conover CARES."

"Well, I have news for you too. Steve Mitchell called from *The Gazette* and said they're going to publish Chapter Fourteen of *Snow Job* in the last February or first March issue! Can you believe it? And they want to include an interview on the book and how it came about."

"Good. Then we can follow up with the series of articles I want to do. And the *Snow Job* chapter will be a great lead-in to an article on Conover CARES, because it will take the substance abuse issue and bring it down to earth with a personal story. When are you meeting with Mitchell?"

"Next week, over lunch."

But our pleasure at working with *The Gazette* was to be short-lived. Although Steve Mitchell was pleasant and seemed genuinely interested in the substance abuse issue, early on in our conversation, two concerns emerged for me: he wasn't asking the hard questions and then as he repeated his version of my answers back to me, I worried about being misquoted – in print, for all to see. "Look, I don't mean to be a backseat editor," I said, "but I don't want anyone to be hurt by what I have to say in this interview. The material is very sensitive. How about if I write my own questions and answers, and you look them over, and we work on any editing together?"

"You can even come in and look at the typeset copy," he offered. His generosity and graciousness amazed me, particularly after I spoke with a reporter friend in Washington. "Ursula, if you'd told me you wanted to write your own Q & A, I would have told you to go straight to hell!" she said. "Frankly, I'm surprised that a local paper would agree to publish your chapter at all. Forgive my cynicism, but these days, small town papers rarely exhibit any courage, and when they do, they usually win a Pulitzer Prize!"

After ten weeks, people in town who'd been working with Devon started asking about *The Gazette* pieces. "Artemis Blaine, the publisher, is no longer committing to a date," I told them.

"Well, would it be all right with you if I call her to find out when they're going to appear?" asked Wendy Lerner, a Conover mom who'd been especially active in the schools on the substance abuse issue.

"I guess so," I said, but before Wendy Lerner could get back to me, Artemis Blaine called. "We've decided not to publish your chapter and interview."

After all the delaying, this did not surprise me. "May I ask why?" I said.

"We're only interested in writing about Conover CARES," she said, "and this is a personal story."

"All substance abuse stories are personal stories," I replied evenly. "You knew exactly what this was when you originally agreed to publish it. And this decision in no way impairs my ability to work with you on a story about Conover CARES," I added.

But by then Devon had already made arrangements for us to be jointly interviewed by *The Conover Observer,* another area paper. "*The Observer's* being responsive, so we'll work with them first," she said. "*The Gazette* had its chance, and I'll be happy to explain that to Channing Murray, their reporter." Both of us had admired Channing's work over the years. "I'll tell her we'll work with her later in year."

The Observer wasted no time. Their reporter, Clarice LaChessy, contacted me immediately, arranged a breakfast interview with Devon and me at Ted's Place, and promptly published a straightforward introductory piece on Conover CARES.

Not long after, I ran into Sterling Smythe in the Conover Grocery Store. She had been Amanda's English teacher in fifth grade, the year all hell had broken loose in our lives. "How are all of you getting along now?" she asked with concern. "I've often wondered how you are." I hadn't seen her for two years.

"We're doing all right," I said. "It's not easy at times, but we're slowly putting our lives back together."

"Tell me about your book. How is it coming? Are you still writing?"

"Yes. I'm working on the last third of it. *The Gazette* was going to publish Chapter Fourteen, which tells what happened when we went to court for child support. They were also going to publish an interview I wrote, but at the last minute, after everything was typeset, *The Gazette* reneged, saying the chapter was a 'personal story.' I guess if you're ever going to read *Snow Job*, it won't be in the local paper!" I laughed.

Then I told her about Conover CARES and the work I'd been doing with Devon.

"Devon's been doing a great job in the schools," said Sterling. "She has so much to offer, and she's really making a difference. I keep meaning to call her to see how we could do even more with the fifth grade. It's such a perfect age to be addressing these problems."

"Well, I have a few ideas about that," I said, "if you don't mind my putting my two cents' worth in."

"No, I don't mind. What do you suggest?"

"When the children and I were at the beginning of all this, back in 1989, I received a lot of help and insight from my former high school French teacher in Ohio, Ginny Bartlett. A long-time recovering alcoholic herself, she had done a lot of work in the schools, and what she told me is that it's the elementary school kids who are just itching to tell someone outside the family about what's going on at home, and they have *no one* to talk to. Schools tend to put programs in place for middle and high school students, but little exists for the elementary school age children."

"That's certainly true in the Conover System," said Sterling, "but what about the privacy issue? Don't we have to protect people's privacy? Parents might feel very threatened if they knew children were talking at school about what's going on at home."

"That may be," I countered, "but in the long run, I believe more damage occurs if we don't break the ring of silence that keeps substance abuse going in a family. These children need a safe place to go to break that silence, and the schools are in a position to provide that."

"I hear what you're saying Ursula, and I'll speak to Devon about it."

It was to be my day for running into the past at the grocery store. In the checkout line, I turned around and found Lee Malley staring at me. We had not spoken in years. Lee had been our first interior decorator when we had moved to Conover. "How are you enjoying your new house?" she asked referring to the Inverary Lane Cotswold, I guessed.

"Well, it's hardly new. We moved in four years ago, and the following summer Duncan moved out, as you must have heard," I added, for she was gazing at me hesitantly, as if she were leaving something deliberately unsaid. Wanting to know what it was, I continued. "We had thought Duncan was seriously ill, which is why I might have seemed a little tense to you when we were working together, but eventually we learned it was a substance abuse problem."

She continued to look at me, still with no trace of surprise. "Oh, I knew he had a drinking problem years ago," said Lee Malley.

"You knew?! – years ago?" I was stunned. "How could you have known? *I* didn't even know!"

"Ursula, I smelled liquor on Duncan's breath at the meetings all of us used to have in the middle of the day, and when you smell liquor on a man's breath two times in a row in the middle of the day, you know he has a drinking problem. Furthermore, I'm Irish, and I've had experience with this sort of thing. I know it when I see it. Nice man, but he had a real problem. I just assumed you knew."

"No, I didn't know!" I protested. "Why didn't you tell me? Why didn't somebody tell me?"

But she said nothing, and in my mind I had to acknowledge that I knew her unspoken answer: I would not have believed her if she had told me, and at that time, so many years before I caught on, I would also have resented her intrusion.

"Look, if you ever want to talk about it, you can call me sometime," said Lee. "If I had been closer to your family, maybe I would have said something back then." Tears stung behind my eyes, but I managed to hold them back until I got out of the store.

It was another sharp reminder that many around me had seen Duncan for what he was, but I had not. I could accept that "love was blind," but I was having a lot of trouble accepting that I had been stupid to a degree that allowed me to be so incredibly and repeatedly deceived. Lee Malley's words had put me back on "the pity pot," as Al-Anon friends called it. Or rather, I had let them.

Minutes later, as I unloaded groceries at Inverary Lane, Spencer put me back on track.

After Amanda told him why I was crying, Spencer said, "Mom, do you ever wonder why God has been so bad to you?"

"But God hasn't been so bad to me," I protested in response. "I have two beautiful, healthy children to bring up, a functioning brain that has enabled me to learn new things, worthwhile work, a good job, good health, plenty of energy to do all before me, and loyal friends."

He grinned back at me. "So . . . what's the problem?"

I am, I didn't say.

XXXII

Sic Transit Ursula

In your patience possess ye your souls.
— Luke 21:19, *The Bible*

If I was the problem, then I was also the solution.

"I am still not free of Duncan, and I want to be," I said to Ginny Bartlett on the phone a few days later. "I've done so much of the hard work. I admitted I was powerless over alcohol, that my life had become unmanageable. I've been in Al-Anon for more than two years. I'm part of a spiritual community now. My work is going well with *Molecular Modelling News*. The children are thriving, if at a lower material standard of living. I'm getting my finances in order. I've learned to accept help from others. I'm trying to help set up Conover CARES. My health is great; my energy has never been higher. Why then, do I still feel pulled down in some way?"

"Maybe you haven't completely let go," suggested Ginny Bartlett. "There are three sets of mental fetters you have to give up if you want to be completely free: judging, comparing, and needing to know why. Needing to know why is co-dependent."

In reality, I *was* still judging. I *was* mad at a System that attacked nurturers like Julia Holliday and me. And how could I *not* judge attorneys, who'd been bought? Or judges, who put children out on the street?

Yes, I *was* still comparing. "If I quintupled the size of *Molecular Modelling News* while I was operating under such difficult circumstances, simultaneously trying to save my home, preserve my children's world, retain my sanity, and function as a single parent," I reasoned, "what greater heights might I have achieved during these years, if life had been stable and normal?" This question tormented me chronically.

"The System can't make you a victim," said Ginny. "Only you can do that. And you make yourself a victim, when you keep asking 'Why?' 'Why?' is the question of the victim; 'What next?' is the question of the survivor."

Well and good in theory, I thought, yet the question "WHY?" remained.

"*Why* had Duncan thrown his life away? *Why* had he behaved so cruelly to a family who loved and respected him? *What* had I done to make him hate me? *Why*, in his own words, was he still trying to destroy me?"

At night, I often sat on the windowseat in my darkened room and pondered these imponderables, under the moon's eye. "Well, Old Crater Face," I bantered one evening, "Why?"

Old Crater Face seemed to wink back at me, and say in Ginny Bartlett's somber tone: "The question 'Why?' is irrelevant." Then, assuming the features and voice of Gabriel G. Reed, Old Crater Face suddenly boomed at me: "Lighten up, Ursula, lighten up!"

"The next thing I suppose you're going to say is that you are 'the Great Oz!' " I snapped at the moon.

I laughed at the sound of my words in the dark. But I must have lightened up a little bit already, for I was referring in humor to a metaphor Duncan had regularly used to describe Calvin Germane and the inexplicable behaviors that went on at Germane Engineering. Duncan used to liken GEC's venerable, corporately despotic CEO to The Wizard of Oz: on stage — powerful, terrorizing, iconoclastic, and manipulative; and behind the mask — a frightened, inept, powerless old man, wreaking havoc in the lives of those around him. And GEC was like Emerald City. Green, moneyed, sprawling in influence, arrogant, and pretending to have all the answers.

In retrospect, there had been warnings along the way: from Eleanor Bertucci and from Duncan himself.

I'd met Eleanor Bertucci, a Conover psychiatrist, through Jackie Melrose, the first week we moved to Conover in 1981. All of us had two year-olds, and Jackie had invited me to join their weekly playgroup of six moms and toddlers. Eleanor asked why we'd moved to Massachusetts, and she expressed concern when I said Duncan had taken a job at GEC. "Oh, not Germane," she sighed, shaking her head. "Half my patients are Germane executives. I don't know what's going on over there, but they take reasonable, decent people and turn them into monsters. You should be watchful, Ursula."

It seemed an odd thing to say at first meeting. "Oh, you wouldn't say that if you knew Duncan. He's the calmest, kindest person I've ever known. Nothing rattles him. Certainly not some corporation. We'll be fine." I'd totally discounted her words, and thought no more about them for a decade. But something must have made me file her warning, for it was here now, accessible, swirling between the layers of my mind.

Duncan, too, over the years had expressed misgivings about Calvin Germane. "He's got a 'moth-and-candle approach' to his management team, Ursula. He sucks all the vitality out of those who get close to him; and then, when he has no more use for them — he consumes them. I watched him do it to Gil Borden (the brilliant engineer who had designed the company's operating systems and left with his health and spirit in ruins), and I've seen him do it to others. If I get too close to him, it could happen to me."

But I discounted his concerns. "Nonsense, Duncan, you're strong. And intelligent. Nothing like that could ever happen to you," I would say in a reassuring but naïve tone, wrapped in Duncan's arms under cozy blankets. Now, ten years later, I revisited these thoughts in a cold, black night. In effect, I'd had so much foreshadowing, that I'd been completely in the dark!

"They take reasonable, decent people, and turn them into monsters," echoed Eleanor Bertucci, as cloud wisps danced across the moon.

Ginny Bartlett was right. Knowing why was not going to extract me from any of it. I had to deal with the here and now, without the benefit of that knowledge. My task was to create a new life, not bury myself in the old one.

And in my struggle to completely let go, a parallel struggle continued through spring: Duncan was still trying to hang on. He was still trying to control my medical insurance reimbursements and access to my medical insurance records; he was preventing me from refinancing Inverary Lane; and he was eagerly awaiting abatements on overpaid taxes I'd discovered from the small trust fund my grandfather had established for me. In the eyes of the law, I was still chattel.

"Continue to extract yourself, step by step, Ursula," counseled Jackie Melrose. "Take one problem at time, and keep chipping away at Duncan's control over you until he no longer has any. And put on blinders – think about only what's in front of you at the moment. If you look at the big picture, it will paralyze you. Tackle one problem at a time."

I began with the medical insurance. Duncan was not allowing the John Hancock Insurance Co. to send my medical reimbursements directly to me. He was insisting they come to him first, which apparently was "his right" since I was still on his policy at Germane. The reimbursement records included details of which doctors I'd seen and why. "What about my right to privacy?" I asked Jonah. "Can't you do anything about this?" Then I appealed to Jane Herrick, a kind supervisor in the Hancock office. "I have nothing to hide, but the intrusion is offensive. I'm divorced from this man. My medical information is none of his business."

"Well, it is wrong," she agreed, "but the rules say that as long as it's *his* policy, we need *his* permission to reimburse you directly for your out-of-pocket expenses. Until he gives his permission in writing, we have to send him the money and the information, but I agree with you, Mrs. Charbonnier, it doesn't seem right."

"Particularly since we have major cash flow problems at our house, and he sits on the checks for months before signing them over to us. Isn't there anything I can do?" I appealed to Jane.

"We still need his permission, and he's ignored all the previous release forms I've sent to him. But I'll keep trying. We're only allowed to send him the release forms every ninety days, and I'll keep doing that. In the meantime, I suggest you tell each of your healthcare providers exactly what the situation is, and ask them if they will accept delayed payments from you and the children. Send your medical bills directly to my attention (that will save time in the system), and I'll pay your doctors just as quickly as I can."

"But that hurts all of the doctors," I said, "and it isn't the greatest use of your time."

"True, but as long as Duncan is withholding his permission, Ursula, it's the best we can do." To my amazement, every single doctor we dealt with was totally understanding, and agreed to Jane Herrick's proposal. Once again, Duncan's behavior was causing a lot of people a lot of inconvenience, but he didn't seem to mind; and Jane Herrick's repeated efforts to obtain signed release forms didn't embarrass him in the least. Finally, Chubb MacIntyre came to the rescue and convinced Duncan to authorize direct reimbursements to me. One down, and two to go! Jane Herrick deserved a medal. Duncan Charbonnier had cost John Hancock dollars and productivity over the years, starting with his four sets of EEGs and CTs and years' worth of unnecessary medical bills from neurologists, and ending, hopefully, with this. And America wonders why medical insurance rates are rising!!! Too bad John Hancock couldn't go after Duncan for all the money it spent on his unnecessary medical tests!

My next tussle with Duncan came over Inverary Lane. His name was no longer on the deed, thanks to the divorce agreement struck by Jonah McCoy, but his name could not be taken off the note, since my salary was so low. Now Hub Safe was offering a very attractive opportunity – a loan conversion, which would lower my mortgage rate by nearly three whole points for an unusually small fee. But because Duncan's name was still on the note, I needed his permission to go ahead with the conversion. This he steadfastly refused to give. "You mean Duncan can prevent me from lowering the mortgage on my own house?" I asked incredulously.

"Yes. I never expected this to happen," said Jonah apologetically. "It's in his interest to let you lower your mortgage, and it costs him nothing! It never occurred to me that this would happen."

So the reality was that Jonah and I had worked hard to salvage an asset over which I now had no control. "He still wants us to lose the house, and he has no intention of making life easier for me and the children; that's what he told me Jonah. What do we do now?" Jonah asked Duncan's attorney to intervene.

"But it won't cost you a dime," protested Chubb MacIntyre to his unyielding client. "There's no reason not to let her do it, *and* it helps your children!"

Chubb called Jonah a few days later. "Duncan is not a happy camper," he relayed. "He hasn't seen much of his daughter in more than a year."

"Well, what does he expect?" I said to Jonah. "Why would she want to see a person who had tried to take away her house, and who had said in her presence that he was going to destroy us?"

Instead of answering that question, Jonah said, "Why not ask Amanda what he could buy for her, maybe a new dress or something she really wants?"

I couldn't believe Jonah McCoy was asking me such a question.

"Duncan Charbonnier has a long journey ahead of him, Ursula. And he's not even close to taking the first step!" Jonah's voice was filled with a compassion I didn't share. Buying a new dress didn't seem to me like a way to make amends for the past four years, but what did I know?

So I relayed Jonah's question to Amanda, and found my daughter was as surprised and offended by this tack as I had been. "Tell your lawyer I'm not a material girl!" she snapped.

Spencer walked in on the middle of this conversation. "Mom, you're leaving something out. Dad told me that child support is based on the mortgage. If he lets you lower the mortgage, then child support for Amanda and me will be lowered."

"That's completely untrue, Spencer! The court doesn't care if our mortgage is zero dollars a month or a million dollars a month. They don't even consider one's housing payment in determining child support – though I think they should. If your father told you that, it's incorrect information."

Spencer looked confused. He knew I had never lied to him, and that Duncan had, but he still wanted so much to believe Duncan. I hated having a confused child, but there was nothing I could do about it but furnish him with accurate information, and then let go. "The fact is Spencer, that if we were able to convert our house loan, there would be a lot more money to spend on you and Amanda every month. As things stand now, we are throwing away hundreds of dollars a month for no good reason. It's crazy." But I could see I wasn't reaching him. "Spencer, what do you call people who steal from others?"

"I call them lawyers!" he laughed sardonically, and walked out of the room.

Amanda had taken all this in, and seeing my frustration, adopted a more conciliatory stance. "Look Mom, I'll spend some time with him, if it will help you get the mortgage lowered, even though I don't want to."

"I'm not asking you to do that," I said. "Jonah McCoy and I worked hard to preserve your and Spencer's freedom to spend time with whomever you want, whenever you want."

Amanda continued, "I'm sick of all these people who keep saying I'm going to be messed up because I don't spend time with my father. Look, if I'm mature enough to accept what he did, and he's not mature enough to admit it, then I'm a better person than he is, and I'm better off."

I threw up my hands in despair. This was going nowhere. I had one child who was confused, another who was calling a heart a heart and a spade a spade, and I was no closer to getting extricated from Duncan, who was continuing to eat up my time and my energy – not to mention my money.

I called Rod McLaren, the kind person in Hub Safe's Mortgage Department, who for weeks had been looking at The Charbonnier Matter, six ways to Sunday, trying to figure out a way we could put through the loan conversion without Duncan's permission. But the bank's Legal Department was very clear, and so were the Debtor-Creditor laws on the books in Massachusetts and plenty of other states: without the permission of both parties, banks are unable to amend existing notes signed by those parties.

In all of my dealings with him, Rod McLaren had expressed feeling badly over what had happened to me and the children two years before.

"You know, I'm the kind of person Hub Safe should want to do business with," I had told him in our first phone conversation. "Nobody ever went after Duncan Charbonnier two years ago when he announced that he wasn't going to pay our mortgage anymore. Look at the records, Mr. McLaren. Did you ever once go after Duncan? No, Hub Safe came after *me*, a mom with two kids and an income one-sixth of Duncan's."

"Actually we did call him once," said Rod McLaren, as he skimmed the bank records on his desk.

"And what happened?" I asked, not letting up for a second.

"It says here that he told us you were handling the mortgage, that we should deal directly with you on this. So that's what we did."

"You just accepted his word without question. And you'd do business with him again if you could, because there's no record of what he did, and there's no penalty for it.

"With stock options, he makes more than $200,000 a year. I paid for more than two-thirds of our first house Mr. McLaren, with my inheritance from my grandparents. Duncan had no mortgage for years! And then at age forty, he tried to render me and the children homeless. I was left holding the bag for Duncan Charbonnier, and you've been left holding the bag by the Probate Court system. And children and nurturers are getting thrown out in the street, while lawyers and dropout breadwinners are getting rich, and the banks are getting the short end of the stick by having to be the bad guys. When are the banks going to wake up and see what's really happening here? As long as conduct is irrelevant in Massachusetts, this nonsense will go on," I exclaimed, dumping my frustration on him. "In this Commonwealth, lawyers and judges think they've legislated and adjudicated conduct right out of existence!"

But kind Rod McLaren, to his credit, didn't take my outburst personally. In fact, he couldn't have been more gracious. "Look Mrs. Charbonnier, I'd like to screw this guy if I could."

"Well, I don't want to screw anyone, I just want to get my life back in order and take good care of my children. And I'd like to see some leadership and courage on the part of the banks.

"Why can't Hub Safe give children and their nurturers some reprieve? I'm not talking about cases where the money isn't there to pay mortgages. I'm talking about cases where the primary breadwinner has willfully announced, with malice aforethought, that he's going to pull the financial plug on the family, and that nobody will be able to stop him. In the eyes of the law and in the eyes of the bank, he did nothing wrong."

Then I told him about Conover CARES, and how we were trying to help the families of substance abusers in getting advice and in saving their homes. "We need a banker for Conover CARES, someone with vision, energy, and courage. Is there anyone over there I could talk to about this?" I asked.

"I want you to go see Mr. Gordon Neville. He's our Vice President for Community Affairs," said Rod McLaren.

"Well, I'll be sure to give him a call eventually. But first I want to straighten this out." I filed Neville's name in my "Healing The System" folder, and continued to work for Duncan Charbonnier's signature on my loan conversion.

Through Chubb, Duncan finally sent a message that he would assent to the deal, provided that half the savings were sent to him each month over the life of the loan. Initially, even Jonah and Chubb said that this would be a nightmare to manage. Then they tried to talk me into accepting it. All I could see were more attorneys' fees and new complications which I would then be stuck with monitoring, and worst of all, another connection with Duncan. "I'm trying to get him *out* of my life, not back into it," I told Jonah.

"Look, you have several options," said Jonah. "Do nothing; get someone else to replace Duncan on the note; agree to Duncan's offer; or take him back to court and see if a judge will order him to sign the loan conversion." Jonah was urging that I negotiate with Duncan, but every fiber of my being was screaming, "Do nothing! And turn this one over to your Higher Power!"

And that wasn't my only 'Mopping Up After Duncan' Project. Now that I was managing my own money, I'd learned that Duncan had failed to take a Massachusetts (and before that Michigan) tax deduction for all the income earned from the government instruments in my grandfather's trust. Not only had he convinced me to use this interest income to pay for all family clothing and furniture (because *we* were saving for college), he had overpaid our taxes for fifteen years! I called Frank Stoughton immediately, and learned that we could only go back for three years' worth of abatements, and because the lawyers had made me file jointly in 1988 and 1989, Duncan was owed half of this money – or close to $800! "But he was trying to render us homeless during those years," I protested to Frank, who in addition to being a financial advisor was also an attorney.

"I know Ursula, but that's the law!"

"Well, my grandparents would die all over again if they could see this latest turn of events!"

Jonah concurred. "It is the law Ursula, and you must abide by it." So I made all the arrangements for the abatements, filled out all the forms, notified Duncan, and obtained his signature. "If you are ever in a position to benefit from another woman's trust income," I said in the memorandum I fired off to him, "don't forget to take the deduction for government instruments! It will save you a bundle in taxes."

The Massachusetts Department of Revenue said the abatements could take up to two months to process. The refunds were to be made out to us jointly and mailed to Inverary Lane. Within a month, the refund appeared for the year in which I had filed singly; but two-and-half-months later, the other two checks still hadn't turned up.

I called the DOR. "Those checks were mailed out more than two months ago, Mrs. Charbonnier, but according to our computers, they're still active. That means they haven't been cashed. We should put stop payments on them right away. We can do it over the phone, right now, but I'll be sending you the appropriate forms to fill out and return to us. Then new checks will be issued. And if those missing checks turn up in the meantime, you are not to cash them under any circumstances. They'll bounce. Do you understand? And here are their numbers. Now remember, don't cash them!"

"I won't," I promised.

A few weeks later, Spencer handed me a check from Duncan for close to $800, dated three weeks earlier. Duncan had sat on the DOR checks for more than two months, then delayed a little longer before cashing them and sending my portion to me. When he phoned that evening, I told him that the DOR had put "stop payments" on their two checks a few weeks earlier. "Why did you sit on them for more than two months?" I asked. "I know they were sent in mid-April and made out jointly, so how could you have cashed them without my signature?"

"Oh, that was easy," laughed Duncan. "They were sent to me and made out only to me, because, I'm *the man!*"

"That's impossible," I said. "The DOR said abatements on joint returns are made out to *both* parties. At any rate, they'll be contacting you."

"I wrote you a check for your half," continued Duncan, "but you really owe me two-thirds, because I did your taxes all those years."

"Well, you did them wrong, all those years," I said dryly.

"You're not taking responsibility. You're blaming the tax errors on me," accused Duncan.

"I am taking responsibility," I said quietly. "I found the errors; I sorted them out; and I absorbed the expenses of rectifying them. What more do I owe you Duncan? Should I send you the other half, as well?"

"Oh, you owe me a lot more. Now what are you going to do about refinancing your house?" taunted Duncan.

"I can't do anything," I replied almost nonchalantly, "because you won't let me. You know even your lawyer thinks you're off-base on this one. Candice & MacIntyre were in Simon Rumborough's court last week, representing a woman whose former husband wouldn't allow her to refinance her house, and according to Jonah they did a brilliant job."

"You're twisting everything around," said Duncan angrily. "You are a totally fucked-up person and a terrible mother. You don't care what kind of values your children have or what kind of people they turn out to be!" And he slammed down the phone.

I marveled to myself that I was still calm, bemused even. I called my cognitive lawyer. "Jonah, will you help me work this out and do what's right?"

"*Yes!* But something is very fishy," said Jonah. His choice of adjective tickled me. "Ursula, find out from the DOR what you should do with Duncan's check, and if they now have the canceled checks, ask them to send you a copy of both sides, to see if he cashed them with only his signature or if he forged yours."

"Oh, is there a penalty for that in Massachusetts?"

"Yes, there's a penalty for it! Straighten this out as best you can with the DOR, and then call or fax me tomorrow."

"The Excursions of Miss Vanilla Through the DOR," as I entitled my next day's fax to Jonah, was to be another test of my rejuvenated sense of humor. After several layers of polite but not helpful bureaucrats, a delightful gentleman came to the phone.

"I want to help you, Mrs. Charbonnier."

"Who are you?" I asked incredulously.

"I am Mr. Solomon Arnold, second in command at the DOR, and I care about The Public."

"Oh good," I began again, this time hopefully.

He listened to my story – all of it. "Now can we put a stop on the stop payment, so I can go cash this check from Duncan?"

"No. There is no way to put a stop on a stop payment, but there are three things I want you to do right away Mrs. Charbonnier. First, call back and ask for the Abatement Department. Find out whether both of your names were on the checks. They can't send you copies, because according to our computers, neither has been cashed yet, but they can look up and see who they were made out to, and what address they were mailed to.

"Second, if there is a branch of Duncan's bank in your town, I want you to go there immediately and cash his check at his bank."

"Can I do that? I don't even have an account there."

"Maybe yes, maybe no, but I want you to try so that you can get your money right away. Otherwise, you may have to wait another three or four months, and I don't want that, and I don't think you do either. Third, I want you to call me back and let me know if you were successful."

"Are you sure this is all right? How will Duncan get his money?"

"That's his problem. You are in a perfectly harmless position if you cash his check. Duncan will then have to come back to us to get the new checks we'll issue. But at least it won't be your problem anymore."

"Thank you, Mr. Arnold!"

The Abatement Department confirmed what Duncan had said: the checks were in fact made out only to Duncan. "But how could that happen?" I asked. "It was a joint return, and it was his mistake and my money! Why weren't the checks made out to both of us?"

"Because we go by *the man's* social security number. According to that, Duncan moved to Farboro, so we sent the checks to Farboro. End of story. That's how we do it. If you don't like it, contact the Office of the Commissioner of Revenue. Here's their number."

I didn't like it, but when I tried to complain, the Office of the Commissioner of Revenue told me, "Yes, it is unfair, but that's how we do it. We go by the man's social security number. And until there's some reason to change our policy, that's the way it is. But if you feel strongly about this, and if you'd like to file some written complaints, and then go through our process . . ."

I'd had enough "process" for one day. Too bad there wasn't some way to alert the women of Massachusetts.

Next stop: Bay Bank in Conover Center. "The Department of Revenue advised me to cash this check immediately. Now I don't have an account here, but I was wondering if . . ."

"No problem," said the teller. "But if it's over $500, you will need to show two pieces of identification, one with a photograph. Here, take a brochure, read about our services; maybe you'll decide to open an account here."

"Thank you," I said, taking the proffered brochures after I cashed my check.

Next stop: Conover Trust, two doors down. "Lynne, you'll never believe this!" I said waving a sheaf of bills in her direction as I walked in.

"Oh, try me." She laughed when she heard the story. "Finally something worked in your favor, Ursula."

"Yes, Duncan's greed and need to control. If he hadn't sat on those checks for two and half months, the DOR wouldn't have told me to put stop payments on them! It's just another waste of everyone's time!"

Then I reported back to Mr. Arnold. "Okay, I did what you said, and I got the cash. Thanks for all your help."

"It was my pleasure, Mrs. Charbonnier! Have a nice spring."

Actually, I was having a nice spring, the nicest one I'd had in years. Gradually I was beginning to get back in circulation. People were asking me out – to plays, to dinners, for walks. Most of them were close to sixty, but I didn't mind.

"Why are you going out with all these old men, Ursula?" several well-meaning people inquired.

"I'm not doing midlife crisis twice," I told my friends, "I flunked it the first time."

"You mean Duncan flunked it," one of them edited.

"Well, it's just not something I ever want to do again." Actually, I was a long way from being ready to get serious about anyone new. "I just want peace," I told Jonah. And if peace came in sixty year-old packages, then that was okay with me. It was a pleasure just to find out that there were kind, intelligent, ethical men out there.

As I was coming back to life, Spencer and Amanda were also awakening in social respects. They were now teenagers, and the parties, the phone calls, the affectionate notes had also begun for them. Going through this all at the same time had its entertaining moments. After my third date with one fellow, Amanda expressed concerns that I might be getting involved. "There are just two things I want to say to you," she sternly announced to me over a Saturday morning breakfast after a Friday night date: "Number One, Safe Sex. Number Two, I have to live in this town too, so don't go getting a reputation like all the other divorced moms!"

This required a response. "Amanda, although I'm a long way from it now, someday I hope, I am going to fall in love again, and what I do about it will be my responsibility and nobody else's business. 'Til then, if people are going to gossip about events that aren't even happening, that's their problem, and let's not make it ours."

Jackie Melrose also took the philosophical view. "You're not just Mom anymore when you start dating again, Ursula. It's bound to be an adjustment for Spencer and Amanda. But just remember how far you've come, and don't let anything or anyone get you down. Remember, two years ago, it wasn't even clear that you were going to have a roof over your head. And now you do."

XXXIII

Home for the Hollidays

Bad laws are the worst sort of tyranny.
— Edmund Burke, *Speech at Bristol*

And that was more than I could say for Julia Holliday.

For more than a year, she had been in and out of courtrooms from Walden to Westbury to Cambridge and back to Walden again. And as the parade of lawyers lengthened, she and the boys drew closer and closer to homelessness. The two latest lawyers had grown so outraged by what The System was doing to a Mom and four boys — that they were now working for free. But this was a recent development.

Last autumn, the lawyers were still raking in the dough: Roger Cornwallis from Hobart's hidden assets, and Jeannie Curtin from claims against Julia's portion of Hobart's pension. Although Julia was still in the Pigeon Place manse, Hub Safe was rapidly closing in. Because Hobart had transferred the property into Julia's name only and stopped paying the mortgage two years before, in the eyes of the law he was off the hook. That he was continuing to deduct all the mortgage payments (which he wasn't making) from his own taxes, was of no concern to anyone but Julia. Even the IRS hadn't done anything about it. Like Duncan, Hobart was fond of saying that the law didn't apply to him, and so far it hadn't. And because Hobart had taken out second and third mortgages against Pigeon Place in Julia's name only, the full-time mother of four little boys was now in bankruptcy. As far as Hub Safe was concerned, their claims were entirely against Julia. And that was about where things stood in late October, when Julia was summoned to Probate Court in Walden.

Jeannie Curtin, in her early morning phone call, did not mince words. "Yes, Julia, I know you have a fever, fluids dripping out of both eyes, that you're in bed on doctor's orders, and the four boys have the day off from school, but I repeat, get over to this courthouse immediately, before everyone settles this case without you!"

"What about the children?" asked Julia. It was the question that always went unanswered. "I have no place to leave them, and no money to pay a sitter."

Jeannie ignored the question. "I said, get over here, Julia!" And she hung up.

"Come on, boys," said Julia wearily. "I guess we're spending your day-off in court."

The walls of Judge Simon Rumborough's courtroom, in the Walden Probate courthouse, are devoid of right angles, like the Roman arenas where early Christians were devoured in public view. The trappings in Walden are more modern, however: a climate-controlled environment with thick carpets, lots of attorneys and official paperwork to make all that takes place within it — "legal."

Hobart and Roger Cornwallis had already been with Judge Rumborough for an hour on that Friday, before Julia and the boys arrived, and the case seemed pretty much settled by then anyway, at least in Judge Rumborough's mind.

"Let's get one thing clear," began the black-robed magistrate, repeatedly jabbing his left index finger through space, as if he were trying to revive an imaginary broken doorbell. "You remind me of *Gone With The Wind*," he said glowering at Julia. "Everything has crumbled. The '80s are over. All your dreams were coming true. You had everything, but . . . whatever happened, happened. Your dreams were shattered." Then warming to his subject, "It's like the last scene, when Rhett Butler walks in and says, 'Frankly, my dear, I don't give a damn' — and in those days, Mrs. Holliday, that movie was almost banned for such language — and Scarlett O'Hara is distraught — it reminds me of you, Mrs. Holliday. But, tomorrow *is* another day. And Mrs. Holliday, that's my advice to you. Don't live in today!"

Julia wiped the continuing ooze away from her eyes, and blinked at the Judge. "But, Your Honor, I'm in a Twelve Step Program. You know, live one day at a time?"

This did not register with Simon Rumborough, as he rifled through papers and bobbed his head horizontally, as if the words on the pages had transformed themselves into a tennis match, which in a sense wasn't far from reality: the litigious balls had bobbed since summer, from Hobart's court, to Julia's court, to Judge Tracy's court, to the Westbury District Court, to Cambridge Superior Court, and now back to Rumborough's court, and this was still a long way from being over.

"Don't live for today, Mrs. Holliday," continued Judge Rumborough, rocking back and forth in his blue vinyl chair, and furiously rubbing his face and chin, for no apparent reason. "Don't live in today, Mrs. Holliday. Think about how good tomorrow will be! Madam," he said, engaging her face with a sneer, "you must learn how to let go emotionally. Now you and Mr. Holliday go with nice Mr. Norris," he said jabbing at the air again, and motioning them to exit with his assistant.

Nice Mr. Norris led them out of Rumborough's courtroom into an ante-chamber off the main corridor. "Sir," said Julia, "I can't tell you what a pleasure it is to be in a courthouse that doesn't smell like a urinal!"

"Oh, so you've been to Cambridge?" laughed Norris.

"Yes, I've been to Cambridge. Now you get something clear," said Julia Holliday. "I let go of this marriage emotionally a long time ago. I'm only holding on to it for the stability and security of my children. Hobart is the one who's rejected and hanging on. He was physically abusive to me at Disneyworld. He beat me up in front of my children for no reason whatso-ever, and he smashed down a door in our hotel. That's all right with the Court. But the fact that I want to raise my children with some stability is not all right with the Court.

"It's all right for Hobart to improve his standard of living," continued Julia. "He has two houses and two new Volvos – while our living standard is lowered. That's all right with the Court, too. Is that Justice, Mr. Norris? Is this the guy who cares so much about his family that he won't even pay for his children to go to the dentist? I'm no dummy."

Knowing he couldn't argue with the facts she had presented, because they were all true, Norris turned to Hobart. "You're still trying to control her life, aren't you? That's really stupid." Hobart started to cry.

"Now I realize you're just upholding The Law, Mr. Norris," continued Julia, "and The Law says that Hobart may have a second new car this year, but that he is not required to pay for shoes for his children. Isn't that right, Mr. Norris? It's within his right, isn't it? It's not a legal issue."

"That's right, Mrs. Holliday."

"Well, you didn't make the laws, Mr. Norris, I realize that. I'm not blam-ing you. So don't take this personally."

"I've heard all this before, many times, Mrs. Holliday. And I don't make the laws."

"There's just one thing I want to know, Mr. Norris. Why does *The Law* condone this?"

"Because we can't print money," replied Mr. Norris.

Then Julia turned to Cornwallis, Hobart's lawyer. "You're a father, Roger. Have you no sense of shame? Your client is running around town in his new car, his three-piece Armani suits, and his children can't go to the dentist. You know I shouldn't be here. You know I'm just a mom trying to raise my kids and preserve the roof over our heads."

"It's true Julia, that you are not the person that Hobart and Rob Rhana painted. You're not like that," said Cornwallis quietly. "So let's just settle this case today." But Julia, despite her eye infection, could still see. Cornwallis was clearly uneasy. Maybe he was remembering his interchange last summer at Westbury District Court, with Mortimer Hives, the Hub Safe Attorney who had come to court to evict Julia and the boys, and with Sherman Franklin, Julia's real estate attorney. "I'm afraid of Julia Holliday,"

Hives had said to the attorneys.

"Well, what would you do if you were Julia Holliday?" Sherman Franklin had asked.

"I would hope that I would have the balls to do what she's doing!" Hives had replied.

A screaming Julia brought Cornwallis back to the moment. "You want me to settle this case now?!"

"Yes, Julia," said Jeannie Curtin. "Let's settle this case now."

"Well, I demand a trial!" said Julia. "You're not going to railroad me like you have all the others. I have nothing more to lose. It's my right as a citizen to have a trial, and I'm going to have one!"

"Isn't that my right, Your Honor?" said Julia when they returned to Judge Rumborough's courtroom.

"Yes, it's your right," said the Judge, his tiny head bobbing back and forth, in tennis-watch mode. And then again jabbing his left index finger violently toward Julia, he declared, "I'm not going to say that it's going to be any different for you if you have a trial, but it is your right." Then he turned to the attorneys. "Now how long is a trial going to take?"

"Maximum three hours." "Minimum couple of days," said the two attorneys in unison.

"Oh God, I can see it now," said Mr. Norris. "Eviction on Christmas Eve!"

Back outside in the lobby, there was no order in the courthouse. "Julia, I don't want a trial!" declared Jeannie Curtin. "And get these kids out of here!" She was referring to Ethan, Evan, Enoch, and Ezra who had wandered into the proceedings.

"I'll take these kids," said Hobart, pulling Ezra's arm.

"Oh no you won't! Don't you touch my kids!!!" screamed Julia.

"Julia, they're going to file a 51A on you," warned Jeannie Curtin. "Stop, stop . . ."

"Why should I stop?" Julia demanded of her attorney. "You haven't done a goddamn thing for me and my kids."

"Hey Mom, remember Legal Sea Foods . . ." said Ethan devilishly.

"Yeah, Mom, remember Legal Sea Foods?" repeated Evan, Enoch, and even Ezra, who had now freed himself from a still tearful Hobart, and wriggled into his mother's arms. "Should we Mom, should we?" they laughed.

"No boys!" said Julia sharply. *"Not here!"*

"Hey Hobart, why don't you just take these kids and go get a baby-sitter for them?" suggested Cornwallis.

"Oh God, I need a drink so bad – I'm gonna get so stoned and drunk. I would take the kids today, but I need to go get shitfaced," said Hobart to his attorney.

"Yeah," agreed Cornwallis, "I need a drink too."

"Well, I don't do that anymore," said Julia. "I'm going to take my boys home, *while* we still have one."

At Pigeon Place, a disturbing message waited on her answering machine. The voice on the tape was fuzzy, but explicit. "You're gonna die bitch, you're gonna die real soon."

The following week, Julia Holliday played it over for me several times. The words were slurred to disguise the voice, but the menacing tone came through loud and clear. "The Conover Police have heard it, Ursula, and they are appalled. I also played the part where Hobart says he's going to see to it that my life is ruined, as if he hasn't already done that."

"He hasn't Julia. He can control your possessions, but he can't control you. When's the next court date?"

"Tuesday. In Cambridge. Eviction in Land Court. And Hobart is re-opening the custody suit in Probate. I can't do this much longer. I can't go on. Look what this is doing to my kids, Ursula. They don't want to spend their lives with shrinks. They want to play soccer with their friends, live in their house, be normal." I knew. This was precisely the way Spencer and Amanda had felt two years before, when I had been as powerless as Julia to prevent the long and expensive parade of paid enablers.

A few days later, another Conover ex-wife in trouble asked me to accompany her to the Walden courthouse to witness the signing of a document. While she fiddled with paperwork, I slipped into Judge Rumborough's courtroom to listen to the proceedings. A man in the front row turned around, and smiled in dim recognition. The look on his face said, I know you. Why do I know you? Then he disappeared into a room off the court. Minutes later when he returned, Seth Wright marched straight to my row and motioned me to make a space for him.

"Did you get my recipe?" he asked, without saying hello.

"Yes, I got your recipe," I said. "I haven't tried it yet, but it looks good."

"It is good," he said proudly. "It's practically all I know how to make."

"Here, look at this," I said taking out a rough draft of *The Snow Job Cookbook*, which I always carried in my briefcase, in case I ever got a few spare minutes to write.

Wright read through the Table of Contents, and then slowly through the very funny Foreword, and burst out laughing.

"I couldn't believe it," I later told Jonah. "There I was, sitting in Judge Rumborough's courtroom with a laughing Seth Wright reading *The Snow Job Cookbook*. What's gonna happen next, Jonah?"

"I don't know, Ursula, but I love your cookbook!" said Jonah. "By the way, how was Seth's recipe?"

"Almost as good as his 1990 miracle!" I said alluding to the unexpected settlement of our case at Christmas the year before.

But for Julia and her four boys, the approaching holidays of 1991 were to hold no miracles. Superior Court in Cambridge was scheduled to issue a decision about eviction from Pigeon Place by mid-January, and the divorce trial was set for early February. Julia and Jeannie were finding it hard to exchange a civil word.

"Ursula, I know this sounds crazy, but it's like my own lawyer has suddenly turned against me," said Julia over tea one late December afternoon in the Pigeon Place kitchen. "I know that doesn't make any sense, but that's how I feel. And actions speak louder than words. She's no longer fighting for us. I feel like I've been sold down the river by my own lawyer. But why?

"And now that woman we met in court last year when we were in Cambridge with Rob Rhana – remember Amelia Emilios? – she called me, out of the blue, and said I should get *another* lawyer. I don't know what to do. I'm so sick of lawyers, and I don't trust any of them anymore. But Amelia said he was a good person, and that he would give me a free hour to learn about the case."

"They all say that; the first hour is always free," I said, unimpressed. "But who is this potential new lawyer?" I asked, softening, since it was clear Julia was considering him.

"Quentin Corey."

"Oh, I've heard of him – at Al-Anon, but other than that, I don't know anything about him. Are you going to call him?"

"I already have. And are your ready for this? When I told him I felt like Jeannie was selling me down the river to Cornwallis and Hobart, he told me that Jeannie and Cornwallis have been having an affair. Can you believe that, Ursula? Does that beat all?! The two opposing lawyers are sleeping with each other!"

"Well, it explains all," I said quietly. "So you're considering going with Quentin Corey. But something's making you hesitate. What is it?"

"Oh, it's partly that I don't trust lawyers anymore. Will a new one really make a difference? And it's partly that Rumborough hates Quentin. You may remember what Amelia told us about her case last year."

"Only vaguely. Refresh my memory."

Julia launched into a rambling tale of how Amelia's ex-husband, a wealthy owner of grain elevators up and down the whole East Coast, had arranged to have Amelia declared dangerous and incarcerated at McLean's, and Rumborough had collaborated by saying that Amelia had issued a death threat against him, the Judge in The Emilios Matter. The bottom line was that even though Amelia managed to get out of McLean's, she was officially barred from ever entering Judge Rumborough's courtroom. And, because Quentin subsequently brought Rumborough up before the Judicial Board of Conduct, because of how the Judge handled himself during Amelia's case, Rumborough loathes Quentin.

"Well, those are good reasons to hesitate," I agreed. "In our case, Judge Tracy was no fan of Gabriel's or Chubb's as you'll recall, but he did like

Jonah, and *that* served me well in the end."

"Yeah," continued Julia, "but since the feelings Rumborough and Quentin have for each other are so widely known in greater Boston legal circles, Quentin thinks we can get Rumborough to recuse himself from the case, and then we can get a judge who's more likely to be impartial."

"Not a bad tactic," I had to agree.

"At the same time, we'll get Jeannie to withdraw from the case."

"When is all this supposed to take place?" I asked my friend.

"On the eighth of January, Quentin has us scheduled to appear before Rumborough. Did you hear a car?" she asked suddenly. "Hobart must be early to pick up the boys." On my way out, I offered to move my station wagon, which blocked Hobart's way into the garage.

"Don't bother," he replied nastily. "I'll go through you!"

I laughed. "Oh, that's been tried Hobart. It doesn't work!"

Home for the Hollidays was to hang in the balance through yet another Christmas, but many of us in Conover hoped that a new year would make a difference, and Quentin Corey was already hard at work with Sherman Franklin to make it so.

Sherman's first step in the New Year was to go into Superior Court in Cambridge to appeal the eviction order that Mortimer Hives had obtained from Westbury District Court. Superior Court rendered a swift decision: "Be out by January 15 or the bank will move you out!"

Meanwhile, Quentin Corey tried a different tack: dealing directly with Mortimer Hives on an attorney-to-attorney basis, once he realized the events since last summer *had* indeed pricked Hives' conscience.

"I would now favor giving Julia and the boys a reprieve, at least until after the divorce trial in February," said Hives to Quentin Corey. "You know that Julia Holliday is the smartest fucking little bitch I've ever seen. And beautiful too! And I hate that combination," he added with more than a touch of admiration and respect.

"I think I'm beginning to like my new client even more," smiled Julia's latest attorney. "So then, Mr. Hives, will you agree to defer the eviction process and court proceedings against Mrs. Holliday until after the divorce?"

"Let me see what I can do," said Mortimer Hives reasonably, in what was to be the only short-lived spark of hope in the holiday season.

His immediate boss, Attorney Lilly Lockhart, would have none of it. "I've waited long enough for the bank's money!" she snapped. "I want that woman and those children out by January 15. The law is on our side!"

Then Sherman Franklin appealed to Lilly Lockhart directly. "But my client has offered to pay you rent until she gets back on her feet. She's willing to negotiate monthly payments. Please! She doesn't want to lose her home and uproot her children. She's willing the pay you two-thirds of her child support!"

Lilly Lockhart remained unmoved. "If Julia Holliday doesn't come up with the mortgage balance — $480,000 by the fifteenth — then they're out. Hub Safe will take physical possession of the property."

Sherman Franklin was dismayed. "Julia, that Lilly Lockhart has no family values, and she's totally insensitive to the children's needs. I've been a real estate attorney for close to thirty years, but I've rarely seen such a hard-hearted person. She's just in it for the money," he said, shaking his head sadly. "Even Mortimer Hives favored holding off until after the trial. Maybe Quentin should try to reach her." But Lilly Lockhart ignored all of Quentin Corey's subsequent correspondence and refused to return his many phone calls.

Which meant the Holliday crew and assorted attorneys were back in Walden Probate court on the eighth for: relief from the housing issue; Withdrawal of Appearance by Jeannie; and a request to recuse Judge Rumborough from the case.

I was mildly amused when Amelia Emilios entered the courtroom and flashed a smile of distaste at Judge Rumborough, as if to say, come and get me, Judgie, in front of all the oblivious spectators in the gallery!

Then Quentin, who was close to seven feet tall, marched into the courtroom, peered down at tiny, elegant Amelia, and said in a loud voice, "Have you been properly searched, Mrs. Emilios? Are there no weapons on you this day?" The idea of Amelia's being armed was ludicrous. Then Quentin turned to Julia. "Ah, it's Scarlett O'Hara!" he boomed in greeting, just within range of Judge Rumborough's hearing. It was to be the last note of humor in the morning. The Walden magistrate was *not* amused.

"The Holliday Matter," intoned a court clerk, and Hobart, Julia and the various attorneys approached the bench. Roger Cornwallis had the first words. He cited Julia's failure to find a decent and affordable place to live, the imminent eviction from Pigeon Place, and how irresponsible she had been to bring the four boys to this courthouse last October. "Your Honor, I request a Pre-Trial for February 5."

Then Quentin stepped forward to ask for Jeannie's Withdrawal of Appearance; more time; and Judge Rumborough's recusal. Jeannie was glad to be relieved of The Holliday Matter, now that Julia was cued in to her relationship with Attorney Cornwallis, but Rumborough refused to recuse himself, saying, "I have no instant recall about the case you're referring to, Attorney Corey," even as Amelia Emilios glowered from the gallery.

"Are you prepared to try this case, Mr. Corey?" asked the judge.

"I'd prefer not to, but I will," said Quentin Corey.

Then Cornwallis launched into a monologue about the "difficulties of dealing with Mrs. Holliday," and how "Mr. Holliday has bent over backwards to be understanding about her drinking problem, and the month she spent in Appleton Hall," and that they'd like to request "a 38 percent decrease in child support, and immediate custody of the four boys."

Judge Rumborough suddenly interrupted. "Is custody going to be an issue in this case?"

Hobart said that the boys needed a place to live, and Julia was about to be evicted. "As far as I'm concerned, she can have the children back once she finds a place to live in Conover, and once she can prove she's a responsible adult. She's in bankruptcy, Your Honor," said Hobart in a patronizing tone. Naturally Hobart didn't explain how Julia had come to be in bankruptcy. Not that the court would have cared.

"I'm having trouble recalling your case," said Judge Rumborough again. "Look, the bank won't throw her out." Then he waved at both attorneys, "Now you just tell the bank that this case is being heard on the fifth, and they can wait until then. Motion to vacate is denied. Motion for custody is denied."

"I'll fight you on this!" Cornwallis scowled at Quentin out in the lobby.

"Go ahead, my meter ain't ticking – and yours is!" said Quentin, referring to his recent decision to charge Julia no further.

Within days of the eviction, Quentin Corey phoned Julia Holliday and announced, "Your assignment for today is to go rent a house."

"But I have no money. I'm in bankruptcy, remember?" Julia reminded her lawyer.

"I'll take care of it. Now you just go find a house."

"Right."

By the end of the day, Julia had found a small ranch house owned by the Day family on Bradford Road, not far from Inverary Lane. She put down a deposit her parents had loaned her, and told the boys they were moving two days later, on the weekend of Martin Luther King's birthday. On Saturday morning, like manna from heaven, tens of people from AA, Conover, and surrounding communities descended upon the Pigeon Place manse. In forty-eight hours, the manse was entirely packed up and contents moved; the children had come home to Pigeon Place from school on a Friday, and on Monday morning, the bus picked them up at Bradford Road. If I hadn't been part of the moving crew myself, I would not have believed it possible! So that Julia could resume her catering business once she got back on her feet, an electrician from AA completely dismantled the Pigeon Place kitchen which Julia had designed and installed, and packaged it up for reassembly at a later date. After the last box was carted off, Julia stood silently in the cavity that had been her kitchen, remembering the many magnificent meals that had been launched from this spot during her Conover Caterer days. Footsteps in the back hall brought her back to the moment.

It was Hobart. He gaped in disbelief at the emptiness around him. He started to cry. "It's really true. You really did it. You moved out of here, and you've trashed our kitchen!"

"That's right Hobart. This house is now as trashed as your life," and she walked out, leaving him sobbing in the applianceless cavern.

That same week, Hub Safe sent an inspection crew over to Pigeon Place, saying a wealthy biotech marketeer wanted to buy the property. The crew found dangerous levels of microwaves in the cables that surrounded the property, lead paint throughout the interior, and a dead septic system. The house was acting out, again, as Julia liked to put it, and because of these unanticipated findings, Hub Safe now had a practically unmarketable property on its hands. Family values aside, in a strictly financial sense, Hub Safe would have been far better off to let Julia and the children remain, and take the hefty percentage she had offered them from child support.

"I could move back in," suggested Julia helpfully through her attorney, Quentin Corey.

"Do I smell a lawsuit coming?!" responded Mortimer Hives thinking of the microwaves and Massachusetts' laws about lead paint, which were enforced much more vigorously than child support statutes.

And there was something else the bank wanted to know: "Where is the kitchen?"

"Oh, my lawyer needed it for his condo in Vermont. That's how I'm paying him," said Julia breezily, as Quentin Corey had instructed her to do.

Not taking that lying down, Hub Safe's attorney, Lilly Lockhart swiftly called the Conover Police, and got Deputy Chief Avery Boland on the line. "Yes, I'll look into it," he said wearily, knowing full well the hell that Julia and the boys had been through.

"Yes, I took the kitchen," Julia freely admitted when Avery dropped by later that day. "That bank didn't give a damn about me and the children. I put that kitchen in, and I took it out! Hub Safe wouldn't wait two weeks longer, like the judge wanted them to, like their own attorney Mortimer Hives wanted them to. Avery, the children and I would have stood a much better chance of keeping our home if Hub Safe had just waited a few more weeks until the divorce trial!"

Avery shook his head sympathetically, patted Julia on the shoulder, and returned to the Station to phone Lilly Lockhart. "Ms. Lockhart, this is Deputy Chief Avery Boland of the Conover Police Department, responding to your complaint against Mrs. Julia Holliday. And I just want to tell you that as far as the Conover Police Department is concerned, no crime has been committed, and we see no reason to file criminal charges. This is a civil matter, and Ms. Lockhart," he added, as a suggestion and warning all in one, "don't go wasting the taxpayers' money with a trial."

Avery recounted this to Julia when he stopped by Bradford Road the next day. "Now how are you all getting along?" he inquired with his usual good cheer and quiet concern, as he looked at the disarray around him.

"We're doing fine, Avery," said Julia Holliday. "I could hug you for what you did yesterday. It's going to take a little time to fix this place up, but the boys are helping, and we'll be fine. Thank you for stopping by to tell me about the bank."

"Not at all. Just doing my job," smiled Avery Boland as he waved good-bye.

I, too, had a warm spot in my heart for the Conover Police Department. Two years later, they still had Duncan's unregistered gun safely locked up at the Station, and Sergeant Allenbury told me that they regularly kept an eye on me and Inverary Lane, after all that had taken place. "You mean, if anything ever happens to me, you'll know where to look?" I half-kidded.

"Yes, we'll know where to look!" They were aware of Duncan's threat to destroy me, and that it had been made in Amanda's presence. In large part thanks to our very caring police department, Conover was the sort of town where citizens were glad to pay their taxes.

The first week of February, the Hollidays' divorce trial opened right on schedule. Hobart admitted under oath that he regularly watched pornography, sometimes in the presence of the children, but he denied that he had beaten Julia up at Disneyworld or ever forced her to have kinky sex.

Then Quentin informed Judge Rumborough that Hub Safe in fact hadn't waited, that foreclosure and possession of the property had taken place, and that his number one concern in The Holliday Matter remained housing. "My client has found a temporary place to live and agreed to pay rent for three months, at which time she must come up with a deposit to purchase. I intend that her down payment come from the divorce settlement." He said his second major concern was Julia's car, which was close to undrivable. "She requires a car in good operating condition for the children's safe transport."

Cornwallis told the judge that his client had "done everything by the book" and cooperated, but that he still had many problems with Mrs. Holliday. "It's time for Julia to understand that there's a real world out there, Your Honor. Mr. Holliday is tired of being generous."

And here's what Judge Rumborough said: "Mrs. Holliday had no right to move from Pigeon Place without permission from the court." Had he forgotten that Hub Safe was about to throw her and the boys out on the street? "Mrs. Holliday must learn to live more economically, so I am reducing child support by 30 percent, and awarding her some alimony. This will leave Mr. Holliday with roughly as much to live on as Mrs. Holliday and the children, and that is fair." With what Julia would now have to pay in taxes on the alimony, this amounted to a radical reduction in support. "Mrs. Holliday will pay 100 percent of her uninsured medical expenses, and 25 percent of the children's out of the awarded child support." The court ruled that Julia's nearly undrivable car was an asset worth

$500, but that Hobart's two Volvos were not assets, because he leased them through his company. Judge Rumborough also took into consideration that Hobart owed the Bank of the Region $250,000. He did not take into consideration that Hobart had told the bank he'd give them ten cents on the dollar over the next five years, and that they had accepted his offer. The Judge also did not express concern that Hobart had taken more than two years' worth of income tax deductions on mortgage payments for Pigeon Place that he had never paid. Julia was to be awarded no property and no cash settlement. Each Holliday would be entitled to take tax deductions for two children apiece (in The Charbonnier Matter, Judge Tracy had awarded all tax deductions for children to Duncan; it didn't matter that I was contributing a greater amount to their support). Finally, Hobart would be obliged to maintain $500,000 in life insurance, of which Julia was to be the beneficiary. Judge Rumborough's decision was handed down on Valentine's Day, on what would have been the Hollidays' fifteenth wedding anniversary.

Shortly thereafter, Hobart canceled his life insurance. And Quentin and Julia had to return to court.

"My client terminated his insurance, because he was in fear for his life," stated Roger Cornwallis. "He's had death threats!"

You mean, he's made death threats, Quentin refrained from saying. "Your Honor, according to the orders you yourself handed down at the time of the Divorce, Mr. Holliday is obliged to maintain life insurance in the amount of $500,000."

Judge Rumborough scratched his head, rubbed his chin, wrinkled his face, and bobbed up and down in his swivel chair while he decided. "I think carefully about all my decisions," he began (somewhat defensively I thought). "My most recent judgment is to be amended to reflect Paragraph 11 of the Divorce Agreement pertaining to life insurance."

I couldn't believe Julia, who was buried behind the front page of *The Boston Globe,* was actually getting a fair deal in Judge Rumborough's courtroom. Hobart was furious, and she was missing the whole show, until Jimmie, our familiar court clerk, came up and reprimanded her. "You can't read a newspaper while court's in session," he said. "You must show respect for this Honorable Court," and he snatched the newspaper from Julia.

"You won," I said.

"I did? I don't believe it, but Quentin's smiling so it must be true," said Julia.

As we exited the courtroom, I couldn't resist nudging Jimmie, who was relaxing in a chair by the door. "Jimmie, see that man over there," I said. "He's reading a newspaper!" I exclaimed in mock horror. "He should show more respect for this 'Honorable' Court!'"

"Where? Where?!" said Jimmie, jumping up like a Boston bulldog to do his duty.

With the divorce final, Julia and the boys came into their first stretch of normalcy in years, and they were reveling in it. But Hobart grew increasingly furious that he had been unable to gain custody of the boys. "My goal is still to have Julia crumble and be committed to Appleton Hall," he told one of the family psychiatrists, who immediately phoned Julia.

"Do you know this man is a psychopath?" said the shocked psychiatrist, obviously upset.

Julia listened calmly, then said, "Ryan, where have you been for the last four years while all this was going on? And where were you during the divorce trial? You were writing reports to the Court, telling everyone what a wonderful father Hobart is."

"I was wrong," said the psychiatrist.

"That's not going to help us now," said Julia. "Did you know Hobart's planning to initiate another custody suit?"

"Well, he'll have to find another psychiatrist to help him."

"That shouldn't be a problem," said Julia. "Finding new paid enablers is relatively easy in Massachusetts."

Then Hobart told Enoch's school teacher that he wouldn't rest until he'd gotten all four boys away from their mother.

"Even if it means you have to destroy them in the process?" asked Ms. Keele, who over the years had taught most of the Holliday boys and knew Julia well.

"I have to do this," said Hobart, eyes blazing.

"I will get those boys if it's the last thing I do," Hobart repeated to Quentin Corey. "There will be another custody battle, mark my words. I'm going to destroy your client."

"Oh, no you won't," said Quentin Corey, "because I am going to watch her like a hawk for the rest of my life."

The remainder of February progressed uneventfully, and Julia settled into making Bradford Road a comfortable place for the boys. It was a quarter the size of Pigeon Place, but they were just glad to be in Conover, and with careful budgeting, Julia found she could send more than half of child support to the Days for rent. Quentin was confident that he could appeal to the court for a cash settlement that would enable Julia to put a down payment on the house by the fifteenth of April. But then Julia's car gave out again.

"It's undrivable, Mrs. Holliday," said Vic, the mechanic in Conover Center, one blustery March day.

"But I can't buy another car," protested Julia. "I'm in bankruptcy."

"I'll buy one for you," offered her father, who had already put a good portion of his retirement nest egg toward Julia's legal fees. He came to Boston to shop for a new car, only to learn that Massachusetts will not permit someone to purchase car insurance if that person is in bankruptcy, and it's illegal to drive an uninsured car in Massachusetts, but it is not illegal to arrange it so another person is in bankruptcy, as Hobart had so cleverly done. Oh the things we were learning about the law!

"What kind of a cockamamie place is this state?" asked Julia's father in total frustration. "How are you supposed to drive my grandchildren around safely in that wreck? My God, doesn't Hobart care about the safety of his own children?!"

Mechanic friends in AA said not to worry. They would find a way to make that car work. And they did. At no charge. And they continued to, throughout the spring and summer. But April 15 was rapidly approaching, and Quentin had still not extracted a cash settlement from Hobart.

"If I don't come up with a down payment for Bradford Road, I'm out on the street again," Julia told Quentin. "It will be my second eviction in six months."

"Appeal for more time," said Quentin. "I'm trying."

"The Days told their broker they want to sell if I don't come up with a $10,000 deposit by the fifteenth, that they won't accept rent money after that."

"Who's their broker?" asked Quentin.

"Adolf Carlson from Most Sold Realty."

"Look, if we haven't come up with a cash settlement by the fifteenth, let Carlson show the house, but tell him we're still trying, and that you and the boys want to buy."

Adolf Carlson was not gracious when Julia's deposit failed to materialize on the fifteenth, and the boys found an eviction notice on the floor when then came home from school.

"When I got home Ursula, they waved the paper in my face and said, 'Look Mom, we're getting evicted again!' It wasn't even in an envelope – it was shoved under the front door, in plain view for the boys to see!" exclaimed Julia. "Now the two little ones are having nightmares again, and scared about where we will go. They tried appealing to Hobart, saying 'Daddy, we need your help.' And Hobart said, 'I can't help you. Your mother takes all of my money and spends it on herself. I have no money.' "

"Duncan used to tell my kids the same thing, but they don't believe him anymore. Did yours fall for that line?"

"Of course not!" said Julia. "Ethan said, 'Dad, how come you had enough money for my fancy Bar Mitzvah?' and Evan said, 'How come you had enough money to take us to the Ritz for dinner twice last month?' and Enoch said, 'How come you have enough money to pay for all these shrinks we don't need?' And now they're refusing to see Hobart. So then I did what Quentin said: I appealed to Adolf Carlson for just a little more time, and I wrote a letter to the Days, explaining our predicament, and said we're doing our best to come up with the deposit."

"Who actually sent the eviction notice?" I asked.

"It was from Denise Goferbucks, the Days' attorney. She lives here in Conover and practices out of her home. Here, read this letter she sent."

The letter was short and addressed to Sherman Franklin, Julia's real estate attorney:

RE: *Day v. Holliday*

Dear Attorney Franklin:

Enclosed please find a letter sent by Ms. Holliday to the Days. Please inform Ms. Holliday that she is not to contact my clients directly.

As far as we are concerned, your client is a trespasser, and we are beginning the civil suit for the loss of the $335,000 sale forthwith.

The best your client can do is to take the rental in her letter and pray that I can salvage the sale to the Church with which she maliciously and wilfully interfered.

Sincerely,
Denny Goferbucks, Esq.

"She spelled 'willfully' wrong. Maybe she could run for Vice President," I said, handing the letter back to Julia. "What's this about the Church?"

"You know how the Episcopal Church has a new minister? Goferbucks claims the Church was going to buy Bradford Road for the minister's family, but pulled out when they found out there was an eviction in process that involved children. Now I'm to be sued for damages in the amount the Church would have paid for the property."

"Is that true?" I asked. "Why don't you call the Church? They're just across the way from First Parish, and this doesn't sound like the way St. Paul's operates, Julia."

"Well, I did call them, just as soon as this letter came, and the Church said they had decided on another house, and the decision had nothing to do with me, and they'd be willing to say so."

"Good."

"So Sherman fired off a letter to Denny, stating her advice about 'prayers' was unprofessional, that her threats were becoming tiresome, and that she should know the consequences of filing groundless, frivolous lawsuits. Then she hauled me back into Westbury District Court the other day, and the Church's lawyer just sat there and didn't say a word. I went *pro se* and told the judge I needed time to get representation. Sherman doesn't think anything will come of it. Denny Goferbucks yelled at me in the courthouse. She said, 'The way we're going to get you out is by taking your children away from you. Who do you think you are, trying to stay in that house with four children?' and I said, 'Who do *you* think you are? Have you no regard for innocent families?'"

Adolf Carlson of Most Sold Realty was equally unsympathetic. "I'll show this house whenever I want to," he snarled at Julia. "I have a job to do. What's the matter with you? There's money to be made here."

The four boys continued to express their anger to Hobart. Evan refused to go play tennis with him. "No thanks, I'd rather go to an AA meeting with my mom!"

And Enoch would not allow Hobart to drive him home from the next baseball practice. Motioning in Hobart's direction, Enoch shouted to his baseball coach Stanley Leonard, "Who is that man? I don't know that man!"

"I'm your father!" said Hobart angrily.

"Fuck you, you asshole!" shouted nine year-old Enoch.

"Don't talk to your father that way!" reprimanded the coach.

Poor Stanley had to drive Enoch home. After the fourth week of the boys' refusing to spend any time with Hobart, Cornwallis got a court order forcing the children to see their father and opened a third custody suit in Judge Rumborough's court in Walden.

"On what grounds?" I asked Julia.

"Failure to provide adequate shelter, since I'm about to be evicted again."

"This is looneytunes!" I said. "You stay home for fourteen years and take care of everyone, and Hobart is not required to provide shelter for you and the children, but he can take them away from you, even though they've told numerous shrinks and the *g.a.l.* that they want to live with you!"

At the end of May, Judge Rumborough appointed Robina Braverman, a friend of his, to serve as attorney to the Holliday boys. "What about Ken Wouk, the other *g.a.l.* who said the children should live with you?"

"They're disregarding his recommendation."

"On what grounds?" I fired back. "Ken Wouk is highly regarded by every person I've met in The System, including Jonah McCoy!"

"Rumborough's a judge, Ursula. You know he doesn't have to give grounds."

"What about Ryan, the family shrink who told you Hobart is a 'psychopath'? Can't he help here?"

"Hobart hired a new shrink. His name is Bing Levine and the kids have to start seeing him now, but at least it's on Hobart's nickel. Evan saw Hobart give Levine a check for $375 the other day."

"Who's paying for Robina Braverman, Julia? I hear she's not cheap."

"Hobart is. A $10,000 retainer, according to Quentin, and she's $300 an hour. She came out here last Sunday to interview me and the boys, and she assured me that custody was not an issue in this case. Then she turned in a twelve-page report to Rumborough, recommending that Hobart have sole custody of the boys, at which point the boys called her up and fired her for lying to them, and told her they smelled a big payoff!"

"They *fired* their lawyer?!" I laughed.

"That's right, Enoch, on behalf of all four boys, fired her over the phone, and she faxed a notice saying that they were not allowed to contact her directly anymore. Is that too much?!"

Ethan walked in the midst of all this. "How's it going?" I asked trying to be cheery. "It's fine," said Ethan, "about the same really. I have a new shrink."

"How is he?"

"He's a major geek, a dork – actually I think he's a faggot, Mrs. Charbonnier."

"Oh, Amanda used to say that about her *g.a.l.*, but I don't really think he was. She used to do imitations of him: 'so tell me about the sitch-uuuuu-aaayyy-shun.'"

"Oh cool, that's just what our new shrink says, same voice and every-thing, Mrs. Charbonnier. I've told him about fifty times that I want to live with my mom. We all have. Anyway, I think he had a long talk with Dad and said, 'The children want to stay in the house with Julia,' so hopefully this will be the end of it."

It's too bad you have to go through all this, but it's making you strong and wise. That's what it did to Spencer and Amanda."

When he left, I said, "I can't believe I'm having a conversation like that with a child. We should be talking about soccer games and camp and summer. Not attorneys and shrinks and evictions. There are times when I don't recognize this country anymore. Have you thought about going back to Hub Safe and seeing if Pigeon Place is still available, if you could work out some kind of a deal? With all the property's problems, maybe they'll reconsider."

"I thought of that. In fact I called up that man you told me about in the Mortgage Department at Hub Safe."

"Rod McLaren. Was he able to help you?"

"He was very nice, Ursula. You were right about him, but after he lis-tened to my story all he could say was, 'It sounds terrible Mrs. Holliday. What is it with these guys from Conover?' Then he asked Lilly Lockhart to call me, remember her? And she told me Pigeon Place is 'under agree-ment.' So that's that."

"Are you doing anything for fun these days, Julia?" I asked, trying to change the subject.

"I just go to AA meetings and take care of my kids and try to figure out how to keep a roof over our heads. And do you know what Robina Braverman said about *that* in her report to Judge Rumborough? 'Mrs. Holliday is a full-time mother who goes to AA meetings; consequently she's a very limited person.' Do you love that? Devoting myself to nurturing the next generation makes me 'a very limited person' in the eyes of the court. Would they prefer I was an alcoholic in denial, farming out my children to be reared by someone else?"

"Isn't there someone else in the court system you could talk to about all this?" I asked.

"Funny you should mention that. There was a party after an AA meeting last night, and for two hours I cried in Judge Tracy's arms. I couldn't stop. I just cried and cried."

"Our Judge Tracy? The same Judge Tracy who was so offensive to you in court three years ago?"

"The same. And you should have heard what he told me: that he hates his job, that the Probate Court system is corrupt, that he doesn't even know what he's saying or deciding on half the time, that people just go hire rich lawyers and expect judges to solve all their problems for them, that he's chronically depressed, and that he thanks God he only has one more year before retirement. He also said that during the years he was an active alcoholic, he did terrible, terrible things in his personal life."

"I don't see that he's doing much better in his professional life," I sighed. "Given the current state of affairs, what does Tracy suggest you do?"

"He said he doesn't know. He thinks I'm in a terrible position, that Rumborough and Braverman and Cornwallis will screw me, and the fact is they will if I don't find another place for us to live before the custody case on September 17. Tracy says there's very little hope for me and the boys – unless a miracle happens between now and September."

XXXIV

Emerald City, Just Around the Corner!

*. . . but vether it's worthwhile goin' through so much to learn so little,
as the charity-boy said ven he got to the end of The Alpha Bet,
is a matter o' taste.*

— Charles Dickens, *Pickwick Papers*

Julia wasn't the only one who needed a miracle. My life was wired together with gossamer threads, too. Life at Molecular Innovations was precarious again; rumors about upheaval at Germane were ripping through the industry; and closer to home, one of my favorite fellow-moms in Conover criticized me for not spending enough time with Spencer and Amanda.

"If I were you, Ursula, I would have different priorities," she announced.

"What could be a higher priority than putting food on the table and clothing on my children's backs? You know I'm supporting our family now. Duncan barely sends us enough for the mortgage, which he won't even let me lower." Then I started to cry. "If you'd been dealt my deck, what would you have done? What would your priorities be?" I challenged.

"I don't know," she replied coolly, "but they'd be different from yours."

"Do you have any idea what my life is like?" I said quietly through tears.

"Well, how could she, Ursula?" said Julia Holliday when I relayed the conversation over early morning coffee at Bradford Street. "You know she's a wonderful person, and . . ."

"Yes, she's a wonderful person, Julia. And we wouldn't have made it through the past four years if she hadn't been so repeatedly marvelous to Spencer — I've thanked her many, many times for her kindnesses and hope I can do something for her children someday. But doesn't she know how hard I work? That I hardly ever rest? That everything I am doing is *for* my children?"

"Look Ursula," Julia replied, "a lot of women in Conover just play tennis and raise their kids. It's their job, just like being an editor and raising your kids is your job. What they do isn't better or worse than what you do. It's just their lives, that's all, and you can't expect them to understand yours. They have no idea what goes on in Probate Court. I mean, would you have believed it, if you hadn't actually lived through it?" She had me there. "And you're doing a fine job with your children. Don't let anyone tell you differently."

"But it's such a double standard! Why is she not critical of Duncan for lying about his alcoholism and walking out on our family and his responsibilities? She's not criticizing him. But when I do everything in my power to pick up the pieces and keep the kids' world whole, I get criticized. Why am I called to a higher standard of behavior than Duncan?"

Julia looked at me with a mixture of sadness and frustration. "Even if I could answer that question, Ursula, what would it buy you?"

"Understanding," I said.

"You've been hanging around scientists too long," she sighed. "Not everything can be understood."

"But it's important to understand. People who don't understand the past are doomed to repeat it."

"Even if that were true, knowing why *still* won't get you anywhere – because there's no guarantee this couldn't happen again."

"What are you saying? That's crazy!"

"No, I'll tell you what's crazy . . . what's crazy is going over the 'Why?' question day after week after year. It's getting you nowhere and dragging you down and around in circles – like a whirlpool in the ocean."

"With no escape," I agreed. "I just can't seem to break free of this thing. Why do I think I was doing better two years ago?"

"Because you were."

"But why? – if you don't mind my using the 'W' word again!" I laughed ruefully.

"Because two years ago you were in 'What Next?' Mode. You decided that an empty bed was better than a bed with a liar in it; that a marriage without love wasn't good enough for you; that a home without a dad was better than a home with deception in it. And you did something. You took action."

"So how come things aren't better now?"

"Maybe because of what Jonah tried to tell you on the night before the divorce. Do you remember?"

"Like it was yesterday. He said "You've been under a lot of pressure for a long time . . . and don't be surprised if it takes a while to feel normal again."

"Jonah was right. It is taking time, and it's going to take a lot more time.

You were under *a lot* of pressure, Ursula. A lot of pressure takes a long time to dissipate."

"Now who's sounding like a scientist?!" I quipped. "Thanks for the coffee, Julia. I better get going. I have a breakfast meeting with Kevin Wilder at the Vista – to talk about the future of *Molecular Modelling News.*"

We were barely seated when our CEO, who'd been partying all night, cut right to the chase. "*MM News* would be nothing without you," he began.

"On the contrary, Kevin. I would be nothing without it. Work has helped keep me whole in recent years. And I have a lot of ideas for new directions we can take with the publication."

I had thought we were meeting to discuss my long-range vision for building *MM News.* Instead, Kevin talked about eliminating my job. "It's not an immediate question," he said "but it is a critical one. We are going to have to address it soon." And then in a threatening tone, "What are you going to do if I decide to pull the plug on this thing?"

I looked up from my oatmeal and said with a calm uncharacteristic of me, "Oh, I think I'll go write bubble bath commercials." This did not go over well.

"Oh my God, I can see the furrowed brow from here," said Kathleen Farmer, the MarCom Manager at MII's California competitor, where Wilder had been VP of Marketing, two jobs ago. I had called Kathleen to verify rumors that her firm was close to being acquired – by a major Japanese trading firm or a Fortune 100 company in the U.S.

I would soon learn through various sources (long before Kathleen confirmed it) that Ike Peters' company was the one that was going to acquire hers – Ike Peters of Wheaton Glass and the beautiful Cincinnati dinner, the computational scientist who had been my teacher, guide, and friend from the earliest years of *Molecular Modelling News.*

This news I kept to myself, even as Kevin Wilder began pumping me about the rumored acquisition. One day he stopped by my desk. "You look like the cat who swallowed the canary!" I said brightly, knowing what he had come for and that he stood to make a financial killing from this deal that I would neither confirm nor deny.

"No, *you* look like the cat who swallowed the canary!" he retorted, his blue eyes all flash and anger beneath wire rims.

"Too bad neither of us sings well," I said, terminating the conversation and returning to my computer screen, but not before I noted the furrowed brow Kathleen had so accurately described. The little voice inside said, be mindful; you're endearing neither yourself nor your work to Kevin Wilder.

According to the Boston high-tech rumor mill, corporate waters were no less turbulent over at Germane Engineering. To outsiders, Germane wore the masks of corporate sanity and apparent success. But in the past four years, GEC stock had declined by nearly 75 percent; two years ago, its competent and highly regarded Chief Financial Officer had abruptly resigned (with no new job and no interviews to the press); and now the co-worker of Duncan's, who in 1989 accused me of creating a scene in a restaurant about gallium arsenide, had been named Germane's new CFO!

A Wall Street analyst's quote in *The New York Times* said it all: "This is a completely illogical choice." Germane's new CFO selection was right up there with Ivy Parrish's appointment to head all of science at GEC in 1990. Duncan's high-profile project continued to be touted in the press worldwide as the GEC product that was going to "save the company," but by mid-July, Calvin Germane announced he was resigning as Chief Executive Officer of the company he had founded more than thirty years before. Then GEC posted a nearly $2 billion loss for its fiscal year, a near-record disaster in American business history! According to *The Boston Globe*, Calvin Germane was still firmly in control. Behind the scenes, nothing had really changed; the resignation was merely for show. When people asked me what I thought about all this, I would simply shrug, remind them Duncan had been out of my life for three years, and quote Harry Truman: "I feel sorry for the poor son of a bitch who reads the newspapers and thinks he knows what's really going on." And that would usually end the discussion.

But it was harder to pull this off when Ike Peters phoned. "Ursula, I told you I'd keep my ears open about Duncan's project at GEC and let you know anything I heard. Well I have some things to tell you, kid, and they're not good."

"I have something to tell you, too," I said. "Remember the Germane exec who accused me of creating a public scene about gallium arsenide?"

"Yep. I sure do. I couldn't forget that story!"

"Well, that's the guy they just named CFO."

"Jesus!"

"Despite what people are saying, Ike, I still consider most of the rumors unconfirmed."

"Well, I'm going to confirm them for you, and tell you loud and clear that Duncan's project is going to be a year late and yesterday's news. The whole thing has been poorly managed. I've seen everybody's stuff under non-disclosure, and I know."

"That's not my idea of great news, Ike. If Duncan loses his job, we lose Inverary Lane. And then the kids and I really are back to square one. My long struggle to keep them in their home and community will have been for nought."

"Well, since I have nothing good to say to you about Germane, maybe we should talk about something else," he suggested.

"Okay. Could I ask you a science question?"

"Always," he laughed, for over the years, Ike Peters had spent many hours making up for all those courses I'd never taken in college. It was something he did with dependable delight. No question was too stupid or simple. When it came to teaching, this world-class scientist had all the time in the world. "What'll it be today, kid? Physics, materials design, or metallurgy?"

"Oceanography, with pickles, hold the mayonnaise," I teased. Then I turned serious. "I want to ask you about whirlpools."

"Shoot."

"How does one escape from a whirlpool – or, put differently, what makes a whirlpool stop?"

"Well first, do you know what makes one start?"

"Yes, two sideways currents meeting."

"They don't just meet, Ursula. They collide, and the collision is what sets a vortex, or whirlpool, in motion. We call that a metastable state."

"Which means . . . ?"

"Which means a whirlpool can persist for a long time, even though it's not the natural state of the water that composes it. The momentum of the colliding waters is what keeps the whirlpool going. Think of it as moving water surrounded by still water. Are you with me so far?"

"I think so. The whirlpool sort of sucks its own currents into itself?" I asked.

"I guess you could think of it like that. Yes. What eventually slows down the whirlpool is the viscosity, or friction, of the water."

"Friction against what?"

"The friction of the water in motion, i.e., the whirlpool, rubbing up against the still water that surrounds it. Friction kills the whirlpool's energy by transforming it into heat; then that heat is transferred to the surrounding water. So what you're left with, when it's all over, is warmer, calmer water where once there was a whirlpool. But it's an iterative, slow process. The water in motion has to go around and around, covering the same territory again and again before for all that energy finally spins itself out."

I smiled. "Let me see if I can play that back to you. It's interaction with the surrounding environment that does the trick. And the net result is warmer, calmer water. Is that right?"

"That's right," said Ike Peters. "Did I just say something profound?"

"Quite possibly," I replied.

"Can we talk about it over dinner at The Four Seasons, the next time I'm in Boston?"

"It's a deal, Dr. Peters!"

XXXV

Gateway

. . . pause and review the past: the learning and the joys, the tests and tribulations, all that it took to bring you here. Bless it, and release it all. For in so doing you reclaim what is truly yours — your power in the universe.

– Ralph Blum, *The Book of Runes*

Even as Ike's fresh insight buoyed me up with hope, the next news from the Holliday camp plunged me into despair: Julia and her four boys could stave off their second eviction of the year no longer. Judge Tracy's hoped-for miracle had not come.

In that summer of 1992, as the politicos of the moment waxed eloquent about family values, Julia and millions of nurturers across America were reaping the bitter harvest of court-induced homelessness. And lawyers like Gabriel G. Reed and Denny Goferbucks were getting rich off it!

"The hands that knock the cradle rob the nation!" I wanted to shout at them, in my parody of a phrase from a bygone era. Julia Holliday, on the other hand, only wanted to shout at expectant mothers: "Don't go to Lamaze Classes – go to law school!" I longed to take out a full page ad in *The Boston Globe,* but I didn't have the money. It would have said:

> Would you take a job that carries a 50 percent risk that you will lose your medical insurance, your home, your financial security, and maybe even your children? If you've stayed home to nurture your family in Massachusetts – you already have that job!

Instead, a legal reform group used my statement as a cover quote for a report it prepared for Barbara Morgan-Fauth, a lawyer from the Judicial Conduct Commission. Or as I put it to Morgan-Fauth directly when we met some months later, "You know, when you hold a new baby in your arms and your mind runs through all the bad things that could happen to it – you think of illness or accidents, but it never occurs to you that the two greatest threats to its well-being will be the other parent and the United

States Legal System!" And knowing full well the mounting horror stories of judicial misconduct in the Commonwealth, just starting to come to light, Morgan-Fauth did not argue with my assessment.

In fact, American nurturers in 1992 actually had fewer legal rights than a hired housekeeper, who for the duration of her caretaking, by law at least, was to be provided with: a roof over her head, OSHA-approved working conditions, unemployment benefits, social security, and a safe automobile in which to drive the children. That Julia transported Ethan, Enoch, Evan, and Ezra in a nearly undrivable minivan with 120,000 miles on it, while Hobart squired them around town in two new sports cars offended Boston-area family court judges not in the least.

But the car issue was minor compared to what happened next in The Holliday Matter. The week before, with eviction from the Day's house imminent, tough-talking, cigar-chomping Sherman Franklin had told her to find another rental rapidly. By the next day, ever-efficient Julia had found a modest ranch house on November Street, just blocks from Inverary Lane.

"Well, at least it will be easier for us to cook!" I quipped in an allusion to *The Snow Job Cookbook*, now very much in process.

"You don't understand," said Julia. "Denny Goferbucks, the Day's attorney, called Sherman and he called me and said, 'Julia, I don't want to upset you, but Denny wants $5,000 from you by the day after tomorrow, or she said she's going to fudge the deal for November Street.'"

"Now I don't understand," I said to Julia. "Five thousand dollars for what?"

"To pay her off. Hobart called up Denny yesterday and said, 'What's the deal with my kids?' When Denny told him about my new rental on November Street, and that we're supposed to move in mid-September, Hobart saw another opportunity to get custody of the kids, this time with Denny's help. The bottom line is, Hobart is taking the boys on a two-week vacation, and while they're gone Denny said it would be a 'perfect time for an eviction.' Then when they return from vacation, and I have no place to live, their friend Judge Rumborough will give Hobart physical custody of the boys."

"Wait a minute, back up," I protested. "I thought Denny gave a verbal recommendation for you to the new landlord on November Street – to get you *out* of the Morrow's house, and that Hobart wrote a letter *guaranteeing* the lease, which you are paying from child support. How can they *now* go ahead and stop the deal? I don't get it."

"Don't you see, Ursula? Denny's getting money from Hobart to get me evicted, and then turning around and trying to get me to pay her off not to go through with it. She makes money both ways! She said if she can't kill the deal with the November Street landlord, she's going to get the court to throw me out of this house two weeks before the new lease starts. Denny told Sherman if don't I come up with five grand in two days, she'll have us back in Superior Court for an eviction next week."

"Is that the law's idea of ethical conduct for a lawyer? Jesus Julia, where are you going to come up with $5,000. You're in bankruptcy!"

"Sherman said he'd give me $3,000, and I'm going to borrow the rest from friends. Now my lawyers are not only working for free, they're actually loaning me money!"

"I know. Jonah did that for me too, when I didn't have the money to pay for the court-ordered house appraisal during foreclosure. Jonah paid the appraiser. And when I protested, he said, 'I'll put it on the bill, Ursula,' but I don't think he ever did. What does Sherman think your chances are?"

"Not good. We'll probably be back in Superior Court next week to try to stay where we are until the new lease starts. Since the boys will be safely away with Hobart, Denny's counting on a judge not caring, and given what goes on in Middlesex County, we both know that's a safe bet. Sherman's so discouraged that he's thinking of joining the Peace Corps. Yesterday he said, 'Maybe other countries could use my legal expertise. Maybe I could go to Russia. At least there I'd be making a difference.' And we're really up against it now, because guess what Sherman found out? Guess who one of Goferbucks's best friends is?"

I random accessed quickly across our colorful cast of characters, and then the light went on in my brain. "Robina Braverman!"

"You guessed it! Judge Rumborough's latest hand-picked *guardian ad litem*. The one who told me custody wouldn't be an issue in this case, and then promptly turned around and said I was too limited because I'm a full-time mom and my children are my whole life."

"So they're all in bed together: Rumborough, Hobart, Goferbucks, Braverman, and Cornwallis!"

"Right. That's why Quentin and Sherman think we haven't got a chance. We're surrounded."

So this was what we had come to in Boston, the cradle of American liberty: a legal system so corrupt that it took bribes against the innocent. These thoughts churned in my soul the following Sunday as Paul Revere's bell called me into the chapel of First Parish. On this glorious New England morn, much of Matthew Hale's sermon turned to matters in the Book of Micah: ". . . That they may do evil with both hands earnestly, the prince asketh, and the judge *asketh* for a reward; and the great *man,* he uttereth his mischievous desire: so they wrap it up . . . the best of them is as a *brier.*" So the Commonwealth's legal system deserved no points for originality. How closely Micah's world paralleled our own! As I surveyed my surroundings and all that had brought me here, Matt's words filtered in and out of my thoughts.

"Micah summons us how to live: to do justly, to love mercy, to walk

310 Snow Job

humbly . . . and Micah understood the linkage among these ideals . . . we must use our influence to confront and to condemn heartlessness and collective unfairness . . . the Spirit of Mercy wills the welfare of others . . . Does Mercy govern *our* lives, even where there is risk? . . . do not sit at the head table, but sit at the back, that you may be asked to move up . . . Micah advocated National Repentance . . . know that the broken heart is received."

The broken heart *is* received, I thought. Mine had been received right here in this room, as I'd cried silently in the dark, more than two years before. On that cold winter's night, during the slide show on hurricanes, I had been afraid, alone, lost, and unable to discern my surroundings. But I had felt their warmth. Now in the light of this August day, I could see every detail of where I was and all it had taken to bring me here. In this cool, oblong chamber built in the early English Gothic tradition, every feature blended into a true and harmonious whole, just as the fragments of my broken life were healing themselves into a new and stronger oneness of being.

All of the materials that now surrounded me were true: the graceful walls and chancel arch of French limestone; bright Wilbur Herbert Burnham windows; an altar of Spanish marble front-paneled in Venetian glass mosaics; a cross and candlesticks fashioned from holly wood and burnished with gold leaf; richly carved woodwork depicting birds and flowers – symbols of the joy of God in the creation of the world.

Here, in the back corner where I liked to sit, a continually lighted cabinet encased the manuscripts of an earlier minister to this Parish. This chapel bore his name, and how accurately his nineteenth-century carol had presaged its light! For Edmund Hamilton Sears, "It Came Upon A Midnight Clear." For Ursula Charbonnier, it had taken a lot longer, as I'd toiled "along the climbing way, with painful steps and slow." Some of those steps had taken my feet across this smooth floor of French Vaurien stone. Others had taken my eyes upward to the high vaulted ceiling, painted in many colors after the manner of early Italian churches.

This morning sunshine streamed over me through windows of delicately colored glass, deliberately chosen to admit maximum light. On that first night as I'd brushed away my tears, light had also met me, but from hanging colored glass lamps that harmonized with roof and chancel.

The dignity in this room came from a harmony that had been planned from its inception. Color, texture, shape, and pattern had fused with light to form a perfect whole. And isn't this the way that dignity arrives in a human life? When every element that has been expressly made for it interacts with light, the spirit knows and behaves with authenticity. But nothing proceeds without the illumination, for it is the alteration of light that transforms. Only in total darkness do we produce the recognition of the glimmer. John Milton had got it right after all: "Long is the way and hard, that out of hell leads up to light."

Upon reflection, my most fearsome torturers had been my greatest teachers: Ian Ruddway had taught me to dream and persevere; Duncan Charbonnier to sacrifice and love; Gabriel G. Reed to fight; Chubb MacIntyre to show mercy. And then there was Jonah McCoy: the healthy man in our unhealthy system, who had tutored me in the ways of being swallowed alive and tossed back up whole and intact. What awesome teachers; such splendid lessons!

And what had I learned about the law in the end? That it is ours to re-shape. And about Tracy and Rumborough and all who colluded with them? That they are the briers in our midst; and we must root them out if we are to protect the next generation. There are those who devour the earth, and there are those who stand by and watch them do it. In our time, these are bankers happy to do business with wealthy breadwinners who walk out on mortgages; lawyers who get rich by taking houses from children; fellow parents who see outrage and then say they cannot judge; abusers who are in pain and express it by inflicting pain on others.

That's what our *Snow Job* had been all about: Duncan's pain, which came from Elsie's pain; Tracy's pain; and Gabriel's pain. For all this, I held a new respect. For who among them was not abused as a child? Long ago, Gabriel had told me that The System was the *Snow Job*. But he was wrong: Our Silence is the *Snow Job*.

And while I could now acknowledge all of these people's collective and individual pain and bear them no malice, I could not exonerate or absolve them of their actions. Duncan Charbonnier had had a responsibility to protect and nurture his family, a responsibility not to perpetuate his pain unto the next generation. The most I could do for him was to acknowledge his pain, but I could not fix it. And I could not take it on as my own. This agonized man and the current laws of the Commonwealth notwithstanding, my job was to protect and nurture Spencer and Amanda.

Could I now truly bless all that had brought me to this point? I thought so. For these lessons in agony had not come without gifts. Above all, I had learned the meaning of perseverance: a state of grace that continues until it is superseded by a state of glory.

XXXVI

The Home Stretch

. . . And he who gives a child a home
Builds palaces in Kingdom come . . .
— John Masefield, *The Everlasting Mercy*

Although glory felt very distant as Julia moved into the final five months of 1992, without knowing it, she had in fact entered the home stretch — that long leg of narrow, straight track between the last turn and the finish line. Emphasis on long. The next five months were to be a painfully extended tour of individuals throughout The System who turn their backs on children: judges, attorneys, bankers, journalists, even purveyors of food — people who knew what was happening to children and turned away, people who were so easily able to find a reason why they couldn't help. When I think back now about what kept Julia going during the autumn of 1992, it was this: an unyielding determination to take the knowledge she had gained and use it to help others.

The fourth week of August found Julia Holliday and her lawyers back in Cambridge Superior Court, before Judge Francis Foyle, to plead for one extra week at Bradford Road, for the Hollidays had no place else to go in the seven days between the Bradford Road and November Street leases.

Having failed to shake down Julia for the $5,000 bribe, Attorney Denny Goferbucks was determined to get Julia evicted this time. Although she had advised her clients, the Days, to refuse Julia's rent checks all summer, Denny now demanded all back rent be paid immediately in one lump sum.

"Why should Mrs. Holliday have to pay now, if you wouldn't take her checks all summer?" implored Sherman Franklin, Julia's real estate attorney.

"I have to agree, Attorney Goferbucks," said Judge Foyle, a man who had kindness written all over his face.

"Then I'm going to contact the November Street landlord and see to it that your deal falls through," Goferbucks then said to Julia – right in front of the His Honor!

"Attorney Goferbucks, let me remind you of the first rule of tort," said Judge Foyle. "A lawyer may not interfere with a signed contract. And Ms. Goferbucks, what you do outside of this courtroom I cannot control, but let me tell you this – you will be held accountable for your behavior!"

Sherman Franklin was elated. "Get ready Julia," he said to his client, "you are about to have a normal life."

But as it turned out, Sherman's pronouncement was more than a little premature. In mid-September, Julia Holliday and Quentin Corey were back in Judge Rumborough's courtroom, this time to stave off *another* custody suit by Hobart. This was Cornwallis' third attempt to take the children away from Julia, and he'd made tens of thousands of dollars off every one. As for Hobart, the custody suits had cost him more than money: Pansy had postponed their wedding when she learned of them.

"Julia is making up stories about custody suits, Pansy," Hobart had explained. "You know how she lies about everything. I have no intention of going for custody." So Julia, who actually thought Pansy was a pretty nice person, produced all the paperwork from the court, saying, "From what I've seen of you, I don't think you would want to be a party to taking four little boys away from their mother."

Not that any of this deterred Hobart from proceeding, so intent was he on hurting Julia. And as long as he could profit from it, Attorney Roger Cornwallis was happy to go along. Robina Braverman, the court's second appointed *guardian ad litem* was in tow for this third initiative, but this time without a leg to stand on. By making it possible for Julia to provide a home for the boys in Conover, Judge Foyle had effectively torpedoed Hobart's game plan to take the boys.

Nonetheless, Robina Braverman was not about to admit defeat gracefully. "Your Honor," she began in her summary of Ethan, Enoch, Evan, and Ezra to Judge Simon Rumborough, "These children have an attitude of entitlement . . ." and she proceeded to recount all of the new possessions that had been bought for the boys in quadruplicate: skateboards, surfboards, boom boxes, etc.

"Hey, I can't buy them that stuff!" Julia protested in Quentin's ear. "Why isn't she telling the court that Hobart bought all that stuff for them!"

"Be patient, Julia. We'll have our turn. She doesn't have a leg to stand on, because we've complied with every item on her list to the Court." He looked at his client with a mixture of frustration and compassion. "I don't know how I got you for a client," he said gently. "Sometimes I get stressed out just talking to you!"

Robina Braverman droned on. "Nevertheless, Your Honor, Julia has complied with all of our recommendations." Disappointment tinged her voice, and Quentin smiled at Julia. "In fact, Your Honor, I have to say that

I'm quite pleased with the outcome, and I am going to recommend that you dismiss this case."

"That's fine with me," said Judge Rumborough, looking straight at Hobart's attorney.

Roger Cornwallis went wild. "I protest most strenuously, Your Honor! We have many objections. Julia is not working! This is a complete charade of the Court! My client should have sole custody of his children!!!"

"There are no grounds," said Judge Rumborough quietly.

"But what about the emotional abuse these children have endured, Your Honor? These children are being neglected. And they are being played against Mr. Holliday."

Rumborough turned his attention to Hobart. "It is, Mr. Holliday, your legal right to pursue this. That's your business, but we've been around the block a couple of times on this matter, already. I encourage you to pursue this, if you wish, but not on the Court's time. You must go through Attorney Braverman, and only with her authority will I have another custody hearing – on your time and on your nickel – but remember, I have the option of not agreeing with her."

Now it was Hobart's turn to go wild, but Judge Rumborough didn't seem to notice. "Case dismissed," he said pounding his gavel. "By the way, I forgot to tell you folks – I wrote about the two of you in a law journal. The couple who married for better and better and better and best, and they got worse and worse and worse, until they were the worst. Goodbye. That's all I have to say to you folks."

The following week, as Julia was packing up Bradford Road, Hobart telephoned. "Your children just called me. They're hungry. Why aren't you making dinner?"

"I'm packing. I'm being evicted, remember? Maybe you could take them out for dinner."

"I'm busy. I have a date with Pansy," said Hobart. "Why don't you order something, and I'll pick it up and bring it over to them."

And so Julia ordered about $100 worth of Chinese food. Hobart was fuming when he arrived at Bradford Road with all the sacks of food in tow. "Oh how rude of me," said Julia as she carried them into the house. "I didn't even thank you for it. In fact, we'll be eating it for the next three days, because we have no money to buy anything else." She was referring to the court's order that she pay all moving expenses.

As Julia was transitioning to her third home in ten months, I got a call from Clarice LaChessey, the reporter from *The Conover Observer,* who had written about Conover CARES last spring. "We want to do a story on what happens to the living standards for single mothers after a divorce," she began. "Would you be willing to be interviewed for it?"

"Of course," I said, "and I'd even be willing to supply you with other people to be interviewed, if that would be helpful." Julia Holliday was at the top of the list.

The following week, a worried Julia called me at work. "*The Observer* wants to interview Hobart – to corroborate or deny my story. Should I let them?"

"Of course you should let them, Julia. That's standard and proper journalistic practice," I said. "Furthermore, you have only told the truth, so you have nothing to hide and nothing to fear. I told them they could interview Duncan. He'll probably deny my story or tell them that I need to be psychiatrically evaluated. But I haven't said anything I can't document. I even told Clarice about how Duncan won't let me lower my own mortgage, and that I spend more than 92 percent of child support on it. In fact, now that I think of it, I should ask her if she'd like to interview Rod McLaren over at Hub Safe. You know, a quote from the bank, corroborating my story, would really strengthen her article. So by all means, Julia, allow her to call Hobart."

When I asked Clarice if she would like to interview the bank, she said yes, and that *The Observer* had decided to expand – translation delay – its story. "All right, I'll call the bank and see if they'd be willing to speak to you."

And that was how I came to be speaking with Rod McLaren for the first time in five months. "Hello Rod McLaren, this is Ursula Charbonnier, and I still want to lower my mortgage! Remember me?"

"I sure do, and now we can offer you an even better rate than last spring. How does 5.75 percent sound?"

"It sounds great, but Duncan still won't grant his permission. That's why I'm calling. A local newspaper wants to write about what happened to me and others like me, and I thought it would strengthen their article if the bank would be willing to go on record about what has happened to me with regard to the mortgage."

"Let me talk to our Corporate Communications Department."

"Okay. In the meantime, if it would help, I could fax you a page of quotes and comments that I have already given to the reporter. I have no problem with your showing them to your colleagues at the bank. Everything is true, and it puts the story into context."

"Yes, please. That would help. Go ahead and fax it to me."

McLaren kept his word about talking to Hub Safe's Corporate Communications Department, and their representative, Simon Semple, began several rounds of phone tag with me. But before he caught up with me, Hobart Holliday threatened *The Observer* with a multimillion dollar lawsuit, so the paper backed down and decided not to run the story.

When Simon Semple finally did reach me one morning at Molecular Innovations, several minutes of phone conversation went by before I could get in a word. He began in the most official of tones, "I've read 'your article,' Mrs. Charbonnier, and we cannot take a public position on what is, in essence, a dispute between two co-signers on a mortgage. The bank does not take a position in a dispute between co-signers. And we cannot side with one person or the other, because this matter falls squarely into the area of client confidentiality. It is a long-held policy of this bank not to take sides."

He talked on, making this point another four or five times, as if he didn't think I'd gotten it the first time. "In terms of dealing with the media, for reasons of client confidentiality, we cannot takes sides . . ."

Finally when he came up for air, I said, "Thank you for explaining the bank's policy, but the information I sent you was not 'the article.' It was backup information for the reporter. And you needn't worry, because one of the deadbeat dads in the story has threatened to sue the paper, so they will not be running the story. But this story is a lot bigger than Ursula Charbonnier. And here's what I want to know, Mr. Semple: why does Hub Safe still want to do business with Duncan Charbonnier? Why are you still sending him letters soliciting his business, even though he deliberately walked out on his mortgage, and laughed that you would do nothing to him for it?"

"I already told you, Mrs. Charbonnier, the bank does not take sides in its dealings with clients."

"Well, what about conduct?" I asked. "The legal system says that conduct is irrelevant. Is it also irrelevant to the bank? What about ethics? Doesn't character enter into whether you give someone a loan?"

"I can't speak to that question," said Simon Semple.

"But don't you see a connection?" I continued. "When someone deliberately walks away from a responsibility to pay a mortgage, and laughs that he will be in no trouble for it, that hurts bankers too. Think how much time and money your bank spent on coming after me and the children, and foreclosing on us. Wasn't that a waste of your resources?"

"I can do nothing," said Simon Semple. "If you have a specific question that you would like to ask, I can direct you to someone, but the bank does not take a position on these matters in our dealings with clients."

"All right, I have a specific question for you," and I briefly told him about Conover CARES. "Could you direct me to someone at Hub Safe who might have an interest in participating? Someone who could offer advice to the families of substance abusers − families in danger of losing their homes?"

"I'm afraid I couldn't, Mrs. Charbonnier."

I hung up the phone with a new insight: no wonder the New England banks were in so much trouble. They were happy to do business with the Duncan Charbonniers of the world, regardless of their conduct and record of financial irresponsibility.

In the race for ethical wimpdom, the banks, the newspapers, and the courts were running neck and neck. I could only wonder how long it would take before some banker besides Rod McLaren recognized the linkage between lending attitudes and the foreclosures on their balance sheets. And I still held the risk of becoming one of those foreclosures, according to Ike Peters and others who knew what was going on at GEC, if I didn't find a way to make more money soon.

And with this concern very much on my mind, I stopped in to say good-bye to Jeff Abbott during his final week at Molecular Innovations. He wanted to chat about his new job – heading up a startup to produce environmental software. "Maybe we should start a newsletter for the industry, Ursula."

"You mean something like *Molecular Modelling News?*"

"Yes, that's exactly what I mean. Now by the terms of my contract with MII, I can't hire you away, but you could work for me as a consultant."

"I might have an interest," I began, "because Duncan still won't let me lower the mortgage, so I'm thinking of taking a second job at night to make ends meet. I'm determined to keep my children in their home and their community. You know Jeff, I overestimated Duncan's commitment to the children – and he underestimated mine. Poor people use knives and guns on their spouses – rich ones use lawyers!"

"Well, think about what I said. Maybe we can work something out."

"All right, and thanks. *MM News* prospered under your tenure at MII, and I wish you well."

I was now overpaying the mortgage by nearly $800 per month (because Duncan wouldn't give permission for me to refinance). This was more money than I brought home in a week. A second job at night to make ends meet was looking more and more like a necessity.

I gave it to the children straight: "Spencer and Amanda, I may have to take a second job at night. I want to take care of you as best I can, but I'm just not in a position to throw away nearly $10,000 a year on the mortgage and still meet your material needs."

This waste was unconscionable, and it hit me at every turn: every time I had to say no the children; every time I had to ask the school to postpone due dates for deposits for class trips and other activities; every time something broke at Inverary Lane or I had to deal with unexpected medical bills or car repairs.

Money was also Julia Holliday's problem. Hobart had convinced Judge Rumborough to temporarily put aside his wage assignment if Hobart would pay the November Street rent directly to Julia's new landlord. So at the first opportunity, Hobart simply stopped paying all of the child support (minus rent) to Julia. When Julia protested, Hobart laughed in her face and said, "Don't annoy me. I'm going antiquing in New Hampshire with Pansy this weekend. I know no one is going to make me pay."

"You can't do that! We have no money for groceries!" protested Julia.

"Who's going to stop me?!" he taunted.

"Certainly not Cornwallis or Judge Rumborough!" I said to Julia when she told me. "You know, this gives me an idea. What if we could get the grocery store in Conover Center to set up a donation box or offer gift certificates to families who did not receive their child support? Cindy Bannister told me she hasn't received any child support for her four kids either – not a dime since last April, when Henry left the state. The Conover Grocer has a box for Boston Hospital's 'Failure to Thrive,' program. Why couldn't they have a donation box for children right here in Conover?"

When I mentioned the idea to Trudy Hale over at First Parish, she was not encouraging. "You could try Ursula, but I think you'll encounter some real problems. You'd be better off trying to get the laws changed."

"But do you know how bad the laws really are?" I asked, feeling sure she didn't.

"Yes, I do," she said in her quiet and firm tone. "And it will take a lot of work. I've been through it with regard to children with special needs. Matt and I worked for years with the legislature and various government offices. It takes a long time. But The Law is the place to start, Ursula. The Law is what needs to be changed. That is the place to put your effort."

I had no idea how to change the law. I didn't know anything about the intricacies of government and legislation. It seemed much more reasonable to trot across the street to the Conover Grocer and ask Store Manager Rick Bennett about setting up a donation program for kids in Conover.

"It's not that I don't care, Ursula," began Rick, "but there are several problems with what you're suggesting. First, how would we be able to verify that a family didn't really receive its child support check? People could take advantage of such a program."

"But people wouldn't do that!" I protested. "People wouldn't lie about not receiving child support just to get some free groceries!"

"Maybe you wouldn't. But you'd be surprised. And another thing. We have to protect the confidentiality of the parent."

This I could not believe! "Do you mean that protecting the confidentiality of a parent who doesn't pay child support is more important than feeding that person's children?!"

"I didn't say that exactly. It's just that there are a lot of problems associated with setting up what you're suggesting, and the store can't assume any responsibility for . . ."

"Well, would you be willing to work through Conover CARES?" I asked him, "or maybe come to a meeting to explore how the store and the community might work together to help Conover families in need? Would you be willing to talk to Devon Carmody about it?"

"Sure, I'll talk to her. She can call me at the store anytime. Look, as an individual I'm not opposed to what you're trying to do, but there are a lot of obstacles. I've run food banks. I have years of experience. I just don't see how the store can get involved. There's the verification problem, and we do have to protect confidentiality. We can get in trouble if we don't."

"I tried, Julia," I said, as I dropped off some food to the Holliday household, "but the grocery store was more concerned about protecting Hobart's confidentiality than feeding your kids. And they had to be – because of the law. They're not bad guys. Rick Bennett is a decent human being. But he has to be careful because of the law."

"Well, you can put *The Conover Observer* in the same category," said Julia. "Their reporter, Clarice LaChessy, won't even return my calls now. Can you believe it? A newspaper knows that children, right here in Conover, are going without child support, and they don't want to talk about it, because they have to protect the confidentiality of the deadbeat dad. What about the rights of the unfed child?

"And catch the latest from Hobart. Now he's decided to deduct all the children's shrink fees from child support, even though *he* is the one who got the court to order the children's therapy. And are you ready for this? He's thinking about initiating a fourth child custody suit, and he's going to sue me for all the costs associated with the third suit, which I repeat, *he* initiated!"

"Well, he won't get very far Julia. After all, Hobart hasn't paid child support in weeks. Even Judge Rumborough might be offended by that."

"I'm not counting on it. Let me tell you what happened at the boys' shrink appointment last night. Listen to this. When their session was up, Bing Levine invited me into his office, told me to sit down, and said that the boys were now going to critique me.

'Boys, we are going to go around the room and I want each of you to take a turn and tell your mother the things you don't like about her.' 'What is this?' I shot back at Bing. 'Do you call this *therapy*?' 'I'm just trying to bring a little sunshine into the Holliday Home,' smiled Bing. 'Don't worry Julia. Next week it will be Hobart's turn to be on the hot seat. Now boys, what's wrong with your mother?' 'Sometimes she embarrasses us,' said Ethan. The others remained silent. 'Come on boys, it's okay to speak up. Are you afraid you're going to be punished when you get home? Are you afraid you're going to be hit?' They laughed. 'She doesn't hit us!' At that point I exploded, 'If you think this is therapy, Bing, you're nuts! Who are you, the King of Denial?! I'm not going to stay here and be mom-bashed. This is an abusive situation, and you are nothing but a paid enabler! Come on boys, we're going home!' 'Oh Mom, that was cool,' said Enoch. 'Yeah Mom, you totally dissed him!' said Evan. Little Ezra remained silent. 'Do I have to go back there again?' said Ethan. 'Mom, I'm sorry I said you embarrassed me.' 'Ethan, all thirteen year-olds feel embarrassed by their parents at one time or another. My mother embarrassed me when I was your age too. That's not the issue. Your doctor's behavior isn't healthy. That's the issue.'"

As Thanksgiving approached, the Holliday boys' support remained unpaid. One afternoon on the way home from work, I dropped off more groceries and stayed to have tea with Julia. She made no effort to hide her increasing despair. "The banks don't care what these guys do; the courts don't care; the newspapers don't care; my parents have used up most of their retirement savings to help me; I'm in bankruptcy; and Hub Safe is still doing lots of business with Hobart's company, even though he walked out on *their* mortgage! I have eight bleeding ulcers, and my doctors are giving me free medicine because they know Hobart is pocketing all my medical reimbursement checks from John Hancock, who in turn says they can't do anything about it. Where does it end, Ursula? Doesn't anybody in Massachusetts care about children?"

"The Governor's Office," I replied.

"Don't be funny, Ursula!" snapped my exhausted friend.

"I'm not being funny. Look at this clipping from this morning's *New York Times*. I brought it over to cheer you up."

"What's this?"

"It's an article about an initiative from the Lieutenant Governor's Office. They're going to get serious about going after people who don't pay child support. They're talking about taking away driver's licenses, professional licenses, putting some teeth in wage assignments, arresting child support evaders if they leave the Commonwealth, and so on and so forth. What do you think about that?"

The phone rang, and Julia went to answer it.

"You'll never believe who that was," said Julia coming back into the room. "It was my parents, calling from Los Angeles, to read me a story from the front page of *The LA Times*. It said that Massachusetts is going to lead the nation in clamping down on deadbeat parents."

"It made *The LA Times*, too? Maybe we should offer to help them, Julia. We certainly know about the cracks in The System. In fact, on my next vacation day, I'd even be willing to go talk to someone down at the State House. Why don't you think about coming with me? And we could get others in the various legal reform groups to help. Now that we're affiliated with Monica Getz's group in New York – The National Coalition for Family Justice – we have even more resources to draw on. If the Weld Administration is really serious about 'cleaning out the barn,' you know we could help them."

"I'll think about it, Ursula. But we're on our fourth week of no child support. I went back to Mr. Norris in Judge Rumborough's court, and he said even though I have a wage assignment back in place, I still have to come back to court with an attorney to get it enforced. Quentin said we'll go back to court next week, and in the meantime he got some writ of something or other that says Hobart will be arrested if he leaves the state – he can't even go to Connecticut on business."

"So why doesn't he just pay up?"

"I don't know. His own attorney even quit on him."

"Cornwallis . . . quit?!"

"That's right. Roger said Hobart wasn't going back into a courtroom with a wage assignment in place because in today's political climate, he'd lose. He said he also didn't want to continue on a case where Hobart's only purpose was to hurt me. And Roger told Quentin that all our numbers were right about the child support and medical reimbursements owed, and he advised Hobart to pay up. Since Hobart's still refusing, Quentin got a court date for next Monday — in Cambridge, so we won't have to deal with Rumborough, who as you know isn't crazy about Scarlett O'Hara and her attorney!"

As I'd listened to all this, an idea was hatching in my brain. "What are you doing this Friday?" I asked.

"I have an appointment."

"Change it and come to Beacon Hill with me. Let's go talk to someone in the Governor's Office."

"Just like that? How do you know if anyone will even see us?"

"Well, I don't, but I'm going to call and ask. Julia, we have access to a lot of information they could use; we can furnish them with plenty of documentation that showcases cracks in The System and what's really going on in the Commonwealth. Look, if I can get an appointment, will you come downtown and tell your story?"

"I don't know. I'll think about it."

And then Julia beat me to the punch. The next morning, she called me at Molecular Innovations. "Ursula, I've got a name for you: Raoul Fernandez. He's an aide to Lieutenant Governor Cellucci. I thought about all you said when I was trying to fall asleep last night, and an hour ago I called to ask about this legislation they've drafted. Fernandez listened to my story and told me to follow up with a letter. Here's his number. I think you should talk to him too. Tell him about all the unbelievable things that have happened to us. And if you can get an appointment with someone down there, I'll go with you Friday. Ursula, he sounded sincere. I don't want to get my hopes up, but just in case they really mean business, I think we should try to help them."

Several days later, on a bright November Friday, Julia and I wandered into the State House on Beacon Hill. In all the years we'd lived in Massachusetts, this was our first visit. The gold dome sparkled against a cold sky, a gift of light to our weary eyes. We found Raoul's office in a tangle of basement hallways and sat down at a small round table in an anteroom. Within minutes a young man appeared. "Hi, I'm Raoul Fernandez," he said shaking our hands.

"I'm Ursula Charbonnier," I replied, meeting his gaze, "and this is Julia Holliday. We're here to learn more about the Governor's legislative initiatives and to tell you about our experiences with the legal system. As two

Massachusetts moms, we'd to help the Weld Administration, in any way we can."

"Let's sit down and talk," Fernandez said. Then he launched into a description of the proposed legislation (yes, it would have real teeth in it) and an acknowledgment that the Governor's Office did recognize that child support collection in fact *was* part of a much larger problem in the Commonwealth. "We are very concerned about what is happening to children. We've been getting a lot of phone calls since we announced our proposed legislation and began our search for the 'Ten Most Wanted' — did you know we've caught nine of the ten already!?"

I had brought along a file for Raoul Fernandez. Labeled "A Citizen Who Cares," it included a memorandum from Julia and me, entitled "Cracks in The System We'd Like to Help you Fix." In it we applauded the new efforts to collect child support, but we mostly talked about the larger problem of how nurturers and children are treated under the law in Massachusetts. It was a chronicle of our outrageous odysseys through the Registry of Motor Vehicles, Hub Safe, John Hancock, the Probate Court System, the Board of Bar Overseers, the Judicial Conduct Commission, and sundry attorneys' offices. We also brought information about other cases, far worse than our own. "These problems took years to create," we told Fernandez, "and they will take years to resolve. But having seen them at close range, and knowing what we know, we cannot turn away."

Then we launched into our respective stories. When I got to the part about fighting to save our house, only to have Duncan refuse to let me lower our mortgage, Fernandez showed the first moment of emotion. "Can you imagine how that feels?" I asked him. His dark eyes blazed in anger when I said, "and I paid for more than two-thirds of our first house with my inheritance from my grandparents — we had no mortgage for years, only to have Duncan threaten me and the children with losing our home many years later. He didn't even level with the court about his true income. Child support was based on a figure far below what he makes."

Then I told him about Judge Tracy's inviting Duncan to an AA Meeting, Fernandez interrupted me. "Oh, I've had *a lot* of calls about Judge Tracy, and although we're not allowed to talk about it publicly, rest assured that this Administration knows plenty about what's going on, and we are quietly, behind-the-scenes doing things here and there to rectify matters. There's a lot more that needs to be done, but please know that we are trying — and we care."

"Well, if you read nothing else in the file I've brought you, be sure to check out the worst Judge Tracy story — that would be the Jennie Stanford case in the report our group submitted to the Judicial Conduct Commission." Fernandez scribbled her name on his legal pad. "Tracy turned the small children over to a father who'd repeatedly been in prison for alcohol- and drug-related offenses," I continued, "and what happened to the children next is horrifying. If Governor Weld knew what we knew . . ." I paused, groping for the exact words . . . "he would cry."

Fernandez looked at me. In his face I saw a concern that did not doubt my words. "It's much more than a matter of law," he said quietly. "As far as this Administration is concerned, it's a matter of morality."

Julia and I nearly fell out of our chairs. "Someone in government is using the word 'morality'!" I exclaimed.

"You think morality matters?!" Julia asked unbelieving.

"Yes, morality matters!" said Fernandez.

"It's just that after Judge Tracy said to me, 'Mrs. Charbonnier, ethics have nothing to do with this case!' and after so many lawyers and judges have said to us that 'conduct is irrelevant in Massachusetts!' – well, it's hard to believe that someone in government actually thinks morality matters."

"This is really refreshing!" said Julia.

"I'm going to read through what you've brought me," he said, "and then I'm going to give all this information to someone I know on the Lieutenant Governor's staff, someone I know will be very interested in what you have to say. I'm also going to make a copy for Mitchell Adams's office. Do you know who he is?"

"No," we said.

"He's the Commissioner of Revenue, and he's very serious about cracking down on deadbeat dads. I should say parents, but in fact, in 97-98 percent of the cases, it's mothers who are not receiving their child support payments."

"We think its a breadwinner-nurturer issue, too," I added. "We know plenty of men who've been hurt by The System because a woman walked away from her responsibilities."

"You should call Mitchell Adams," said Fernandez turning to Julia, "because his office can help you with your problem. I already forwarded them your complaint and the letter you sent to Lieutenant Governor Cellucci earlier this week. But you should talk to them, too. The DOR has a lot of complaints to investigate, but rest assured they will follow up on yours. Also, I want to make you both aware of the Governor's Council, elected officials who meet at the State House every Wednesday. One of its duties is to approve judicial appointments. You should get in touch with Conover's representative on the Council and make your views known. Here are the various names," he said, showing us an information sheet, "and here is the number to call to find out who represents your town."

"I'll follow up on that one, and Julia will contact the Commissioner of Revenue," I said, "but after we leave here today, we want to have ongoing contact with someone in the Governor's office. We know a lot of people who want to help you. We don't want what happened to our children to happen to anyone else's children. Thanks for meeting with us today."

"Thank you for coming in. And be watching for the package I'm sending to each of you with our legislative proposals – and we'll stay in touch."

We shook hands and left.

"Do you think he'll be able to help?" I asked Julia as we strode down the steps to Beacon Street.

"I think he'll put our information into the hands of someone who can," said Julia. "I do believe that."

The following Monday at 9 a.m., Julia returned to Probate Court in Cambridge. The smell of the urinals and usual teeming human disarray greeted her. "Go to Courtroom Four," a Court official instructed, "and we've lost your file."

Quentin did not turn up, even though his sister (and law partner) insisted he was on his way, and Julia waited until after four o'clock, then returned home to take care of the younger boys. Another day shot in Probate Court with nothing to show for it.

Quentin called at the end of the day. "Where were you?" he asked.

"Where were you?" said Julia. "I was in Courtroom Four all day, waiting as the clerk instructed me."

"Oh, that's just great," said Quentin. They put me in Courtroom Five with Judge Lowoil, and they lost your file! Hobart never showed up, and Lowoil argued with me and said he didn't care if Hobart hadn't paid child support despite a court order; he wasn't deciding anything without Hobart and your file!"

"You mean Lowoil didn't even charge Hobart with contempt for not appearing?"

"That's right," said Quentin in total exasperation.

"Now what?" asked Julia wearily.

"I called Hobart, and he's agreed to meet at my office tomorrow. He was very conciliatory in view of the Writ and said he wanted to settle the matter of child support and your medical insurance reimbursements he pocketed from John Hancock. And since Cornwallis quit, he's agreed to come to my office without a lawyer. So I'll see you tomorrow."

"God forbid I ignore a court date, I'd be in contempt," roared Julia when I dropped by that evening on my way home from work. "But Hobart can laugh at The System and not show up whenever he pleases, and that's just fine with the courts! You know, before I left the courthouse yesterday, I started talking with a woman and her young attorney who'd been waiting in my courtroom for hours. They were so excited, because the judge granted her an automatic wage assignment. So I told them my story and said, 'Look, an automatic wage assignment isn't going to guarantee you anything. It's just a piece of paper. I have an automatic wage assignment, and my ex hasn't paid child support for weeks!' So this young attorney looked at me and said, 'But he can't do that. That's against the law!' 'Oh really?' I laughed.' Where does it end, Ursula? Where does it end?"

The next day, as Julia was walking out the door to leave for Quentin's office, Raoul Fernandez called. "I just wanted your address," he said (in fact he already had both of our business cards) "and I wanted to find out what happened at Probate Court yesterday (the real reason for the call). We just wondered, how are you doing, Mrs. Holliday?"

"Well, thank you for calling," said Julia, as she recounted her day long wait, the lost file, and Hobart's absence without penalty. "He sent part of the back support, but not the whole thing."

"Well, if he didn't send it all, he's still in default, Mrs. Holliday. Look, the Department of Revenue is following up. You can take my word on that. What is happening to you sounds awful, but we wish you the best, and be sure to write a follow up letter to the Lieutenant Governor and tell him what happened at the courthouse yesterday."

"I will," promised Julia.

"They don't usually call people – you have to call them," said Quentin Corey at his office the next day, surprised that the Governor's Office had followed up. "It sounds good, but I've had very bad luck with politicians. Nevertheless, I guess you have to hope. Oh, oh, look who's here."

'Ivan the Terrible,' as Quentin had begun to call Hobart, stormed into Quentin's disorganized and unpretentious office with a force that seemed inconceivable for a man who was only 5'4". Within minutes, it became clear that full payment of child support was not in the cards, as Hobart began bouncing around the office, enraged that Quentin and Julia would even entertain the notion of his paying any of the owed funds. Pulling his fists in the air, Hobart lunged at Julia's 6'6" bear-of-a-man attorney. "Come on Quentin, come and get me. Punch me, punch me, give it to me, give it to me! Come on Quentin, put up your dukes and fight!"

Quentin Corey leaned back in his chair and laughed, waving 'Ivan the Terrible' away. "Oh, I don't partake of that sort of thing, Hobart – I don't hit people, especially in my office!"

"Come on Quentin, come and get me, go ahead and hit me!" continued Hobart, dancing around the furniture, fists flashing through the air. "Do it to me, Quentin. Oh, I can't stand your office. There's no comfortable place to sit – and there's no round table. How can you have an office without a round table?"

"Well, Hobart," said Quentin mildly, "this is the only office I have," as the not-to-be-believed scene continued. The wealthy financial advisor and father of four continued to carry on, and Quentin Corey leaned over to Julia and inquired under his breath, "Just where did you manage to find this fucking, flaming, latent faggot?"

Julia was too stunned to reply.

"I mean you told me about his breaking down the door at Disneyworld, but really Julia, I've never seen a grown man carry on this way. Criminal law has always been my favorite, but this guy is worse than any murderer I've ever seen."

Hobart hadn't heard a word Quentin said. Then after several more minutes of Quentin gazing imperturbably from his chair, Hobart grew tired of waving his fists in the air and pulled out his checkbook. "All right, all right. I want to get this done, too. I'll pay the back child support."

"And you'll pay Julia the money that she is owed by John Hancock for her out-of-pocket medical expenses."

"No way!" fumed Hobart, re-entering rage mode. "I intend to make it as financially tough on Julia as possible. This is all her fault. Everything that's ever happened to me is her fault. Did you know she's worthless Quentin? She does nothing. She's a complete waste of a human being."

"She brings up your four children, Hobart. That's not worthless," said Quentin. "Nurturing children is the most important job there is."

"She's worthless!" snarled Hobart. "Did you know that *The Conover Observer* briefly thought about doing a story on her? But she's not that important. What makes you think, Julia, that you're actually important enough that anyone would care about you, that anyone would care to write about you and your life? You and your crazy friend Ursula Charbonnier!"

"Then I guess we'll see you in court, Hobart," said Julia's attorney placidly.

Quentin roared with laugher and rolled his eyes at Julia, as Hobart stormed out of the office. "Oh my God, to hear Hobart carry on about the little *The Conover Observer*. If he only knew that someone at NBC wants to get you and Ursula on national television!"

But Julia and I had made a pact to discuss that with no one but our respective attorneys. I still hadn't told Jonah McCoy, and we didn't even mention it at the next weekend meeting of our political group, now officially affiliated with the National Coalition for Family Justice in New York.

A few people from State Government had come to address our group, including one attorney who asked for anonymity. She spoke of her long struggle with the court system, from both professional and personal perspectives.

"I am a recovering litigant," she began, after the manner of a recovering alcoholic at an AA Meeting. "You see, many of the things you are describing happened to me in the court system two decades ago too, and that's part of why I became an attorney. I wanted to make a difference. I know how long it takes to get over the pain. But I haven't made very much of a difference after all, because all of these atrocities are still going on in the legal system."

And this was how she ended her talk to us, "You are all pioneers, and you are all going to be punished for what you are doing – for having these meetings and trying to make these changes and fight this rotten system. In one form or another, you will all be punished. It is never easy to change laws. But you must try. We must all continue to try."

November drew to a close with the arrival of the press package from Raoul Fernandez, and the joint press release in it minced no words: "Asserting that 'the financial neglect of children should be considered no less a crime than other forms of child abuse,' Lieutenant Governor Paul Cellucci and Revenue Commissioner Mitchell Adams today submitted legislation which would substantially strengthen the state's ability to establish and enforce child support orders, making Massachusetts' child support enforcement program the most aggressive in the nation . . ."

With these words the political winds had shifted for children in Massachusetts. Julia and I approached December with a cautious, but fresh, breath of hope.

XXXVII

Winter Solstice

Labour to keep alive in your breast
that little spark of celestial fire, called conscience.

— George Washington,
Rules of Civility and Decent Behaviour

But the political fortunes for nurturers remained very much at a standstill, or so it seemed, as December brought no improvement on the work or home fronts. At MII, thanks in part to the arrival of a new Marketing VP who had no love for *Molecular Modelling News,* work was not going well; and at home, the children's expenses were again starting to exceed my income. Then Duncan downgraded our medical insurance. Even friends stopped phoning and returning my calls. Or so it seemed. I took all this personally. Like our planet, plunged in December darkness, I felt entirely at the mercy of forces beyond my control. And would I ever again see the return of light?

"Julia, what's the matter with me?" I asked when I dropped off her Christmas present. "I've come through so much, the kids are doing well. Why am I in this funk? I've lost my perspective. I keep trying to get out of the whirlpool, but the currents are winning!"

"It will pass," assured Julia Holliday, whose troubles greatly outweighed my own.

"I have no right to complain — to you or anyone else. I *do* count my blessings, but when am I going to feel completely normal again?"

"When Ursula forgives Ursula."

"When Ursula forgives Ursula? For what?" I asked.

"Maybe for having chosen Duncan, whose behavior brought you and your children so much pain. As long as you continue to blame and not forgive yourself, you perpetuate the illusion that you are in control. In this whole mess, there was nothing you could have done that you didn't do. You were powerless over alcohol; you will become powerful again,when you forgive yourself, Ursula.

"Here, eat this new appetizer I just invented and stop beating yourself up!" said my friend the Conover Caterer. "Frankly, I thought it was amazing this didn't happen to you before. Look at all the crummy stuff you've been through in the last four years. You have every right to feel sad, angry, betrayed and just plain fed up! So *feel it!!!*" shouted Julia Holliday. "Let yourself feel every last ounce of pain. Admit to yourself that yes, something horrible has happened to you; that yes, Duncan betrayed your trust; and yes, The System sucks. Then remember that you saved your house against all odds; you kept your kids' world together; you built *MM News*, from the bottom up – with *no* background whatsoever; your book is almost done; you're in great health, and you look fabulous."

"Appearances are deceiving. I am not fabulous."

"You still haven't acknowledged your own pain," said Julia, shaking her head. "And when you do, Ursula, it will go away."

Instead I went home to toss some potatoes in the oven and go through the mail before I left to drive the basketball carpool. Amid the Christmas cards and bills I found yet another envelope from Hub Safe Deposit & Trust, addressed to Mr. Duncan Charbonnier. "Why do they keep sending him wonderful offers to do business with them?" I shouted at our cat. "Why do they keep sending him videocassettes that offer financial advice? Don't they remember that he walked on their mortgage for this house? *What* is the matter with these bankers?"

The cat brought me her rabbit's foot, and rubbed sympathetically against my leg. "Let's see what they want this time, Streak!" I said mischievously as I tore open the envelope. Normally I don't read form letters, particularly when they're addressed to someone else, but I am a sucker for good writing, and I have to admit that this one was well written. Under the signature of the President of The Hub Company, which owned Hub Safe, was a request for "five minutes of my time," – which was about all I had to offer anyway on this busy evening! What for? Why, to complete a survey on my level of satisfaction with their mortgage department. *This* was irresistible. All right, Mr. Whitaker, you can have five minutes of my time between my fourteen-hour workday, dinner prep and the b-ball carpool. And if what I write in the next five minutes makes any sense whatsoever in the morning – heaven help you Mr. President, because I am going to send this form directly back to you and not your designated market research firm!

The next morning, my responses made even better sense than they had the night before. What does Hub Safe do well? "Provide information promptly!" What could we do better? "Believe that conduct *is* relevant and do business accordingly!" I also told Mr. Whitaker how baffled I was by Simon Semple's comment that "the bank doesn't take sides," how I'd paid for most of our first home in cash with inheritance from grandparents, and how Duncan had laughed that *only I* would bear the consequences for his having walked on the mortgage. "I wish that someone in a senior position at Hub Safe would review our case and try to help. What I want for Christmas is the ability to refinance my home and use the savings to invest in my kids."

Then I tossed the survey into an envelope, marked it "personal" and on a last-minute impulse enclosed a copy of Amanda's 1990 letter to Judge Tracy, the one in which she said that all she wanted for her birthday was her house. In the cover note I wrote: "Dear Mr. Whitaker – As requested I took five minutes to fill out the form you sent me. Would you please take five minutes to read my reply?" and as I dropped it into a post box on the darkest day of the year, I whispered, "Godspeed!"

Then thought no more about it, for there was plenty to occupy me at Molecular Innovations: thirteen out of thirteen scientists had just said yes to my invitation to join *MM News* as new Editors and Technology Sector Advisors. By spring we would have a much stronger organization behind the publication, an organization that spanned industrialists, academics, and even MII competitors in the software field, who had all agreed to put aside individual concerns to share in the task of keeping the entire CAMD community better informed. This was the part of the job I loved – the building part, getting everyone to work together for the benefit of us all. I drafted that first memorandum to the TSAs in a spirit of joy: "The forces of complexity, velocity, and information overload have brought us together for what I hope will be a more effective and enjoyable way to cover our world."

While I was personally thrilled about this development, I wasn't sure how the new VP of Marketing was going to handle it, especially when he found out that one-quarter of the TSAs worked for rival firms. To my astonishment, he said, "Well, that's okay, Ursula," and walked away.

"I don't understand," I said to Frank Morrow, my Chief Science Editor. "Suddenly, all opposition to *Molecular Modelling News* has vanished. What is going on?"

Frank Morrow laughed. "You really don't understand why this is working, do you?"

"No," I said, feeling clueless.

"Because it is the right thing, in the right place, at the right time. That's why."

"Oh," I said, still not fully comprehending, still spinning round and round in the whirlpool of self-questioning that continued to blur many of my perceptions.

Too often I needed corroboration from outsiders before I could register one of my own observations in my own brain. I think it was the effect of having experienced so much that was unbelievable. I'd never been this way before, but it's how I was now. And part of why I listened so intently when Janey Thayer phoned from Ann Arbor, just before Christmas. For decades she had lived around the corner from Elsie Charbonnier. "Ursula, I was just writing your Christmas card and said to Rodney that I *had* to call you and . . ."

"Oh, you got my card!" I interrupted.

"No, I didn't get your card," said Janey.

"Well then this really is amazing, because in it I promised to call you soon."

"Your card hasn't come yet, but I hope it has a picture in it. Ursula, I just had to call you and talk to you. Rodney and I saw Duncan at a family wedding up in Vermont a few months ago, and I just have to tell you . . . "

"He looks great, doesn't he?" I interrupted again. "Like he's about thirty years old and hasn't a care in the world."

"No, Ursula, he looks just horrible. It was apparent to everyone at the wedding, and I want to tell you about it. He is emaciated – he has no meat on his bones whatsoever, and when I hugged him, well it was just like hugging some skinny old woman. His behavior was meek and withdrawn. He didn't even act like himself. He had no interest in anything, wouldn't make conversation, wouldn't interact with anybody at the rehearsal dinner. He came with some blond floozy from work, and they left the table before dessert was even served. Something is horribly, horribly wrong with Duncan." She was talking faster than I could process. "Ursula, you were so smart to get out, so smart to get divorced." I couldn't speak. "Others noticed it too. Alcohol alone doesn't do that to someone."

"I know," I said quietly, remembering what Ginny Bartlett had told me years before.

"I was sitting with your brother and sister-in-law at the rehearsal dinner," continued Janey, "and they know something's wrong. When I asked where Duncan can gone, they just rolled their eyes and said he'd 'gone up to bed with that blond floozy.' Don't you care Ursula?"

"Not particularly."

"Well, don't you think he's lost a lot of weight?"

"Janey, I rarely look at Duncan anymore, and when I do, he looks like the picture of Dorian Gray – inside and out. He's soul-less, like a mannequin in a store window. Just empty. This is not the man who used to bring me to elegant dinner parties at your home."

"No, it isn't," she agreed.

"And it's not the man I fell in love with and had babies with . . ."

"But, you've got it all together, Ursula. I know it's tough, but you came through. You've got it all together," she repeated.

I didn't feel like I had it all together, despite what Julia, Janey, and others continued to say.

Something still troubled me, but nothing I could pinpoint. I dropped by First Parish to talk with Trudy Hale. "I'm not here for sympathy," I began.

"I'm getting plenty of that from my friends. What I'm here for is guidance on how to jump-start my spiritual engine! No matter what I do to straighten out my life, I just keep spinning in circles like a trapped current."

But Trudy didn't see it that way at all. "You are doing all of the right things. Trust me, Ursula. I've watched situations like yours over a long span of years. I've been in this business a long time."

"But Duncan appears to have been right: Conduct really is irrelevant."

"I know it seems that way to you now. But in time, you'll see that the hard choices you made really did make a difference. I've watched you and the children at close range now, for nearly five years, and I have no doubt that all three of you are going to be fine. It's not what happened to you that matters; it's what you did with it. The doubt you are feeling is just a threshold – a threshold to a deeper understanding. And this is not a bad thing, Ursula, because it will lead you to a new place."

Then she gave me a book to take home. It spoke eloquently of the depth and nature of the inward renewal I was seeking, something "not within our active power to bring about. What we have to do is to prepare ourselves for the power that will effect it. Our preparation is our openness, our vulnerability to the power of God dwelling in us. This is prayer."

Some days I could apprehend this message, and on others I could not. It was like a code that I couldn't quite break. Yet on balance, I sensed we were doing better. At least I was trying – trying to be more forgiving, more aware, less angry, most of all open to new possibilities on the horizon.

Then just before Christmas, two surprises arrived in the mail: the copyright notice from the Library of Congress for "A Canticle of Dawn," a hymn I'd written; and a small envelope addressed to me, from an Executive VP at Hub Safe. The first sentence of his letter said it all:

Dear Ms. Charbonnier,

Kip Whitaker has asked me to dig into your situation and report back to him . . .

Days later I sent Mr. Whitaker a thank-you note and "Best wishes for a new year filled with light.

XXXVIII

Ursula Accepts Cash

To live is like to love –
all reason is against it,
and all healthy instinct for it.

— Samuel Butler, *Note Books*

"Congratulations, Ursula – you have reached a human being!" said Jonah McCoy, when I told him about the letter from Hub Safe. Ike Peters, the Wheaton Glass scientist, had a similar reaction: "You know Ursula, sometimes, just sometimes, people get to the top because they really deserve to be there. Let's hope your Kip Whitaker falls into that category."

Events soon suggested he did. Within weeks, a second letter arrived from Hub Safe, again under the signature of Jay Davis, the EVP who headed the Mortgage Department:

Dear Mrs. Charbonnier:

On behalf of Kip Whitaker and Hub Safe, I'd like to thank you for bringing to our attention the financial hardships you face and the opportunity to try to help . . .

And he went on to say that while the bank was unable [by law] to amend the existing note, they were able to reduce the interest rate on my adjustable rate mortgage – for the next year – without Duncan's approval, and they'd be willing to do so in time for the very next morgage payment.

I raced to the phone to call Jonah with the news. "I didn't know banks could do such a thing Jonah, did you?"

"No," said my equally amazed cognitive lawyer. "At least, I've never heard of one doing this before. *You are amazing, Ursula!*"

"No, Jonah. You are. I've learned so much from you about how to make good things happen. How am I ever going to thank the bank? I am at a complete loss for words." Then, perhaps out of recently formed habit, caution returned and subdued, I asked, "Well, should I just go ahead and sign this form and return it, or should you or Frank Stoughton look it first?"

"Normally, your cognitive lawyer would say bring it in and let me go over it, but I'm telling you to sign it Ursula. If you want to be extra careful, you could run it by Frank Stoughton for his perspective, but I think it's fine, and I never tell a client to just go ahead and sign something. But this is so unusual."

Frank Stoughton, the financial advisor who with his brother Rob had stood by me through all the great troubles of the past four years, was equally enthusiastic. "Just make certain there are no hidden costs, and check on whether any other terms of the loan have been modified. If everything still seems all right, then sign it. And Ursula, congratulations!" added Frank with unprecedented verve.

The next day I called Rod McLaren at Hub Safe to thank him. "You obviously went to bat for us, and I'm very grateful for all you did. I also called to ask you one or two questions about the agreement they mailed to me. I just want to make sure that my understanding is the same as the bank's."

"I think you should talk to my boss, Jay Davis. It would be much better if you dealt directly with him, Mrs. Charbonnier."

"All right. I'll hold. And thank you again for all that you did. Someday I hope to meet you, so that I can say thank you, in person."

Within seconds, Jay Davis was on the line, and he could not have been more cordial. He confirmed there were no additional or hidden costs. Only the interest rate was being modified. The change would appear beginning with next week's statement, if that was okay with me.

Was it ever!

Then I sat down to write a thank you letter to all three of them: McLaren, Davis, and Kip Whitaker. But for two days no words came. What would I really like to tell them, I asked myself. Hub Safe had done so much for me, and they had been hurt by this mess, too. What could I do for them? I wondered. At about this time, Amanda was asked to fill out a survey too — it must have been survey season in Massachusetts — and one of the questions was: "What is the best thing about your house?"

"And what did you say to that?" I asked.

"That *I* live in it!" said Amanda. "Nobody else gave that answer."

I smiled to myself. A long, deep, satisfying smile. And then I knew what to say. And here is how I began:

Dear Mssrs. Whitaker, Davis, and McLaren:

On behalf of our family, I am writing to thank you for the highly creative and just resolution you proposed, regarding my mortgage situation. After years of feeling "up against The System" (legal and financial), I cannot tell you how wonderful it has been to encounter the human side of a commercial enterprise. The fact that you took the time to find a way to assist, and indeed greatly help this little family, says a tremendous amount about the caliber of particular people at The Hub Company and the value of the human spirit in business at its best . . .

And here is how I ended:

The situation faced by me and my children was not unique — anyone who cares to look will find that there are other "Ursula L. Charbonniers" in your files and in the mortgage portfolios of banks across the Commonwealth and nation. As matters now stand, the courts are getting away with passing along problems that cost banks money, waste their time, jeopardize their image, and divert them from doing what they do best: investing in communities where people can flourish. It seems to me that bankers have a tremendous opportunity before them: to find a way to put a stop to this nonsense — at a legal, financial, and/or human level. In our case, where the law failed to provide justice, Hub Safe stepped in and made a difference — and helped itself in the process. And that is as it should be.

If you ever want to tell the world that there's a lot more to banking than bureaucracies and bottom lines, I know someone who would be happy to help: the lady who, against all odds, still lives in the Cotswold cottage at 1 Inverary Lane.

Sincerely,

Ursula L. Charbonnier

Since I never expected to have Kip Whitaker's attention again, it seemed wise to have seized the moment. After all, as the President of a holding company that had banks (and mortgages) in thirty-eight states, he was certainly in a position to do something about the mess that was being dumped on the courts and the banking system by the Duncan Charbonniers and Hobart Hollidays of this world.

I stopped one step short of suggesting he add up all the financial losses.

The Holliday Case alone had cost Hub Safe three-quarters of a million dollars, and they were still doing a lot of business with Hobart! But if any bankers had added up all the numbers in all the states, they'd have been talking many millions of dollars nationwide. And pain – horrific human pain. If Mr. Whitaker was as intelligent as he was kind, he'd get the message from what little I'd said, and if that happened, well he just might do a little more digging. Something he'd already proved he could do quite well.

The Holliday Matter was also moving in mysterious ways. For months, Quentin and his private detective Paul Mallard, had been telling Julia they "had something" on Hobart, "something really big," but they refused to supply Julia with any documentation, ostensibly "for her own good," on the very remote chance she'd reconcile with Hobart and "spill the beans." But Quentin did allow Julia to overhear part of a phone conversation he had with Hobart in early January, 1993:

"Well, Mr. Holliday, Paul Mallard and I hope you had a very happy New Year's. This is Quentin Corey, and it's not every day, Mr. Holliday, that you get to see your ex-spouse's lawyer on the front page of the Business Section of *The Boston Globe,* and with one of the biggest private investigators in the country – in a color photo, too. Paul and I were there, Hobart. We found out exactly what was going on. Julia never had a lawyer like me. By the way, did you know Paul's been investigating you for six months?"

"Is that where she put all the money?" said Hobart.

"I can't disclose that, Mr. Holliday. But let's just say we have enough on you to make Mrs. Holliday quite content. Now do you want to go the hard route or the easy route?"

"Anything but court," said Hobart.

"Then let's do this neatly. Outside of court would be my preference as well."

"And that's all I know," said Julia. "For my own protection, that's all they'll tell me, except that Hobart and Quentin are having lunch next week."

But the lunch never happened. Hobart canceled, and by the third week of January, Julia and I were absorbed with other matters, anyway. The previous month, we'd put Personals Ads in *Boston Magazine,* since both of us were ready to start dating again.

I decided to play mine straight: "Luminous, coherent, and slim DWF, writer/editor seeks intelligent company of . . . male who is whole, happy, and excited about life." From the dearth of responses, I quickly realized that Ian Ruddway had been right again: or as he'd so succinctly put it at the Ritz, "Ursula, that's not what most people want." Julia, however, *did* send me all the esoteric types who answered *her* ad, and I was looking forward to lunch with the laser physicist, coffee with the investment house founder, and dinner with a nationally acclaimed author, before fate intervened.

Julia, on the other hand, had judiciously decided to go for the hook, as they say in marketing circles: "Scintillating and sensitive DWF seeks . . . male who will always believe that romance is a part of love" – and was immediately deluged with calls and letters from men in their forties who were whole, happy, and excited about life, most of whom had been married to incurable shopaholics or unfaithful princesses!

"Gee, maybe I should run another ad in the spring that says, 'Stunning Conover brunette . . . !'" I laughingly suggested to Julia.

"Maybe you should," she said, as she recounted all the engaging possibilities now before her. "Ursula, I'm overwhelmed. I simply can't deal with this many men." Of the more than thirty responses, four or five real contenders rapidly emerged – all wonderful, two outstanding: Dr. Curt Rivers, the new Director of Marketing and Public Affairs for Appleton Hall; and urbane Bentley Bowman, who appealed to Julia on every level!

"Well, just imagine if you ended up with Curt Rivers!" I laughed. "Hobart would have an awfully hard time ever having you declared psychiatrically incompetent in Massachusetts!"

"I know," she laughed. "Isn't it just too much, Ursula!"

"Has Dr. Rivers checked out your medical records?" I couldn't resist asking.

"I asked him that," said Julia, and he said, "'Of course not. That would be unethical.'"

"A man with ethics!" I exclaimed. "Now there's a change of pace!"

But of all the respondents, the rapidly emerging front-runner was Bentley Bowman, an ex-Conover dad, who lived in a swish Boston hotel, owned car dealerships all over the world, and had one son who had been Enoch Holliday's best friend for the past five years! The child's nanny, who had dealt with and liked Julia the entire time, had also moved out of the marital home – in hopes that Bentley would be granted custody of twelve year-old Josh Bowman and she could resume taking care of him. The trial was scheduled for early March in Judge Robert A. Trophy's Court in Farboro. And what Bentley Bowman wanted was nothing more than to become a Conover dad again, or as he put it, "I'm a Conover refugee living at The Four Seasons, and all I want is to come back to my community." To complete his vision, he needed a Conover Mom.

"This is not to be believed!" I said. "In addition to turning you on, being nice, wanting to be a dad and live in Conover again *and* having a nanny who likes you, your children have been pals for years!!!"

"And guess who is representing Bentley's wife at the upcoming trial before Judge R. A. Trophy?" said Julia. "Gabriel G. Reed!"

"And who's representing Bentley?" I asked.

"Malcolm Rohrschach!" exclaimed Julia.

"Oh God, the grandpappy emeritus of all Boston divorce lawyers! The one who begot all the corruption and greed in our fair city's Family Law system! Absolutely too much!" I laughed.

"I know. I'm scared, Ursula. Bentley Bowman is too good to be true. You know what Ethan said yesterday? 'Boy, will this dis Dad!' If someone were reading this in a book, they would say it was contrived."

"Well if I have my way, a lot of people *will* be reading this in a book Julia, and it is all absolutely true, and I say take a chance and trust this guy!"

"You're telling me to *trust* someone?"

"That's exactly what I'm telling you!" I said firmly. "And someday, if I am *ever* lucky enough to be in your position, it is exactly what I want *you* to say to *me!*"

Listening to Julia and truly reveling in her long-awaited good fortune was having an unexpected effect on me: it was making me long for Ian Ruddway. After not allowing myself to think or daydream about him for the longest time, many suppressed feelings began to stir. One Monday afternoon, they stirred with an intolerable intensity, and I was actually grateful when Spencer and Amanda called me at the last minute to drive their basketball carpools. Resolved: I will banish Ian Ruddway from my thoughts for the rest of the day and immerse myself in writing and motherhood! I left work a little early, filled with maternal purpose, glad for once that dinner wouldn't be over 'til 9:30. Late in the evening, a long-time friend dropped by Inverary Lane; it was Christina Perrine, a close friend since our move to Conover in 1981, who knew about Ian and me.

"I can't help it," I said. "I've tried really hard to put him out of my mind and heart, but he's still there. I guess he'll always be there. I am no further along then I was twenty years ago, and I am getting a little old for unrequited love."

"This is not unrequited love, Ursula, and you know it. The two of you have something that's real. You both made that clear to each other at the Ritz and in the Public Garden. And you did the right thing by sending him back to his wife. What Jonah McCoy told you was right. Two years ago, you did everything in the one way that would allow you and Ian to rebuild for the long run. Rather than being sad about all that's happened between you, I say you should take comfort from it. "

She continued. "Do you realize how rare it is for two people to have what you two do? And how even more rare it is that he came back after so many years and told you he was sorry about the past, and you told him too? That you both apologized to each other? Practically no one ever takes or gets a chance like that, not after so many years."

"If only I could have some sign that he still cared too."

"You may have to wait a long time for that. But why don't you just try to go to sleep now and think about all the good and rare feelings that the two of you still share, after all these years? Even from afar. And take comfort in it, Ursula."

Christina's advice had been good. I looked up at the moon and whispered, "Couldn't I have some small sign?" Then all the feelings of gratitude and love swept me into a long, full night of sleep, and I awoke refreshed and ready for anything – anything but what I found on my voice mail the next morning.

Two messages waited from the evening before, the first poor in sound quality and very garbled: "Ursula, this is Ian Ruddway. I'm on a plane to Boston. I want to have dinner with you tonight. This is a lousy connection. You can't hear me. I'll call when I land." The voice, taut and urgent, confessed a need at least as great as my own.

A second message rapidly followed. "This is Ian, I'm on the ground. You're not there. I still want to have dinner with you. I'll call you later in the week when I get back to New York."

I was so flustered that I didn't push the save button so that I could have the pleasure of hearing that wonderful voice again. All I could do was swear at the telephone. "Damn it, not again. How come after all these years, we still can't connect with each other? Not now! Not now! Not again! Damn it!"

I rapidly dialed his New York office, knowing he checked his messages frequently, even when on the road. The tape said he'd be back in the office Monday, which would have been yesterday. This confused me, but I left a message anyhow. "Ian, this is Ursula. It's Tuesday morning. I just got your messages. Sorry we missed, but I was driving basketball carpools last night. If you get this and are still in town, maybe we could have lunch today. There is *so much* to catch up on. I'll look forward to talking with you later in the week!"

In a reprise of the Rolodex story, we both wanted each other at the same time – again! Last night wasn't just some dim, goofy excursion into memory and longing. That was the miracle of the thing – it had been two-way! Hunch rapidly melted into faith: *it will always be two-way.*

"I wonder what business brought Ian to Boston," I mused as I recounted the voice mails to Amanda that night. My darling daughter frowned at me in great consternation. "What is it?" I asked her.

"Honestly, sometimes you are *so dumb,* Mom! He didn't come to Boston on business. He came to Boston to see you – and only to see you."

"How do you know that?"

"Because when you called his office, his machine said he was due back in New York on Monday, but he didn't go to New York. He came to Boston – to see you. You two are still in love, and I think it's really, really stupid that you aren't doing anything about it."

"Amanda Charbonnier! Ian Ruddway is still married, and he has a daughter and responsibilities. He is not the sort of man to walk away from his responsibilities, and I wouldn't respect him if he were."

"But isn't it dumb for you two to go on caring about each other and staying apart?"

"Not as dumb as breaking apart a family, Amanda. The best thing in the world for that little girl," I said referring to Cam, "would be if her parents straightened out their lives with each other and kept her world whole."

"That's where you're wrong, Mom. I'm going to tell you what it's like from a kid's point of view. Everyone thinks it's so bad that I live in a home without a dad, but it's much better than having him here and not being in love with you. Believe me, it's much better for a kid not to have a parent around who doesn't love the other parent. That's what it's like for a kid."

"But I loved your father," I protested. "We all loved him."

"Well, he didn't want to be here anymore, and I'm glad you and Dad got divorced. I just wish you could be married to someone you did love, and someone who loved you, too. And I still say it's stupid for you and Ian to be apart if you're still going on caring about each other."

"Well, you and I just don't see it the same way," I said walking out of the room.

I called Christina Perrine to tell her about the messages. "I'm thunderstruck, Ursula. Absolutely thunderstruck. After what happened last night, well, I have chills."

"How do you think I feel?" I said. "This is the Rolodex story times ten!"

"I'm having a little trouble absorbing this, Ursula. I think it's great you called him back, but now leave the ball in his court. Don't do another thing. Go out on all those dates you have scheduled over the next five days and forget about Ian Ruddway. Let Higher Power take it from here."

Higher Power, to put it tersely, wasted no time. All those dates from Julia and *Boston Magazine* were not to be. The next morning on my way to work, I was not thinking of Ian as I waited for traffic to clear so that I could turn right at the end of a 128 exit ramp. I was thinking about all the work I had to do at the office. Why doesn't that guy hurry up, I wondered, as I sat stopped, waiting for a slow car to go by. Then: CRAAA-AAA-AAACK!

A sound that resembled the wrath of God gashed across my brain and blasted me into a dark, but beckoning, void. Time out of time and a place with no fear in it. Just fullness and emptiness simultaneously. And then I fought: God, please don't let anything happen to me happen to me happen to me . . . who will take care of my children?

Split from their surroundings, mind, body, and soul tumbled into the blackness. "Go limp!" commanded a voice from inside. I obeyed. Then a bolt of light flashed us back to this world; and car and I slid helplessly down the road, like bubbles plunging into a flume. My head pitched around violently, three or four times, a mindless wind-up toy, out of control.

A pasty-faced man leaned into my window. "My foot slipped off the brake," he said.

"Huh?" I blinked up at him, trying to stay conscious, as I looked into his empty face. "I have no money, I'm a single parent . . ." I babbled. He wanted to exchange papers. Papers? What are papers? I couldn't deal with papers. I felt an urgent need to get to my office, to people who would take care of me. He told me to write down his information. I struggled to draw a zero and stopped in mid-circle. The pasty-faced man said he would write everything down. I couldn't read any of it. How would I make it to my office? I wondered. The pasty-faced man said he would follow me. In the parking lot I saw Vanessa DiStella, Frank Morrow's Assistant at Molecular Innovations.

I tried to get out of my car, but could not. "Are you all right?" she said.

"No," I said, dropping back into my seat.

"Come on, I'm taking you to the Lahey Clinic."

I didn't want to go to the Lahey Clinic. Duncan had just downgraded our medical insurance to an HMO, and the only thing I knew about it was that I needed Dr. Arthur's orders or referrals to get any medical treatment anywhere. There wasn't an extra dime in the budget for car accidents or medical emergencies. Arthur's office didn't even know we were on an HMO. "I can't explain it to them," I said to Vanessa, still struggling to stay with it. "You tell them."

Everything was rapidly slowing down for me. It was hard to think and harder to talk. "Please take me to Westbury General," I said.

"All right. My sister works there. In Quality Assurance. I know it's a good place."

"What did he look like?" I asked.

"The man who hit you, you mean?"

"Yeah."

"He was just a man. He was plain. He had a blank face."

"I thought so too."

I remember the rest of the day only as islands of consciousness. It has never come back to me as a continuous flow. People kept asking me how to spell "molecular." It wasn't hard, but it had *so* many letters in it.

"Your HMO won't cover this," said the woman in Admitting.

"We have to leave," I said to Vanessa. "I can't stay here. We have to leave right now. I don't have any extra money."

"No, no," protested the woman behind the desk. "I'll call your insurance company. We'll find a way. We never turn anyone away at Westbury General." I fumbled for all the cards, and realized my fine motor skills were ebbing too.

She made a phone call. I couldn't follow it. "Your car insurance will pay for everything. I know what it's like," she said, launching into a personal story that was too complicated for me to follow. Someone slapped a hospital bracelet on my wrist, and put a collar around my neck that made me look like Queen Elizabeth I.

"Thank you," I mumbled.

Then they hustled me into a curtained room, and everything slowed further. "Take off all your clothes," said a nurse.

A tall doctor with a British accent and a funny necktie came into the room. He made gooney faces at me, and asked me to make gooney faces back at him. "Close your eyes," he ordered. "No! Really tight, like this! Squeeze my fingers! Open your mouth! Aaaah! Lift your arm! Lift your leg! Look at the wall!"

"Oh shut up!" I wanted to yell back at him, but I didn't have the energy.

Everything kept getting slower. He said his first and last name, which I instantly forgot, and reached out to shake hands.

"Ursula Charbonnier," I said blankly, startled at the disembodied sound of my own voice. "Why didn't you stay at the Lahey Clinic?" he kept repeating. I gestured toward Vanessa and time and again told him, "Ask her. She can tell you."

This tiresome doctor was making me mad. My lower lip pushed out as our eyes locked in fierce, silent combat. Then he shouted at me, "No, I want *you* to tell me!"

You know, I really don't like you!, my eyes flashed back – and why are you harassing me when I need to be left alone? I hadn't said one of these words out loud, mind you, but he'd understood every one of them. And I really don't give a tinker's damn what you think of me, I added with a final blink.

"What do you do?" he said, rolling right past my irritation.

"I'm a writer – and an editor." I thought I might say something about computational chemistry, but the cotton in my mouth was expanding rapidly. My tongue felt more fuzzed up than my mind, and I gestured toward Vanessa again.

I think he realized that being inarticulate was intolerable for me, and he softened his gaze, but the piercing never-give-an-inch eyes didn't let up for second. "NO! I want *you* to tell me!" he roared in my face, "because I am trying to determine how *out of it you are*."

An oh now I get it, registered across my face. His eyes acknowledged the apology in mine, and I put my lower lip away.

"Bureaucracy," I said softly, in the most civilized tone I could muster. Saying the word was even more of an effort than usual. "HMOs are new to me. I don't understand the bureaucracy," I said. This seemed to satisfy him, and Vanessa started filling in the blanks. "Ursula didn't even want to come to the hospital at first," she told him. "All she wanted to do was come up to the office and work!"

From the way he grimaced at me, I knew that under the same set of circumstances, this irritating person would have behaved in the identical way.

"Do you have a headache?" he asked.

"Yes, but not a bad one."

"Where does it hurt?"

Actually I wasn't sure. It was a vague dull feeling. "It's like having had just one glass of wine too many," I said. That seemed to satisfy him. Talking was a chore. I didn't want to.

"What's the matter with me? I . . . feel . . . slow."

"Maybe you're just stressed out from the accident. A little hyper, and all the stress of coming to a hospital."

"I am not stressed out! I do stress very well. You can ask Dr. Arthur!" I don't know why he thought that was funny, but he did.

I don't remember very much after that until he told me to go to sleep for an hour. At some point, Vanessa's sister from Quality Assurance came in, and I remember trying to talk to her, but not being able to very well. Then someone brought me a hot blanket – it was like being wrapped in an enormous *o-shibori* towel. And I went to sleep.

A long while after I woke up, he came back. "What's your name?" I asked. "I don't remember."

"Will Gowell."

"It's time for me to go."

"I said one hour," he snapped, "Isn't that what I said?! And it's only been half an hour!"

"It's been an hour," said Vanessa and I in unison.

Dr. Gowell was out-numbered, not to mention wrong. Then he told me I was in shock, and had a concussion, and that I could leave after the attending physician looked me over. "That's my boss," he added gratuitously, as if I were ignorant of the term.

"Yes, I know," I snapped irritably. "My father is a cardiologist."

"I think you need to just go chill out for awhile. But I want you to go back to work instead for the rest of the day, because you have to be observed every two hours, in case you get any of these symptoms." Then he showed me some list on a yellow form. I couldn't follow it.

"And you're not to drive the rest of the day."

"Can't I drive at the end of the day? I have to get home!"

"Now look . . ." he started to shout.

"All right," I said, conceding defeat. "I'm not stupid, and I don't want to hurt anyone else."

"I think you should go chill out. Take a bubble bath when you're sore tomorrow. I used to do it all the time, whenever I fell off my motorbike!" Then he turned serious. "Not being able to talk awhile ago, that really scared you, didn't it?" he asked.

"Yes," I replied, still concerned that I wasn't right on the inside, even though I was trying so hard to be right on the outside. He knew.

"Can she keep the collar?" Vanessa asked Dr. Gowell. "I told her it would do wonders for her."

"Yeah, like if I've been up for twenty hours writing."

"If you've been up for twenty hours writing," he thundered, "*go to bed!* Here, let me put this around your neck to make sure it's the right size."

"You are . . . impossible," I grinned. "Thank you."

That was to be my final quip of the day. As the afternoon progressed, my mind dulled further. I couldn't even coherently parcel out the tasks that needed to be done to get *Molecular Modelling News* to the printers. Everyone at MII wanted so much to help, and I couldn't even say what I needed. After a long stretch of confusing and stuttering, I looked up at everyone around me and said, "Why can't I talk?" The fear in their eyes collided with the tears in mine.

Venkat, an MII scientist, tried to cheer me with a joke: "Maybe now you will become a great mathematician," he kidded. "Please alert me if this has enabled you to find prime numbers in a jiffy!"

But most people were somber, serious: "You looked like a scared and wounded animal that afternoon," said a co-worker later – a week *after* the aphasia had disappeared.

I decided to work from Inverary Lane the rest of the week. The next morning when I woke up, my neck was in agony, and I couldn't lift my head from the pillow. It felt like an abused and overused bowling ball – a twenty-five pounder – and it wasn't budging. I thought of Dr. Gowell and his obnoxious advice ("Take a bubble bath when you're sore tomorrow!") and all the swear words I suddenly couldn't scream out loud. Then I marched into the bathroom and filled the tub – to the top!!!

I called John Arthur to update him on what had happened in the ER. It was the first time we'd talked to each other since the accident. What I said to him couldn't honestly be described as talking. I just stuttered and stammered my way through and expected him to roll right over it, which for the most part he did. This man always knew how to make "the other guy" feel more comfortable, especially when "the other guy" was in pain, or under pressure. "This just goes to show you, Ursula, how dangerous it can be just to leave your home!"

"J-j-just so you'll know my s-s-sense of humor is intact, I'd s-s-ay-ay in m-my c-c-ase, being in home was m-more dan-anger-rous!" And we laughed together, albeit ruefully.

Later that morning, Frank Stoughton stopped by to help me with taxes and was gracious about my stuttering and inability to speak my thoughts. Julia called in the midst of our meeting. "Is isi-isi-i it st-still all right if-f-f- she c-c-calls you?" I asked, turning to Frank. "She's in much worse t-t-trouble than I am."

"Of course. I told you that before. I'd be happy to try and help her."

Then we plunged into income taxes, and when we were done, I showed

Frank all the correspondence that had taken place between me and Hub Safe on the refinancing of Inverary Lane. When he got to my thank-you letter to Kip Whitaker, Jay Davis, and Rod McLaren, Frank paused at the part that said, ". . . anyone who cares to look will find that there are other 'Ursula L. Charbonniers' in your files and in the mortgage portfolios of banks across the Commonwealth and nation. As matters now stand, the courts are getting away with passing along problems which cost banks money, waste their time, jeopardize their image, and divert them from doing what they do best: investing in communities where people can flourish."

"I guess I never thought about it that way before," said Frank.

To underscore the point I had made in the letter, I told him more about what Julia had experienced. "You know Hobart t-took income t-tax de-de-de-deductions for h-h-house payments – he never made on all the mortg-ga-gages – for m-more than two ye-ears, and IRS did-didn't even c-care!"

"Ursula, fewer than one percent of tax returns ever get audited, so Hobart's chances of getting away with that were very good."

"T-t-tell me something, F-Frank. Wh-why are all the f-f-inancial people in Bos-B-oston and beyond still hap-happy to do business with a ga-guy like that? Someone who would st-st-st-steal from his own cli-lients and al-l-llow his w-wife and ch-ch-children to lose the rooo-oof over their h-heads? Is there j-ju-ust some Gentlemen's Agree-eee-ment in the f-f-f-inancial c-c – com-mu-munity, that th-they l-look the other way wh-when one their own do-oes these th-things?"

"Hobart's not in as great shape as you seem to believe, Ursula. Westbury Ventures has a very bad reputation, and while the clients don't know the full extent of what happened to them, enough of them know the basics of what was done to them. And word has gotten around. I'd be surprised if Hobart had two nickels to rub together."

"Then wh-where does he he he get all the mon-money he's spending on the k-k-k-kids and himself? Did-did he stash it – way someplace?"

"I don't know, but the final year Rob and I were at Westbury Ventures, it was clear that there were serious problems. But despite Hobart's faults and fiduciary lapses, you should understand that he's been a victim too, a victim of the other partners in the firm, who robbed the clients of millions of dollars – and for the most part got away with it. It's nothing anyone can prove in court, you see," said Frank. "And now enough years have gone by that if anyone tried, the statute of limitations has probably run out on what they did."

My brain, even in it's below par state, took in what Frank was telling me. I combined it with comments from Julia ("Hobart's partners demeaned him all through the years, even referring to him in public as 'the selling schmoe'") and fragments I'd read in *The Boston Globe*. Paul Mallard hadn't been stringing Julia along, after all.

"Hobart has a lot of talents Ursula," continued Frank, "which isn't to say he wasn't also flawed."

"Aren't w-we all-all, Frank?" I replied sadly. "Even D-d-duncan, and those c-c-corrupt Proba-ate C-court judges, as ba-ad as th-th-they are and as m-much dam-m-mage as they've inflicted on Boston fam-m-m-milies, even they m-must have some r-r-redeeming fea-features. I really belie-eve that, Frank."

"And any decent person would have to," said Frank.

Throughout the weekend, I continued to chip away at the next issue of *MM News* from home, but the stuttering wasn't improving, and neither was the aphasia. Asa phoned twice from Ohio, thoroughly enraged about the medical care I'd received — or rather hadn't received, and so were all the scientists at Molecular Innovations, not to mention my intellectual property attorneys, here and abroad. They were surprisingly of one mind: I might have brain hemorrhaging or other damage; seizures might ensue in the time ahead, owing to brain scarring from the accident; I should have been hospitalized; I should have had a CT or MRI; I should have been immediately referred to a neurologist; I had a serious condition that wasn't being taken seriously; no one thought I was thinking clearly.

Asa said I might be talking like this for the rest of my life and threatened to call John Arthur and read him the riot act. So I asked Jackie Melrose to intervene and forewarn Arthur, to tell him that I, myself, was displeased with no one. I also wanted her to explain to Dr. Arthur why she was down on Westbury General's form as my "next of kin," and that she was the person he should deal with — not any family members. I was unable to put this thought into any simple English sentences, or for that matter, any simple English words. My mind danced a silent, if spirited, jig around these thoughts. Speech finally spilled forth in a sort of telegraphed phrase, "T-tell him that you are priority person!"

Shortly after they spoke, John Arthur tried to telephone me, but I was so frustrated at my inability to spit out a decent English sentence, that I just sat there and listened to his voice on the answering machine. I think he knew I was listening, but would not pick up the phone. He indicated he understood. The man deserved a response, but I couldn't give him one. "G-get his f-f-f-fa-ax number," I'd said to Jackie. "T-t-talking isn't f-f-un." The day before, John Arthur had advised me not to return other people's calls, and to "write a lot of memos for awhile" and communicate by electronic mail and fax. "I think you're right," I said in my afternoon fax to him, "so I'm starting with you. Above all, I want to be clear, and I want to be understood . . . if you want to communicate with me, why don't you fax back?"

My cognitive internist turned out to be as cool, calm, collected and constructive, as my cognitive lawyer always had been. Arthur assured me the aphasia was temporary and a result of the "flashout" I'd had at the moment of impact. Bill Wales, my Materials Sciences Editor, who was due in from St. Louis that weekend, told me virtually the same thing: the aphasia was temporary and would heal completely. Armed with this confidence and a lot of internal faith, I decided to treat the days ahead as "a science experiment." Maybe in my broken frame of mind I could learn some things.

Which isn't to say I didn't have some frustrating and despairing moments. It was just that I believed in their transience. Friday night, when I finally had a chance to come up for air, I faxed a memo to Ian Ruddway in New York:

12 February 1993

M E M O R A N D U M

TO: Ian Ruddway
FROM: Ursula L. Charbonnier
RE: Communicating

Dear Ian

I tried to leave you a return voice mail on Tuesday, but your machine was full. I can't call you again very well, because on Wednesday morning someone smashed into my stopped car as I was waiting to turn off a 128 exit ramp, on the way to work, and I have a brain concussion which has bruised the speech part of the brain. It will heal *completely*, so not to worry, but for the time being I am somewhat out of commission verbally.

Nevertheless, I can write and think and reason beautifully – and best of all, *listen* maybe better than I ever have before. My internist said I should just communicate by memo for awhile to anyone I need to talk to. He wasn't thrilled when started doing it to him too, but at least he is being a good sport about it.

It is ironic that you tried to reach me Monday, because I wanted to reach you too, at the same time. I'll explain later. Anyway, if you want to call or write, the home fax is kids' line after the sixth ring. You will be at a verbal advantage for the first time in twenty years – unless I have a writing implement in my hand!

Regards – U. L. C.

Later that night, as I lay in bed thinking clear thoughts which came out garbled whenever I tried to give them voice, I felt sad and upset. It was time to sing a song to comfort myself, and I chose the hymn I had written the summer before, "A Canticle of Dawn":

"Where Truth meets light, and shines in grace, The soul slips free, of its carapace. We strike the dawn, and find our way, where Truth meets light and shines in grace . . ." I began. *Wait a minute! No stuttering.* Whoa, I thought to myself. Is this a singing versus speaking problem, or is it a spontaneous speech versus memorized speech problem?

Let's try Shakespeare: "The quality of mercy is not strained. It droppeth as the gentle rain from heaven, upon the place beneath. It is twice blessed: it blesseth him who gives and him who takes . . ." This was amazing. How about the Lord's Prayer? I wondered. "Our Father, who art in heaven, hallowed be thy name!" Well how about that. Could I still do the Gettysburg Address? I could! All right, let's get really fancy. How about tongue twisters: "Sally sells seashells by the seashore," I said without a stutter — then faster and faster and louder and louder. H-h-h-ha Ha! And then I went back to my favorite verse in "A Canticle of Dawn." "When you see hate, know it is fear. Where you hear weak blame, value courage dear. The heart betrayed, that still beams light, Can open minds and set worlds right!"

"I can sing, I can sing, I can sing," I sang, "b-b-but I c-c-c-an't t-talk, I c-c-c-an't t-talk, I c-c-c-an't t-talk," I stuttered.

The next day Jackie Melrose phoned to say she was taking me on errands, including the dump and the grocery store."

"Y-y-you c-c-can't . . . n-n-no no d-d-ump!" I protested.

"Ursula, don't argue with me, and I'll be over around 1:30."

I was unprepared for the horror that awaited me in the grocery store. I was feeling pretty confident. After all, I'd spent the previous day writing about computational chemistry, sending coherent faxes to the world, and demonstrating to myself, at least, that I could still sing. The grocery store should have been a piece of cake.

My troubles began, not far from the door, in the Produce Section. I couldn't say any of the words, but I could say numbers for how many I wanted. After some going around with Jackie about the abundant variety of apples offered at the Conover Grocery, I grunted in frustration at the Granny Smiths. I couldn't say "Granny Smith." I couldn't say "green." I couldn't even say "apple." I could say "f-f-f-four!"

Selecting bread was also an unnerving experience. The children's ultra-detailed description was hard to locate: Pepperidge Farm Country White — I found Toasting White, and Thin-Sliced White, and several other Whites. Finally, Jackie Melrose found the last loaf of Country White — on the bottom shelf, at the back. Buying bread was daunting. I didn't like this.

On down the aisle, I collided with the angled wall of cereal. "Small Cheerios" said the list. I picked up a box, but couldn't tell if it was big or small. I rummaged around for other boxes of Cheerios and compared them. It was small. Only by comparing two sizes could I tell what was big and what was small. The other cereal on the list was a brand I'd never heard of. The flashy bright boxes took on a life of their own, as if the cereal wall were coming at me. It was too much. Conceding defeat, I passed the list to Jackie Melrose.

Spencer and Amanda had made an outrageously long list, as if they believed it would be my last trip to a grocery store. "I censored their cookie list," said Jackie. "They simply don't need five different brands for the next week!"

We moved on to soups. "What kind?" asked Jackie Melrose. I knew beef bouillon. Along with oatmeal, it is one of my main comfort foods. I know most people go for chocolate, but for me it's beef bouillon with lemon slices floating on top. That's what does the job. But I couldn't say it. I couldn't say any of it. I looked at all the soups and wanted to cry. "Wh- who who c-c-cares?!" I spluttered, aimlessly tossing a bunch of the nearest cans and boxes into the cart.

"Ursula, this is like Beethoven going deaf!" said Jackie sympathetically.

By the time we got to frozen food, I'd had it. Jackie, after some effort, located some obscure brand of chicken pie for Amanda. "Gee, I'm learning about all sorts of new products!" kidded Jackie.

Our eyes met, and we didn't know whether to laugh or cry. We made a fierce decision to laugh. A friend of Jackie's heard us and came over. Jackie made introductions, and the other woman tried to engage me in small talk. When I realized I couldn't talk to her, I walked away in despair.

Jackie retrieved me. "It's all right Ursula. This is temporary. It's like going to a grocery store with an eighteen month-old. But you and I have done that before, and it's all going to be all right," she soothed. "And don't worry about the cereal aisle . . ." How could she have known that's exactly what I was worrying about? "I have trouble with that one on a bad day too! It's not you. It's because of the way the cereal wall is angled!"

As we exited the grocery store, I made a promise to myself: the next time I see a grownup berating a toddler in a grocery cart, I will go over and hug the kid and tell the grownup to be kind. I now knew what it felt like to be in a grocery store, to know every word, and be able to communicate none of them.

When we got home, Jackie was in the midst of sending me off to a hot bath and a nap when Bill Wales, my Materials Sciences Editor called. He needed directions to Inverary Lane. I couldn't give them. "G-g-get his f-f-ax at h-ho- wh-whwhere, oh . . . oh," I threw up my hands in total frustration. "Ursula, I'll tell him how to get here. You go take that bath!"

I felt much better by the time Bill arrived, though not up to dealing with a restaurant and the outside world. Amanda ordered a pizza for us, and the evening passed pleasantly. A scientist who'd worked with me for close to eight years, Bill was unflappable and kind, no matter how much I stuttered and groped for words. The next day, Sunday, I woke up early and spent the morning reading *The New York Times*. When I'd finished by 11, I was exhausted and spent the rest of the day asleep, threw a quick dinner together for Spencer and Amanda, went back to sleep, and slept all through the entire next day, which thankfully was Presidents Day, so I could sleep. The office was closed!

Asa continued to phone throughout the weekend, but I couldn't bring myself to pick up the phone. I didn't have the energy to deal with any negativism, no matter how well-intentioned. On Tuesday, when I no longer sounded like Flub-A-Dub, I called John Arthur as he had asked, and explained why I had stopped answering my phone. "I'm just not good at dealing with hysterical and angry people – despite all the experience I've had, I'm still not good at it. Thanks for being such a good sport when I played 'escape and evade' even with you. But I really couldn't talk to you."

"I know, but you sound fine now, and at least I got to learn how to use the fax machine. I'd never used it before!" he said. "How do you feel you're doing now?" I told him about the grocery store – the wall of cereal and my inability to verbally select apples – "Do you know what that's like?" I asked him.

"Not firsthand, but I've had patients tell me."

Then I thanked him for talking with Jackie Melrose, and said that although Asa and many of the scientists around me were upset at me and at him, that I personally had no problem with him, or Dr. Gowell in the ER – "though I don't think I was very nice to Dr. Gowell because I couldn't talk to him very well. You know, everyone wants me to sue the guy who hit me. And we both know how I feel about courtrooms and lawyers, well not all lawyers," I edited.

"Ursula, when something like this happens, a lot of people want to blame someone."

"Well, I don't want to blame anyone. I just want to be well. I wish I could stop getting into so much trouble. All I've ever wanted is to take care of my family and write – that is all I have ever wanted, and sometimes it all seems so unattainable." My good doctor listened sympathetically.

Then I asked him whether it was a good idea for me to see a neurologist. Everyone who cared about me – all my scientists and all my lawyers – were insistent that I be referred to one. "But I don't want to waste a doctor's time," I said. "Don't they have sick people to see? I'm having trouble deciding what the right thing to do is. Can you help me sort this out, walk me through the pros and cons, tell me what you would do if you were in my place?"

"I'm going to give you an answer that's part philosophical and part medical," he replied.

"At their best, they're not mutually exclusive," I said. And then I listened.

In the end he said, "You know if you forget one thing in the summer of 1994, everyone is going to blame it on the accident, and maybe you could get rid of some of the pressure being put on you by going and getting another opinion now."

"Caving in to pressure is not the way I've lived my life."

"I know," he said.

"Pressure is not the right reason to order more tests and waste a doctor's time," I continued.

"True. But Ursula, it's also not entirely the wrong reason."

"Well, you're the quarterback. But you still haven't answered my original question. What would you do if it were you?"

"If it were myself with no one to bounce the question off of, I'd probably do nothing. If I were talking to my wife about it, I'd probably get checked just to satisfy her," he said.

"We're too much alike," I said.

"I don't know if that's good or bad," said John Arthur. I didn't reply, because it was so obviously both.

"There are already too many neurologists in *Snow Job,*" I commented dryly.

John Arthur laughed.

"But all right, I'll go see one. In the interests of saving time, tell me, who's in the neighborhood?"

"Well, a lot has changed over the years," he began, alluding to Duncan's contact with four neurological practices over the years, "but you could go see Thorensen and Strangebach . . . Thorensen has a little more grey hair on his head . . . if you don't mind seeing someone your family's already had contact with."

"I'm a separate issue," I replied tersely. "And I never dealt with him anyhow. Look, five years ago, I didn't know an epileptic from an alcoholic – end of story. It's not a problem for me, if it won't be a problem for Dr. Thorensen." I was trying to remember which one he was. It took a moment. I rummaged out loud through names. Arthur helped me. Then I got it straight. He had been Neurologist Number 2.

"I think that's right," said Dr. Arthur.

As things turned out, I never made it to Neurologist Number 2 – he couldn't schedule me as soon as Arthur wanted, so they referred me to Neurologist Number 4, Hugo Schell of Westbury, the grand pooh-bah of all neurologists of the western Boston suburbs, as we'd jokingly called him way back in 1987, another lifetime ago. Duncan had been sent to Schell because other Boston-area neurologists considered Schell to be utterly brilliant, the one who regularly solved so many of their own unsolvable cases. Christina Perrine had even seen him once, and Schell had zeroed in on problems which all previous neurologists had missed.

In Duncan's case, Schell ordered a fourth CT and a 24-hour EEG, which had necessitated sending a technician out to our house. She smeared jelly on Duncan's scalp, and wired him up to some gizmo that would record his brain waves for the next night and day. It had meant missing two days of work, and it had taken some fancy verbal footwork on my part for the children not to be alarmed by Duncan's appearance. He had gamely gone along with it all.

I have no idea what Schell finally concluded about Duncan, for he and I never discussed it. This hadn't stopped Duncan from telling his psychiatrist, Dr. Culp, a few years later that Schell and I had discussed the whole case behind his back. But in fact, Dr. Hugo Schell and I had never exchanged a blessed word until I walked into his office on a late February afternoon in 1993.

His receptionist was not glad to see me. I still hadn't gotten the hang of the HMO, and had shown up without all the appropriate paperwork. "We don't bill accident victims," she kept saying. "That should all go through your lawyer!" I obviously wasn't grasping her point. She had to say it two more times.

"I'm just trying to get all the lawyers and doctors out of my life!" I said with detectable exasperation. "So I don't have a lawyer." She looked at me in disbelief.

"I hate HMOs," she snapped between non-stop phone calls. "I don't have papers for you. Where's your authorization number?"

"What authorization number?" I didn't know what she was talking about. "Just call Dr. Arthur," I replied, trying to be helpful, remembering only that he was my medical quarterback and the HMO's bureaucratic clearinghouse. "And I know he's at his office," I said firmly, not wanting to postpone this another day, "because Spencer's seeing him. I dropped him off on the way here."

Spencer had strep, I had a brain concussion, and Duncan was off having fun skiing, following the advice of good old Dr. Culp, the first of our paid enablers, to put himself first. What made me think of this now was a tall fellow dressed in tweed, who kept mentioning Culp's name, as he trotted in and out behind the receptionist's desk. The reminder irritated me, but it wasn't the tweedy man's fault, and I somehow mustered a smile. He grinned back, especially when he heard me say, "I'm just trying to get all the lawyers and doctors out of my life!"

Five minutes later, the tweedy fellow returned. "You must be Ursula!" he boomed jovially in a delightful South African accent. He sounded just like my new editor in Pretoria.

"I must be!" I said, surveying his eyes: two azure marbles spinning with spirit and wit. "Hello again," I said wryly. "Where do you want me to go?"

"Straight ahead."

So this was the great Hugo Schell. Well, this made it official – I had absolutely not scrambled my neurologists four years ago. A voice like his I would have remembered. This was definitely our first conversation, and it was devoutly to be hoped, our last. I needed a brain that was 100 percent, and I needed him to certify to the world that mine was.

Perhaps he read my thought. "What can I do for you?" he asked.

"I want you to tell everyone that I am absolutely fine!" I said. "I'm getting faxes and e-mail from three continents, from scientists and lawyers – and many people are convinced that I've had bleeding in my brain, and need MRIs, and should have had dye injected into my brain, and will have all these residual symptoms six months or twelve months or two years down the road."

"Lawyers?" he asked quizzically. "Why do you have lawyers?"

"My publication does a lot with intellectual property!"

"Now tell me what happened." he said. "Tell me about the accident."

"It was the loudest noise I've ever heard," I began. "I know that seems odd for what it was. Later I found my sunglasses had been thrown into the backseat, and tapes were all over the car . . . Anyway, everything went black for a second. I was struggling to stay conscious, and then I looked up and saw this sort of pasty-faced person staring in my window . . . I guess he was an honest person. He pulled over and tried to exchange insurance information. I couldn't read what he wrote. I tried to write, but I couldn't make a zero . . ."

"Was it hard to read later?"

"Well, actually, it's right here. Let's have a look at it," I said, reaching into my briefcase, where all the accident paperwork was neatly clipped together. "Gee," I said, "it's not too bad. It's not great, but I can read it today."

I handed it to him. "Not too bad," he agreed, nodding. "Well go on, tell me what happened next."

I recounted the difficulty I'd had getting to my office and how I'd run into Vanessa DiStella in the parking lot, and we'd gone to the Lahey Clinic and later Westbury General. Then I told him about the frustration of dealing with Dr. Gowell in the ER. "I couldn't really answer his questions. I knew what had happened, but I wasn't able to tell him . . . Well, how much do you want to know?" I asked, suddenly interrupting myself.

"You keep going. You're doing just fine," he laughed. "Did you hit your head?"

"I don't think so, because wouldn't I have had a bump or bruise?"

"Probably, but not necessarily."

"My head was tossed around a lot. And my speech got all messed up in the days that followed."

"What was it like?"

"Here, read this fax I sent Dr. Arthur. This paragraph on the second page, describes it perfectly, as it was, at the time. My talking was like a

Parkinson's victim trying to walk – the words just keep tripping over each other, and bouncing like a hot potato."

Then I told him about Asa's anger, and the grocery store, and sending faxes to people because I couldn't speak properly over the phone, and working at home, and how Dr. Arthur said I should slow down for a while. "And I thought, all right, I'll compromise. After all, his definition of slow is different from my definition of slow!"

At this, he smiled. "Now, through all this time, how was your drive?"

"Well, 128 was a little hard; after all, I couldn't turn my neck very well."

I saw him suppress a laugh. "Not your driving! Your drive, your drive, your drive!!!"

"Oh, my drive," I said, as the differences between his English and mine slowly penetrated. Really, having been raised by British nannies, I should have got that one much quicker! "Well, I guess it was all right. No, maybe a little slower. And now for a low-tech question: What do I do about my stiff neck and back muscles?"

"Hot water bottle, in bed, for twenty-five minutes before you go to sleep!" That sounded sensible.

I continued with my story. "By Friday, I was pretty frustrated at not being able to talk properly. I fully believed Dr. Arthur that it was temporary, but it was still upsetting. And when I'm upset – I sing!"

And I recounted how I'd made the discovery that I could sing. "Software engineers at MII later told me that, indeed, singing and talking are in different parts of the brain."

"That's right," he said. "We use singing to help people who've lost their speech – we call it melodic therapy."

Then I told him about being able to recite Shakespeare and the Lord's Prayer, without stuttering, and even "Sally sells seashells by the seashore" over and over, really fast, but that I couldn't manage spontaneous speech. I also told him about doing experiments, keeping notes, and trying to use the experience as an opportunity to learn about my brain. "It's neat in there, and there is tons of backup. But there was one experiment I didn't think of until it was too late. Might I have been able to sing the directions to my house to my Materials Science Editor?"

"Most probably, yes!" said Hugo Schell with delight. "Now did you experience any fatigue through all this?"

"Why, yes!" And I told him about Sunday and Monday, which I dubbed, "The Big Sleep." He was not surprised, but I was. "For me that's so unusual. I hardly ever need any sleep, compared to most people. I have this supersonic energy level that just won't quit. I mean sleeping for two days – I'd never do that!"

Then I told him about the travails of going to the grocery store. How I couldn't say Granny Smith or apple, or even green. And how I couldn't say what kind of soup I wanted, but I could answer questions about Soup

A versus Soup B. And about wonderful Jackie Melrose, who had helped take care of me when I was verbally out to lunch, and how she understood me, and nothing absolutely nothing ever rattled her, not even being with me in stutter-mode.

"Look, I don't know much about neurology," I told him, "just a little about MS, my mother's illness, and epilepsy . . ." I trailed off for moment. "I am the woman who didn't know an epileptic from an alcoholic . . . my former husband . . . one of your former patients . . ."

"Tell me about him . . ."

"Oh, he's in your files – and let's just keep him there!" I said.

"Well, what was his name?"

"Duncan Charbonnier. It's too long a story to tell. It's all in my book, *Snow Job*. And you're in it – it's always a pleasure to meet another character! If you're really interested, you can read about it in the book."

"Oh, I'd love to!" he said.

Then he asked a lot questions about family illnesses: "How about your dad?"

"A cardiologist who's had one heart attack."

"How about you?"

"Well, how far back do you want me to go? Let's see . . . I had pneumonia when I was . . . fourteen. And toxo when I was thirty . . ." and I told him about all the twists and turns in diagnosing it; and then I finished, hoping that would satisfy him. But it didn't.

"Well, had you gone anywhere?"

"I'd gone to New York and eaten a lot of raw fish, but there's nothing unusual in that."

"Any history of mental illness?" he asked. Oh dear, maybe I shouldn't have told him about the raw fish! "Have you ever seen a psychiatrist?"

"Oh, I saw Dr. Culp once, when we were back in the middle of all this family mess, and my husband was seeing him, and I had to go as the spouse of . . . anyway, I said to Dr. Culp, 'Don't *you* want to see me again?' and he said, 'NO, I don't want to see *you* again!' It's all in *Snow Job*."

"Any alcohol in the family?"

"Alcohol????" I looked at him, incredulous, as if to say, alcohol in *our* family?

He burst out laughing.

"How about drugs?"

At which point, we both laughed. *This guy knew.* If I were a betting woman, I'd have bet Duncan Charbonnier hadn't fooled Neurologist Number Four for an instant. Culp and his social worker, Irena Cossell, might have been paid enablers, but not this guy! Schell was too smart. I'd have bet money on it.

"How old are your kids?"

"Fifteen and thirteen."

"And how are they doing?"

"Splendidly, considering what they've been through in the past four years!"

"The divorce, you mean?"

"Not the divorce. The total change in their father . . . the complete inversion of values. Seeing someone change that much."

"So Ursula, tell me again, throughout all this, how has your drive been?"

And again I launched into the difficulties of highway driving with a stiff neck . . . and felt instantly foolish, not to mention forgetful, when he once again said, "No, not your driving – your drive, your drive, your drive!"

I grimaced and changed the subject. "So now, Dr. Schell, after listening to all this, can you give me a name for what happened to me?"

"You had a cross between aphasia in the Broca's part of the brain," he said showing me a plastic model, "and aphemia."

"Well, I can spell practically anything," I said, "but you'll have to spel that one for me!" Then he pointed to various parts of the plastic model and explained how speech is generated by the brain, and that the very last stage of that function was what I had not been able to do.

I made some notes on what he said. "So is this a recovery, or merely a reprieve as so many around me think?"

"It's a recovery."

"No chance of a brain scar or any future trouble?" I asked, echoing the fears of my colleagues and father. Schell didn't think so. That was good enough for me. I was thrilled with his diagnosis. "You know," I said alluding to my office friends, "I think they're just worried because nobody knows how to do my job"

"Show me your palm," he commanded.

"Which one?"

"It doesn't matter. Lift your arm. Show me your thigh!"

"I can't – I'm wearing pan . . ."

"Lift your leg!" laughed the grand pooh-bah!

"Oh, here!"

"Let me look at your eyes before you go. Come over here. You just look at that picture on the wall. You're fine!" he pronounced. "You're a super woman, Ursula, 100 percent, 100 percent!"

"Good. Now hopefully that will satisfy all my scientists, and all my lawyers, and maybe even my father!"

"Maybe!!" he said, in a tone that suggested only a snow ball's chance in hell of satisfying Asa. "Now take care of yourself, Ursula! Take care of yourself," he instructed, for what seemed the zillionth time. Right, I thought, if someone could just keep the unethical lawyers and corrupt judges and in-denial alcoholics and sloppy drivers out of my path, I *would* be just fine. I might even be super, fine, 100 percent!

"And I see no point in doing an MRI," said Dr. Schell.

"I agree. It's overkill."

"Now take care of yourself, Ursula. Take care of yourself!"

"Well, I'm trying to, but I just keep standing still, and I just keep getting in more trouble!"

"Take care of yourself, Ursula," he repeated yet again. "Take care of yourself."

I waved good-bye to his receptionist, still in phone-overload mode. "Thank you, good-bye, and I hope I never see you guys again. And I really mean it!" I called cheerily. Then I realized that might have sounded mean, but from the way she grinned, I knew she'd understood exactly what I meant. "Don't take that personally," I amended.

"I won't!" she smiled.

I prayed that I was now done with this little episode and could put the brain concussion behind me. Schell's assurances to the contrary, neither all my lawyers nor some of my scientists nor Asa were pleased. I sent Asa a fax: "Saw Duncan's Neurologist Number 4 yesterday, and I *had* a cross between Broca's aphasia and aphemia. All better now. Any muscle stiffness (and it's minor!) that remains will be solved by time and heating pads. It's a low-tech solution, but it works. Now writing a poem called *The Joy of Speech*. Please Relax."

This did not have its intended effect. "It doesn't mean anything!" sputtered Asa regarding Schell's diagnosis. "Aphasia, aphemia — what can he possibly know without an MRI, and how can he possibly ascertain that you won't have trouble from this down the road?"

"Number 4 is utterly brilliant," I replied "and I feel absolutely terrific!" That seemed to quiet him.

The following week, someone from an insurance settlement firm that was representing the guy who hit me called and peppered me with questions: Would I settle? Could they interview me? Would I authorize the release of my medical records? Who was my neurologist? I just wanted any medical bills, now and in the future that were a traceable to the accident, to be paid by the other guy's insurance company. But didn't I intend to sue them for pain and suffering? Only if they didn't pay my medical bills. Too bad I couldn't sue Duncan for all the pain and suffering he'd caused me and the kids!

"Pain and suffering" suddenly struck me as an absurd legal term. The law would not allow me to sue Duncan for pain and suffering, Duncan whose intent with malice aforethought, had been to put the children and me out of our own home and to destroy me. But it was okay for me to sue someone for pain and suffering, someone I didn't even know who never intended any harm toward me whatsoever. It was just another outrageous inconsistency in our System, and I couldn't help but notice it.

All I really wanted was be well and get on with my life: to work, to write, to love, to take care of my family, and to be well. And now that I had been pronounced "completely well . . . a super woman . . . 100 percent" by the grand pooh-bah of all neurologists, of the western Boston suburbs, that was just what I intended to do. Lucky, lucky me!

I had to have been the happiest person in the store, when I walked into the Conover Grocery a few days later. I laughed openly at the wall of now-unthreatening cereal boxes; and I reveled in my decisiveness when it came to selecting soups. But my finest moment came in front of the apple bin in the produce department: "I want four Granny Smith Apples," I declared clearly and joyfully to all those shiny little green pieces of fruit.

And I didn't care who heard me!

XXXIV

The End of the Line

Racehorses do not recognize when they have crossed the finish line, for it takes time to realize that the race has been run, in the same way that ancients pondering the sky at winter solstice needed several days to confirm the actual and inevitable return of light. Much like the horse who knows the racetrack, but nothing of the race, and the human who knows the sky, but is ignorant of astronomy, Julia and I stumbled through the final weeks of winter, unaware of greater forces at work — forces too formidable, too far away, and much too large for us to see.

Denny Goferbucks, the attorney for the Days (Julia's former landlords) struck first. Nearly a year later, she was following through on her threat to sue Julia for more than $100,000 — in fact she was going for treble damages, alleging that Julia had "engaged in a campaign of threats, vilification, and harassment to dissuade . . ." St. Paul's from buying the Bradford Road property. For such "tortious interference," Denny was seeking $30,000 alone! And that was only one of seven complaints she'd filed against Julia.

"What do you think of that?!" exclaimed Julia.

"I think the next thing that will happen is Hobart will try a fourth custody suit," I replied tersely.

"You do?"

"I do." After years of dealing with Boston's legal establishment, I could practically smell it coming! "Otherwise, Julia, Denny's complaint against you makes no sense. Think about it. Why would any self-respecting attorney initiate such a ridiculous lawsuit? Apart from the suit's being groundless — St. Paul's parishioners can attest to that — you are bankrupt. There's no way the Days could collect damages. So what's the point?"

The very next day, Julia heard it from Ethan first: "Dad is going to marry Pansy, and buy a nine-bedroom house in Conover, and make it so we have to live with him. But we want to live with you, Mom. He can't really take us away from you, can he?" Within hours, Robina Braverman, Bing Levine, and the other assorted Holliday shrinks and paid enablers descended upon Julia. What it boiled down to was this: a fourth custody suit – in Judge Rumborough's court.

Sherman Franklin, Julia's real estate attorney, and Quentin Corey, Julia's divorce attorney, rapidly downshifted into warrior mode – *pro bono* warrior mode! "Sherman asked Denny why she was doing this to me, and you know what she said? 'I have personal reasons for wanting to do this to Mrs. Holliday!' It looks like you were right, Ursula. Quentin told Denny he was going to countersue for malpractice and conflict of interest, because of her connections with Hobart and Robina Braverman and Judge Rumborough. This is so sick. And now Hobart is coming into the house whenever I'm out on a date with someone, and calling me and telling me what time I have to be home. He must think he's still married or something, and can dictate where I'm to be and when!"

"What about your restraining order?" I asked.

"It expired."

"Then get another one! Enough moms have been murdered in Massachusetts this year. The political climate is changing. Surely you can find a judge who will take your concerns seriously and give you a restraining order."

A few weeks later, a new judge in Westbury District Court, the Honorable Marcus Hay, gave Julia a year-long restraining order. Hobart hadn't even bothered to show up for the hearing, *after* insisting that the judge postpone it to a more convenient time. As Julia was pulling away from the courthouse with signed restraining order in hand, she saw Hobart running up the street, a full hour after the hearing had been scheduled.

She called me when she got home. "They can't take the restraining order away from me Ursula, can they?"

"I don't see how. It's all signed and everything, isn't it?"

"Yes."

"And it's good for one year?"

"Yes."

Nevertheless, Julia called the following day with this news. "They've revoked my restraining order because Hobart didn't show up for the hearing!"

"They what?"

"You heard me, Ursula!"

"This is unbelievable, Julia. First Hobart doesn't show up for court. Then he asks for a postponement. Then he doesn't show up for court again, and you're granted the restraining order, and then the court takes it away from you and schedules yet another hearing!"

"That's right. Right here in Westbury District Court!"

"You know, if you hadn't showed up for court twice in a row, you'd have been found in contempt! This is absolutely outrageous. Why don't you call the Governor's Office and tell them about this. Let Raoul Fernandez add this to his file on us!"

"That's a good idea. I think I will."

That night, exhausted but wanting to fulfill Devon Carmody's request, I showed up at the Conover Town Hall to speak before the Board of Selectmen, which included Jeff Melrose. The Board was again considering whether to extend Devon's position as Conover's Substance Abuse Prevention Coordinator. Devon and her committee were going in to lobby for a half-time position for one more year, but what was really needed was a full-time position – *for the foreseeable future*. Family therapist Davis Fenway was there, along with the Chief of Police, Amanda's Phys. Ed. teacher, my Al-Anon sponsor, her in-recovery spouse, and all the others who had spoken at the appeal we'd made last year to the Conover Finance Committee. Once again, I hadn't had enough sleep the night before. But this time, I knew what I wanted to say.

"Hello again," said Amanda's teacher as we gathered in the lobby to wait our turn. "Hello, again" and "Here we are again," we murmured to each other. Jeff Melrose wanted very much for the Substance Abuse Prevention program to continue, one Selectman was on the fence, and the third had historically been opposed to the entire matter. If it was continued for even one more year, she argued, then substance abuse prevention should be placed under Education or the Board of Health, under one particular budget. She saw substance abuse prevention as neither a pressing nor all-encompassing problem. Devon had charged us, citizens of Conover, with the task of convincing her otherwise. It was a tall order.

Davis Fenway spoke eloquently, as he had the year before, about the need for teaching children how to deal effectively with peer pressure. Amanda's teacher told how Devon's work had made a real difference in the schools, and the Chief talked of the reduction in D & D complaints to the Conover Police over the past year, which he credited to Devon's hard work. Then my Al-Anon sponsor and her spouse spoke openly of the pain and enormous difficulty of confronting alcoholism in the family during an era when there had been no Substance Abuse Prevention Coordinator in Conover. There was a lot more talk about helping kids deal with pressure to do drugs and drink. And then it was my turn.

I prayed that I would be more coherent than the year before. I looked around me at the people of our town, and then I zeroed in on the reluctant Selectman. She was my audience. She had become my audience the moment she asked, "Does education *really* make any difference?"

I took a deep breath and began.

"Tonight, we've heard a lot about education as prevention, and particularly how it can help youngsters to deal with pressure from their peers. I would argue that an equally important function of education is to prepare children to deal constructively with the world around them — *the world as it is* — not as we wish it were. With education, we can give our children the tools to cope with the *adults* in their lives who may be abusing substances.

"The world as it is — a case in point. Several years ago, one spring afternoon in the parking lot of the Isaiah Jones Tavern, just across the Green from here," I nodded, "two Conover children, one in the Middle School, the other an elementary school student, after months of upheaval at home, confronted their mother with this question: 'Is our Dad on drugs?'

"Even now, I can't tell you if their mother was more astounded by the question, or that it came from her children. Several months later, those same two children and their mother were sitting in a doctor's office at Appleton Hall, and the doctor asked the little girl, 'Your father's told you that he's stopped. Don't you believe him?' And the child replied, 'Well, maybe he has and maybe he hasn't. But stopping isn't enough, Dr. Ballard. It isn't enough just to stop. You have to go and get help for yourself. I learned that in school.'

"What these children learned in school gave them the tools to confront a substance abusing parent in their own home and the tools to talk constructively with a physician at Appleton Hall. Today these two children are thriving — *by any standard* — so if you ask me, does educating our children about substance abuse really make a difference? I give you a resounding '*Yes*'!"

And then I sat down, very tired, and not knowing if I had really moved any minds.

A few minutes later, our reluctant Selectman returned to the subject of trying to pigeonhole substance abuse into some particular budget, be it schools or the Board of Health or whatever. Again, people spoke of how substance abuse cuts across budget lines, how it could not be pigeonholed if it was to be honestly addressed by the town. "It's a town-wide problem," asserted the Conover Chief of Police.

I waved my hand toward Jeff Melrose. "Mrs. Charbonnier has something to say," he announced.

"When Devon and I were deciding what to call Conover CARES, we spent a lot of time on it. The name was well-thought out. And I'd just like to remind everyone here that the 'C' in CARES stands for COMPREHENSIVE! And there's a reason for that."

Lights went on in the eyes at the head table. Wonder of words! They had been moved. Before Devon and her Committee were dismissed, the reluctant Selectman suggested that maybe instead of a part time position for one year, they should be approaching the town about funding for a full-time position – five years and beyond, or as Jeff Melrose put it, "There will always be a new generation of youngsters coming along who need to be educated."

But it wasn't just a new generation that wanted for education. Our generation, that older generation, was also in need of learning, the kind of learning that was spelled out in the serenity prayer that opened every Al-Anon meeting: "God, grant me the serenity to accept the things I cannot change, the courage to change the things I can, and the wisdom to know the difference."

I now accepted that all that had happened to me – that our system as it was currently structured – enabled me and other spouses of substance abusers to be attacked, simply because the abuser felt like doing it. And while I'd learned to channel my angry energy into productive endeavors: starting Conover CARES, working with others for legal reform, rearing two children, and working on *MM News,* this was not the life I had envisioned for myself.

How right John Arthur had been when he said four years ago, "Things will never be the way they were."

"But they can be better," I had said at the time.

Well, they were better, but not in any way I might have foreseen. I would never again be an adoring young wife with an unshakable trust in her husband. That love-struck creature died the day I stood at Armstrong Field with an empty, brown-bagged vodka bottle in my hand. And I have mourned her – and her happy dream: a marriage with love that would last a lifetime.

Nor would I ever again be a citizen with the assumption that high ethical standards were required to be admitted to the Bar or to serve on the Bench. That citizen had been stripped of her illusions in Gabriel G. Reed's office, and in Judge Tracy's chambers.

And who had emerged in her place? Maybe a woman, who could wholeheartedly embrace a less-than-perfect man, and a citizen who could still work toward justice in a less-than-perfect system. For what we forge out of betrayal is ultimately up to us.

Today, Duncan Charbonnier's salary and stock options from Germane Engineering total more than a quarter of a million dollars a year; only a small fraction of this wealth is shared with his children. Ivy Parrish is a cover girl on a *Time-Life* publication chronicling cultural revolution in American Business. Hobart Holliday continues to steal millions from his unsuspecting clients, for as Frank Stoughton put it, what Hobart does "cannot be proved in court." The two biggest launderers of drug money in Massachusetts still live in Conover; the authorities know who they are, but can't touch them. Judge Rumborough and his peers continue to take children away from honest parents and place them with parents who are tax evaders and convicted drug felons; Judge Tracy is still telling tasteless sex stories in his chambers, where conversation is not a matter of public record; Gabriel G. Reed and his colleagues continue to grow rich by taking houses from children. And Life goes on.

Justice doesn't always triumph. Evil isn't always conquered or even revealed.

So where is the end of the line? It's where we draw it, when we discern what is authentic with our own eyes. But we do not cross that line until we take action – action that snaps its suffocating grip on our lives, action that acknowledges *the truth around us*.

XL

✒️ *Serenity*

. . . When I learn to live serenely, cares will cease.
From the hills, I gather courage, visions of the day to be,
Strength to lead and faith to follow,
All are given unto me . . .

— Janet E. Tobitt, *Peace of the River*

It was almost predictable after so many years. I was holding the Rolodex card in my hand when the phone rang. "This is Ian, Ursula."

Before I could get in more than an "Oh, hi," he was off and running about literary agents, termination agreements, and various legal procedures that had to do with book publishing.

"How are you?" I asked when he finally came up for air.

"Fine, fine," he said, in his best-foot-forward voice.

"Uh huh," I replied in my I-don't-buy-a-word-of-it tone.

"Well, actually we had a bad car accident a few weeks ago, on the New York Thruway. We're all all right, but the car was totaled. I saw it coming, Ursula, and I had to make a choice. But the car's all cracked up. It's all cracked up," he said, a kernel of self-doubt not so embedded in his words.

"I'm sure you did the best you could," I tried to reassure. "Ian, there are only two things you can do when you see trouble coming: slow down to minimize impact or speed up and try to get out of the way." He had slowed down. "But when you're trying to decide which to do, there's such an interplay of forces you have no control over, so you really must try to be at peace with what you did. And the three of you are all right. That's what really matters. You can always replace a car. It's a lot harder to replace the people in your life.

"And now onto a different subject," I said, taking command of the conversation. "There's something I want to talk with you about. For some time, I've wanted to tell you how much I . . . admired . . . what you started to say at the Ritz, but I just haven't been able to do it . . . and there are things I've left unsaid. "

For a moment I thought he was going to change the subject. "Did . . .

you . . . hear . . . me, Ian?" I repeated, spacing out the words for emphasis. "There are things I've left unsaid, things we've both left unsaid."

"That's true; you're right," he acknowledged.

"We've never really put things straight between us."

"You're right," he said again.

"In every part of my life, I've been full and forthcoming, except with you. So this is my New Year's Resolution: to put things straight between us."

"That's just what we're going to do," said Ian Ruddway, "the next time that we see each other."

I hung up the phone with that much resolved. And I couldn't help but think how in real life, you can't tell which leaf on a full, beautiful tree will be the first to fall – nor which in a mass of russet October glory will be the one to hang on through a cruel winter and ride out all storms. Twenty years before, the betting had looked so easy. How was it, then, that Duncan Charbonnier, the serious young man who embraced responsibility so gracefully, and Ian Ruddway, the wild man who lusted so fiercely after his own freedom, had come to trade places? I could not say. I only knew that this switch had taken place, and in the violent upheaval that accompanied it, I had found courage and faith and peace.

And as the year unfolded, here I was two decades later, getting free of the past, looking forward to the future, but mostly focused on Aujourd'hui – Ike Peters' favorite Boston restaurant, where we planned to meet for dinner.

We were deep into a fragrant, full Boston spring, where nearly every flower had burst its bud. For a long while the blooms had been poised to go, but inadequate sun and a long, harsh winter had taken their toll: many of the blossoms had not come to full flower. I frowned as I looked over a spray of almost blooms.

Ike Peters read my thought as he came up behind me. "It's just part of the cost of living kid," he said, giving me a teddy-bear hug hello.

"Welcome to Boston," I said looking up at him.

"Looks like you survived winter nicely," he nodded approvingly.

"I did – with a lot of help from my friends," I added.

"I brought you a sort of toy," Ike said, handing me a large Wheaton Glass box, topped by their signature red fiberglass bow. "How about we get a table so you can sit down and open this?"

I gently shook the box, as I liked to guess about contents. But this package didn't shake. It sloshed.

Ike Peters delighted in the surprised look on my face. "I'll give you a few clues," he said. "It's bigger than a molecule; it's something you can simulate; and I didn't buy it at that fancy toy store across the street. This is something I made in my own laboratory. In fact, I liked it so much that I made another one for my five year-old."

"Sounds very sophisticated!" I quipped.

"It is. Go ahead, open it."

Inside I found a large Lucite box filled with water; it had knobs and buttons on one side and a battery pack and thermometer on the other. "What does the thermometer say?" asked Ike.

"Seventy degrees."

"Okay, now shake it. No, really hard. Like this. Turn the box upside down."

"Why it's a snow box, like those paperweights we used to have in the 1950s! Is this a Wheaton Glass special?"

"It's more than that," said Ike. "I told you . . . I made it in my laboratory. Okay, let the snow settle down. Now, press that red button on the left and the other one on the right." The buttons activated a mechanism that set up two sideways currents that collided. "Why it's a simulated whirlpool. Very cute!" I exclaimed.

"Okay, now twirl the green button."

"The one that says 'Faster'?"

"That's right."

I turned it in both directions. "Nothing's happening," I said.

"Well then, try the blue button, the one that says 'Slower.'"

"Nothing's happening again! And the whirlpool's still spinning, albeit less intensely."

"Then you better try the orange button, the one that says 'Stop.'"

Nothing happened again.

"Okay, now in another five or ten minutes, I want you to record the temperature."

"Is this a science experiment?" I asked mischievously.

"It's a *Life* Sciences experiment," edited the Wheaton Glass physicist.

"Well, how does Drew like the one you made for him?" I asked.

"It's been interesting," he said. "Drew's just learning to read in school. He can manage simple words like 'stop,' and it's only a little harder for him to read 'slower' and 'faster,' and then reach for the appropriate knob. But he gets frustrated as all get out when he can't control the whirlpool. 'This toy's broken, Dad! I can't make it work' — when in fact the toy is operating just fine. It's going to be a long time before Drew realizes that a lot of control buttons are just for show. But you didn't get upset, Ursula, because you understand how it works." He glanced at his watch. "Time to check the thermometer. What do you get for a reading?"

"Seventy-two; an increase of two degrees. And no more whirlpool. Just warmer, calm water," I smiled. "It's a great toy, Ike. I love it! Thank you."

"A toast to your serenity, kid," said Ike Peters as he raised his glass.

"You do know what you're drinking to, I hope."

"Serenity, peace, contentment, deceased whirlpools . . . did I leave anything out?"

"The root," I said. "Did you know 'Serewen' is Old High German for 'to dry out.'"

"No. That's amazing. I'm hearing this for the first time — over cocktails with you."

"To serenity then, and to a new season," I said.

"To a new season," said Ike. "Well kid, now that you've got Ursula Charbonnier banged out, what do you think you're going to do for an encore?"

"Oh, that's easy," I laughed. "Now I'm ready to take on Ian Ruddway — the biggest Life Sciences experiment of all."

"Oh my God, I can see the headline now, kid: 'Life Imitates Science.'"

And so it does.

Serenity is a most invisible reality. Striking in its clarity; comforting in its immutability. It is fullness and emptiness simultaneously. It is knowledge of danger, unaccompanied by fear. It is looking at Death and seeing the transcendence of Life. It is at last understanding the irrelevance of the question "Why?" It is Faith.

. . . he leadeth me beside the still waters.
He restoreth my soul . . .

A Canticle of Dawn

Words and Music by Barbara F. Graham, © 1992.

Verse 1
Where Truth meets light and shines in grace,
The soul slips free of its carapace.
We strike the dawn, and find our way,
Where Truth meets light and shines in grace.'

Verse 2 – *Confront Deception*
When shadows fall, concealing blight,
Confront the dark which leads up to light.
Incline your eyes, ears, heart, and mind.
Seek ye the truth, and ye shall find.

Chorus
Neap tide, spring tide – the moon calls our tunes,
That conceal, then reveal – as the timeless runes.
Security ushers dusk – and the dusk deceives.
Serenity welcomes dawn – and the dawn relieves.

Verse 3 – *Fight for Survival*
When you see hate, know it is fear.
Where you hear weak blame, value courage dear.
The heart betrayed, that still beams light,
Can open minds and set worlds right.

Verse 4 – *Acknowledge Dawn*
When new worlds bright beckon from afar,
Take the wilderness path, that leads on to stars.
Through brambly ways, there lies a place,
Where truth meets light and shines in grace.

Chorus
Neap tide, spring tide – the moon calls our tunes,
That conceal, then reveal – as the timeless runes.
Security ushers dusk – and the dusk deceives.
Serenity welcomes dawn – and the dawn relieves.

Verse 5 – *Dare Tomorrow*
As spring's return, melts the winter snow,
So a silence broken, can prime love to flow.
New journeys start, when we embrace,
Where truth meets light and shines in grace.

Verse 6
Where Truth meets light and shines in grace,
The soul slips free of its carapace.
We strike the dawn, and find our way,
Where Truth meets light and shines in grace.